Domain-Specific Development with Visual Studio DSL Tools

Microsoft .NET Development Series

John Montgomery, *Series Advisor*
Don Box, *Series Advisor*
Martin Heller, *Series Editor*

The Microsoft .NET Development Series is supported and developed by the leaders and experts of Microsoft development technologies including Microsoft architects. The books in this series provide a core resource of information and understanding every developer needs in order to write effective applications and managed code. Learn from the leaders how to maximize your use of the .NET Framework and its programming languages.

Titles in the Series

For more information go to www.awprofessional.com/msdotnetseries/

Domain-Specific Development with Visual Studio DSL Tools

- Steve Cook
- Gareth Jones
- Stuart Kent
- Alan Cameron Wills

✦✦ Addison-Wesley

Upper Saddle River, NJ • Boston • Indianapolis • San Francisco
New York • Toronto • Montreal • London • Munich • Paris
Madrid • Capetown • Sydney • Tokyo • Singapore • Mexico City

The publisher offers excellent discounts on this book when ordered in quantity for bulk purchases or special sales, which may include electronic versions and/or custom covers and content particular to your business, training goals, marketing focus, and branding interests. For more information, please contact:

U.S. Corporate and Government Sales
(800) 382-3419
corpsales@pearsontechgroup.com

For sales outside the United States please contact:

International Sales
international@pearsoned.com

This Book Is Safari Enabled

The Safari® Enabled icon on the cover of your favorite technology book means the book is available through Safari Bookshelf. When you buy this book, you get free access to the online edition for 45 days.

Safari Bookshelf is an electronic reference library that lets you easily search thousands of technical books, find code samples, download chapters, and access technical information whenever and wherever you need it.

To gain 45-day Safari Enabled access to this book:

- Go to http://www.awprofessional.com/safarienabled
- Complete the brief registration form
- Enter the coupon code RRDU-2SLC-SDJH-JSC3-V1ZX

If you have difficulty registering on Safari Bookshelf or accessing the online edition, please e-mail customer-service@safaribooksonline.com.

Visit us on the Web: www.awprofessional.com

Library of Congress Cataloging-in-Publication Data

Domain-specific development with Visual studio DSL tools / Steve Cook ... [et al.].
   p. cm.

Includes index.

ISBN-13: 978-0-321-39820-8 (pbk. : alk. paper)

ISBN-10: 0-321-39820-3

1. Microsoft Visual studio. 2. Computer software—Development. I. Cook, Steve.

QA76.76.D47D644 2007

006.7'86—dc22

                                                                            2007011960

ISBN 13:   978-0-321-39820-8
ISBN 10:   0-321-39820-3

Text printed in the United States on recycled paper at RR Donnelley in Crawfordsville, Indiana.
First printing, May 2007

To Hazel, Laurence, Oliver, and Imogen.
You make it all worthwhile.
—SC

To my grandparents, Muriel and Keith, whose constant love and support
have made any and all success in my chosen career possible.
—GJ

To Gabrielle, Nathanael, Madeline, Raphaelle, Isolde, and Elsa.
You can have your weekends back now.
—SK

To Kath, with love and thanks.
I owe you many dinners.
—ACW

Contents

Figures

Tables

Foreword

Ludwig Wittgenstein once compared a language to a city. In the historic center were gnarly lanes, in the middle were broad avenues and gardens with diverse architecture, and on the edges were geometrically planned suburbs. He was, of course, speaking of what we now call "natural" languages, but the analogy holds to our computer languages as well. We have low-level languages that fit the historic centers. And the boxy modeling techniques we use are the Stalinist apartment blocks in the suburbs.

It's the broad avenues and diverse architecture in between that have evaded the conventions of most of our computer languages. If you look at the workings of the city, there are street layouts, traffic patterns, zoning maps, architectural codes, and landscape maps; in the buildings are structural, plumbing, electrical, telecom, ventilation, and security plans; and in the factories, you'll find more specialized process, fluid, machine, and automation schemas. These are a few of the domain-specific languages of the real world. Each has a rigid set of semantics and an established body of practice. Each has been created because the prior alternatives were insufficient for the tasks at hand.

Of course, people now use computers to draw all of these things. In every case, some enterprising vendors (or occasionally users) have created packages that implement the specific modeling tasks for the domain. The applications have been limited to the domain, and the cost of maintaining the infrastructure has been considerable.

At the same time, in the world of computer systems, the most frequently used design tool is the whiteboard. And there is some kind of (usually manual and highly tacit) process in which the whiteboard sketches eventually get translated into code. Ideally, this would be a smooth progressive rendering of design, moving from broad concepts to precise code.

Unfortunately, today it's not so smooth. Whether developers use generic modeling languages like UML (in the minority case), or go from dry-erase marker to 3GL, there's always an abrupt shift from the human-readable world of the domain to the computer-executable world of the software. The goal of the Microsoft DSL Tools is to bridge that gap.

What if we could make it as easy to sketch a design in the language of the problem domain as it is to draw on a whiteboard, and then progressively annotate the sketch until it were sufficiently rich to become an executable model? That technology isn't here yet, but the DSL Tools are a huge leap forward.

The DSL Tools democratize the creation of domain-specific languages that can capture high-level design in an idiom familiar to domain experts and transform the designs into running software. This is a big step toward mass customization—the idea of capturing the domain patterns of a family of related software solutions and assembling the specific results from well-defined components. Almost every successful industry has learned to do this, but software has lagged.

When we achieve mass customization, the economics of software will change from the craft era to an age of software supply chains with component marketplaces and well-defined rules for reuse. The DSL Tools will be remembered as a pivotal step in that transformation.

There are no better individuals to write this book than Steve Cook, Gareth Jones, Stuart Kent, and Alan Cameron Wills. They are the creators of the DSL Tools. They have decades of experience in the use and design of prior generations of modeling tools. This depth of knowledge informs a passion and an expertise that can't be matched in the industry. Their work is a great contribution.

Sam Guckenheimer
Author, *Software Engineering with Microsoft Visual Studio Team System*
Redmond, WA
March 2007

Preface

This book is a software developer's guide to using the Microsoft Tools for Domain-Specific Languages ("DSL Tools"), which are included in the SDK (Software Development Kit) for Microsoft Visual Studio 2005.

The software industry is showing considerable interest in using "domain-specific languages," an approach to building software that promises to reduce software development costs, especially in large projects. A domain-specific language (DSL) is a language specially geared to working within a particular area of interest: a vertical domain such as telephone design, or a horizontal one like workflow. It may be a programming language or a specification or design language. It may be textual or graphical, or a mixture of both. The language is expressed in terms that are used in a particular domain, such as "connect," "ringtone," or "work item," uncluttered by the details of how those concepts are implemented. Software, configuration files, resources, and other documents can be generated from instances of the language—often many of those artifacts can be generated from one DSL—or the language may be interpreted directly. This makes it much easier to discuss the software at the requirements level, and to make changes in an agile way. In vertical domains, the accessibility of the language to business users helps when discussing requirements with them.

DSLs are not a new idea—HTML and SQL are well-known examples of DSLs. Less widespread, however, is the idea of creating your own DSL for your own project. The purpose of the Microsoft DSL Tools is to reduce the upfront cost of doing so. You can quickly create a range of diagrammatic languages, such as workflow, class, or entity diagrams, and you can create tools for generating artifacts from them.

Goals and Scope

This book is for you if you are a software developer or architect using, or thinking about using, the Microsoft DSL Tools. It explains how to create and use languages, how to tune them to your needs, and how to employ them within the context of your project. The book should also be of significant value to readers who are interested in the broader general topic of domain-specific languages, or who wish to compare and contrast different approaches to model-driven development, or tools that support model-driven development. Chapters 1 and 11 discuss the more general topic of domain-specific languages, and how you go about designing one. The middle chapters focus exclusively on providing a detailed yet readable reference on building DSLs and code generators using the DSL Tools.

The book's authors are the main designers of the Microsoft DSL Tools. They have worked together on the product since its inception, and are responsible for most of the key design decisions.

Why You Might Want to Use DSL Tools

If you (or your organization) are writing the same or similar code repeatedly, whether within a single large project or over the course of multiple projects, then such code can probably be generated. If this is the case, you should consider using the DSL Tools as a way to generate this code. This is especially the case if the code can be generated from structures that can easily be understood by domain specialists rather than software development specialists. After reading this book, you should be able to assess the capabilities of the DSL Tools to address problems of this kind, either directly or after some customization.

Organization of This Book

- Chapter 1, *Domain-Specific Development*, explains the DSL approach, compares it with similar techniques, and introduces typical scenarios in which a DSL is used.

- Chapter 2, *Creating and Using DSLs*, looks at the various parts of the DSL Tools system, shows how they fit together, and introduces the main examples that will be used through the remainder of the book.

- Chapter 3, *Domain Model Definition*, details how to define the concepts of the language.

- Chapter 4, *Presentation*, deals with defining the visual appearance of your language.

- Chapter 5, *Creation, Deletion, and Update Behavior*, covers these important aspects of the behavior of your language.

- Chapter 6, *Serialization*, deals with how models and diagrams in your language are represented in files.

- Chapter 7, *Constraints and Validation*, shows you how to ensure that the users of your language create valid statements.

- Chapter 8, *Generating Artifacts*, shows you how to use your language to drive or configure your system by creating configuration files, program code, resources, and other artifacts.

- Chapter 9, *Deploying a DSL*, explains how to create an installer that will install your finished language on multiple computers.

- Chapter 10, *Advanced DSL Customization*, shows you how to make specialized features of your language (or specialized behavior in the editor) in addition to those provided by the standard definition facilities.

- Chapter 11, *Designing a DSL,* provides a lightweight kit of principles and procedures for developing and evolving languages within the context of your project.

Updates and all of the main examples are available for download at the website www.domainspecificdevelopment.com.

What You Need to Use This Book

To get the full value of this book, you need to be reasonably familiar with the facilities that Visual Studio offers to developers of program code, including the code editor and XML editor. A basic knowledge of the C# programming language and the main aspects of the .NET class library are needed to understand the programming examples.

DSL Tools can be downloaded as part of the Visual Studio SDK and used with Visual Studio Professional Edition and later. Tools created using the DSL Tools can be deployed on Visual Studio Standard Edition and later. The website http://msdn.microsoft.com/vstudio/DSLTools/ is the entry point to information about the DSL Tools. There you can find links to where the SDK can be downloaded, a popular online forum with active discussions about the DSL Tools, weblogs containing discussions about the DSL Tools by the authors of this book and others, a tool for reporting bugs and making suggestions, white papers, chats, and other resources.

Acknowledgments

The authors would like to acknowledge the contributions of the following people who contributed materially to the design, development, documentation, and testing of the DSL Tools:

Annie Andrews, Steve Antoch, Austin Avrashow, Bhavin Badheka, Andy Bliven, Anthony Bloesch, Scott Chamberlin, Frank Fan, Jack Greenfield, Howie Hilliker, Ashish Kaila, Jesse Lim, George Mathew, Niall McDonnell, Blair McGlashan, Grayson Myers, Kirill Osenkov, Duncan Pocklington, Anatoly Ponomarev, Jochen Seemann, Keith Short, Pedro Silva, Patrick Tseng, Steven Tung, Dmitriy Vasyura, and Yu Xiao.

We would also like to acknowledge our community of early users, including participants in the DSL Tools Forum, who have stayed with us through a sequence of technology previews. The feedback of these early users has been immeasurably helpful in the process of getting the DSL Tools completed.

The following reviewers have given us invaluable detailed feedback on the contents of the book, which has improved it considerably:

Victor Garcia Aprea, Edward Bakker, Dan Cazzulino, Patrick Cooney, Dragos Manolescu, Jean-Marc Prieur, Jezz Santos, Gerben van Loon, and Markus Völter.

Joan Murray and her team at Addison-Wesley kept us going with patient moral support throughout the writing process.

We would also especially like to thank Bonnie Granat for her accuracy and responsiveness in making sense of and polishing our prose.

Finally, we thank our partners and families for putting up with the evenings and weekends when we have been working on the book instead of spending time with them.

About the Authors

Steve Cook joined Microsoft in 2003 to work on the DSL Tools. Previously, he was a Distinguished Engineer at IBM, which he represented in the UML 2.0 specification process at the OMG. He has worked in the IT industry for 30 years, as architect, programmer, author, consultant, and teacher. He was one of the first people to introduce object-oriented programming into the UK, and has concentrated on languages, methods, and tools for modeling since the early 1990s.

Gareth Jones is a lead developer in the DSL Tools team. He's been at Microsoft since 1997 doing various developer jobs such as building bespoke enterprise solutions, running the development of Microsoft UK's small business portal, and managing a consultancy team. Before joining Microsoft, he spent seven years leading development projects in the intelligence analysis, simulation, and aerospace industries.

Stuart Kent joined Microsoft in 2003 to work on the DSL Tools. Previously, he was an academic and consultant, with a reputation in modeling and model-driven development. He has over 50 publications to his name and made significant contributions to the UML 2.0 and MOF 2.0 specifications. He is a member of the editorial board of the journal *Software and Systems Modeling*, and on the steering committee for the MoDELS series of conferences. He has a Ph.D. in computing from Imperial College, London.

Alan Cameron Wills was a methodology consultant for almost a decade, and used to get very frustrated when people asked about good tools to support the methods. So he was very pleased to join Microsoft in 2003 to help in the DSL Tools project. He has a Ph.D. in computer science, and was joint creator of the Catalysis approach to component-based development. He gets excited about software factories, photography, sailing, and hills.

▪ 1 ▪
Domain-Specific Development

Introduction

This book describes the Microsoft Domain-Specific Language Tools (the DSL Tools). The DSL Tools are part of the Visual Studio SDK, and may be downloaded from http://msdn.microsoft.com/vstudio/DSLTools/. The DSL Tools extend Microsoft Visual Studio 2005 to support a powerful way of developing software called Domain-Specific Development.

Domain-Specific Development is based on the observation that many software development problems can more easily be solved by designing a special-purpose language. As a small example, think about the problem of finding every occurrence of a particular pattern of characters in a file, and doing something with each occurrence that you find. The special-purpose textual language of *regular expressions* is specifically designed to do this job. For example, using the .NET class `System.Text.RegularExpressions.Regex`, the regular expression `(?<user>[^@]+)@(?<host>.+)` applied to a string of characters will find email addresses in it, and for each address found, assign the substring immediately before the @ sign to the `user` variable, and the substring immediately after the @ sign to the `host` variable. Without the regular expression language, a developer would have to write a special program to recognize the patterns and assign the correct values to the appropriate variables. This is a significantly more error-prone and heavyweight task.

Domain-Specific Development applies this same approach to a wide variety of problems, especially those that involve managing the complexity of modern distributed systems such as those that can be developed on the .NET platform. Instead of just using general-purpose programming languages to solve these problems one at a time, the practitioner of Domain-Specific Development creates and implements special languages, each of which efficiently solves a whole class of similar problems.

Domain-Specific Languages can be textual or graphical. Graphical languages have significant advantages over textual languages for many problems, because they allow the solution to be visualized very directly as diagrams. The DSL Tools make it easy to implement graphical DSLs, and they enable Domain-Specific Development to be applied to a wide range of problems.

Domain-Specific Development

Domain-Specific Development is a way of solving problems that you can apply when a particular problem occurs over and over again. Each occurrence of the problem has a lot of aspects that are the same, and these parts can be solved once and for all (see Figure 1-1). The aspects of the problem that are different each time can be represented by a special language. Each particular occurrence of the problem can be solved by creating a model or expression in the special language and plugging this model into the fixed part of the solution.

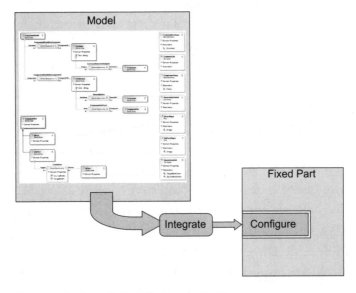

FIGURE 1-1: Domain-Specific Development

The fixed part of the solution is written using traditional design, coding, and testing techniques. Depending on the size and shape of the problem, this fixed part of the solution might be called a framework, a platform, an interpreter, or an Application Programming Interface (API). The fixed part captures the architectural patterns that make up the domain and exposes extension points that enable it to be used in a variety of solutions. What makes the approach applicable is the fact that you create the variable part of the solution by using a special-purpose language—a DSL.

As we observed in the introduction, the DSL might be textual or graphical. As the technology for domain-specific development matures, we expect to see tools that support the development and integration of both textual and graphical DSLs. People have a range of feelings about which kind of language they prefer. Many people, for example, prefer textual languages for input, because they can type fast, but graphical languages for output, because it is easier to see the "big picture" in a diagram. Textual expressions make it much easier to compute differences and merges, whereas graphical expressions make it much easier to see relationships. This chapter discusses both kinds, but the first version of DSL Tools and hence the remaining chapters of the book focus solely on graphical languages.

To create a working solution to the problem being addressed, the fixed part of the solution must be integrated with the variable part expressed by the model. There are two common approaches to this integration. First, there is an interpretative approach, where the fixed part contains an interpreter for the DSL used to express the variable part. Such an approach can be flexible, but it may have disadvantages of poor performance and difficulty in debugging. Second, the particular expression or diagram may be fully converted into code that can be compiled together with the remainder of the solution—a code-generation approach. This is a more complex conversion procedure, but it provides advantages in extensibility, performance, and debugging capability.

Graphical DSLs are not just diagrams. If you wanted just to create diagrams, you could happily use popular drawing programs such as Microsoft Visio to achieve a first-class result. Instead, you are actually creating models that conceptually represent the system you are building, together with diagrammatic representations of their contents. A given model can be represented simultaneously by more than one diagram, with each diagram representing a particular aspect of the model, as shown in Figure 1-2.

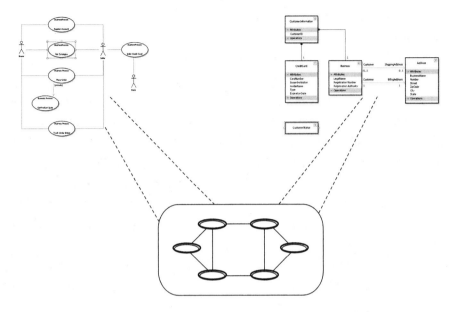

FIGURE 1-2: Two diagrams and one model

Examples

Let's first have a look at a couple of examples where the DSL Tools have been applied in practice. The first example comes from an Independent Software Vendor (ISV) called Himalia. Himalia has created a set of DSLs for implementing complex graphical user interfaces without doing any coding. The Himalia Navigation Model, shown in Figure 1-3, defines the navigation through the user interface.

Use Cases, regarded as heavyweight flows of control consisting of activities and transitions, are explicitly defined in a state machine view in order to address their complexity. Use Case states and transitions are related to Navigation Model elements and actions, respectively. The Use Case Model is shown in Figure 1-4.

The User Profile Model shown in Figure 1-5 defines user states that affect the behavior of the user interface.

The complete Himalia system integrates these models with others into Visual Studio 2005 to implement complete user interfaces based on Microsoft technology, including Windows Presentation Foundation (WPF).

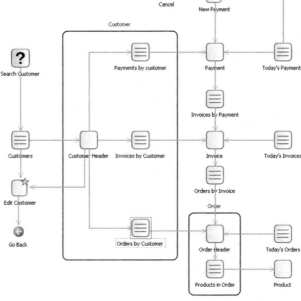

FIGURE 1-3: Himalia Navigation Model

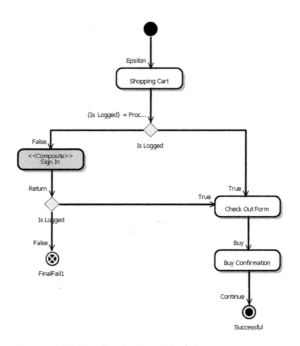

FIGURE 1-4: Himalia Use Case Model

The second example is a Systems Integrator (SI) called Ordina that is based in the Netherlands. Ordina has built a complete model-driven software factory within its Microsoft Development Center, called the SMART-Microsoft Software Factory. This factory uses four connected DSLs. To enable these DSLs to collaborate, Ordina has created a cross-referencing scheme that allows elements in one DSL to refer to elements in another DSL.

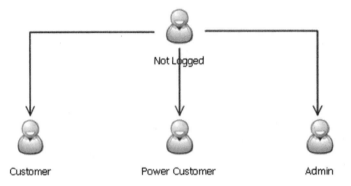

FIGURE 1-5: Himalia User Profile Model

The Web Scenario DSL is used to model web pages and user actions, and to generate ASP.NET web pages. An example is shown in Figure 1-6.

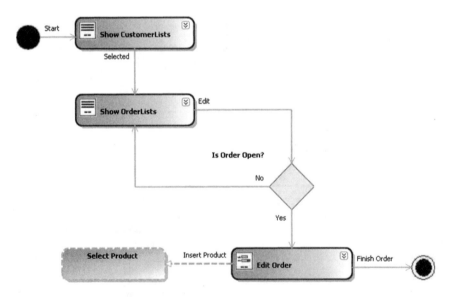

FIGURE 1-6: Ordina Web Scenario DSL

The Data Contract DSL is used to define the data objects that are transferred between the different layers in the architecture. An example is shown in Figure 1-7, which illustrates several different kinds of data objects.

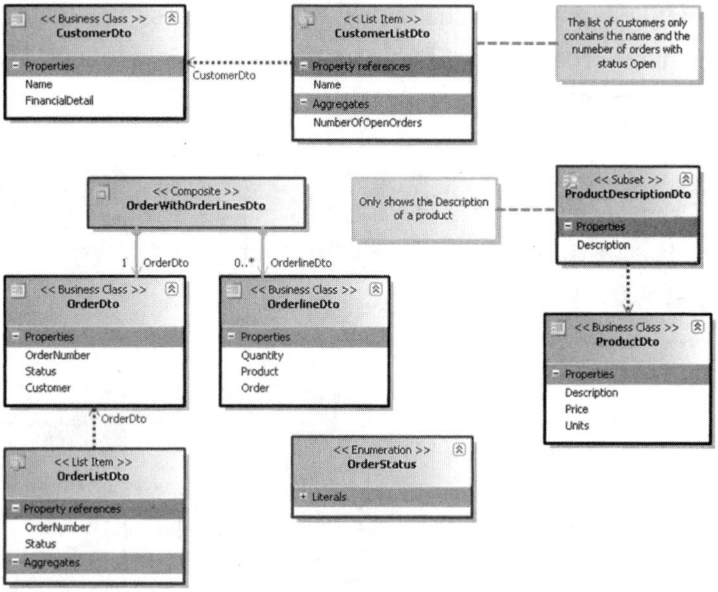

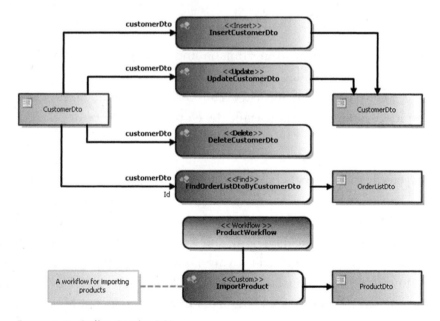

FIGURE 1-7: Ordina Data Contract DSL

The third DSL in the Ordina factory is the Service Model shown in Figure 1-8, which is used to generate service interfaces and skeletons of the business processes that implement the services.

FIGURE 1-8: Ordina Service DSL

The final DSL in the Ordina factory is the Business Class Model that is used to generate code for the Business Class and Data layers. This model is shown in Figure 1-9.

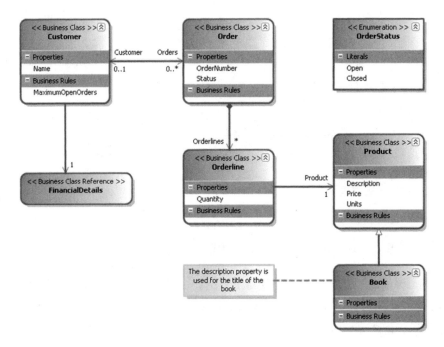

FIGURE 1-9: Ordina Business Class DSL

These two examples from Himalia and Ordina are for "horizontal" DSLs, where the intended customer for the resulting software does not belong to any particular industry. Here are some other more "vertical" examples of where domain-specific development might be applied.

Software Defined Circuitry

Many electronic products have circuitry that is programmed using software. For example, FPGAs (Field Programmable Gate Arrays) are programmable chips used in areas such as software defined radio, digital signal processing, medical imaging and speech recognition. Programming such chips directly in their Hardware Description Language (HDL) is a very low-level and painstaking task. A Domain-Specific Development approach can be used to raise the level of abstraction until it represents much more directly the domain being implemented; for example, a DSL approach to software defined radio is discussed in the paper by Bruce Trask of PrismTech at www.mil-embedded.com/articles/authors/trask/.

Embedded Systems

Many real-time embedded systems can be conceptualized as a set of communicating finite state machines. Separating the design of these systems into explicit state machines, plus a generic platform for executing state machines, can greatly simplify thinking about such systems. In this case, the DSL is the language for expressing state machines consisting of states and the transitions between them, while the execution platform is most likely built using custom code.

Device Interfaces

Many modern devices, such as mobile phones, HiFi equipment, and so on, have complex user interfaces. These interfaces are typically organized via rules that make the interface predictable, such as a rule that pressing a cancel button always takes you back to a known state, or inputting text always follows the same set of predictive rules. A DSL can be created for designing such systems, where the graphical appearance of the language corresponds accurately to the appearance of the actual interface being designed, and the interaction rules of the interface are captured in the structure of the language. Good examples of this approach can be found at the Domain-Specific Modeling Forum website at www.dsmforum.org.

Software Development Process Customization

The example that is used throughout this book to illustrate the DSL Tools shows how to use DSLs to define aspects of a software development process, such as the processing of bugs and issues, and how to use the models to configure the tools used to enact the process.

All of these examples and many others share the same approach: (1) identifying aspects of the problem that are fixed for all occurrences and capturing those aspects in a common framework or platform, and (2) identifying the other aspects that vary between occurrences and designing a Domain-Specific Language whose expressions or models will specify a solution to the problem.

Benefits

Now that we've looked at some examples, we can see the benefits of Domain-Specific Development.

- A DSL gives the ability to work in terms of the problem space, with less scope for making the errors that come from representing it in a general-purpose language.
- Working in terms of the problem space can make the models more accessible to people not familiar with the implementation technology, including business people.
- Models expressed using DSLs can be validated at the level of abstraction of the problem space, which means that errors in understanding or representation can be picked up much earlier in the development lifecycle.
- Models can be used to simulate a solution directly, providing immediate feedback on the model's suitability.
- Models can be used to configure an implementation consisting of multiple technologies of different types, which can reduce the skill and effort required to implement a solution using these technologies.
- Models can also be used to generate other models, and to configure other systems, networks, and products, perhaps in combination with other enabling technologies such as wizards.
- A domain-specific language provides a domain-specific API for manipulating its models, thus improving developer productivity.
- The artifacts generated from a DSL need not all be technological implementation artifacts; a suitable model can be used to generate build scripts, purchase orders, documentation, bills of materials, plans, or skeletons of legal contracts.
- Once important business knowledge is captured in a model, it becomes considerably easier to migrate a solution from one technology to another, or between versions of the same technology. This can often be done simply by modest modifications to the generators or interpreter.

In combination, these factors can offer considerable increased agility. For example, in the software defined radio domain mentioned earlier, Bruce Trask reports that "users of the tool report a minimum of 500 percent increase in productivity."

Of course these benefits are not free. To get them, you must invest in designing and building a DSL and integrating it into your overall solution. This will involve the cost of development—which is considerably reduced using DSL Tools. But it will also include costs for testing, deployment, documentation, staff training, development process modifications, and so on. When setting out to implement a DSL you must balance these costs against the expected benefits. You'll get the benefits when the costs can be paid off from the benefits of applying the approach to lots of systems. Hence the approach is particularly attractive to Systems Integrators, who often have to carry out many similar software development engagements for one customer after another. For a small company that does not specialize in particular business areas, it may be worth investing in DSLs that describe technological domains, such as web services and databases; for a larger company that is vertically organized into industry specializations, it may also be worth investing in DSLs that describe corresponding business domains.

Languages

At this point, we offer a definition of Domain-Specific Language:

> A Domain-Specific Language is a custom language that targets a small problem domain, which it describes and validates in terms native to the domain.

Most computer languages are textual, with their statements and expressions consisting of sequences of characters in a standard character set. Graphical languages have become increasingly popular in recent years, particularly with the emergence of the Unified Modeling Language (UML) as a popular set of standard notational conventions for depicting elements in an object-oriented software system.

When computer experts talk about languages, they usually mean general-purpose textual programming languages such as Visual Basic, C#, or Java. In Domain-Specific Development, our interpretation of the word *language* is widened considerably—it includes graphical languages such as UML, flowcharts, entity-relationship diagrams, state diagrams, Venn diagrams, and so on. We also include other textual languages such as XML and domain-specific varieties like SQL and regular expressions. We even think of tabular and form-based formats such as spreadsheets or the Windows Forms Designer as being languages. Special languages also exist for domains such as music notation and direct-manipulation interfaces. With the power available in modern computers, there is absolutely no need to be restricted to simple linear textual notations to convey our intentions to the computer; we want to exploit the power of the computer to provide means to express the author's intent as directly as possible, thus increasing the efficiency of our development. This includes interactive aspects such as dragging and other gestures, context menus, toolbars, and so on.

There are two main forces at work driving the evolution of languages. The first of these is the progressive lifting of the level of abstraction at which we express our intentions about what we want the computer to do. Originally, programmers had to express their algorithms and data structures in terms directly accessible to the computer hardware, which was efficient for the hardware but very tedious and error-prone for the programmer. Subsequent developments such as symbolic assemblers, filing systems, third- and fourth-generation languages, databases, class libraries, and model-driven development have moved the languages in which developers express their intentions further from the computer hardware and closer to the problems they are trying to solve.

The second force driving language evolution is the increasing variety of available digital media. Originally, computers were used purely to compute with numbers, then also with symbols and texts, and then with bitmaps and images. The evolution of computing has reached a point where the limitation on how we express our intentions is no longer the physical capabilities of the computer itself but the limits of our understanding of how to construct and manipulate computer languages. In Domain-Specific Development, instead of building on a general-purpose language in order to solve a problem, we use a language that is *itself* designed to suit the problem being solved.

Related Work

Domain-Specific Development is not new. In 1976, David Parnas introduced the concept of families of programs in his paper "On the Design and Development of Program Families" and talked about the possibility of using a program generator to create the family members. In 1986, Jon Bentley in his column in the journal *Communications of the ACM* pointed out that much of what we do as programmers is the invention of "little languages" that solve particular problems. Later, in 1994, the popular and seminal book *Design Patterns: Elements of Reusable Object-Oriented Software*, by Gamma, Helm, Johnson, and Vlissides (also known as the "Gang of Four" book), introduced the *Interpreter* pattern. According to the authors, the intent of this pattern is: "Given a language, define a representation of its grammar along with an interpreter that uses the representation to interpret sentences in the language." But it is only relatively recently that Domain-Specific Development has begun to gain widespread acceptance in the IT industry.

Domain-Specific Development is closely related to many emerging initiatives from other authors and organizations, of which the following is a partial list.

Model-Driven Development

Many vendors of software development tools are offering Model-Driven Development tools, which allow users to build a model of their problem, often using a graphical language such as the Unified Modeling Language (UML). From these models, a code generator or model compiler is used to generate some or all of the code for the resulting application. The Object Management Group has a branded initiative under this heading called Model Driven Architecture (MDA). We'll talk more about model-driven development and MDA later in this chapter.

Language-Oriented Programming

Sergey Dimitriev, co-founder and CEO of JetBrains, uses the term "Language Oriented Programming" to describe the approach of creating a domain-specific language to solve a programming problem in his article "Language-Oriented Programming: The Next Programming Paradigm" at www.onboard.jetbrains.com/is1/articles/04/10/lop/.

Language Workbenches

Martin Fowler, popular industry author and speaker, also refers to Language-Oriented Programming and uses the term "Language Workbench" to refer to the kind of tools required to support Language-Oriented Programming and Domain-Specific Development in his article "Language Workbenches: The Killer App for Domain-Specific Languages?" at http://martinfowler.com/articles/languageWorkbench.html.

Domain-Specific Modeling

The Domain-Specific Modeling Forum (www.dsmforum.org) is a body that promotes the idea of specifying domain-specific languages and generating solutions from them. Their site contains several interesting and compelling case studies.

Generative Programming

The book *Generative Programming: Methods, Tools, and Applications,* by Krzysztof Czarnecki and Ulrich W. Eisenecker, discusses how to automate the generation of applications, with a particular focus on domain engineering and feature modeling, and presents a detailed discussion of several different techniques for program generation. There is a regular conference called Generative Programming and Component Engineering (GPCE) dedicated to this topic.

Intentional Software

Intentional Software (www.intentionalsoftware.com) aims to develop an environment in which all programming is domain-specific. Its Domain Workbench technology represents programs and models as data, and provides multiple ways to render and interact with them using domain-specific textual and graphical syntax.

Software Factories

Software Factories are described in the book *Software Factories: Assembling Applications with Patterns, Models, Frameworks, and Tools*, by Jack Greenfield and Keith Short, with Steve Cook and Stuart Kent. Software Factories are a strategic initiative from Microsoft that proposes to use a combination of passive content such as patterns, models, DSLs, assemblies, and help files, with dynamic content such a customized tools, tailored processes, templates, wizards, and tests, all integrated into Visual Studio for producing a particular type of solution. DSL Tools form an important part of this initiative.

Textual DSLs

Before talking about graphical DSLs, let's look briefly at textual DSLs. We'll see how Domain-Specific Development involves a particular way of thinking about a problem, and we'll look at how to implement this approach using textual languages.

Imagine that we are designing a graphical modeling tool and have the problem of defining a set of shapes that will be displayed on a screen to represent the various concepts that can be depicted by the tool. One way we might do this would be to invent a new textual language for defining the various shapes. A fragment of this language might look like this:

```
Define AnnotationShape Rectangle
      Width=1.5
      Height=0.3
      FillColor=khaki
      OutlineColor=brown
      Decorator Comment
            Position="Center"
      End Comment
End AnnotationShape
```

In order to process this language, a program must be written to parse and interpret this text. As a programming exercise from scratch, this is a big job. But a parser-generator might be used, which itself takes as input a description of the grammar of the new language, such as the following, based on BNF (the Backus Naur Form, originally developed for defining the Algol language):

```
Definitions ::= Definition*
      Definition ::= Define Id Shape
      Width Eq Number
      Height Eq Number
```

```
        FillColor Eq Color
        OutlineColor Eq Color
        Decorator*
End Id

Shape ::= Rectangle | RoundedRectangle | Ellipse

Eq ::= "="

Decorator ::= Decorator Id
        Position Eq Position
End Id

Position ::= Center|
            TopLeft |
            TopRight |
            BottomLeft |
            BottomRight
```

The definitions for Id, Number, and Color are not included here; it's assumed that they are built into the grammar-defining language.

We need an algorithm to convert this BNF into a parser for the language it describes. We'd either use an existing parser-generator such as Yacc, Bison, Antlr, or Happy, or an expert might write one by hand in a normal third-generation programming language such as C# or Java.

Notice that the BNF is itself a DSL. We might "bootstrap" the BNF language by describing its grammar in itself, causing it to generate a parser for itself. Perhaps the hand-written parser will be quite simple, and the generated parser would handle a more complicated version of BNF. This pattern of using languages to describe languages, and bootstrapping languages using themselves, is very common when defining domain-specific languages.

Implementing a textual DSL by implementing its grammar like this can be a difficult and error-prone task, requiring significant expertise in language design and the use of a parser-generator. Implementing a parser-generator is definitely an expert task, because a grammar might be ambiguous or inconsistent, or might require a long look-ahead to decide what to do. Furthermore, there is more to implementing a language than just implementing a parser. We'd really like an editor for the language that gives the kinds of facilities we expect from a programming language editor in a modern development environment, like text colorization, real-time syntax checking, and auto-completion. If you include these facilities, the task of implementing a textual language can get very large. Happily, there are alternative strategies for implementing a textual DSL that don't involve implementing a new grammar.

The first strategy is to use the facilities of a host language to emulate the capabilities of a domain-specific language. For example, the following C# code has the effect of defining the same shape as the previous example:

```
Shape AnnotationShape = new Shape(ShapeKind.Rectangle,
                                  1.5,
                                  0.3,
                                  Color.Khaki,
                                  Color.Brown);
Decorator Comment = new Decorator(Position.Center);
AnnotationShape.AddDecorator(Comment);
```

This kind of code is often called *configuration code*, because it uses previously defined classes and structures to create a specific configuration of objects and data for the problem that you want to solve. In effect, the definitions of these classes and structures are creating an *embedded DSL*, and the configuration code is using that DSL. The capabilities of modern languages to define abstractions such as classes, structures, enumerations, and even configurable syntax make them more amenable to this approach than earlier languages that lacked these facilities.

The second strategy is to use XML—Extensible Markup Language. There are many ways in which the definition can be expressed using XML. Here's a possible approach.

```
<?xml version="1.0" encoding="utf-8" ?>
<Shapes>
  <Shape name="AnnotationShape">
    <Kind>Rectangle</Kind>
    <Width>1.5</Width>
    <FillColor>Khaki</FillColor>
    <OutlineColor>Brown</OutlineColor>
    <Decorator name="Comment">
      <Position>Center</Position>
    </Decorator>
  </Shape>
</Shapes>
```

The syntax is obviously limited to what can be done using XML elements and attributes. Nevertheless, the tags make it obvious what each element is intended to represent, and the meaning of the document is quite clear. One great advantage of using XML for this kind of purpose is the widespread availability of tools and libraries for processing XML documents.

If we want to use standard XML tools for processing shape definitions, the experience will be much improved if we create a schema that allows us to define rules for how shape definitions are represented in XML documents. There are several technologies available for defining such rules for XML documents, including XML Schema from the World Wide Web Consortium (defined at www.w3.org/XML/Schema.html), RELAX NG from the OASIS consortium (defined at www.relaxng.org) and Schematron, which has been accepted as a standard by the International Organization for Standardization (ISO) and is defined at www.schematron.com. Schematron is supported in .NET: A version called Schematron.NET is downloadable from SourceForge, and it is possible to combine the facilities of XML Schema and Schematron. We'll use here the XML Schema approach, which is also supported by the .NET framework.

An XML Schema is an XML document written in a special form that defines a grammar for other XML documents. So, using an appropriate schema, we can specify exactly which XML documents are valid shape definition documents. Modern XML editors, such as the one in Visual Studio 2005, can use the XML schema to drive the editing experience, providing the user with real-time checking of document validity, colorization of language elements, auto-completion of tags, and tips about the document's meaning when you hover above the elements.

Here is one of many possible XML schemas for validating shape definition documents such as the one presented earlier. Writing such schemas is something of an art; you'll certainly observe that it is significantly more complicated than the BNF that we defined earlier, although it expresses roughly the same set of concepts.

```xml
<?xml version="1.0" encoding="utf-8"?>
<xs:schema
  xmlns="http://schemas.microsoft.com/dsltools/ch01"
  attributeFormDefault="unqualified"
  elementFormDefault="qualified"
```

```
  xmlns:xs="http://www.w3.org/2001/XMLSchema"
  targetNamespace="http://schemas.microsoft.com/dsltools/ch01">
  <xs:element name="Shapes">
    <xs:complexType>
      <xs:sequence>
        <xs:element maxOccurs="unbounded" name="Shape">
          <xs:complexType>
            <xs:sequence>
              <xs:element name="Kind" type="kind" />
              <xs:element name="Width" type="xs:decimal" />
              <xs:element name="Height" type="xs:decimal" />
              <xs:element name="FillColor" type="xs:string" />
              <xs:element name="OutlineColor" type="xs:string" />
              <xs:element maxOccurs="unbounded" name="Decorator">
                <xs:complexType>
                  <xs:sequence>
                    <xs:element name="Position" type="position" />
                  </xs:sequence>
                  <xs:attribute name="name" type="xs:string" use="required" />
                </xs:complexType>
              </xs:element>
            </xs:sequence>
            <xs:attribute name="name" type="xs:string" use="required" />
          </xs:complexType>
        </xs:element>
      </xs:sequence>
    </xs:complexType>
  </xs:element>

  <xs:simpleType name="position">
    <xs:restriction base="xs:string">
      <xs:enumeration value="Center" />
      <xs:enumeration value="TopLeft" />
      <xs:enumeration value="TopRight" />
      <xs:enumeration value="BottomLeft" />
      <xs:enumeration value="BottomRight" />
    </xs:restriction>
  </xs:simpleType>

  <xs:simpleType name="kind">
    <xs:restriction base="xs:string">
      <xs:enumeration value="Rectangle" />
      <xs:enumeration value="RoundedRectangle" />
      <xs:enumeration value="Ellipse" />
    </xs:restriction>
  </xs:simpleType>

</xs:schema>
```

To summarize, in this section we have looked at three ways of defining a textual DSL: using a parser-generator, writing configuration code embedded in a host language, and using XML with a schema to help validate your documents and provide syntax coloring and autocompletion. A further option would be to define an equivalent to the DSL Tools that targeted textual languages.

Each of these approaches has its pros and cons, but they all share a common theme—investing some resources early in order to define a language that will make it easier to solve specific problems later. This is the basic pattern that also applies to graphical DSLs, as we shall see.

The DSL Tools themselves provide no facilities in version 1 for defining textual domain-specific languages. The Tools' authors have taken the view that XML provides a sufficiently good approach to start with, and so they have designed the DSL Tools to integrate XML-based textual DSLs with graphical DSLs.

Graphical DSLs

So far we have looked at some of the background behind Domain-Specific Development and discussed its benefits. We have also looked briefly at textual DSLs. Let's start our exploration into graphical DSLs by looking at an example that captures data for deploying and managing distributed applications.

Figure 1-10 shows a simple model built using a graphical DSL for designing logical data centers. This DSL is part of Visual Studio 2005 Team Architect. The elements of this language include *zones*, depicted by rectangular areas surrounded by dashed lines; *hosts*, depicted by rectangular areas surrounded by solid lines; *endpoints*, depicted by small shapes (squares, circles, and hexagons) placed on the edges of hosts; and *connections*, depicted by arrows between endpoints. This model corresponds exactly to an XML file that contains information according to the rules of the System Definition Model (SDM), which is used for configuring and managing data centers.

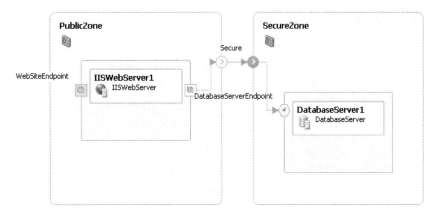

FIGURE 1-10: Data center design

System Definition Model

SDM was created as part of Microsoft's Dynamic Systems Initiative, which promises to deliver self-managing dynamic systems that will result in reduced operational costs and increased business agility. A later version of this model, called SML (Service Modeling Language), is being standardized by industry leaders, which should eventually enable distributed systems with components from multiple vendors to be managed using these models.

We can build up graphical DSLs like this one from a set of simple diagrammatic conventions such as the following. Many of these conventions are derived from UML, which we discuss in more depth later.

Conventions for Representing Structure

See Figure 1-11 for examples of structural conventions, including:

- Nested rectangle or rounded rectangles, to represent structural containment
- Rectangles with headers, sections, and compartments, to represent objects, classes, entities, devices, and so on
- Solid and dashed connectors with multiplicities, names, arrowheads, and other adornments, to represent relationships, associations, connections, and dependencies

- Connectors with large open triangular arrowheads, to represent generalization, inheritance, and derivation
- Ports on the edges of shapes, to represent connectable endpoints

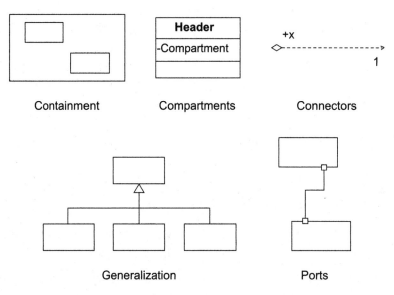

FIGURE 1-11: Structural conventions

Conventions for Representing Behavior

See Figure 1-12 for examples of behavioral conventions, including:

- Lifelines and arrows, to represent sequences of messages or invocations with a temporal axis
- Rounded rectangles, arrows, swimlanes, diamonds, transition bars, and so on, to represent activities and flows
- Nested ovals and arrows, to represent states and transitions
- Ovals and stick people, to represent use cases and actors

Using the DSL Tools, it is possible to build your own graphical language that combines conventions like these in a way that matches your particular problem (although version 1 of the Tools does not fully support all of the conventions listed). You can map them onto the concepts of your own domain and construct a customized graphical modeling language that solves your own problem. We saw an example in the data center design language shown in Figure 1-10, and we'll see many other examples as we proceed.

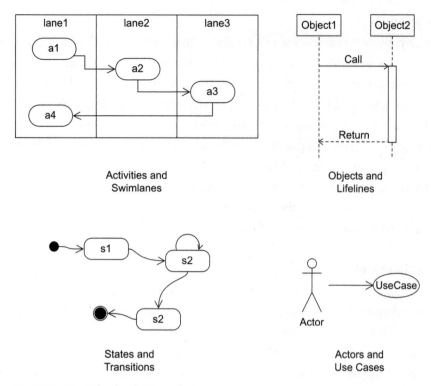

FIGURE 1-12: Behavioral conventions

Building your own graphical language on top of a given set of notational elements and conventions is analogous to building an embedded textual DSL, where instead of writing type wrappers and methods to make the language convenient to your domain, you define a mapping from the notational elements to your own domain concepts. If you want to define a graphical language that uses different notational elements and conventions, you have to be more expert and know how to create new diagrammatic elements from lower-level constructs. This is analogous to building your own parser for a textual DSL.

Aspects of Graphical DSLs

A graphical DSL has several important aspects that must be defined. The most important of these are its notation, domain model, generation, serialization, and tool integration.

Notation

In the previous section we talked about the notation of the language and how it can be built by reusing basic elements, often derived from well-established conventions, particularly those that originate in UML. For the kinds of graphical DSLs that we support, the basic building blocks are various kinds of shapes and connectors laid out on a two-dimensional drawing surface. These shapes and connectors contain decorators, which are used to display additional information such as text and icons attached to the shapes and connectors in particular places. In Chapter 4 we'll see full details of how to define these shapes and connectors and how to associate them with the other aspects of the language.

Domain Model

The domain model is a model of the concepts described by a language. The domain model for a graphical language plays a rather similar role in its definition to that played by a BNF grammar for a textual language. But for graphical languages, the domain model is usually itself represented graphically.

The basic building blocks for a domain model are *domain classes* and *domain relationships*. Each domain class represents a concept from the domain; each domain relationship represents a relationship between domain concepts. Typically, domain concepts are mapped to shapes in order to be represented on diagrams. Domain relationships can be mapped to connectors between those shapes or to physical relationships between shapes, such as containment.

Another important aspect of the domain model is the definition of *constraints*, which can be defined to check that diagrams created using the language are valid. For example, the class diagram in Figure 1-13 uses the correct diagrammatical conventions but defines a cyclic class hierarchy that is semantically invalid. Chapter 7 describes how to define constraints in the DSL Tools and discusses the differences between hard and soft constraints.

Generation

You define a language because you want to do something useful with it. Having created some models using the language, you normally want to generate some *artifacts*: some code, or data, or a configuration file, or another diagram, or even a combination of all of these. You'll want to be

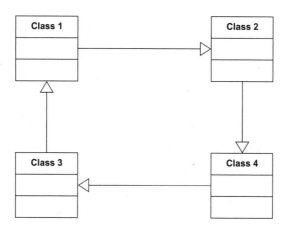

FIGURE 1-13: Invalid class diagram

able to regenerate these artifacts efficiently whenever you change a diagram, causing them to be checked out of source control if necessary.

Chapter 8 explains the DSL Tools generation framework, which enables the language author to define how to map models into useful artifacts.

Serialization

Having created some models, you'll want to save them, check them into source control, and reload them later. The information to save includes details about the shapes and connectors on the design surface, where they are positioned, and what color they are, as well as details of the domain concepts represented by those shapes.

It's often useful to be able to customize the XML format for saving models in order to help with integrating these models with other tools. This flexibility increases interoperability between tools and also makes it possible to use standard XML tools to manage and make changes to the saved models. Using an XML format that is easy to read also helps with source control conflicts. It is relatively straightforward to identify differences in versions of an artifact using textual differencing tools and to merge changes to artifacts successfully at the level of the XML files.

Chapter 6 explains how to define and customize the serialization format for a graphical DSL.

Tool Integration

The next important aspect of a graphical DSL design is to define how it will show up in the Visual Studio environment. This involves answering questions such as:

- What file extensions are associated with the language?
- When a file is opened, which windows appear, and what is the scope within Visual Studio of the information that is represented?
- Does the language have a tree-structured explorer, and if so, what do the nodes look like—with icons and/or strings—and how are they organized?
- How do the properties of selected elements appear in the properties browser?
- Are any custom editors designed for particular language elements?
- What icons appear on the toolbox when the diagram is being edited, and what happens when they are dragged and dropped?
- Which menu commands are enabled for different elements in the diagram and the associated windows, and what do they do?
- What happens if you double-click on a shape or connector?

Chapters 4, 5, and 10 describe how to define these behaviors and show ways of customizing the designer by adding your own code.

Putting It All Together

From the previous sections you can see that there are a lot of aspects to defining a DSL. This might seem rather daunting. Thankfully, the DSL Tools make it easier than you might think. Many of the aspects are created for you automatically, and you only need to worry about them if you want to change the way that they work. Complete languages are provided as starting points so that you don't need to start from scratch. Having defined your DSL, the DSL Tools are also used to generate code and artifacts that implement, test, and deploy the DSL as a designer fully integrated into Visual Studio. If you want to step outside of the set of features easily supported by the DSL Tools, we've provided many code customization options for that purpose.

The DSL Tools have even been used to define and build themselves. The DSL designer that is used to define domain models and notations is itself a DSL. Just like a compiler that can be used to compile itself, the DSL designer was used to define and generate itself.

DSLs in Visual Studio

Visual Studio 2005 has several graphical domain-specific languages integrated into it. These are the Distributed System Designers, which come with Visual Studio 2005 Team Edition for Software Architects, and the Class Designer which comes with Visual Studio 2005 Standard Edition and later. These designers are built on an earlier version of the DSL Tools; the current version is based on this earlier version and has evolved separately. The two versions are incompatible, which means that the DSL Tools cannot be used to extend the integrated designers.

Nevertheless, these designers illustrate very well some of the motivations for using domain-specific languages. Let's look at a simple example, using the Application Designer. This is a tool for modeling applications in distributed systems, with a particular emphasis on the endpoints that the applications implement and use, so that the user can wire the applications together into more complex systems. Figure 1-14 shows a simple design consisting of a Windows application, called **InvestmentCalculator**, that talks to an endpoint called **StockPrices**, which is implemented as a web service by an ASP.NET web application called **StockPriceApplication**. The **StockPrices** web service is shown as a *provider endpoint* on the **Stock-PriceApplication** node and is wired to a corresponding *consumer endpoint* on the **InvestmentCalculator** node.

Having created this design and chosen the implementation language, the Application Designer can generate the skeleton of an implementation for it using standard code templates installed with Visual Studio. The diagram context menu item "Implement All Applications …" causes the generation of two new projects in the solution, including the files needed to implement the solution, as shown in Figure 1-15. Implementing the application by generating these files like this requires much less work than does creating these files by hand. This is one clear benefit of defining a DSL—we can more quickly generate code that would be tedious and error-prone to write by hand.

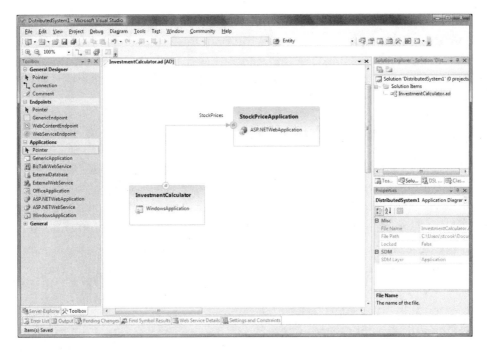

FIGURE 1-14: An application diagram

It's interesting to look into this solution and see where the name of the web service—**StockPrices**—appears. There are several places, in fact, including:

1. The name of the file StockPrices.cs.

2. The body of the generated file StockPrices.cs, containing the following code, which mentions StockPrices as the name of the class in the Name parameter of the WebServiceBinding attribute and in the Binding parameter of the SoapDocumentMethod attribute.

```
namespace StockPriceApplication
{
  [System.Web.Services.WebServiceBinding(Name = "StockPrices",
     ConformsTo = System.Web.Services.WsiProfiles.BasicProfile1_1,
     EmitConformanceClaims = true),
   System.Web.Services.Protocols.SoapDocumentService()]
  public class StockPrices : System.Web.Services.WebService
  {
    [System.Web.Services.WebMethod(),
     System.Web.Services.Protocols.SoapDocumentMethod(Binding="StockPrices")]
```

```
  public string GetPrice(string Symbol)
  {
    throw new System.NotImplementedException();
  }
 }
}
```

3. The name of the file StockPrices.asmx.

4. The body of the file StockPrices.asmx, containing the following template, which mentions StockPrices as a class name and a file name.

```
<%@ webservice class="StockPriceApplication.StockPrices"
            language="c#"
            codebehind="~/App_Code/StockPrices.cs" %>
```

5. The two SDM (System Definition Model) files. These are XML files that describe operational requirements for the applications and can be used to match these requirements against the operational facilities provided by a data center. This is not the place to go into the details of these files; suffice it to say that they both contain references to the service called **StockPrices**.

6. The web reference in the InvestmentCalculator application, which contains a URL such as http://localhost:2523/StockPriceApplication/StockPrices.asmx?wsdl.

7. The app.config file for the InvestmentCalculator application, containing the following section, which includes a reference to the filename StockPrices.asmx as well as the name **StockPrices** embedded in the longer name for the setting.

```
<applicationSettings>
  <InvestmentCalculator.Properties.Settings>
    <setting name="InvestmentCalculator_localhost_StockPrices"
                serializeAs="String">
      <value>
          http://localhost:2523/StockPriceApplication/StockPrices.asmx
      </value>
    </setting>
  </InvestmentCalculator.Properties.Settings>
</applicationSettings>
```

FIGURE 1-15: The generated solution

Now imagine that you want to change the name of the web service. Instead of **StockPrices,** you'd prefer to call it **StockValues.** Working in a modern coding environment, this should be a simple refactoring operation, such as the ones available from the "Refactor" menu in the code editor. But unfortunately, opening the StockPrices.cs file and using the "Refactor" menu will not have the desired effect, because many of the occurrences of the name **StockPrices** are not in code.

However, changing the name from **StockPrices** to **StockValues** on the Application Designer diagram does have the right effect. All of the references within the **StockPriceApplication** project are updated immediately, including the filenames and all of the references in the list above. At this point, the consumer endpoint on the **InvestmentCalculator** project is marked with a small warning symbol to indicate that it is referring to something that has changed; the web reference in the **InvestmentCalculator** project has been removed, and the app.config file no longer contains any reference to **StockPrices.** Selecting the "Implement" option from the context menu on the endpoint causes the web reference, app.config, and SDM files to refer to the new name. By using the DSL, the operation of changing the name has been reduced from a time-consuming and error-prone combination of multiple manual edits to a simple two-step procedure carried out at the appropriate level of abstraction.

You may ask what happens if you change the name of **StockPrices** in just one of these generated artifacts. Well, by doing that you have invalidated your solution. In general, it is difficult or impossible for a tool to solve all of the possible round-tripping conundrums that could be created if you allow complete freedom to edit any artifact at any time. In this particular case, you are allowed to insert your own code into the body of the `GetPrice()` method, and that code will be preserved if the endpoint or operation name is changed in the model. But if you manually change the name of the class or method itself in the code, you have effectively broken the relationship between the code and the model, and future changes will not be synchronized. We return to the general problem of keeping models and artifacts synchronized in Chapter 8.

We can summarize the qualities of the Application Designer, which are qualities that any well-designed DSL should possess, as follows:

- It is a sharply focused tool for a specific task.
- The model corresponds closely to the domain being modeled, and the transformations required to generate code and other artifacts are simple.
- Because of these simple transformations, the round-tripping problem becomes tractable.
- The artifacts associated with the language are all files and can be maintained in a source-control system, and the tool is engineered so that it works effectively in this environment.
- The interactive user experience on a modern computer is rapid and intuitive.
- The files manipulated by the tool are user-readable text files, using published formats based on XML.

The Customization Pit

Applying the simple DSL pattern can make it easy to create a solution to your problem as long as the solution can be expressed fully in the DSL. But what if you want to create something slightly different? If there are no other facilities available for modifying the solution, then you have a "customization pit" (Figure 1-16)—within the boundaries of what the DSL can express, things are easy and comfortable, but outside of those boundaries, things are difficult or impossible.

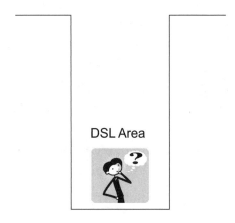

FIGURE 1-16: Customization pit

We'd much prefer the situation shown in Figure 1-17, where stepping out of the area covered by the DSL doesn't cause you to scale the walls of a deep pit but simply to step up onto a different plateau where things may be a little more difficult, but not impossibly hard. Beyond that plateau, there are further plateaus, each extending your capability to make solutions if you are willing and able to acquire the extra skills to go there. Alan Kay, the coinventor of Smalltalk, said, "Simple things should be simple. Complex things should be possible." We'd like to go a little further than that, and have difficulty increase only gradually as things get more complex.

There are several techniques that we can employ to achieve this. The first is to employ multiple DSLs, each one handling a different dimension of complexity in the problem, as depicted in Figure 1-18.

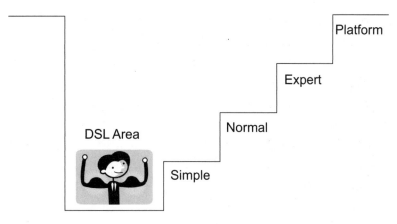

FIGURE 1-17: Customization staircase

A second technique, and one which we employ extensively in the design of the DSL Tools themselves, is to generate code that is explicitly designed to be extended. The C# 2.0 feature of partial classes is particularly helpful here, because part of a class can be generated while leaving other parts of the class to be written by hand. In the case of DSL Tools themselves, where the generated designer is hosted in Visual Studio, these code extensions can call upon facilities provided by the host, such as the user interface or the project system.

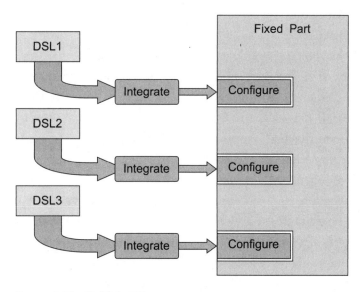

FIGURE 1-18: Multiple DSLs

A third technique, which you might think of as stepping up onto a higher-level *expert* plateau, is to enable the developer to modify the code-generation mechanisms, thus changing the way that the DSL is integrated into its environment. This requires yet more skill, because making it work correctly requires deeper knowledge of the remainder of the code.

The final technique represented by the highest plateau is to alter the implementation of the supporting platform, because it simply isn't capable of supporting the required features.

UML

The Unified Modeling Language, or UML, was first published in 1997 by the Object Management Group. UML unified three earlier approaches for graphically depicting software systems: the Booch method, the Object Modeling Technique, and the Object-Oriented Software Engineering method. The advantage of the UML was that it provided a standard set of notational conventions for describing aspects of a software system. Before the UML was published, different authors used different graphical elements to mean the same thing. Three examples are shown in Figure 1-19. The method described in Grady Booch's 1990 book, *Object-Oriented Analysis and Design with Applications*, represented a class by a cloud; the OMT method described in the 1991 book, *Object-Oriented Modeling and Design,* by James Rumbaugh and his colleagues, represented a class by a rectangle; and the 1992 book, *Object-Oriented Software Engineering: A Use Case Driven Approach*, by Ivar Jacobson and his colleagues, advocated representing a class by a little circle and distinguished diagrammatically between *entity* classes, *controller* classes, and *interface* classes. Many other approaches also existed at that time. UML succeeded in eliminating this "Tower of Babel"— almost all competing diagramming approaches vanished rapidly from the marketplace when UML appeared.

On publication, UML became increasingly popular as a technique for documenting the early phases of software development, especially those using object-oriented technologies. Class diagrams, use case diagrams, and sequence diagrams were especially popular for documenting the results of object-oriented analysis and object-oriented design.

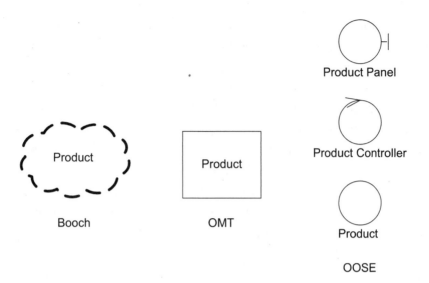

FIGURE 1-19: Different representations for a class

Figures 1-20 through Figure 1-22 show how to use UML to analyze the operation of a very simplified public library.

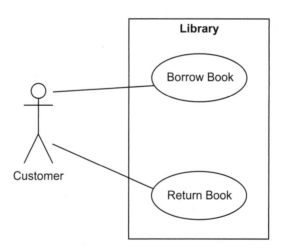

FIGURE 1-20: Use case diagram for simple library

The meaning of these diagrams is relatively informal. Being an analysis model, this set of diagrams does not exactly represent anything that happens in the software system. Instead, it helps the developer to make some early decisions about what information will be represented in the software and how that information may be collected together and flow around when the system interacts with its environment. Translating the analysis model into an exact design for the actual software involves working out many details, such as the design of the database, the design of the classes that represent the business logic, the mapping between business logic and database classes, the design of the user interface, the messages that flow between clients and servers, and so on. Traces of the analysis model will be found in the design, but the detailed correspondence between the analysis model and the eventual programs, schemas, and definitions that constitute the running software will be complex.

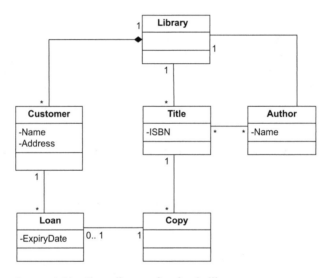

FIGURE 1-21: Class diagram for simple library

When UML emerged during the 1990s, mainstream thinking about object-oriented development assumed that there would be a relatively simple continuity between an object-oriented analysis and a corresponding object-oriented design. Several methodologies proposed that the way to get from the analysis to the design was simply to add detail while retaining the basic shape of the analysis. For simple examples, where there is a single computer implementing a simple non-distributed application, this can work, especially when no data persistence is involved.

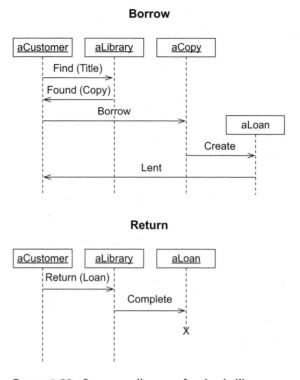

Borrow

Return

FIGURE 1-22: Sequence diagrams for simple library

The design of UML itself is actually based on this concept of adding implementation detail. The UML specification defines the ability to express the kind of detail found in an object-oriented programming language; for example, class members can be marked with the Java-inspired visibility values of `public`, `private`, `protected`, or `package`, and operations can have detailed signatures and so on. This helps to map a UML model to program code, especially if the programming language is Java. Note that there are many inconsistencies between the details of UML and Microsoft's Common Language Runtime, which make it more difficult to map UML effectively to the popular .NET languages Visual Basic and C#. When UML is used for a more abstract purpose such as analysis, these implementation details have to be ignored, because they are meaningless.

UML does offer limited extension facilities, called profiles, stereotypes, tagged values, and constraints. Stereotypes, tagged values, and constraints are mechanisms that add labels and restrictions to UML models to indicate that a UML concept is being used to represent something else. So, for example, a UML class could be labeled as a «resource», or even as a «webpage»—the symbols «» are conventionally used to indicate that a stereotype is being used. But labeling a UML concept does not change anything else about it—a class still has attributes and operations, inheritance, and the rest of the built-in features.

A UML Profile is a packaged set of stereotypes, tagged values, and constraints that can be applied to a UML model. A tool can make use of the profile information to filter or hide elements but may not delete unwanted elements; a profile is effectively a viewing mechanism. These facilities do allow a limited amount of customization of UML for particular domains, and of course individual UML tool vendors can go beyond the published standard to provide increased levels of customization.

However, the world has moved on apace since UML was defined. The Internet and World Wide Web have matured, most of the computers in the world are connected together, and a multitude of new standards and technologies has emerged, especially XML and Web Services. In 2007 and beyond, the likely platform for implementing a business system will involve many distributed components executing in different computers. Logic and data are replicated for scalability and load balancing. Legacy systems are accessed on mainframes and servers. Firewalls and routers are configured to maintain security and connectivity. Browsers and smart clients are distributed to many different devices and appliances. Common artifacts in this world, such as Web Service Definition Language (WSDL) or configuration files, have no standard representations in UML. Although stereotypes and profiles can be used to apply UML in domains for which it was not designed, such an approach gives cumbersome results. In such a world, the transformation from a simple object-oriented analysis to a detailed system design is far too complex to be thought of simply as "adding detail." Different approaches are needed.

If UML is not convenient to be used directly, what happens if we open up the definition of UML, remove all of the parts we don't need, add new parts that we do need, and design a language specifically tailored for the generation task that we want to accomplish? In short, what would happen if we had an environment for constructing and manipulating graphical modeling languages? The answer is that we would eliminate the mismatches and conceptual gaps that occur when we use a fixed modeling language, and we would make our development process more seamless and more efficient. That is the approach adopted in DSL Tools.

Instead of thinking about UML as a single language, we prefer to think of it as a set of reusable diagrammatic conventions, each of which can be applied to a particular kind of situation that we might encounter during software development. For example, sequence charts such as those in Figure 1-22 might be used to describe the flow of messages between applications in a distributed system, the flow of invocations between objects in an application, or even information interchange between departments in an organization. In the first case, the vertical lines on the diagram represent applications, in the second case they represent objects, and in the third case they represent departments.

Note also that it is not only end users that benefit from clean domain-specific abstractions. Developers who build tools that generate code and other artifacts from models and keep models coordinated with one another, need to access model data; providing APIs that work directly in terms of the abstractions of the problem domain is critical to productivity for developers. Developers want the API for the logical data center to give them direct access to the properties of an IIS server or a SQL Server database. Similarly, they want the API for the sequence charts to talk directly about applications, objects, or departments. They'd like to write strongly typed code, such as this:

```
foreach (Department dept in message.Receiver.SubDepartments)
{
  // generate some artifacts
}
```

This contrasts with having to reinterpret a model intended for other purposes (such as a UML model), which can give rise to code like this:

```
Lifeline lifeline = message.Receiver;
if (lifeline.Object.Label = "Department")
{
  Department receiver = lifeline.Object.Element as Department;
  if (receiver != null)
  {
    foreach (Department dept in receiver.SubDepartments)
```

```
    {
        // generate some artifacts
    }
  }
}
else
{
  // handle errors
}
```

SUMMARY

In this chapter we introduced Domain-Specific Development and discussed some examples and benefits of the approach.

We looked at how to define textual domain-specific languages as new languages or as embedded languages within an existing host language, and we saw how XML can be used as a simple and cost-effective substrate for defining textual DSLs. We discussed the different aspects of graphical DSLs, and saw how these are being implemented in several components of Visual Studio 2005. We talked about the customization pit and how to overcome it.

Finally, we discussed UML and saw how it provides a very popular set of conventions for creating diagrammatic documentation of software and how a domain-specific approach helps to overcome its disadvantages.

▪2▪
Creating and Using DSLs

Introduction

The purpose of this chapter is to touch on all of the principal aspects of defining a domain-specific language (DSL) with the Microsoft DSL Tools. We also introduce an example scenario in which the DSL Tools are used. The later chapters will then go into more detail on each topic.

This chapter has three sections. First, we introduce a development group that finds that the DSL Tools improve its productivity, and we look at why that is so and something of the process that the group follows to create and use the DSLs.

Second, we look at the practical steps of creating a DSL, touching briefly on each of the topics that will be discussed in turn in later chapters.

Finally, we take a look at the main components of the DSL Tools architecture.

By the way, we practice what we preach. The DSL Tools are generated, bootstrap fashion, from a DSL definition. Like any substantial DSL Tools-based example, the core of the system is the generated code, and that is augmented with a quantity of hand-written code.

Process: Incremental Development of DSLs

You define a DSL because you want to create models by which software is generated or controlled. It is of course possible to create notations with DSL

Tools that are just used informally, and some DSLs may start life that way. But for the majority of cases, the DSL is essentially a means to parameterize a generic framework; you have an application or a component that you use many times, although with some variation from one usage to the next. A DSL is one way (among many possible ways) of allowing the developer who uses the framework in a specific application to provide specific values for its variable features. Development of the DSL and its framework thus go hand in hand. Toolkits like the DSL Tools have removed one obstacle by making it easy to define the DSL and develop tools to support it. However, developing the framework is still a time-consuming and potentially risky task.

To mitigate the risk, you don't develop the framework and its DSLs all at once from scratch. Instead, you begin with existing code that works for a specific application, and you gradually parameterize it, progressively identifying those parts that should vary from one application to another and making them dependent on DSLs.

Generalizing an Application: Identify Variability, Discover DSLs

The (fictional) consultancy firm of CJKW manages software projects for client companies and provides tools to help that process. One of the key ingredients for success, CJKW has found, is to monitor issues—reports of bugs or other problems that arise during the project—and their eventual resolution. Issue logs are kept in a database; reports can be generated showing what issues are outstanding, how fast they are being resolved, and so on. However, the details of this requirement vary from one customer company to another. Some think of an issue as just being either outstanding or fixed, while others see it as progressing through a detailed set of steps such as approved, assigned, blocked, solution proposed, and so on.

CJKW began by adopting the Issue Tracker Starter Kit, a small application that provides a web client and can run on SQL Server, which the company obtained in source form from the ASP.NET website.[1] (The original version, based on .NET version 1.2, can be found by searching in the ASP.NET website.) Out of the box, the Issue Tracker allows users to create a record of each issue (Figure 2-1) and to query the database to list all the

---

1. It's a mystery that they didn't choose Microsoft's excellent Visual Studio Team Foundation Server for this purpose.

issues that are in a given state. An administrator can define a set of allowed states, and users can set the state of any issue to one of those values. This allows different states to be employed from one client to another. But one of CJKW's earliest customers has a more stringent requirement, that there should be some constraints on how states can be changed—for example, that you can't go straight from *Unassigned* to *Fixed*.

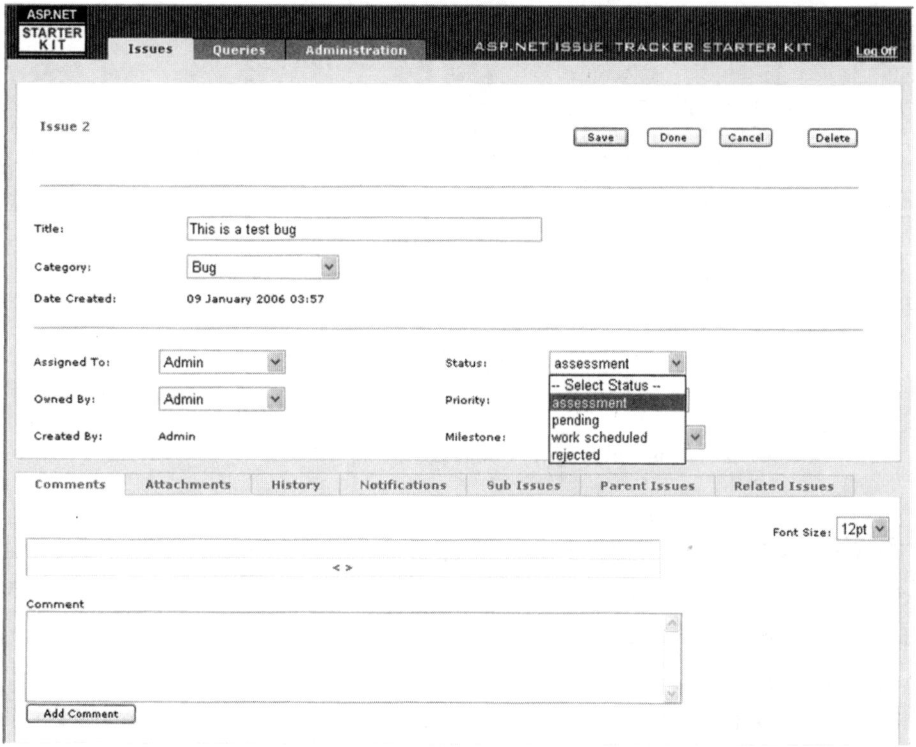

FIGURE 2-1: The web interface to the Issue Tracker application

Looking at the existing code, CJKW's in-house developers identify the point at which the menu of allowed states is presented to the user. They insert some code that computes the set of permitted next states from the previous one. (After an initial test, they realize that they must always include the current state in the allowed list so that the user has the option of leaving the state unchanged.) The relevant fragment looks like this:

```
string[] nextOptions = new string[]{};
if (!string.IsNullOrEmpty(currentState))
{
  if ("Unassigned"==currentState)²
    nextOptions = new string[] {
      "Unassigned" // allow leaving state unchanged
      "Approved",
      "Rejected",
      };
  else if ("Rejected"==currentState)
    nextOptions = new string[] {
      "Rejected", // allow leaving state unchanged
      };
  else if ("Approved"==currentState)
    nextOptions = new string[] {
      "Approved", // allow leaving state unchanged
      "Fixed",
      };
  else if ("Fixed"==currentState)
    nextOptions = new string[] {
      "Fixed", // allow leaving state unchanged
        };
}
else
{ // New Issue
  nextOptions = new string[] {"Unassigned"};
}
```

The first instance of this application works well at the customer site, and CJKW decided to use it with its other clients—though of course with more or less differing requirements in each one. The development team's initial response is to copy the existing code and modify it to meet the new requirements at each customer site. But as CJKW thrives and more customer engagements arise, it becomes clear that this is an unscalable strategy that creates too many variants of the same code. To be fair to CJKW, it wasn't clear at the outset that there would need to be so many variations on the same application, and it wasn't clear which bits would be the same all the time and which bits would vary. So for a while the developers create a new variant for each customer, adapt the code for each new requirement, and often take the opportunity to make some architectural improvements at the same time. But eventually, Devika, the lead

---

2. The CJKW developers show some naiveté with respect to coding practice. The repetitive use of literal strings is inadvisable. And, as they discovered eventually, bolting the state-chart into the UI code isn't the best strategy. However, the fragment serves to illustrate the example.

developer, sits back and surveys with some concern the source repository, full of half-forgotten variations of the same system.

She does a series of text comparisons on the source of the applications that have been developed to date—a variability analysis. It turns out that the above fragment of state transition code is one of the main things that changes from one installation to another. The team therefore decides that this part of the code should be generated from a model. There are other miscellaneous bits of code that change from customer to customer, but this particular aspect is consistently variable, so automating its development would save a lot of time—both in creating the code initially for each new application and in making any changes later.

In this way, the need for generation in a particular area is identified bottom-up, by considering *necessary* variations in the implementation. Some other variations were found in the diff, but they turn out to be incidental, without significant effect on function.

To realize its plan, the team must produce two things:

- A DSL definition
- A body of code, derived from their current code base, the variable parts of which can be generated from the DSL

What kind of DSL is suitable for this purpose? Well, in this case, "states" seem to suggest state diagrams, so let's hope the team didn't spend too long pondering that one. Figure 2-2 shows an example of the DSL they produce.

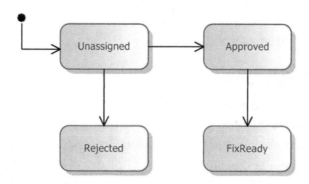

FIGURE 2-2: An Issue State definition

But just for a moment let's consider other possible variations. Some customers may, for example, wish to get a regular report containing a graph summarizing how promptly issues are being dealt with. But perhaps there are two alternative algorithms for cooking them up—some customers favor one method, and others prefer the other method. One way of dealing with this is a compiler switch: `#if ReportType1` ... `#else` ... `#endif`. (There is also of course the option of a runtime flag, which we'll discuss later in this chapter.) Now suppose there are many such choices, some of them multi-valued and some of them interdependent, and some of them requiring more subtle variations in the code than just including a block or not. Some bright team member comes up with the idea of encoding all the choices in XML and then generating the required code from that. This is where the DSL Tools come in, since they can read the XML file and use text templates to generate the code from choices encoded in the XML. In this case, the DSL is just the XML, and the strength of the DSL Tools is in generating the code from this model. In situations where the DSL is more sophisticated, embodying relations between entities—such as workflows or complex static relationships—then it is useful to think in terms of a diagrammatic DSL, and the diagram editing capabilities of the DSL Tools become useful. For most of the examples in this book, we'll discuss diagrammatic DSLs, if only to show off the full feature set.

This DSL looks similar to the UML state diagram notation—a deliberate choice that was made so that newcomers can readily understand its intention. But it is without many of the UML features that are not required here, such as nested states, guards, and other decorations on transitions. The semantics of this language will be expressed entirely by the code generators written for this application.

Top-Down and Bottom-Up

Hearing of the decision to generate code from state diagrams, Annie, the chief analyst, isn't surprised. She recounts that whenever she visits a new client to discuss its project management requirements, the discussion pretty soon gets around to issue tracking. Having now had plenty of experience with these clients, Annie immediately asks them about the states they need in their issue logs. The customers aren't always clear about this at first, but Annie finds it helps to draw a diagram of the states and their possible transitions on the whiteboard and to discuss the situations in which users would change the states and why. Annie remarks that she could have told team members they'd use state diagrams, without their having to go through their variability analysis on the code. And all those binary flags about the reports? Well, for months she's had a form she fills out with new customers, with checkboxes for just those choices. Devika folds her arms and wonders aloud whether Annie can tell her about next month's test results, too.

This illustrates that there are two approaches to developing a DSL, one is observing necessary variations in the code, and the other is looking at the variations at the conceptual level—the states and transitions rather than their code. The virtue of the first approach is that it ensures every feature of the DSL is justified by a generative need; the value of the second is in expressing the variations in terms of the customers' needs and in terms they can discuss. It can be argued, therefore, that the top-down approach tends to lead more quickly to a substantial and self-consistent model, and a longer-sighted one. On the other hand, it can be too easy at the conceptual level to concoct a complex model that is impractical to implement. So, in practice, it is effective to alternate between top-down and bottom-up techniques, working incrementally to avoid the risk of a big upfront investment but regularly standing back to check for consistency.

One of the effects of using a DSL is to bring the implementation work much closer to the user's conceptual space rather than that of the implementation. The DSL is (or should be) expressed in terms of ideas that make sense at the level at which it deals: issue states and transitions rather than database rows and cross-referenced keys. And in a DSL, we're talking here about *issue* states and transitions—not just any old states. Suppose that in each issue log we want to record the reason for the most recent transition and provide that the allowed reasons will be constrained by transition (so that for example, you can say "fixed" or "given up" for a transition to the closed state but not for the transition from "unassigned" to "assigned"). In that case, a list of allowed reasons will be an attribute of each transition.

The DSL captures the variable parts of the conceptual space. The transformations that generate code embody the generic architecture—if you like, the language of patterns—of applications in the DSL's domain: the DSL authors' knowledge about how to create applications or components in that domain, given a statement of requirements in the DSL. Whereas it is an insoluble problem to generate automatically the application that meets a general requirements statement, it is quite easy to generate applications in a restricted domain that meet the requirements expressed by a language specific to that domain.

Developing the DSL: From Sketches to Domain Model

After experimenting with many sketches of state diagrams—and taking into consideration both the variability in the code they want to generate, and the concepts that customers want to express—the developers come up with a definition of the language. The core of this definition is the domain model, which states the kinds of things that are dealt with by instances of the language (individual state diagrams in this case). Using the DSL Tools domain modeling tool, they create the diagram in Figure 2-3 (we'll see how in the next major section).

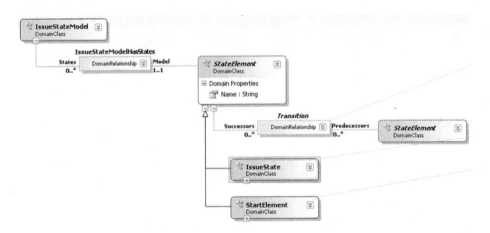

FIGURE 2-3: Initial DSL definition for the Issue State language

A *domain model* is the central part of a DSL's definition. It defines, among other things, *domain classes* (the round-cornered boxes) and *domain relationships* (with square corners). The model defines the classes of elements there may be in instances of the language and the relationships there may be among them. Reading this diagram from the top left downwards, it states that:

- An **IssueStateModel** consists of any number of **StateElements**; the relationship between the two is called **IssueStateModelHasStates**.

The solid line representing the two arms or *roles* of this relationship show that this is an *embedding* relationship. In a running designer,[3] all the elements are linked in a tree of embedding relationships.

- From the point of view of an **IssueStateModel**, its collection of **State Elements** is accessible through its property **States**. From the point of view of a **StateElement**, its parent **IssueStateModel** is accessible through its property called **Model**.

- Each **StateElement** has a *domain property* called **Name**, whose type is **String**.

- There are two kinds of **StateElement**: **IssueState** and **StartElement**. (The **IssueStates** are represented by boxes in the instance example in Figure 2-2, and the black dot is a **StartElement**.)

- Any **StateElement** may be related to any number of other **StateElements** through a relationship called **Transition**. Each **StateElement** has properties **Successors** and **Predecessors**, which provide access to the related **StateElements**. (Transitions represent the arrowed connectors between states on the diagram.) The dotted line representing this relationship shows it to be a *reference* relationship, crosslinking nodes of the embedding tree.

IssueStateModel is called the root of this DSL, and—as is usual—each instance of the root is represented by a whole diagram when the DSL is presented in a designer. It is also the root of the XML tree when instances of the language are saved to file.

Domain models are the subject of Chapter 3.

Domain Model and Presentation Are Separate

The Domain Model—the classes and relationships part of the DSL definition—defines just the concepts dealt with by the DSL. It does not define how to present the material as a diagram. (In fact, as we observed in Chapter 1, it can often be useful to create a DSL without a diagrammatic presentation.) To do this, the team defines a set of Shapes and Connectors—boxes and lines, if you like. In the Issue State DSL, the correspondence between shapes and domain classes

---

3. A "designer" is a graphical or other non-textual editor hosted in Visual Studio.

is straightforward: each **IssueState** is represented by an **IssueStateShape,** and each **Transition** is represented by a **TransitionConnector.**

There is a variety of basic shape and connector types available, and there are several ways of displaying information within a shape, as lines of text, lists of values, or variable icons. Color, line thickness, shading, and other characteristics can be varied.

After defining a set of shapes, the DSL author must define a set of *shape maps.* These define which shape or connector displays each domain class or relationship as well as what determines the text or other variable features of the shapes.

In a running designer, while a DSL user is editing a DSL instance (as in, for example, Figure 2-2), it is of course the shapes and connectors that appear on the screen. However, for the most part the domain properties that are displayed in the properties window when one of those shapes is selected are those of the underlying model element, and the editing or other operations that are performed are defined on the model elements. The shapes and connectors on the diagram are kept up to date by a process known as "view fixup," which is managed by the DSL Tools presentation framework.

The clear separation between presentation and underlying model means that an author of a DSL definition can, within reason, change the way in which the domain model is presented without having to change the model itself.

Another aspect of this separation appears when the DSL user saves an instance to file. Two files are actually generated, one containing just the domain class and relationship instances and their domain properties, and the other with layout information for the diagrammatic presentation. If the latter file is thrown away, the diagram will be recreated automatically. The layout will be a mess, but the shape contents and the connections between them will be correct. The particular value of this separation is that tools can easily be written that accept the model, uncluttered by the incidental layout information.

Presentation is the subject of Chapter 4.

Refining the DSL

How did the team come up with the DSL definition? The essential process is to look at the sketch instances and identify the different types of things you are drawing—not forgetting a domain class for the whole model.

> **■ TIP Work from instances**
>
> We have worked from prototype instances of the notation we want in order to create the domain model—another kind of "bottom-up" working. Sample instances—usually drawn on the whiteboard—are useful for examining the proposed domain model.

Once a domain model is proposed, Annie and Devika draw more example instances of it to see whether it covers the cases they need and also to see if it covers more than they need. A collection of **StartElements** and nothing else would be a valid instance of the model as it stands; would more than one **StartElement** on a state model be allowed? Would a **StartElement** unrelated to any **IssueState** be allowed?

Together with the domain model, the DSL authors can define a set of *validation constraints* (covered in detail in Chapter 7) expressed in C#, which can be used to prevent the DSL user from drawing (or at least saving) such oddities.

In considering what should and should not be allowed as a valid Issue State model, the developers are thinking both about whether such a state model would mean anything useful to its users and about whether they can generate sensible code from it. Once they have defined the bounds of what users can draw, Devika can make those assumptions in the design of the code generators.

Whatever the answers to these questions, they are much easier to ask and discuss in terms of a language than in terms of variations in the source code, tables, or APIs. Working "top-down" from language to code helps ensure architectural consistency.

Driving the Framework from the DSL

Now a generator can be written for the variant pieces of code. The first candidate for generation is the fragment that sets the menu of permitted states. When we saw it earlier, it had been hand-written to support a particular state model. Devika begins by copying the C# file to a text template file (that is, with filename extension .tt instead of .cs) and running the code generator. Without any modification, the file just regenerates the original .cs file. But now Devika inserts code-generation statements at the key places where the code should depend on the content of the state model.

```
// ... preceding section remains as it was in original source
  string [] nextOptions = new string [] {};
  if (!string.IsNullOrEmpty(currentState))
  {
<#
 StateElement startState = null;
 foreach (StateElement fromState in this.IssueStateModel.States)
 {
   if (fromState is StartElement)
     // The actual starting state is that pointed to by the Start Element
     startState = fromState.Successors[0];
   else
   {
#>
       if ("<#=fromState.Name#>"==currentState)
         nextOptions = new string[] {
           "<#=fromState.Name#>", // allow leaving state unchanged
<#
       foreach (StateElement toState in fromState.Successors)
       {
#>
           "<#=toState.Name#>",
<#
       }
#>
         };
<#
   }
 } // end of generating loop -
   // should have seen a start state by now
#>
   }
   else
   {   // New Issue
       nextOptions = new string[] {"<#=startState.Name#>"};
   }
   // Rest of file stays as it was in original source...
```

Code-generation statements are enclosed between the special brackets <# and #>; expressions are enclosed in <#= ... #>. The generator interprets them in the context of the state model. Notice how those statements use the names of the domain classes and their properties from the domain model. The generating syntax is C#. This fragment, which will be run when a user has drawn an Issue State diagram, queries root IssueStateModel to find all of its States and executes a loop for each one. That begins by generating the if statement that compares a state with the runtime current state—be careful not to confuse the generating with the generated code here! Then there is a loop, again in the generating code, that lists each state that is accessible from the starting state. So if we run this generator in the context of the Issue State definition diagram of Figure 2-2, we get:

```
// ... preceding section remains as it was in original source
string [] nextOptions = new string [] {};
if (!string.IsNullOrEmpty(currentState))
{
  if ("Unassigned"==currentState)
     nextOptions = new string[] {
        "Unassigned", // allow leaving state unchanged
        "Assigned",
        "Rejected",
     };
  if ("Approved"==currentState)
     nextOptions = new string[] {
        "Approved", // allow leaving state unchanged
        "Fixed",
     };
  if ("Rejected"==currentState)
     nextOptions = new string[] {
        "Rejected", // allow leaving state unchanged
     };
  if ("Fixed"==currentState)
     nextOptions = new string[] {
        "Fixed", // allow leaving state unchanged
     };
}
else
{   // New Issue
  nextOptions = new string[] {"Unassigned"};
}
// Rest of file stays as it was in original source...
```

Any kind of file can be generated from the models—not just code. For example, Annie would like a summary of the allowed states and transitions in HTML form, so that it can be put up on the project's internal website.

Generation from models is the topic of Chapter 8.

Using the DSL

Now that the DSL has been developed and code can be generated from it, Devika and her team can use it to generate code for the specific parts of

Issue Tracking dealing with state transitions. They may still have to do hand coding for other parts of each application, but at least the most common part has been speeded up and made more reliable. Dave, another developer on the team, has not been closely involved with the state transition logic but finds it easy to draw the state diagrams and press the button that generates those parts of the code.

There's room for potential confusion here when we're talking about "users." Dave is not an end user of the Issue Tracking applications, but he is a user of the DSL—it helps him write those applications. Table 2-1 summarizes the terms we will use for these roles.

TABLE 2-1: Terminology—Roles and Phases

Term	Definition
DSL author	The user of DSL Tools who creates DSLs. Devika was the DSL author in CJKW.
DSL user	The user of a DSL who creates designs in the language to help build applications. Developers Devika and Dave are DSL users. Annie (the analyst) also draws diagrams with the DSL, although she generally passes them to the developers in order to generate material.
Application user	The end user of an application built using the help of a DSL: CJKW's customers and their project staff who use the Issue Tracking systems.
DSL design time	The time when the DSL itself is being authored, together with the generating templates and validation code. The DSL author may also write custom code to augment the functions of the graphical designer.
DSL runtime	The time when designs are being created in a DSL to help build an application. The DSL will typically generate only some of the code, and the rest will be hand-written, or maybe several DSLs will be used.
(Application) design time	The same as DSL runtime. "Application" will be omitted unless the context in which the term is being used demands explicit qualification of this term. We will never omit "DSL" from "DSL design time."
(Application) runtime	The time when the application is being run and used by the end user. "Application" will be omitted unless the context demands it.

Figure 2-4 provides an overview of the process. It's worth taking a moment to reflect on the different stages and the things that can be done there, since it is quite easy to get the different levels mixed up.[4] In authoring a DSL, we use a designer that creates the DSL definition. From this definition, code is generated for the tools that will edit and process instances of the DSL. We can write extra code that enhances the generated designer.

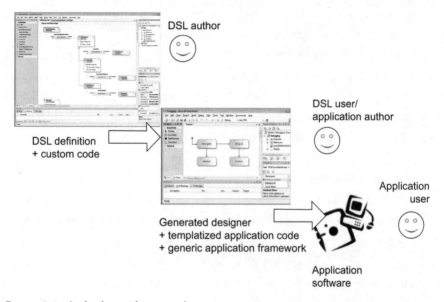

FIGURE 2-4: Authoring and usage roles

In using a DSL, we are also using a designer, and it can also be used to generate code. The code this time is part of an application. Again, we are likely to hand-write code to augment the generated material.

Evolving the DSLs

Developing the DSL and the executing framework is an incremental process. As more target systems are created, more areas of variation will be identified; some of these will vary often enough to be worth generating from a model. In some cases, the new variation might be added to an existing DSL. For example, some customers require that the set of issue fields that must

---

4. All of the authors of this book have had this experience, which we refer to as a "meta-moment" (in the hope that it is usually transitory).

be completed depends on the issue's state. To accommodate this, CJKW finds the existing code in which the transition to a next state is committed. To meet the new requirement, this code must be augmented to check that the required fields are filled. Once again the existing source file is extracted into a text template, and the relevant parts are replaced by script that reads the model. A **RequiredFields** list is added to **IssueState** for this purpose. The generator is written so that if the **RequiredFields** list is empty, the generated code looks just as it would have before—so that older models written before this enhancement still work just as they used to.

This scenario illustrates how a body of source code can progressively be brought under a generative regime, minimizing the upfront investment where there is a perceived risk or uncertainty about the design of the DSL or generating templates. Set against this is the cost of frequent small migrations, in particular, writing code to accommodate older models.

Interpretive Architectures

The code that CJKW has been writing depends on an existing framework, so it's not necessary to create one from scratch. However, the firm eventually gets a customer who wants to run several projects in the same database, each with its own different set of state transitions, and it must be possible to create new projects while the system is running. After some discussion, it is decided that the best way forward is to move the model into the database so that it can be *interpreted* at runtime. The old generated state menu code will be replaced by a generic routine that reads the state options from a new state transition table; rather than generating code, the DSL model will be used to update the transition table. (One convenient way to do that is to generate a script, so we might still use the text template technology.)

> **■ TIP** Generate, then interpret
>
> In general, interpretation requires more substantial change to the existing code, and additional effort to manage the relationship between the model on the DSL user's screen and its internal representation. When devising an incremental development plan, it is therefore worth considering generating the model to code in the early stages, even if it is to be moved inside the application later on.

> Conversely, where you are generating a large quantity of code, there may be an advantage in replacing some of it with more generic code parameterized at runtime. (The DSL Toolkit itself exhibits this progression over its history. Early on, a great deal of code was generated from the DSL definition; in later releases, the generated portion was much slimmer.)

Creating a DSL in Visual Studio

In the previous section, we saw the overall process by which a DSL is designed and used. We'll have more to say about that in Chapter 11.

But now let's look at exactly what steps the developers have to perform with Visual Studio in order to achieve what we've seen. (If you have your own installation of Visual Studio SDK, which contains the DSL Tools, you might like to follow along.)

Creating a DSL Authoring Solution in Visual Studio

The "New Project" dialog in Visual Studio provides a variety of skeleton projects and solutions, and—if you've installed the Visual Studio SDK—under "Extensibility," you'll find "Domain-Specific Language Designer." This template creates a "solution"—a collection of projects—and doesn't give you the option of adding a project into an existing solution. If you want to combine a DSL with another application, you need to create it first and then do some copying later on. (It is in any case better to get the DSL working first.) The dialog takes you to a wizard that asks you details of the DSL you want to create.

The first wizard page (Figure 2-5) provides a set of starting languages on which to base your DSL. Each of them provides a DSL with a fully functioning designer, though without any code generation.

The language templates[5] provided (currently) are

---

5. The term "template " is somewhat overloaded. A Visual Studio *solution* or *project template* creates a skeleton set of files, together with build information. The DSL creation wizard allows you to choose between several different *language templates*. An *item template* is an empty or nearly empty file from which a new file of that type can be created using the Add New Item command in Visual Studio. A *text template* generates code or other material from a DSL.

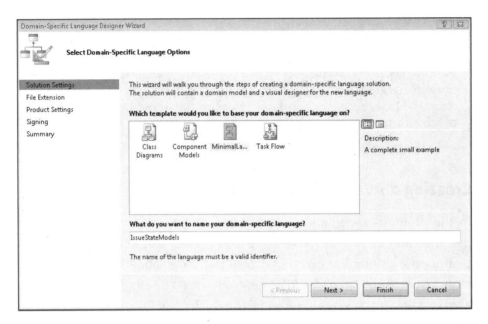

FIGURE 2-5: The DSL Designer Wizard, showing a list of starting languages on which to base the new language

- *Minimal.* Just enough to show one type of box and one type of line.
- *Components.* Boxes with ports—that is, small boxes on the boundaries of the bigger ones.
- *Classes.* Similar to UML class diagrams. The boxes are *compartment shapes*, which display rows of text.
- *Task Flows.* Similar to UML activity diagrams. Boxes can be situated within swimlanes.

■ TIP Choosing a DSL template

Although you can use one of the DSL solution templates just as it comes, the idea is that you choose the one with the features closest to the DSL you want to build, and you edit it. It isn't crucial which one you choose—you'll just have to do more or less editing to achieve what you want.

In addition to these language templates, the Visual Studio SDK comes with a samples browser within which several DSL examples can be found. It's worth taking a look at these, as they demonstrate a variety of techniques for building interesting designers on the templates. (Look under the VS SDK entry under the Windows "Start" menu.)

Devika chose the Minimal language as a basis for the Issue State language. She might have chosen the Task Flows solution, but she knows that she would have to start by deleting the bits that display the swimlanes, and she reckons it might be quicker just to adapt the Minimal solution.

In the later pages of the DSL creation wizard, she specifies the name of the language and the namespace of the source code for the designer and generation tools. She also specifies the filename extension ".iss" that will be used for files containing Issue State models.

The wizard creates two projects containing quite a lot of files. Prominent on the screen once the creation has finished is the DSL definition of the Minimal language (Figure 2-6).

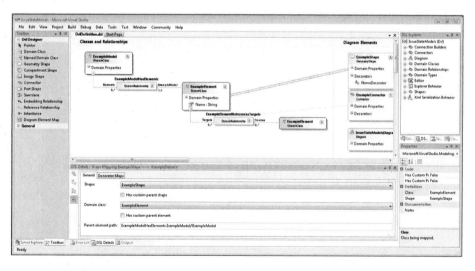

FIGURE 2-6: DSL designer

Nearly all the code in the other files in the two projects is generated from the DSL definition. When Devika modifies the language to change it from the minimal DSL into the Issue State DSL, she will do most of her work on the DSL definition.

The code in these projects (which we'll look at in more detail in the final section of this chapter) defines three main things:

1. The Issue State designer (or whatever language we're defining)—the editor that DSL users will use to draw Issue State models.
2. Code generators—which will take Issue State models and text templates (of the kind we saw in "Driving the Framework from the DSL" earlier in this chapter).
3. A serializer, designed to save Issue State models as .iss files and load them again. The serializer is used in the designer and in the code generator, and can be used in any separate applications the DSL author chooses to write.

The DSL author can modify any of these functions by adding C# code, usually in small amounts—for example, to add menu commands or validation constraints to the editor, or to change the way models are serialized to file (Chapter 6) or the way in which text templates are interpreted and code generated (Chapter 8).

What's in the DSL Solution?

The two projects initially created by the DSL creation wizard are Dsl and DslPackage. The Dsl project provides

*   A serializer/deserializer for reading and writing instances of your DSL to files.
*   Class definitions for processing the DSL and its diagrams in an application.
*   A directive processor enabling you to write text templates that will process your DSL.
*   Essential components of the designer that edits this DSL in Visual Studio.

The DslPackage project provides code that enables the DSL to be edited in Visual Studio. (It is possible to write a stand-alone application that processes the DSL using just the assembly created by the `Dsl` project.) These files are essentially the same as in other Visual Studio SDK packages:

- Document handling code that recognizes the DSL's file extension and opens the appropriate designer
- Menu commands associated with the DSL's designer
- Item template files from which new instances of the DSL can be created

In each project, there is a folder called `GeneratedCode`. This folder contains text template files (extension `.tt`), each of which has a generated file as its subsidiary. In the solution explorer, click the [+] to see the generated file. Most of the text template files consist of references to include files, kept in the DSL Tools installation folder under "TextTemplates."

All of the generated files are derived from `Dsl\DslDefinition.dsl`. You should not modify them, but you can customize the generated code by adding your own partial class definitions in separate files. (See Chapter 10 for a full account of the facilities for customization.)

Trying Out the DSL Solution

Before adapting the language, Devika decides to try out the solution, and so presses the F5 key. (In Visual Studio, this builds the solution and runs it in debugging mode. It is equivalent to the "Debug>Start Debugging" menu command.)

F5 normally has the effect of starting up the application you are designing—perhaps a desktop application in a window or a command line application in the console. But in this case, the users of the DSL are developers—Devika herself, Dave, and her other colleagues—who are going to be building applications with the help of the DSL. They will be viewing the DSL in a designer (graphical editor) that runs within Visual Studio. On pressing F5, therefore, what appears is another instance of Visual Studio, initialized to display a sample of the DSL. In fact, this behavior is common to many Visual Studio SDK examples and templates, allowing you to design enhancements to Visual Studio without fear of causing problems.

The new instance of Visual Studio (Figure 2-7) opens on a small sample project called `Debugging`, and within that, opens a file called `Sample.iss`. This was generated by the DSL creation wizard—you can see it in the file system alongside the main generated project folders.

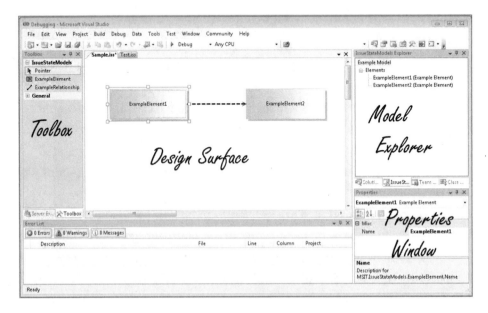

FIGURE 2-7: The designer for the Minimal language

Figure 2-7 shows the basis of the tool that Devika and her colleagues will be able to use—once she has completed her work on it.

- The largest window is the design surface, the main presentation of a DSL instance. Devika will have to edit the DSL definition (back in the main Visual Studio) in order to add, for example, the definition of the Issue State language's start element, the black dot that flags the start state. When the DSL is all working and deployed, DSL users will draw their Issue State diagrams here.

- On the left is the toolbox. To make a new element, you drag from the tool onto the diagram; to make a new connector, you click the relevant tool, click the source element on the diagram and then the target. Devika will have to edit the DSL definition to change the names of the tools to "Issue State" and "Transition," and add a tool called "Start Marker."

- On the right is the model explorer. This shows a tree presentation of the model (that is, the DSL instance). It shows the elements and their embedding relationships. In some DSLs (depending on their design), there are elements that do not appear in the main design surface but will always appear in the model explorer.

- In a separate tab under the model explorer is the usual solution explorer, showing the Debugging project containing the sample file. Devika will change the name of the project to "IssueStates." When it is deployed, copies of this project will run alongside the other code of Issue Tracking applications. She will add text template files that will read the user's DSL instance and create code that forms part of the Issue Tracking application.

- Below that is the properties window. When any element is selected in the main diagram or the model explorer, its properties are displayed here and can usually be edited. Some properties, such as an element's name, are displayed and may be edited directly in the shape. Clicking in the main part of the diagram shows the domain properties of the root element of the model; clicking on a shape or connector shows the domain properties of its corresponding domain class instance or domain relationship link.

(The arrangement of these windows is variable. If any of your windows seems to be missing, find it under the "View" menu; some of them can be found under the "Other Windows" submenu.)

File Extensions, Packages, and the Experimental Hive

When you open any file using Visual Studio, it looks at the file extension— .cs, .htm, .iss, .dsl, and so on—and runs the appropriate designer. Some designers are built in, and some are supplied as separate packages that have to be installed. The package is registered in Visual Studio's section of the Windows registry. When Devika has completed her DSL design, she will package it up for distribution to her colleagues, and they will install it on their machines (see Chapter 9). In the meantime, the build command (F5) installs it on her own machine so that she can try it out.

However, registrations for debugging purposes are made in a separate section of the registry, the *experimental hive.* When Visual Studio starts, it can be made to configure itself from the experimental hive instead of the usual one, and this is what happens when Visual Studio is started for debugging purposes—we say that it is an experimental instance of Visual Studio. An experimental instance can also be started from the Visual Studio SDK section of the Windows Start menu. Once Devika has built her DSL, she can edit it with any experimental instance of Visual Studio. However, the normal instances will not be able to see it until she has installed it properly.

Should she, in the course of development, chance to create a faulty package that prevents Visual Studio from working, it can easily be reset to the state of the normal hive; there is a reset utility in the VS SDK section of the Windows Start menu. The same procedure clears out old experimental language definitions.

The experimental hive is part of the Visual Studio SDK, and there is a full account in the installed help and on the MSDN website.

Defining the DSL

Devika is now ready to author her own DSL. She closes the experimental instance of Visual Studio and returns to the DSL authoring solution. If it isn't already open, she opens `DslDefinition.dsl` in the `Dsl` project. This launches the DSL designer (Figure 2-6). The DSL designer looks not unlike the designer of the Minimal language or any other specific DSL. This is because it was "bootstrapped"—designed using itself.

The main window contains two swimlanes or columns: on the left, the *domain model*—that is, the domain classes and relationships, and on the right, the shapes and connectors that represent them on screen. The names of all of these items can be edited; new ones can be created using the tools in the toolbox. Unlike most designers created with the DSL Tools, this one maintains a strict tree-like presentation of the elements and their relationships. By right-clicking on the domain classes, you find commands for reordering the tree.

Devika edits names of the domain classes, shape, connector, and diagram, so that they become like those of Figure 2-8; then she edits the role names (the labels on the two arms of each relationship), and finally, she edits the relationship names. Each of these can be edited directly in the diagram, except for the role names.

> ■ **TIP** **To change the label appearing on a relationship role, edit the Name of the *opposite* role**
>
> For example, to change "Targets" appearing on the left of the **ExampleElementReferencesTargets** relationship (Figure 2-6), select the opposite role (labeled Sources) and in the properties window, change the **Name** property from **Target** to **Successor** (in the singular). The label on the left-hand role will automatically change to **Successors** (plural). This makes perfect sense—see Chapter 3 for details.

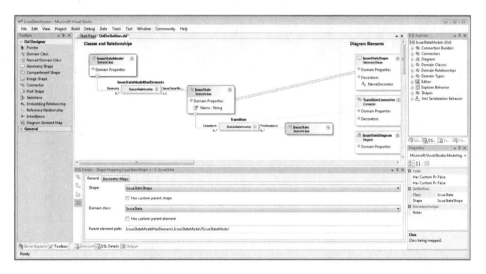

FIGURE 2-8: DSL after editing names

The final step is to change the names of the tools that will appear in the toolbox. These are not represented in the main diagram of the DSL definition—look instead at the DSL explorer; the tool definitions can be found underneath the Editor node. Their names can be edited in the properties window together with the tooltips and captions that are displayed to users.

Generating the Code for the Designer

Code for the designer of this DSL is generated from the DSL definition file. To make that happen, go to the solution explorer (in the main Visual Studio) and click the "Transform All Templates" button in its header (Figure 2-9). All of the code files will be regenerated.

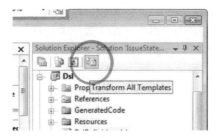

FIGURE 2-9: Solution explorer with "Transform All Templates" button

---

■ **TIP** After editing the DSL definition, always click "Transform All Templates"

The "GeneratedCode" folders contain a number of text template files with the extension `.tt`. Each of these has a subsidiary file that is the generated result. In the solution explorer, click the "[+]" to see it. The generated files include both C# and resource files. Don't edit the generated files!

After regenerating the code, Devika presses F5 to run the experimental VS on the Debugging project. The sample file she first looked at can no longer be read—she has changed the definition of the language, so that the old **ExampleElement** instances of the Minimal language are ignored by the deserializer.

Instead, she creates a new file in the Debugging project (using the "Add new item..." menu command). The file opens, and she can create elements and relationships in it. In fact, it's just like the Minimal language—but the names have changed (Figure 2-10).

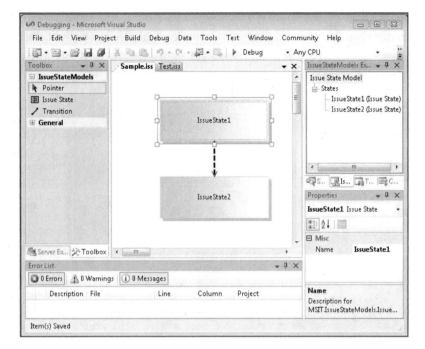

FIGURE 2-10: Issue State designer—first prototype

Adding to the DSL

With the encouragement of a working tool, Devika is enthusiastic to improve the DSL. She again stops the experimental Visual Studio, returning to the DSL definition.

The start element—the black dot that marks the starting state—is still missing from the DSL. Like **IssueStates**, **StartElements** can be connected to **IssueStates**, so Devika reasons that they should be derived from a common abstract base class. Adding some domain classes and a shape, redefining the shape maps, and setting the base class's **Inheritance** property to *abstract* (in the properties window), she ends up with the DSL definition of Figure 2-11.

For the **StartShape**, she uses a geometry shape and sets its "geometry" property to *Circle*. She also changes the default size and color properties of the other shape and connector.

A new tool is required for the **StartShape** that can be added under the Editor node in the DSL explorer window. Devika tries to save the DSL definition at this point but gets an error complaining that no icon has been defined for the new tool. Using the solution explorer, she goes into the

Resources folder in the Dsl project and copies one of the bitmap files there. After renaming the copy to StartElementTool.bmp, she opens it and edits the picture so that it contains a circle. While there, she edits the other tool images as well.

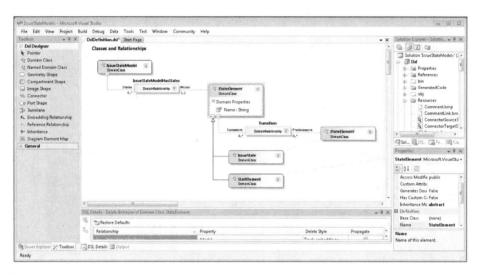

FIGURE 2-11: StartElement and IssueState have an abstract base class

After she clicks "Transform All Templates" and presses F5, she is now able to draw the state chart she's aiming for (Figure 2-12).

Constraints

However, she also finds she can draw many diagrams that would be difficult to assign a clear meaning to, and to generate code from diagrams with multiple start elements, start elements with multiple lines or no lines emerging, arrows targeting start elements, and disconnected groups of states (Figure 2-13).

Devika considers two solutions to this.

One tactic is to move the **Transition** relationship so that it only applies between **States**, and to define a separate relationship from **StartElement** to **State**, with a restricted multiplicity (Figure 2-14). With a little modification to the Tool definitions, the same connector tool can be used to create either type of relationship, depending on whether the user drags from a start element or from a state. And by making the two relationships derive from a common base relationship, the same Connector class can be used to represent both of them on screen. That way, the two relationships appear to the DSL user to be one, but at the same time he or she cannot make multiple connections from a **StartElement**, nor any connections to it. This is an example of a hard constraint that prevents the user from ever breaking the rule.

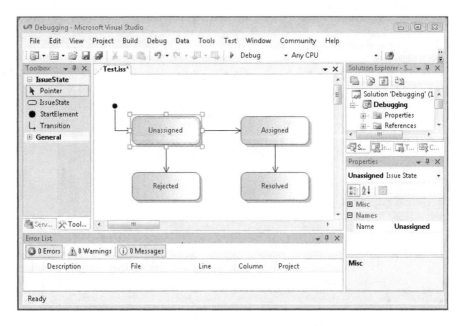

FIGURE 2-12: DSL with StartElement and improved tool icons and arrows

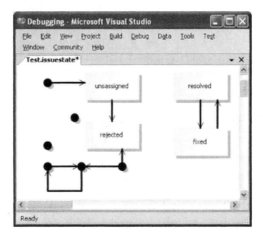

FIGURE 2-13: Invalid state model

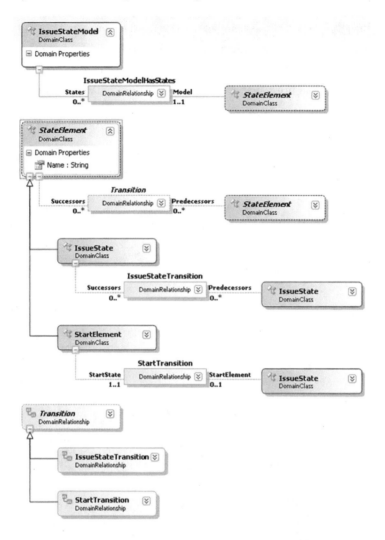

FIGURE 2-14: Issue State domain model with inheritance between relationships

An alternative, more applicable to the sins of disconnected loops and multiple start elements, is the validation constraint. This is a fragment of C# written by the DSL author that checks for invalid configurations of objects and complains about them to the user when he or she tries to save the file. It allows the user illegal configurations while editing is in progress as long as everything is correct in the end.

To create a validation constraint, Devika creates a new C# file in a separate folder alongside the generated code. The file will contain partial class definitions, adding the validation methods into the generated classes. You can see the results in Chapter 7.

Customizing the Explorer Window

Devika now wants to customize the look and feel of the explorer. Specifically, she wants to replace the domain class name, which appears in brackets by default, with icons that indicate the kind of element involved. To achieve this, she adds two "Custom Node Settings" elements under the "Explorer Behavior" node in the DSL explorer, as shown in Figure 2-15.

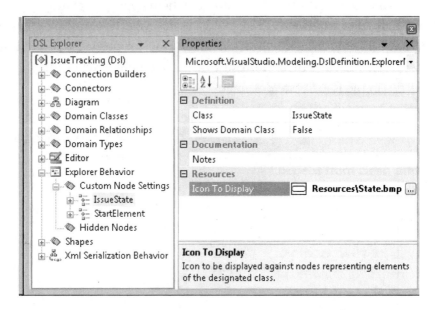

FIGURE 2-15: Explorer behavior definition

When she's done, she regenerates and presses F5 as usual. She opens an existing model and sees the explorer as expected (Figure 2-16).

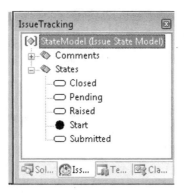

FIGURE 2-16: Result of customizing explorer

The presentation of elements in the explorer is described in Chapter 4. Adding and deleting elements through the explorer is handled in Chapter 5.

Customizing the Properties Window

Next, Devika wants to customize the properties window. Specifically, she wants to categorize the properties and give them appropriate descriptions. She does this by changing settings on domain properties and roles. Figure 2-17 shows the settings for the **DatabaseName** property on **IssueState-Model**. Figure 2-18 shows the result of these changes when displaying properties in the Issue State designer.

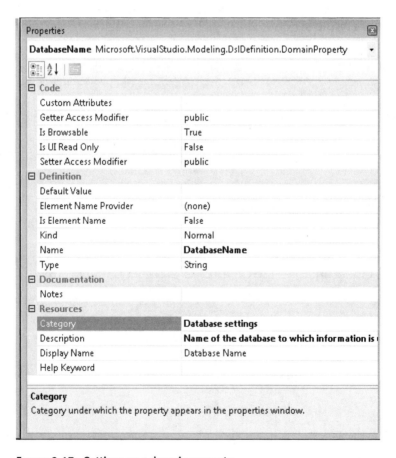

FIGURE 2-17: Settings on a domain property

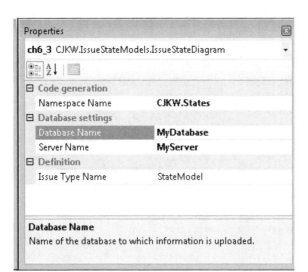

FIGURE 2-18: Result of changing settings on a domain property

Custom Code for the Designers

The DSL definition allows us to specify a wide variety of behaviors in a generated designer and its accompanying serializers and generators. An even wider range is feasible by augmenting the generated classes with handwritten code, and we will see several examples in the chapters that follow. In fact, most of the chapters begin by showing you how to define a range of behaviors in the DSL definition and how to gradually move on to more specialized customizations that require some C#. One typical use for custom code is to add context menu commands to perform some action directly from the designer, a technique described in Chapter 10.

Like validation constraints, custom code takes the form of methods and classes that are integrated with the generated code. Heavy use is made of partial class definitions—the facility for splitting the code of a class between more than one source file. Chapter 10 surveys the full range of available customization techniques.

Serialization Format of the DSL File

Let's take a look at the saved XML form of the model file of Figure 2-12:

```xml
<?xml version="1.0" encoding="utf-8"?>
<issueStateModel dslVersion="1.0.0.0" name="StateModel"
  xmlns="http://schemas.cjkw.com/IssueStateModels" >
```

```
    <states>
      <issueState name="Unassigned">
        <successors>
          <issueStateMoniker name="/StateModel/Assigned" />
          <issueStateMoniker name="/StateModel/Rejected" />
        </successors>
      </issueState>
      <issueState name="Resolved" />
      <issueState name="Assigned">
        <successors>
          <issueStateMoniker name="/StateModel/Resolved" />
        </successors>
      </issueState>
      <issueState name="Rejected" />
      <startElement name="StartElement1">
        <issueState>
          <issueStateMoniker name="/StateModel/Unassigned" />
        </issueState>
      </startElement>
    </states>
  </issueStateModel>
```

Notice that all the elements are represented very simply, using lowercase versions of the names in the DSL definition. Links are expressed in a path syntax using the names of the elements. This makes the file very easy to read and easy to write processing software for. Like everything else, if required, the format can be changed quite substantially within the DSL definition, and can be changed more radically by writing custom code.

Driving Applications from the DSL

The purpose of CJKW's Issue State language is to allow DSL users—the authors of Issue Tracking systems—to define the states and transitions that can be made within an Issue Tracking application.

Generative Application

Devika's initial plan—though as we'll see, the team improves on it—is to generate part of the application's user interface code from the DSL. She envisages that when Dave is writing the code for yet another Issue Tracking system, the Visual Studio project that contains the user interface code will include an Issue State file and one or more text template files that will generate the user interface code. When Dave is actually using the DSL, it will be fully installed in his main VS hive, but for test purposes, Devika works in the experimental VS.

She starts the experimental VS either by pressing F5 in the main project or by using the "Start VS in Experimental Hive" command in the VS SDK section of the Windows Start menu. Now she opens the existing code of an Issue Tracking application and finds the file containing the user interface code. This is the one she wants to depend on the state diagram.

First she copies an Issue State file into the application's project.

Then she proceeds to knock holes in the application code, as we saw earlier, replacing fixed pieces of code with the mixture of generated code and DSL-querying code that we saw in "Driving the Framework from the DSL" earlier in this chapter. To complete the transformation to a text template, she adds some essential header information adapted from the sample .tt files in the Debugging project and changes the file's extension to .tt.

This automatically creates a subsidiary file containing the generated code. Editing the .tt file will update the subsidiary .cs file.

Building and running the Issue Tracking application, Devika is satisfied to see that when an issue log is displayed, the state drop-down menu does offer just the next states her state model dictates.

If necessary, other files in the application can be given the same treatment, progressively turning them into template files and generating their code, which is dependent on the DSL. Whole projects full of files can be generated from a single DSL file—the DSL designer solution is a good demonstration of this.

If the state model is changed, all of the files can be regenerated, using—guess what?—the "Transform All Templates" button. This time, we're using it not to generate the code for the language but to generate a target application from an instance of that language.

Interpretive Application

Devika's solution is shown to customers, who like it. But reviewing Devika's prototype, Annie (the analyst) objects to the design. She points out that part of the way through many projects, the managers want to redefine the states and transitions their issues go through. It won't really be acceptable to regenerate and rebuild the Issue Tracking application for this purpose.

Archie (the software architect) suggests a solution. The Issue Tracking application should be rewritten to be more generic, storing the set of allowed states and transitions in the issues database itself. The DSL will be used to set these tables. As well as making the application dynamically configurable, the same software can now be used for many applications. In theory, there could be a small performance penalty for this more interpretive approach, but the negative effect will be tiny in this case and well worth it. The other issue is of course the extra work needed to refactor the application—making it store the state model and interpret it is a substantially bigger job than punching template holes in the existing code.

Devika is a bit disappointed that her generative solution wasn't acceptable, but the others point out that the DSL design itself need not be changed, and that the generative approach allowed her to prototype and demonstrate the whole approach rapidly, before investing in the more expensive interpretive solution.

The team considers two methods of loading the DSL's state model into the database. One is in a sense generative again. We write a text template that generates an SQL script that sets the state and transition records. After generating the script, it can be handed to the database administrator to run at an appropriate time.

The other method is more direct and involves writing some custom code for the designer. A menu command is added that logs onto the Issue Tracking database and runs the necessary SQL commands directly. The DSL user will draw the Issue State model and call up the menu directly on the design surface; the effects should be immediately visible in the application.

Deployment

Once the DSL and the framework it generates have been developed, they can be packaged in an installer and distributed in the form of a standard .msi (Windows installer) file. The installer can include

- The designer, serialization, and text template processor components for the DSL.
- An item template for Visual Studio's "Add new item" command, allowing the DSL user to create a new instance file of the DSL in a Visual Studio project.
- A project template for the "New Project" command, allowing the DSL user to create a new instance of a project in which the DSL is used—including all the code generation templates for the application in hand.

- Compiled assemblies that are required for the generated application. Typically, the generated parts of an application can be separated from the unchanging generic parts; the latter can be compiled and distributed in that form rather than as source.

- Readme and license agreement files that should be displayed when the installer is run.

The DSL Tools make it easy to create an installer. A "Domain-Specific Language Setup" project template is in the same location as the "Domain-Specific Language Designer" template. Devika uses this to add a setup project to her solution, which, when built, constructs the .msi file. Devika is able to customize what's included in the installer as well as customize the UI that gets displayed when the .msi file is executed, just by editing an XML file (it's actually a DSL file with an XML syntax), and then reprocessing the .tt files in the Setup project. See Chapter 9 for details.

Devika's colleague Dave has a standard edition of Visual Studio, without Visual Studio SDK. The installer automatically begins by installing the DSL Tools runtime and then installs the DSL itself. He can now create, edit, and use instances of the Issue State language even though he cannot author them.

A Second DSL: The Project Definition DSL

One useful aspect of the Issue State DSL is that a state model can be drawn offline and uploaded to the application after it has been discussed. Other aspects of the Issue Tracking application's administration remain uncomfortably immediate, however. For example, an administrator can set up new projects in the database and new categories of work to which issues can be assigned, but the effect is immediate, with no possibility for offline consideration.

Using a similar incremental process to the Issue State DSL, Archie (the architect) and Devika (the lead developer) create a new DSL. The resulting designer is shown in Figure 2-19.

The new designer drives the issue database in much the same way as the Issue State DSL.

An interesting aspect of this is that we now have more than one DSL in use to drive different aspects of the same application.

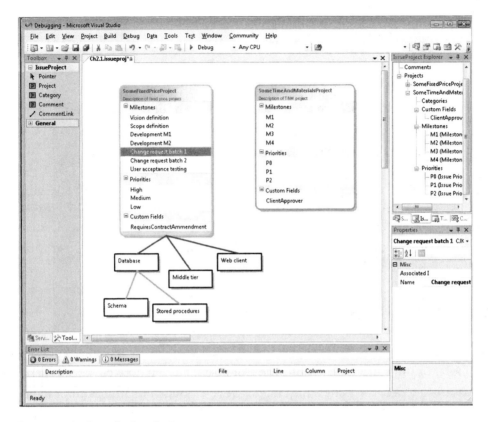

FIGURE 2-19: Issue Project designer

Architecture of the DSL Tools

A new DSL Tools solution in Visual Studio contains two projects, `Dsl` and `DslPackage`. `Dsl` provides code that defines the DSL in terms of the behavior of the generated designer, how it is serialized, and how transformations work; `DslPackage` provides coupling to Visual Studio so that instances of the DSL can be opened and saved as documents.

The Generated Code

Most of the content in both projects resides in the `GeneratedCode` folders and is generated from `DslDefinition.dsl`. While it's instructive to look at the content of these folders, it is never useful to edit them, as the edits will be lost the next time you click the "Transform All Templates" button. When you write custom code for validation constraints or to augment the functions of the generated designer, it should be written in separate files in a "Custom Code" folder.

Looking into the GeneratedCode folders using the solution explorer, the text template files (.tt) are immediately visible; to reveal the generated files, click the "[+]." Opening a typical template file, we see that there is very little code aside from a reference to the DSL definition file and an include directive:

```
<#@ Dsl processor="DslDirectiveProcessor"
                 requires="fileName="..\DslDefinition.dsl'" #>
<#@ include file=îDsl\Connectors.ttî #>
```

The included files are to be found within your Visual Studio SDK installation directory, under VisualStudioIntegration\Tools\DSLTools\ TextTemplates.

Most of the customizations you may wish to perform can be done by adding to the generated code—see Chapter 10 for details. In the rare case in which you need to change the generated code, replace the @include directive in the project's text template file with the text from the included standard template, and then edit that.

DSL Tools Architectural Layers

The generated code is concerned with the variations that make your DSL different from others. The generic features common to all DSLs are provided in a number of compiled assemblies that are installed as part of the DSL Tools.

There are thus three major layers in the architecture of a DSL implementation: the compiled framework, the code generated from the DSL definition, and hand-written code. The major parts are shown in Figure 2-20.

The Framework Assemblies

- Microsoft.VisualStudio.Modeling—The domain model framework is at the core of the system, managing model elements and links—instances of domain classes and domain relationships, which were introduced in Chapter 1 and are covered in detail in Chapter 3. It supports transactions, including undo and redo as well as the propagation of changes using rules and events, for example, to keep the screen presentation synchronized with the internal model.

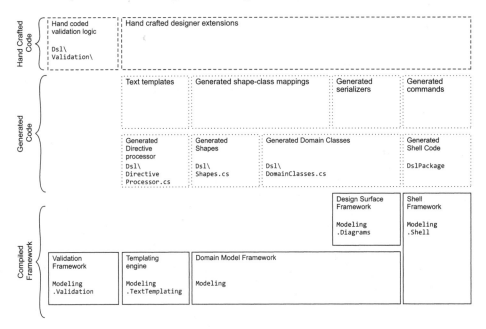

FIGURE 2-20: Architecture of the DSL Tools

- `Microsoft.VisualStudio.Modeling.Diagrams`—The design surface framework is built on top of the domain model framework and deals with the graphical notation by handling the display of elements on the design surface such as diagrams, shapes, connectors, decorators, and so on. These elements are also model elements, so the services of the domain model framework can be exploited for their management. The presentation aspect of a designer, which exploits this framework, is described in Chapter 4.

- `Microsoft.VisualStudio.Modeling.Validation`—The validation framework handles the execution of validation methods over model elements and links, and then the creation of error objects when validation fails. This interfaces with the shell framework to post messages in the errors window of Visual Studio. The use of this framework is described in Chapter 7.

- `Microsoft.VisualStudio.Modeling.TextTemplating`—The templating engine is used to execute text templates for the generation of code and other artifacts. It is an independent component that can be used to execute templates that obtain their input from sources other than DSLs. The use of the templating engine is described in Chapter 8.

- Microsoft.VisualStudio.Modeling.Shell—The modeling shell manages the hosting of the designer in Visual Studio, in particular, dealing with tools, menu commands, and the opening and closing of files.

Content of the DSL Project

The compiled code assembly built by the Dsl project (Figure 2-21) defines the DSL. A stand-alone application can use this assembly to load and manipulate DSL instance files, though without the benefit of the graphical user interface.

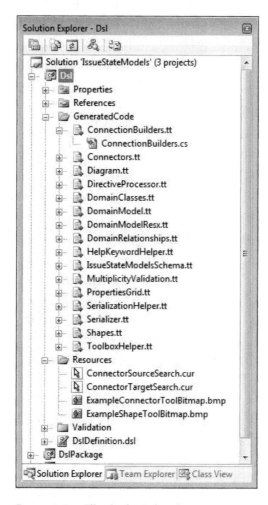

FIGURE 2-21: Files in the Dsl project

- `DslDefinition.dsl`—The file from which all the generated code is derived.

- `DslDefinition.dsl.diagram`—Every DSL instance is stored in a pair of files: one containing the essential information about the domain class instances and relationships, and the other containing the layout of the diagram. If the diagram file is lost, the user needs to rearrange the material on the screen, but no important information is lost. The DSL definition is like any other DSL in this respect.

- `Resources` folder—The images used in the toolbox for cursors and on some shapes. The images may generally be in any of several formats, including bitmap (`bmp`) and JPEG. The files that should appear here are determined by the content of the DSL definition. For example, if you define a new Tool in the DSL definition, it must have an icon to represent it in the toolbox. You provide a name for the file and then supply it in the `Resources` folder.

- `Properties\AssemblyInfo.cs`—Version information that finds its way into the compiled code for your DSL. The entries are derived from the values you supplied to the wizard when you created the DSL.

- `Dsl.csproj`—The project file isn't explicitly shown in the folder, but its content is accessible by right-clicking the `Dsl` project node and choosing "Properties." The assembly name and default namespace are derived from values you supplied to the DSL creation wizard.

Several of the files in the `GeneratedCode` folder correspond to the main sections of the DSL definition as seen in the DSL explorer:

- `DomainClasses.cs`—A class (or two) for each of the domain classes defined in the DSL definition. There are regions in each class handling each domain property, each role (that is, participation in a relationship), and in some cases a handler handling "merges"—linking of one object to another. Each class also contains a nested property handler class for each domain property. (See Chapters 3 and 5 for details.)

- `DomainRelationships.cs`—A class for each domain relationship. All the same code as domain classes, plus handlers for the linkage to each end of the relationship.

- `DomainModel.cs`—A class representing the model as a whole (not the same as the root class of the model). It provides mostly reflective information about the other domain classes.

- `Shapes.cs`, `Connectors.cs`—Implementations of the graphical aspects of the DSL definition. Contain quite a lot of code that can be overridden or augmented to customize the interactive behavior of the generated designer. (See Chapter 4.)

- `Diagram.cs`—Includes code for updating the diagram content when the model changes.

- `ConnectionBuilders.cs`—Implements the detailed behavior of connection tools. (See Chapter 5 for details.)

- `ToolboxHelper.cs`—Code called when Visual Studio sets up its toolbox, which defines the tools for this DSL. This code is generated from the "Editor\Tools" node in the DSL explorer. (See Chapter 5.)

- `Serializer.cs`, `SerializationHelper.cs`—Define how instances of the DSL are saved to files. Generated from the Xml Serialization Behavior section of the DSL definition. (See Chapter 6.)

- `DirectiveProcessor.cs`—Defines parameters to the template processing engine that allow instances of the DSL to be referenced by text templates. (See Chapter 8.)

- *Language*`Schema.xsd`—The XML schema definition for the language.

- `MultiplicityValidation.cs`—Where the DSL definition specifies that the minimum multiplicity of a relationship role is 1, this code checks that the DSL user has indeed created a link, as part of the validation checks on saving the file.

- `DomainModelResx.resx`—A resources file containing strings and image references used in your DSL. (See Chapter 4.)

Content of the DslPackage Project

The assembly generated by this project (Figure 2-22) is concerned with managing DSL instances as Visual Studio documents. Many of the files are standard for packages defined using the Visual Studio SDK and are discussed in the VS SDK help.

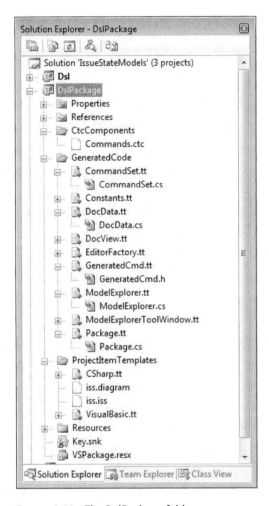

FIGURE 2-22: The DslPackage folder

- Commands.ctc— Modify this file to define menu commands in the standard Visual Studio command table syntax. (See Chapter 10.)

- GeneratedCommand.h—Text that is included by Commands.ctc that defines the standard menu commands for the DSL that appear when you right-click on the diagram—for example, to run validation checks.

- CommandSet.cs—Code for the standard commands for the DSL.

- Constants.cs—The file extension of this DSL, the version number, the Globally Unique IDs (Guids) of the designer package, and so on.

- `Package.cs`—Run by Visual Studio when setting up its toolbox and menus, to register menu commands. Notice the class attributes, which control the registration of the package, tools, explorer, and the mapping of the filename extension to this package.
- `EditorFactory.cs`—Code to start up the designer for the DSL when a file is opened.
- `DocData.cs`—Code managing the loading and saving of a DSL file within Visual Studio.
- `DocView.cs`—Code managing the presentation of a DSL instance in a designer window.
- `ModelExplorer.cs`—Code for the explorer specific to this DSL.

SUMMARY

This chapter has examined a scenario in which a company used DSL Tools and provided an overview of their application. Several points have been made:

- A DSL allows you to quickly and reliably produce multiple variants of a piece of software and to make changes when necessary.
- A DSL and the framework that executes it (or uses it as input) are developed together, preferably in gradual steps to minimize risk.
- In some cases, the system may graduate from a generative toward an interpretive framework, allowing more runtime flexibility.
- A wide variety of functionality may be specified in the DSL definition and may be extended even further by augmenting the generated code with hand-written code. Hand-written code is used particularly in the definition of validation constraints.
- To understand the DSL Tools and their use, it is important to distinguish between the roles of DSL author, DSL user, and the user of the application created with the help of the DSL.

The chapters that follow treat in more detail all the features touched on briefly here. The final chapter discusses in more depth the process for designing a DSL in the broader context of the software development process.

▪ 3 ▪
Domain Model Definition

Introduction

Chapter 2 introduced the different pieces that must be created to develop a DSL: the domain model, graphical notation and toolbox, explorer and properties window, validation, serialization, and deployment. It also introduced the DSL designer, which the DSL author uses to define the different components of the new language. This chapter describes how to define the domain model and what a domain model means in terms of the generated DSL tool.

Every DSL has a domain model at its core. It defines the concepts represented by the language, their properties, and the relationships between them. All DSL users must be aware of these to some extent, because every element that they create and manipulate while using the DSL is described by the domain model. The domain model is like a grammar for the DSL; it defines the elements that constitute a model and gives rules for how these elements may be connected together.

The domain model also provides the foundation for the other aspects of the language to build on. The definitions of notation, toolbox, explorer, properties window, validation, serialization, and deployment are all built on the domain model. It is also used to generate the programmatic API, which you can use to customize and extend the language, and which you access from templates to generate code and other textual artifacts.

The basics of domain modeling are quite simple if you are familiar with object-oriented design or object-oriented programming. This chapter describes all of the basic ideas, using the Issue State example introduced in Chapter 2 as a source of examples. It also delves more deeply into some of the finer points of domain modeling, using some modifications to the Issue State example to illustrate the key issues.

The Domain Model Designer

We start building the Issue State domain model in the DSL authoring solution described in the previous chapter, created using the Domain-Specific Language designer wizard. The minimal language template creates a good starting point. In the wizard, the company name is set to CJKW, the language name to **IssueStateModels**, and the file extension to .iss. From the resulting domain model, everything is deleted except the domain class **ExampleModel** and the **IssueStateModelsDiagram**, which are renamed to **IssueStateModel** and **IssueStateDiagram**, as shown in Figure 3-1.

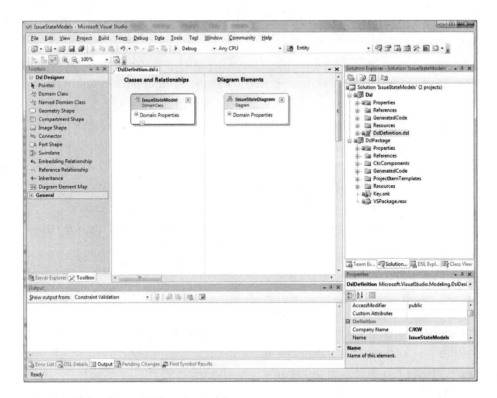

FIGURE 3-1: Smallest valid domain model

The topic of this chapter, the domain model, is the set of elements that appear in the left-hand area of the design surface, marked "Classes and Relationships."

> **TIP Delete invalid toolbox elements**
>
> If you try to validate this domain model by right-clicking over the design surface and selecting "Validate All," you may get a couple of errors because of elements in the Toolbox part of the definition that refer to elements that you've deleted. It is fine to delete these toolbox elements, because this chapter will not discuss the toolbox. Once they are deleted, the domain model should validate; it is in fact the smallest valid domain model, which contains a single domain class associated with a single diagram.

Whenever your domain model is valid, you can create a designer to try out by pressing the "Transform All Templates" button in the solution explorer and pressing F5 to build and run your design. You might even try this on the domain model shown in Figure 3-1. In the resulting designer, each `.iss` file will load as a blank diagram associated with a model explorer that shows a single **IssueStateModel** element and no means to add anything else. When the domain model is completed, the diagram will still be blank but you'll be able to create models using the model explorer, save them as `.iss` files, and reload them. Later chapters will show how to complete the user interface of your designer with shapes, connectors, toolbox entries, and customized behavior.

The In-Memory Store

Before going any further in building the domain model, it is a good idea to understand something of what happens at DSL runtime inside a generated DSL tool. At the heart of a DSL tool is a set of APIs called the In-Memory store. We often call it simply the store; it is implemented by means of a class called `Store`, which is available to the DSL author as part of the DSL APIs. The store provides a set of basic facilities to support the behavior of a DSL tool: creation, manipulation, and deletion of model elements and links; transactions, undo/redo, rules, and events; and access to the domain model.

When a DSL tool such as the Issue State designer is launched, for example, by opening one of its files, a new `Store` is created and initialized by telling it about the domain models that make up the DSL that it will be executing. We'll describe how this is done later in this chapter.

Once the store has been created and initialized, the DSL runtime executes by creating and manipulating *model elements* and *element links*. In the DSL Tools API, the abstract classes `ModelElement` and `ElementLink` provide access to all of the functionality available for creating, manipulating, and deleting model elements and links in the store. As we'll see, the code generated for the domain model when you press "Transform All Templates" in the DSL designer mainly consists of classes derived from these. For brevity, when describing instances of classes derived from `ModelElement`, we often refer simply to model elements, or MELs; we similarly refer to instances of classes derived from `ElementLink` as links.

Consider the simple model of issue states shown in Figure 3-2, consisting of the states *Raised*, *SubmittedForAssessment*, *Pending*, and *Closed*, connected by transitions as shown.

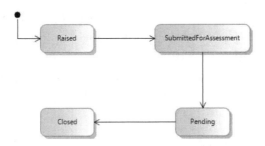

FIGURE 3-2: Simple Issue State model as presented on screen

What we see in Figure 3-2 is the on-screen presentation of a model kept in the store. We'll see later how the actual shapes and arrows are derived from the model, but let's for the present focus on the model itself. In the store at DSL runtime, this model is represented by MELs connected by links as shown in Figure 3-3. Observe that each MEL representing an **IssueState** has a **Name** property. Each of the links has a direction, from source to target. The black circle that indicates the starting state corresponds to a MEL whose class is **StartElement** and which also has a **Name** property.

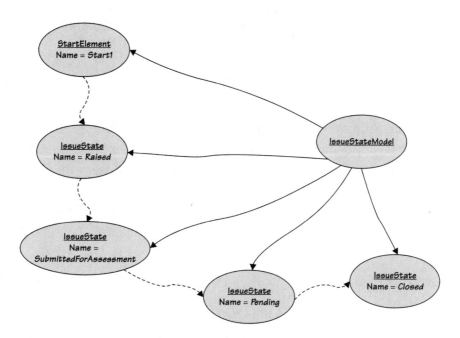

FIGURE 3-3: Issue State model as ModelElements and ElementLinks

In the store, each MEL is an instance of a C# class that is directly or indirectly a subclass of `ModelElement`. These classes are generated by the DSL Tools from the particular domain model defined by the DSL author. In fact, each of these C# classes is generated from an element in a DSL definition that we call a *domain class*. Similarly, each link is an instance of a C# class that is directly or indirectly a subclass of `ElementLink`. These classes are generated from elements that we call *domain relationships*. In fact, `ElementLink` is itself a subclass of `ModelElement`, so every link can do everything that a MEL can do, such as possessing properties.

> ■ **TIP** Creating links between links is possible but can cause complications
>
> It is even possible to create links sourced and/or targeted on links, links between those links, and so on *ad infinitum*. But you would be wise to avoid creating links to links unless you are sure that it really is the best way to get what you want; usually a simpler approach will pay dividends in maintaining your models and avoiding tricky customizations.

To avoid confusion, we will always talk about "domain classes" to refer to the parts of the domain model, and "C# classes" to refer to classes defined in the C# programming language—whether generated from the domain model or hand-written. Sometimes when talking about the generated code we'll also mention the CLR: the Common Language Runtime, which is the basis for all of the Microsoft .NET programming languages.

Domain Classes

Domain classes are created in the DSL designer by dragging the "Domain Class" tool from the toolbox and dropping it onto the "Classes and Relationships" section of the DSL designer's design surface. We've already got a domain class in our domain model, called **IssueStateModel**. This is called the *root domain class*. There can only ever be one of these in a domain model. When you run the Issue State designer to create models like the one shown in Figure 3-2, there will always be a single instance of the root domain class that corresponds to the diagram. The same is true for any DSL; you must define a single root domain class and associate it with the diagram. Thankfully, this is done automatically for you by the language templates from which you start, so unless you delete the one provided, it is already set up correctly.

As we saw from Figure 3-3, the Issue State domain model must contain domain classes called **IssueState** and **StartElement**, both of which must define a **Name** domain property. Later we will define domain relationships to link these states into their owning model and to represent the transitions between them. **IssueState** and **StartElement** share some important characteristics;

they have a **Name** and they participate in transitions. These characteristics are represented by an abstract domain class called **StateElement** from which these domain classes inherit.

On the toolbox is a choice between "Domain Class" and "Named Domain Class." Dragging the latter causes the creation of a domain class that has a **Name** domain property. We use this tool to create a new domain class, which gets a default name of **DomainClass1**. Renaming this to be **StateElement** and setting its "Inheritance Modifier" to *abstract* gives the result shown in Figure 3-4.

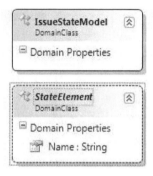

FIGURE 3-4: Creating the StateElement domain class

TIP Use the "Named Domain Class" tool to create a Name domain property

The special tool for "Named Domain Class" actually does more than just creating a domain class and giving it a **Name** domain property; it also creates settings so that the **Name** property has unique default values and special treatment for serializing cross-references. We'll see the details later. As a rule of thumb, if you want to create a domain class whose instances have names, use the "Named Domain Class" tool.

The two domain classes **IssueState** and **StartElement** are created using the "Domain Class" tool—since they will inherit from **StateElement**, they do not need a **Name** domain property. Once the domain classes have been dropped onto the design surface and given their correct names, selecting the "Inheritance" tool and then clicking on the derived class and dragging and dropping it on the base class will create the inheritance connectors, as shown in Figure 3-5.

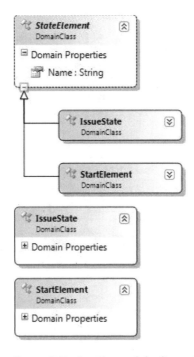

FIGURE 3-5: Creating an inheritance hierarchy

At this point, each of the new classes appears twice on the design surface as a consequence of the way the domain model design is laid out. In any domain model design, a particular domain class might appear many different times, depending on the various relationships that it has with other domain classes. However, only one of these appearances represents the full definition of the domain class; the rest are placeholders. By right-clicking on one of the placeholder appearances and selecting "Bring Tree Here" from the context menu, you can rearrange the diagram so that the definitions are conveniently placed, resulting in the reorganized layout shown in Figure 3-6. Other options to rearrange the layout include "Split Tree," which has the opposite effect of "Bring Tree Here," allowing you to divide up the tree into convenient sections, and "Move Up" and "Move Down," which enable you to change the vertical order of the domain classes. Also, the little square on the edge of the **StateElement** domain class contains a little

"–" sign; clicking in the square will cause everything hanging beneath it to collapse, leaving just the square containing a little "+" sign.

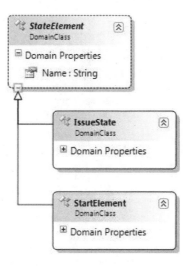

Figure 3-6: Reorganized layout of the
inheritance hierarchy

As we've seen from this example, domain classes can participate in inheritance hierarchies. Each domain class may have zero or one base domain class. The notation for this is borrowed from UML and consists of a solid line with a triangular open arrowhead directed toward the base domain class. The meaning is just as you would expect—the derived domain class inherits all of the domain properties and domain relationships from the base class. A domain class can be marked as *abstract* or *sealed*. An abstract domain class cannot be directly instantiated—it must instead have another domain class derived from it. A sealed domain class cannot be inherited from. Abstract domain classes appear on the diagram with a dashed border, and their names are in italics; sealed domain classes appear on the diagram with a heavy solid border.

Now we would like to give the **IssueState** domain class two domain properties: **Description**, so that the DSL user can give each **IssueState** some descriptive text, and **Icon**, so that the DSL user can associate an icon file with the state. Right-clicking over the "Domain Properties" compartment of the domain class offers a context menu containing the option "Add new DomainProperty;" by using this, the desired properties are created, as shown in Figure 3-7.

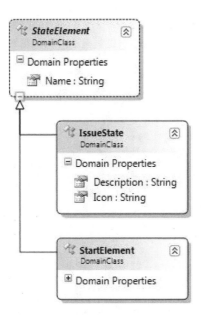

FIGURE 3-7: New Domain Properties added
to IssueState

Figure 3-8 shows the Visual Studio properties window when the domain class **StartElement** is selected on the design surface. The "Description" setting is selected in the properties window. Every domain class has such a description, which is used to generate comments into the code and the XML Schema generated from the domain model. Under the "Definition" category are settings for the "Base Class" from which this domain class inherits, the domain class's name, and the CLR "Namespace" into which code will be generated.

An explanation for each entry in the properties window can be obtained by pressing the F1 key, which will open the appropriate page of the online documentation.

Figure 3-9 shows the properties window when the **Name** domain property of the domain class **StateElement** is selected.

Each domain property has a type, which may be any CLR type. In fact, the most commonly used types in a domain model are String, Boolean, and domain-specific enumerations defined in the DSL explorer (using the "Add New Domain Enumeration" command). A domain property may also be given a default value, which will be used to initialize its value when a new MEL is created.

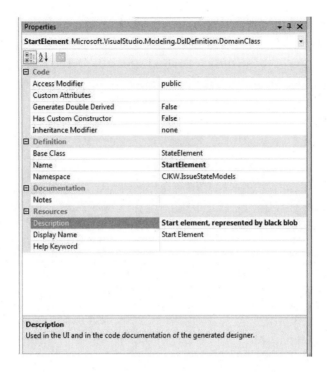

FIGURE 3-8: Properties window for domain class StartElement

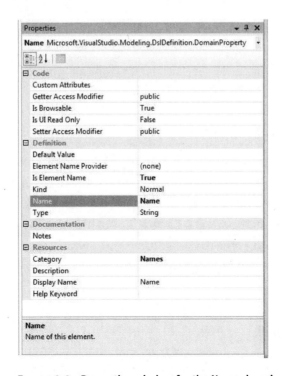

FIGURE 3-9: Properties window for the Name domain property

Up to one domain property in each class may be marked as a name by setting "Is Element Name" to *True* as shown in Figure 3-9. Properties with "Is Element Name" set to *True* are treated specially in the DSL runtime; for example, their "Display Names" will be shown in various parts of the runtime user interface, such as the properties window.

▪▪ **TIP** "Property" has two meanings

The word "property" can cause confusion, because it has two different meanings. In a domain model, a domain class has a set of domain properties, which will govern what exists in the store when the eventual DSL is running. In the DSL designer, every element has a set of properties, which are shown in the properties window when the element is selected. One source of confusion is the fact that a domain property is just such an element. Through the properties window you can see that a domain property, such as the one called **Name**, has a set of properties, such as **Kind**. Similarly Figure 3-8 showed that every domain class has a **Description** property, not to be confused with the domain property called **Description** in Figure 3-7.

We've tried to avoid this confusion by referring explicitly to domain properties wherever possible. But you really have to get used to the fact that every domain property has a **Name** property, and in fact the **Name** property of the domain property shown in Figure 3-9 has the value "Name."

Domain Relationships

Let's add some domain relationships to our domain model. Unlike classes, we don't have to worry about confusing domain relationships with C# relationships, because there is no such thing as a C# relationship! So we usually simply talk about relationships. Each relationship has a direction, from left to right. The left end is the *source* and the right end is the *target* of the relationship. There are two kinds of relationships, called *embeddings* and *references*. Embeddings are represented by shapes connected by solid lines, and references are represented by shapes connected by dashed lines. As we'll see, embeddings and references have quite different characteristics, especially in the way that they influence the way that the language is visualized and serialized. We start by looking at reference relationships.

We'll add a **Comment** domain class to the example and introduce a reference relationship so that a **Comment** can be associated with any number of **StateElements**, and a **StateElement** can have any number of **Comments**. The store at DSL runtime will contain MELs representing **StateElements** and **Comments**, connected by links of the new relationship as shown by the dashed lines in Figure 3-10.

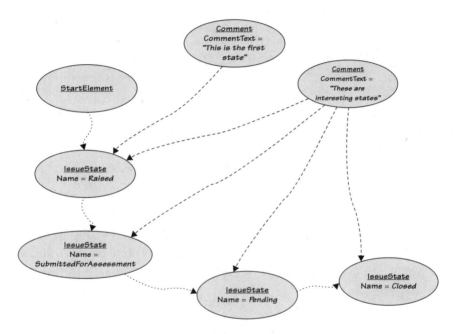

FIGURE 3-10: Comments linked to IssueStates

First we add a new domain class called **Comment** using the "Domain Class" tool. We give it a domain property called **CommentText**, with the type String. Then we select the "Reference Relationship" tool on the toolbox, click over the **Comment** domain class, drag to the **StateElement** domain class, and release. This creates a new reference relationship whose name is automatically set to **CommentReferencesStateElements**. We decide that this name doesn't quite represent the intended meaning of the relationship, so we edit it and change it to **CommentsReferToIssueStates**. The result is shown in Figure 3-11.

Let's take a close look at the relationship in Figure 3-11 so that we can see its various component parts. The relationship itself has a name, **CommentsReferToIssueStates,** in this case. The line at each side of the relationship is called a *domain role,* or often just *role.* Dashed lines indicate reference relationships, as in this case. Each role connects the relationship to a domain class, sometimes called the *roleplayer* for the role.

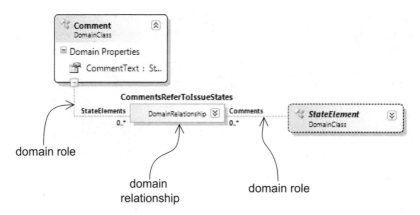

FIGURE 3-11: The CommentsReferToIssueStates domain relationship

A name is shown next to each role. This is called its *property name.* Default property names are calculated by the DSL designer from the names of the roleplayer classes. The property name **StateElements** on the left-hand role is not very descriptive, so we edit it and change it to **Subjects**, resulting in Figure 3-12.

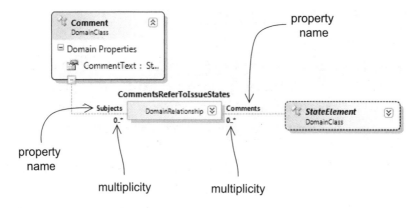

FIGURE 3-12: Property names and multiplicities on roles

Figure 3-12 also shows that each role has a *multiplicity*. In this case, the source role's roleplayer is **Comment**, its property name is **Subjects**, and its multiplicity is *ZeroMany*, which shows up on the diagram as 0..*; the target role's roleplayer is **StateElement**, its property name is **Comments**, and its multiplicity is again *ZeroMany*.

In addition to its property name, a role has a name, which is not shown on the design surface. We'll see later how the name of a role is used when code is generated for the relationship.

We've already seen that default values for the names of roles and relationships are created by the DSL designer. The default name of a role is set to be the same as the name of its roleplayer domain class. The property name of a role defaults to be the same as the name of its opposite role, pluralized in cases where the multiplicity is *Many*. The name of an embedding relationship defaults to be *XHasY*, where *X* is the name of the source role player, and *Y* is the property name of the source role. The name of a reference relationship defaults to be *XReferencesY*, where *X* and *Y* are calculated in the same way. This scheme usually gives a reasonably meaningful set of names for relationships and roles, and avoids a good deal of unnecessary work on the part of the DSL author. All of the names can be explicitly overridden by the author if desired, and we've given a couple of examples of doing that. Selecting "Reset" on the context menu for the property's entry in the properties window will reset it to the default.

Embeddings

Some relationships are embeddings, which are displayed using solid lines. Embeddings provide a way to navigate through your model as a tree, that is, as a structure in which every element (except for the single element at the root of the tree) has exactly one parent element. This is important for several reasons. The first is that models are typically serialized as XML files, and the structure of an XML document is intrinsically a tree of elements, starting at the root element. The embedding defined in the domain model determines the structure of this tree of XML elements. Chapter 6 returns to this topic in much more detail.

Second, recall from Chapter 2 that the generated designer for your DSL has a model explorer. The embedding structure determines the organization of this explorer, because an explorer is also structured as a tree.

Third, the embedding structure also provides a default for how deletion and copying behavior is propagated through a model. By default, the deletion of an embedding parent deletes its children, while the deletion of a roleplayer MEL in a reference link deletes the link but not the other end.

Marking a relationship as an embedding places some special constraints on it, as follows:

1. The multiplicity on the target role must be either *One* or *ZeroOne*, because a MEL can only be embedded once.

2. If a domain class is a target in more than one embedding relationship, the multiplicity of all of those target roles must be *ZeroOne*, because a MEL of the class can only be embedded by one of those relationships at a time. Marking any one of the roles as *One* would make all of the other relationships impossible to instantiate.

3. In a complete domain model, every domain class except the root must be the target of at least one embedding relationship, because it would not be possible to create trees of MELs otherwise, and so the model explorer and serialization would not work.

Let's create some embedding relationships. Taking the domain model created so far and selecting the context menu item "Validate All" produces the warning *"DomainClass IssueState is not abstract, and is neither a root of the model nor embedded within it"* and similar warnings for **StartElement** and **Comment**. These warnings appear because it is not possible to create trees of MELs with the domain model created so far. Therefore, it would not be possible for the Issue State designer to display a model explorer or to save the models as files. To enable the models to be trees, we must create two embedding relationships, one that embeds **Comments** into the **IssueStateModel**, and one that embeds **StateElements** into the **IssueStateModel**. These relationships are created using the "Embedding Relationship" tool, using the same gestures as the "Reference Relationship" tool. The resulting relationships are shown in Figure 3-13. Notice that the multiplicity on the right-hand roles, whose property names have been changed to **Model**, are 1..1, which is the default multiplicity for the target role of an embedding relationship.

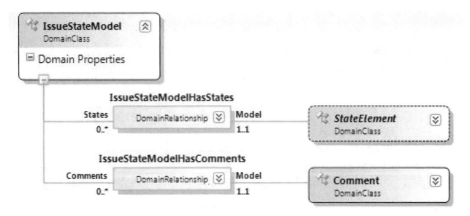

FIGURE 3-13: Embedding relationships

> **▪ TIP Embeddings control nesting in the model explorer**
>
> The best way to think about which relationships should be embeddings is to consider your model explorer. If you want elements to be nested in the explorer, make the relationship an embedding; otherwise make it a reference.
>
> An easy rule of thumb for beginners is to embed every non-root domain class directly in the root domain class and make every other relationship in the domain a reference. This is sometimes not ideal, but should always produce a workable DSL.

The root domain class **IssueStateModel** is not itself the target of any embedding relationship. Any Issue State model created at DSL runtime, such as the one depicted in Figure 3-14, will have exactly one root MEL of the class **IssueStateModel**. In the following chapters that describe how to associate a diagrammatic notation and a serialization with this domain model, you'll see that both the diagram and the top-level element of the serialized file correspond to this MEL.

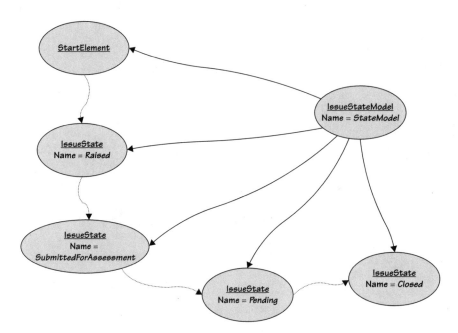

FIGURE 3-14: Root element at DSL runtime

Multiplicity

The multiplicity of a role defines, given a MEL of a particular class, how many links may have that MEL as roleplayer. There are four possible values for multiplicity.

- *One*: Every MEL of this class (or a derived class) must play this role exactly once. For example, every **Comment** must be embedded in an **IssueStateModel**.
- *ZeroOne*: A MEL of this class (or a derived class) may play this role no more than once. This is equivalent to saying that it may be linked via this relationship with zero or one MEL.
- *ZeroMany*: A MEL of this class (or a derived class) may play this role any number of times. For example, each **Comment** can refer to any number of **StateElements**.
- *OneMany*: Every MEL of this class (or a derived class) must play this role at least once.

References

We created a reference relationship earlier. References are not constrained like embeddings. In general, links from reference relationships can refer from any MEL to any other MEL. Indeed, because links are themselves MELs, you can create links between links in order to create complex graphs of objects. Bear in mind, however, that a primarily diagrammatic user interface will be used to interact with the graph at DSL runtime, so it is important to keep the design simple enough to understand through such an interface. Note, however, that although it is possible to create referencing links between any kinds of MELs or links, *embedding* links may not target links.

The next relationship we create is called **IssueStateTransition,** which goes from **IssueState** to itself. Figure 3-15 shows the detail of this relationship. Instances of this relationship are links that represent transitions that connect predecessor states to successor states. The multiplicity of both roles is *ZeroMany*—this is the default for reference relationships. This relationship has been given a domain property called **Action**.

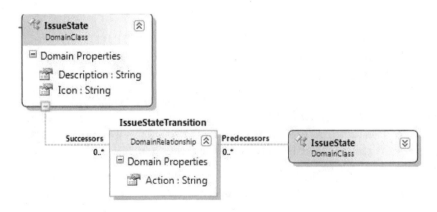

FIGURE 3-15: The IssueStateTransition relationship

Figure 3-16 shows the on-screen presentation of an example model containing links of this relationship between the four **IssueStates** called *Raised, SubmittedForAssessment, Pending,* and *Closed.*

In the figure, there are two transitions between the two states *Pending* and *Closed.* Each transition has a label that specifies the associated action.

Here is a case in which it is permissible to have more than one link of the same relationship between the same two MELs. Because the transitions carry actions, this makes perfect sense; the model says that a pending issue can be closed either by solving it or postponing it. If the transitions did not carry actions, then having two links between the same two states would not really make sense, so the DSL author would like to be able to prevent this.

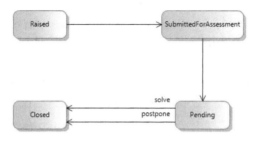

FIGURE 3-16: IssueStates and IssueState Transitions

In fact, the DSL author may specify whether or not to allow duplicate links between the same pair of MELs by setting the "Allows Duplicates" property on the domain relationship object while designing the domain model. If duplicates are not allowed, the DSL runtime will refuse to create a duplicate link.

> ■ **TIP** "Allows Duplicates" can only apply to many-to-many relationships
>
> Having multiple links between the same pair of roleplayers is only ever possible for *Many-Many* reference relationships in which both roles of the relationship have a *Many* multiplicity—any other cases have a maximum multiplicity of one, so they cannot have more than one link in any case.

Relationship Derivation

A further reference relationship is needed that connects **StartElement** to **IssueState**. Remember that a **StartElement** appears on the screen as a black dot connected to an **IssueState**. Figure 3-17 illustrates the result of creating this relationship. Note the multiplicities: Every **StartElement** must be connected to an **IssueState** via a link of this relationship—another way of saying this is that **StartElements** cannot validly exist in a disconnected state—and an **IssueState** can be connected to zero or one **StartElement**, but no more.

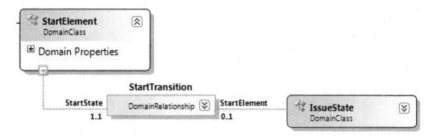

FIGURE 3-17: The StartTransition relationship

Now we are going to do something rather subtle. Remembering that **StartElement** and **IssueState** both inherit from **StateElement**, we observe that the relationships **StartTransition** and **IssueStateTransition** are rather similar. They both connect **StateElements** to **StateElements**. We can actually capture this similarity in the model by introducing inheritance on the relationships themselves. Using the "Reference Relationship" tool, we create a new relationship between **StateElement** and itself, which we call **Transition**. The "Inheritance Modifier" of this relationship is set to *abstract*, which means that it is not possible directly to create links of it.

Now the relationships **StartTransition** and **IssueStateTransition** are both derived from the abstract relationship **Transition**. This is shown by the portion of the domain model illustrated in Figure 3-18. To create this part of the model, the option "Show as Class" was selected on the relationships **Transition, IssueStateTransition,** and **StartTransition**, which caused extra shapes representing the relationships themselves to appear on the DSL designer's design surface (see Figure 3-19). This facility allows inheritance, and indeed any other kind of relationship, to be set up between domain relationships.

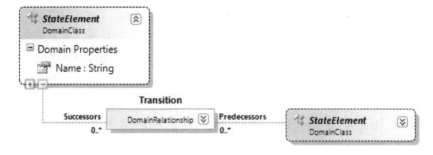

FIGURE 3-18: The abstract relationship Transition

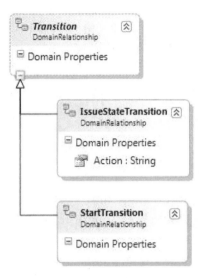

FIGURE 3-19: Relationships shown as classes in a hierarchy

The basic rule for relationship derivation is that a link of a derived relationship can be considered as if it were a link of the base relationship. This is the same as for normal classes: An instance of the derived class can be considered as if it were a link of the base class. Relationships are special, though, because they always have two roleplayer classes. If a link of the derived relationship can be considered as if it were a link of the base relationship, then the roleplayer MELs must have classes consistent with the roleplayer classes of the base relationship. That is, the roleplayer classes for a derived relationship must be derived from, or the same as, the corresponding roleplayer classes for the base relationship.

For example, a link of **IssueStateTransition** connecting two **IssueStates** can be considered as if it were a link of **Transition** connecting two **StateElements**. Similarly, a link of **StartTransition** connecting a **StartElement** to an **IssueState** can also be considered as a link of **Transition** connecting two **StateElements**. Asking the relationship **Transition** for all of its links will give back the total of the **IssueStateTransition** and **StartTransition** links.

Generating a Designer with No Shapes

Having used the concepts described so far to define the domain model in the DSL designer, a working Issue State designer can be generated and launched in the Debugging project as explained in Chapter 2.

The generated Issue State designer has a blank diagram and an empty toolbox, because these elements of the language have not been defined—defining these is the subject of later chapters. However, it does have a fully working explorer and properties window. Figure 3-20 shows the explorer when one **Comment** and three **IssueState** elements have been created, and the menu provides the option to add further elements. Notice that the structure of the explorer corresponds exactly to the embedding relationships defined in the domain model.

> ■ **TIP** Links of many-to-many relationships cannot be created through the explorer or properties window
>
> This designer is not fully functional with respect to the domain model because it is not possible through the explorer or properties window to add new **IssueStateTransition** links. To do that, it is necessary to create links from the toolbox; we'll see how to do that in later chapters.

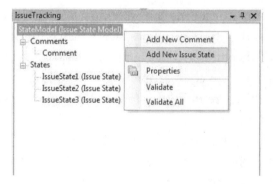

FIGURE 3-20: Explorer for Issue State target designer

The Generated Code

So far we've explained how to create the domain model. On its own, this would just be a structure within the DSL designer that represented the user's wishes about the DSL that he or she would like to build. In order to bring these wishes to life, code has to be generated to implement the domain model using the "In Memory Store" and other features of the DSL Tools. This code is generated by pressing the "Transform All

Templates" button in Visual Studio's solution explorer for the DSL Authoring solution.

From a practical perspective, it is very useful to understand the generated code, not least because customizing the generated DSL tool requires the DSL author to interface to this code and because there are some restrictions to what is allowed in domain models that result from the fact that valid code must be generated. At this point, we focus on the generated code and the elements of the DSL Tools framework that it uses.

The explanation can be considerably simplified by use of another DSL, namely, the graphical language implemented by the Class Designer tool that forms part of Visual Studio 2005. This tool will take a body of code written in C# (or other CLR languages) and create diagrams of the classes in it that show how they relate to each other.

Figure 3-21 shows such a diagram that illustrates the C# classes generated from the domain classes created during this chapter. Each rectangle in Figure 3-21 corresponds to one C# class. Observe in the header of each rectangle the little symbol that indicates the base class. By default, each class inherits from ModelElement. Each class is generated in the CLR namespace specified in the properties window for the corresponding domain class. By default, all classes are generated in the same namespace, which is the one specified in the language wizard when the language template was originally unfolded.

For our purposes, the compartments containing Fields, Methods, and Nested Types, which are only of interest to more advanced developers, have been closed up. What remains are the properties of each class. There are two kinds of property: those that have been generated directly from the domain properties specified in the domain model, and those that have been generated from the roles of the relationships, where the name of the generated property is the property name of the role. These are shown in Figure 3-21 using different display options provided by the Class Designer. The properties generated from domain properties are shown inline in the class symbols themselves, while those generated from roles are shown as arrows on the diagram.

There are two kinds of arrows, those with single arrowheads and those with double arrowheads. The ones with single arrowheads simply mean that the property has the type of the class at the head of the arrow; so for example, the arrow from StateElement to IssueStateModel marked Model means that the class StateElement has a property called Model whose type is IssueStateModel. This is a diagrammatic convention derived from UML that helps to visualize properties whose type is a class shown on the diagram.

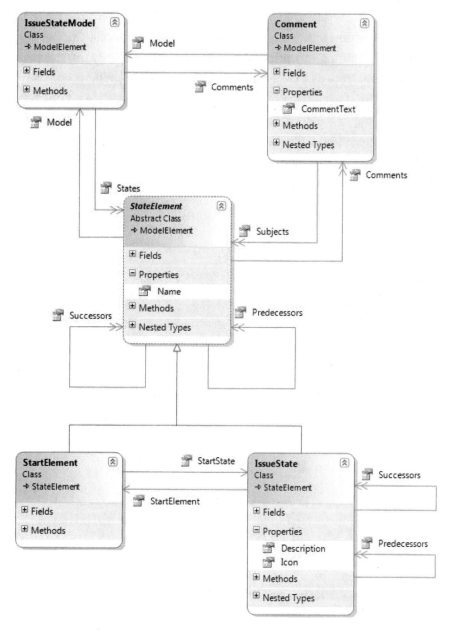

FIGURE 3-21: Class diagram of generated domain classes

The arrows with double arrowheads mean that the type of the property is a collection whose contents are instances of the type at the head of the arrow. This can be illustrated more clearly by expanding the part of the diagram that deals with the relationship `CommentsReferToIssueStates`, as in Figure 3-22. In this figure, the property of `StateElement` called `Comments` is labeled with its type `LinkedElementCollection<Comment>`. The generic class `LinkedElementCollection<T>` is part of the DSL Tools API. Every relationship role that has a multiplicity of *ZeroMany* or *OneMany* generates a property whose type is `LinkedElementCollection<T>`, where `T` is the class at the opposite end of the relationship. Generic classes are a CLR feature introduced in .NET 2.0. One of their important strengths is the ability to define strongly typed collections, that is, collections where it is possible to specify the type of their contents at compile time. This strength has been used extensively in the design of the API generated from a domain model by the DSL Tools.

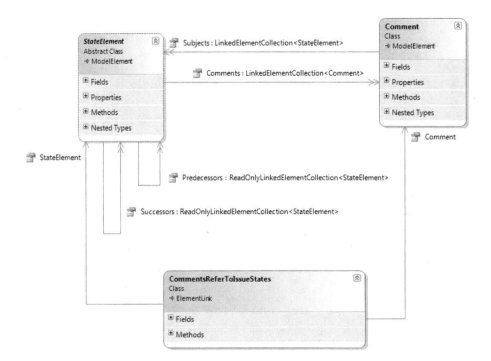

FIGURE 3-22: Class diagram for CommentsReferToIssueStates

Recall that in the domain model the role whose roleplayer is `StateElement` has a property name of `Comments`. This is used to generate the `Comments` property on the C# class `StateElement`. This role has a multiplicity of *ZeroMany*, so the type of the generated property is `LinkedElementCollection-<Comment>`.

Figure 3-22 also shows explicitly the class `CommentsReferToIssue-States`, which is generated from the corresponding relationship in the domain model. The header of the class shows that it inherits from `Element-Link`. It has two arrows leaving it, one pointing at `StateElement` and called `StateElement`, and the other pointing at `Comment` and called `Comment`. These represent properties generated from the domain roles onto the relationship class itself. The names of these properties are generated from the name of the role, as distinct from its property name. Such a property can be used in code to navigate from an individual link to the associated roleplayer object.

> ■ **TIP** The role's name is always singular; the property name is often plural
>
> Note that the *name* of the role is always singular, whereas the *property name* is plural whenever the multiplicity is **Many**. Maintaining this convention can help considerably with the readability of the generated code.

Classes generated from domain relationships such as this one are used in circumstances where the DSL author wishes to deal explicitly with the links of the relationship itself. In this particular example, that is not very likely; the normal DSL author only needs to use the `Comments` and `Subjects` properties on the roleplayer classes to create and manipulate configurations of `Comment` and `StateElement` objects together with their intervening links.

Using the Generated Code

The generated code has been carefully designed to give a convenient API for DSL authors as a basis for their own DSL extensions and code generation templates. Whenever you want to write code against this API, you must include the following using statements:

```
using Microsoft.VisualStudio.Modeling;
using Microsoft.VisualStudio.Modeling.Diagrams;
...
```

First, note that any change to the store must be performed in the context of a Transaction. If you want to add or remove elements or relationship links, or you want to change their properties, you must open a Transaction like this:

```
using (Microsoft.VisualStudio.Modeling.Transaction t =
  this.Store.TransactionManager.BeginTransaction("operation name"))
  {
    // ... change store in here ...
    t.Commit();
  }
```

If an exception is thrown that is not caught within the using block, or if you explicitly Rollback() the transaction, then all the changes performed within the block will be undone. Also, when an Undo() or Redo() operation is performed, all of the changes made in the store within the transaction are undone or redone as a unit. Indeed, the name given as a parameter to the BeginTransaction() method is the name that will show in the eventual DSL as an item on the Visual Studio undo stack.

Having defined the Issue State domain model and generated code from it, the DSL author can write code such as this:

```
using (Microsoft.VisualStudio.Modeling.Transaction t =
    this.Store.TransactionManager.BeginTransaction("example"))
{
  IssueState state = new IssueState(store);
  state.Name = "TestState";
  Comment comment = new Comment(store);
  comment.CommentText = "This is an interesting state";
  comment.Subjects.Add(state);

  t.Commit();
}
```

In fact, before this code will work, the store must be initialized. In addition to the C# classes generated for the classes and relationships in the domain model, a further C# class is generated that corresponds to the domain model itself. This class implements a variety of helper methods for creating and deleting objects, giving runtime access to the domain model, and enabling and disabling diagram rules. For our example, this class is called `IssueStateModelsDomainModel` and is derived from the class `DomainModel` supplied with the DSL Tools framework. This class is used for initializing the store. A store is created and initialized using its constructor:

```
Store store = new Store(typeof(IssueStateModelsDomainModel));
```

The result of this call is to create a new `Store`, initialized so that it can contain instances of the domain classes and relationships defined in the domain models passed in as parameters to the constructor. You can in fact pass in as many domain models as you like; a store initialized with multiple domain models can contain MELs and links from any of those models.

More about Domain Classes

The remaining sections of this chapter delve into some of the finer points of domain models and the code generated from them. Broadly speaking, they are concerned with three topics: customization of the generated code, customization of the generated user interface, and code customization options. Quite a lot of customization is possible using the DSL Tools' built-in code generation, but when the DSL author wishes to stray outside of those possibilities—to step up onto a higher customization plateau—there are additional options to enable this. These options are briefly covered here; later chapters build on these concepts and discuss the topic of customization in greater depth. Readers who are particularly interested in code customization might like to skip ahead and take a brief look through Chapter 10, where all the material on custom code is brought together.

Figure 3-23 shows the properties window when a domain class is selected. In the "Definition" category, the property "Namespace" specifies the CLR namespace where the C# class will be generated. The "Code" category provides further options for customizing the generated code. We've already seen the use of the "Inheritance Modifier" property, which can be set to *none*, *abstract*, or *sealed*, causing the generated class to be correspondingly marked. You should mark a class as *abstract* if you don't want to create any instances of it in your running DSL. If you don't mark it as *abstract*, then the DSL Tools will assume that you want to create instances of it and will generate code and validate your domain model accordingly. Marking a class as *sealed* can be useful for restricting the ways in which a designer can be extended and thus can reduce the costs of supporting it.

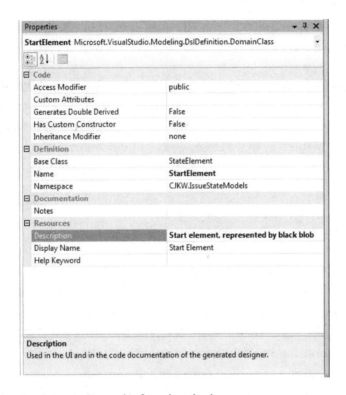

FIGURE 3-23: Properties for a domain class

By default, all of the C# classes generated from domain classes are *public*. You can specify that a generated class is *internal* using the "Access Modifier." Again, this is a way to reduce the ways in which a designer can be extended.

A very common approach to customizing a generated DSL tool is to add methods and properties to the generated C# classes by hand. *Partial classes* are a feature introduced with .NET 2.0 that permit the definition of a single class to be split across multiple files. This is extremely useful in code generation scenarios where part of the class's definition is generated and another portion written by hand; it means that hand-written code is not overwritten when the rest is regenerated. The DSL Tools exploits this capability throughout its generated code. For each domain class a *partial* class is generated so that DSL authors may write their own matching partial class(es) that add custom behavior to that generated by the DSL Tools. Such a partial class might, for example, declare that the class conforms to a particular interface, or add methods, fields, or properties to the generated code.

Sometimes, though, it is necessary to inhibit some of the code generation so that the DSL author can customize at a deeper level. For this purpose, two Boolean flags are available on the definition of a domain class. "Has Custom Constructor," when set to true, will stop the generation of a constructor for the generated class. This is useful where the DSL author needs to apply customized initialization to a particular class. "Generates Double Derived," when set to true, causes the generation of two classes: an abstract base class, containing all of the generated methods, and a concrete derived partial class that only contains a constructor. This pattern allows any virtual member in the generated class to be overridden by DSL authors, who can create their own partial section for the concrete derived class that overrides the base class. Customization sections in later chapters will demonstrate the use of this capability.

A further customization option, which applies to domain classes, relationships, properties, and roles, is given by the ability to add any extra CLR attributes that the DSL author desires through the "Custom Attributes" setting in the properties window. These attributes will be added to the generated code. This can be a useful general-purpose way to add data to the domain model that could be used to extend its use, for example, to help generate code for different purposes.

Properties of a domain class in the "Resources" category govern aspects of the user interface of the generated DSL Tool. These properties generate entries in a resources (.resx) file included in the DSL authoring solution. The "Display Name" is used whenever the domain class is identified in the user interface at DSL runtime. This is useful if the DSL is intended for use in a country that speaks a different language, or if the desired user interface name of the class is one that cannot validly be used as the identifier of a C# class.

Each domain class is also given a "Description." This is used to create a summary comment in the generated code; it is also used to generate annotations on the generated XML Schema, which provide extra IntelliSense assistance to a DSL user hand-writing XML in the target domain.

The "Help Keyword" is used to associate an optional keyword with the domain class that can be used to index F1 Help.

DomainClassInfo

When the store is initialized with a domain model, a `DomainClassInfo` object is created for every domain class in the domain model. Objects like this provide *runtime* access to the domain model, enabling the caller to discover the properties of a domain class, what domain properties it contains, which relationships it participates in, and its inheritance hierarchy. Objects like these are useful for writing programs that need to operate across the store, independently of the specific domain model that is loaded—programs such as generic user interfaces, debugging tools, serialization tools, animation tools, and so on.

This code fragment illustrates how to acquire a `DomainClassInfo` object from a suitably initialized store and query it:

```
IssueState s1 = new IssueState(store);
DomainClassInfo dci = s1.GetDomainClass();
string className = dci.Name;
ReadOnlyCollection<DomainPropertyInfo> = dci.AllDomainProperties;
ReadOnlyCollection<DomainRoleInfo> = dci.LocalDomainRolesPlayed;
```

> **■ TIP** Every DomainInfo object has an Id property
>
> Every Info object—DomainClassInfo, DomainPropertyInfo, Domain-RelationshipInfo, DomainRoleInfo—has an Id property that gives a unique System.Guid for the Info object. Some of the DSL Tools' APIs require these Ids to be passed as parameters, although most require references to the objects themselves.

The class `DomainClassInfo` also provides several static utility methods that are mainly concerned with manipulating the names of MELs. These methods could also have been implemented on the class `ModelElement` but have been made static methods on `DomainClassInfo` in order to reduce the surface area of `ModelElement` and thus improve the IntelliSense experience for generated classes that derive from ModelElement.

More about Domain Properties

The customization settings for a domain property are accessed using the properties window when the domain property is selected, as shown in Figure 3-24.

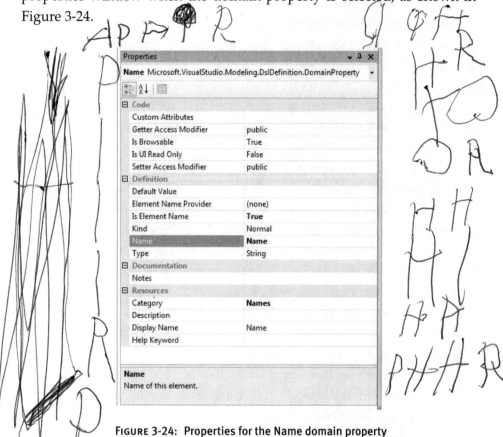

FIGURE 3-24: Properties for the Name domain property

Most domain properties in a DSL are typically typed as String, Boolean, or an enumeration defined as part of the DSL. These enumerations can be specified either as public or internal. An enumeration may optionally be marked as *Flags*, in which case its values are interpreted as a bitfield.

> **■ TIP** Domain properties of Flags types have a custom editor with checkboxes
>
> When a domain property's type is an enumeration marked as Flags, the property will automatically show up in the properties window of the generated tool with a custom editor that allows you to set the bitfield using checkboxes.

In fact, a domain property may have any CLR value type, including types defined outside the DSL. The default value for the domain property, if there is one, must be a string that converts validly to a value of the domain property's type.

Normally, a domain property generates a public CLR property on the generated class. It's possible to separately specify the access modifier for the generated getter and setter via "Getter Access Modifier" and "Setter Access Modifier" to be *private, internal,* or *protected*—in fact, any of the access modifiers allowed by the CLR. The DSL author might place such restrictions in order to limit the way that the domain property can be used, and hence in order to limit support costs.

We earlier saw that one domain property in a class may be marked as being a name (by setting "Is Element Name" to *True*). When this is set, a built-in algorithm is used to create default values for the name domain property that are unique for the MEL and its siblings within the context of the same embedding MEL. The default algorithm appends a number to the name property's default value, or to the domain class name if there is no default value. For example, the **Name** domain property in the **State-Element** domain class has no default value. This means that the default unique names for **IssueStates** within the same **IssueStateModel** will be "IssueState1," "IssueState2," "IssueState3," and so on.

This algorithm may be overridden by defining a class that derives from the built-in `ElementNameProvider` class, implementing its `SetUniqueName()` method with the desired algorithm, and setting the "Element Name Provider" property to refer to the new class.

When the generated designer is running, selecting a shape on the diagram or an entry in the model explorer will cause the domain properties defined for the domain class of the selected MEL to show up in the properties window, named by their "Display Name." Domain properties can be hidden from the properties window by marking them with "Is Browsable" set to *False,* and if they are browsable they will show up in gray and with editing disabled if they are marked "Is UI Read Only" set to *True*. The properties window is organized into categories, and the domain property's "Category" can be specified by a string. If no category is specified, the property will appear in the category "Misc." When a property is selected in the properties window, its "Description" will appear, giving the DSL user some help in understanding its meaning. The "Description" is also emitted in the property summary comment in the generated code and as an annotation in the generated XML Schema.

Calculated Properties

An important customization is the ability to define calculated domain properties. These are properties that have no storage and only a getter. The value for the domain property is calculated, when called, from data acquired elsewhere, for example, from other domain properties on this or other MELs. Setting a property's "Kind" to *Calculated* causes the generation of code that requires the DSL author to implement a method, in a partial class, called `GetXXXValue()`, where **XXX** is the name of the calculated domain property. This method can use the generated API to navigate to the data it needs to calculate the correct result. If the DSL author forgets to implement this method, then the DSL will fail to compile.

There is a subtlety that arises when defining a calculated domain property. We'll see later that making changes to the store causes the firing of *rules*, which are used to update objects in the store, and *events*, which are used to make updates external to the store. In particular, rules are used to fix up the diagram when MELs are changed. When a domain property is defined as *Calculated*, rules and events do not automatically fire when the calculated value changes. Instead, the DSL author must explicitly cause rules and events to be triggered, using the method `Notify-ValueChange()` on the class `DomainPropertyInfo`. We'll describe this class shortly.

A further possibility for the "Kind" of a property is called *Custom-Storage*. A domain property marked in this way will not generate any field to hold its data. Instead, the DSL author must define, in a partial class, some other way to store the value for the property, and must also define methods `GetXXXValue()` and `SetXXXValue()`, which will access and update the property's stored value. This capability can be useful when the "Type" of the property needs special initialization or lifetime management.

DomainPropertyInfo

When the store is initialized with a domain model, a `DomainPropertyInfo` object is created for every domain property in the domain model. This object provides runtime information about the corresponding domain property. It also offers some useful methods:

- The method GetValue(ModelElement element) can be used to get the value of this domain property for the ModelElement passed as a parameter. It returns a System.Object.
- The method SetValue(ModelElement element, object value) can be used to set the value of this domain property for the ModelElement passed as a parameter.
- The method NotifyValueChange(ModelElement element) can be used to trigger events and rules that depend on this property on this ModelElement. This is for use in scenarios where the property is calculated, where these events and rules would not otherwise be triggered when the calculated value changes.

The following code fragment (which must be run in the context of a transaction) shows how to acquire a DomainPropertyInfo object from a suitably initialized store and use it to update the associated domain property's value:

```
IssueState s1 = new IssueState(store);
DomainClassInfo dci = s1.GetDomainClass();
DomainPropertyInfo dpi = dci.FindDomainProperty("Name", true);
dpi.SetValue(s1, "NewName");
string newValue = (string)dpi.GetValue(s1);
```

More on Domain Relationships and Roles

First, note that because relationships are implemented using classes, all of the customization and tuning that applies to a domain class can also be applied to a domain relationship. This section explores some of the extra customization options that particularly apply to the roles of a relationship. The properties window when a role is selected is shown in Figure 3-25.

We explained earlier how domain roles cause properties to be generated on the roleplayer classes. In fact, a setting on the role can be used to inhibit the generation of these properties, if desired. This is done by setting "Is Property Generator"—seen in Figure 3-25—to *False*. The DSL author would normally only do this in order to reduce the size of the DSL's generated API, or possibly to avoid name conflicts in the generated code. Similarly, when the properties are generated, the DSL author can restrict their external visibility using "Property Getter Access Modifier" and "Property Setter Access Modifier," which have similar effects to the corresponding settings on a domain property.

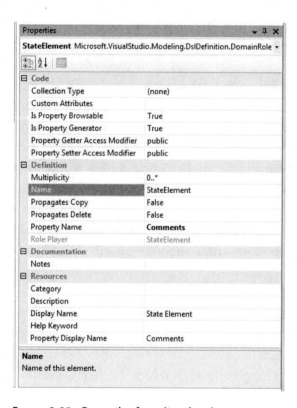

FIGURE 3-25: Properties for a domain role

If the role has a multiplicity of *ZeroOne* or *One*, properties generated from the roles will appear in the properties window at DSL runtime just like any other properties, allowing the single roleplayer to be selected, and similar data may be used to fine-tune these properties: "Property Display Name," "Description," "Category," and" Is Property Browsable."

We saw earlier in the chapter that a role with *Many* multiplicity causes the generation of a property whose type is LinkedElementCollection<T>, where T is the domain class at the other end of the relationship. The DSL author can define a custom collection to be used instead of this, for example, by creating an index to help performance on a collection containing many elements. The setting for "Collection Type" can be used to apply such a customization.

By default, an embedding relationship will cause deletion to be propagated from source to target. If the source roleplayer is deleted, then the embedding link must be deleted—it is not possible for a link to exist without a roleplayer at each end—and as a consequence of the link being deleted, the target roleplayer will also be deleted. On the other hand, a reference relationship will not propagate deletion. This is often the behavior required from a DSL—but not always. Some scenarios exist for which we want to customize this deletion behavior. For example, in the Issue State model, the relationship between a **StartElement** and its associated **IssueState** is a reference relationship. If the **IssueState** MEL is deleted, then the link between them will go, but the **StartElement** will remain. But we would definitely like the **StartElement** to be deleted, too—it makes no sense on its own. By marking the source role of **StartTransition** as **PropagatesDelete**, we can achieve this. Now, when the **StartTransition** link is deleted, the source roleplayer—the **StartElement**—is deleted too. This topic is discussed further in Chapter 5, which describes how to customize the delete behavior using the DSL Details window.

Programmatically, a MEL can be deleted by calling its `Delete()` method. By default this will cause deletion to be propagated as described in the paragraph above. It is, however, possible to specify as parameters to the call to `Delete()` a set of roles through which the delete is not to be propagated. This is done by passing the `Ids` of the associated `DomainRoleInfo` objects, described below.

Accessing Links

If you want to get access to the actual links of a relationship, the generated API provides static methods on the C# class generated for the domain relationship to do this. Three of these for the class `IssueStateTransition` can be seen in Figure 3-26. Their signatures are as follows:

```
/// <summary>
/// Get the IssueStateTransition links between two given IssueStates.
/// </summary>
```

```
public static ReadOnlyCollection<IssueStateTransition> GetLinks
                        (IssueState source, IssueState target)

/// <summary>
/// Get the IssueStateTransition links targeting an IssueState.
/// </summary>
public static ReadOnlyCollection<IssueStateTransition> GetLinksToPredecessors
                        (IssueState nextStateInstance)

/// <summary>
/// Get the IssueStateTransition links sourced on an IssueState.
/// </summary>
public static ReadOnlyCollection<IssueStateTransition> GetLinksToSuccessors
                        (IssueState previousStateInstance)
```

FIGURE 3-26: Generated methods for
IssueStateTransition

The use of the GetLinks() method is illustrated in the following code example:

```
using (Microsoft.VisualStudio.Modeling.Transaction t =
                this.Store.TransactionManager.BeginTransaction("example"))
{
  IssueStateModel model = new IssueStateModel(store);
  IssueState s1 = new IssueState(store);
  model.States.Add(s1);
  IssueState s2 = new IssueState(store);
  model.States.Add(s2);
  s1.Successors.Add(s2);
  s1.Successors.Add(s2);
  ReadOnlyCollection<IssueStateTransition> links =
                IssueStateTransition.GetLinks(s1, s2);
```

```
    links[0].Action = "solve";
    links[1].Action = "postpone";

    t.Commit();
}
```

More on Relationship Derivation

Relationship derivation can be very useful for all of the same reasons that class inheritance is useful—it allows common structure and behavior to be shared in common base classes. For example, if the author of the IssueState model wished to specify some rules or behavior that applied to all transitions, whether they are start transitions or normal Issue State transitions, the **Transition** relationship is the place to do it.

However, it does cause some subtleties in the generated code. Furthermore, it also imposes a few restrictions on which multiplicities are allowed for the various roles. Let's look at the multiplicities first.

Remember that each role causes the generation of a property on the roleplayer domain class. In the case of the **StartElement** role on the **StartTransition** relationship, the generated property on the StartElement C# class is called StartState and returns the associated IssueState. Similarly, for the **Previous** role on the **Transition** relationship, the generated property on the StateElement C# class is called Successors and returns the associated StateElements.

The restrictions on multiplicity are a logical consequence of the fact that the links navigated via the base generated property (Successors) must be a superset of the links navigated via the derived generated property (StartState). This follows from the definition of relationship derivation—every link of **StartTransition** is also a link of **Transition**.

For example, given a **StartElement**, the links navigated via the **StartState** property must be a subset of the links navigated via the **Successors** property. In fact, in this model, they must be the *same* set of links, because there is no other relationship derived from **Transition** that is sourced on **StartState**.

These restrictions imply that it is an error, if the multiplicity of the base role is *ZeroOne* or *One*, for the multiplicity of the derived role to be *ZeroMany* or *OneMany*. Given the multiplicity of the base role, there could never be more than one link.

It's also possible, although unusual, to create misleading multiplicity combinations, which will cause the DSL Tools to issue warning messages. Here are a couple of examples.

- If the multiplicity of an abstract base role is *ZeroOne* or *One*, and there are two or more derived roles that have the same roleplayer class, they must all have the multiplicity *ZeroOne*, because only one of them could validly be instantiated at a time.

- If the base relationship is not abstract and has an end with a multiplicity *One*, then there is no point in creating a derived relationship, because we know that the base relationship has to be instantiated directly.

> **▪ TIP** The DSL designer validates all of the multiplicity rules
>
> If the complexity of this description defeats you, then don't worry. Unless you try something very subtle you are unlikely to trip up against these issues, and if you do, the DSL designer validates all of these rules before it generates a DSL.

There's a restriction of the C# type system that impacts the code that is generated for derived relationships. It is not possible in C# to override the definition of a virtual property with a property of a more derived type—the type of the overriding property must be exactly the same as the type of the overridden one. We can see this restriction by looking at the code generated for the relationship `IssueStateTransition`. Referring to Figure 3-27, there are properties called `Next` and `Previous` on the classes `Transition`, `IssueStateTransition`, and `StartTransition`, all generated from the names of roles. For `IssueStateTransition` and `StartTransition`, their types have not been shown, to avoid clutter on the diagram. In fact, they are all virtual properties that have the same return type—`StateElement`—even though it would be more in keeping with the model for the `Previous` property on `StartTransition` to refer to `StartElement`, and its `Next` property to refer to `IssueState`. But because of the built-in restriction of the language, these properties must all have the same type, and code is generated that actually checks the correct type at runtime.

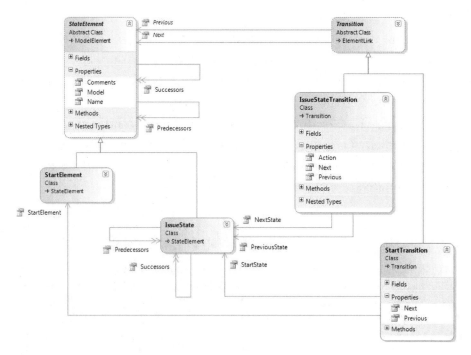

FIGURE 3-27: Classes generated for derived relationships

Slightly different considerations apply for the properties generated on roleplayer classes, such as the properties Predecessors and Successors defined on StateElement. These properties may be superseded in derived classes by properties with a more derived type. This can be seen for the class IssueState, which has also defined these properties to be called Predecessors and Successors. In the generated code, these properties are marked as new, to explicitly specify that they are intended to replace the inherited properties. In fact, because of the semantics of derived relationships, both the inherited and replacing properties will return exactly the same values.

In practice, the effect on the DSL author of these considerations is minimal. A derived relationship may use either the same or different names for the role and property names of derived relationships, and the code generator will take care of it, generating the appropriate pattern for each case.

DomainRelationshipInfo and DomainRoleInfo

`DomainRelationshipInfo` is derived from `DomainClassInfo` and provides runtime access to information about the corresponding domain relationship. It defines the following important properties.

- `AllowsDuplicates` returns a Boolean value indicating whether duplicate links are allowed.
- `IsEmbedding` returns a Boolean value indicating whether the relationship is an embedding.
- `DomainRoles` returns a collection of two `DomainRoleInfo` objects, each of which provides runtime access to information about the corresponding domain role.

More about the Store

This final section offers a few points of interest about the store that can be helpful when writing code customizations. Much more detail can be found in the online documentation, which can be installed when you install the Visual Studio SDK.

Looking Up Elements

The class `ModelElement` defines a property called `Id`. The value of this property is a Guid (Globally Unique Identifier), which is allocated when the element is first created in the store (`System.Guid` is a structure provided by the .NET framework). The value of this property may be used to find the element in the store. Given a store and an `Id`, the following line of code will find the element with the `Id`, or return null if it is not present:

```
store.ElementDirectory.FindElement(id);
```

The method `GetElement(id)` can be used similarly but will throw an exception if the element is not found.

Model serialization, described in Chapter 6, provides the option to save the `Id` of an element so that it can be preserved across model reloads. This would be necessary whenever an element's `Id` can be saved externally and used to access it later.

Partitions

A store can be divided into distinct partitions. When a `ModelElement` is created, it is possible to specify the partition that it is created in. The main purpose of partitions is to enable a single store to contain multiple models; for example, each partition might be associated with a separate model file. The current version of the DSL Tools does not make any use of the partitioning facility of the store.

Rules

Another important concept when working with models in the store is *rules*. We'll encounter these when writing customizations in later chapters, especially Chapter 7 and Chapter 10. A rule is defined when the DSL author needs to propagate changes to elements in the store so that other elements are also affected. For example, rules are used to fix up the diagram automatically whenever the model changes. We'll leave the details for later chapters. For now, notice some essentials, as listed here:

- The rule is a class that inherits from `AddRule`, `ChangeRule`, `DeletingRule`, `RolePlayerChangedRule`, or one of several other categories. The single overridable method provides an argument that yields the details of the change.
- The rule has a `RuleOn` attribute that specifies which class it applies to.
- The rule is executed within the transaction in which the change occurred; it may make changes that cause further rule firings, which are added to the queue to be fired.
- You must register your custom rules in the DomainModel class:

```
public partial class IssueStateModelsDomainModel
{
  protected override Type[] GetCustomDomainModelTypes()
  {
    return new System.Type[] { typeof(MyNewRule) };
  }
}
```

DomainModelInfo

A `DomainModelInfo` object is the top-level entry point giving runtime access to data for the entire domain model. This code fragment shows how to acquire a `DomainModelInfo` object from an initialized store, and how to query it for its constituents:

```
Store store = new Store(typeof(IssueStateModelsDomainModel));
...
DomainModel dm = store.GetDomainModel<IssueStateModelsDomainModel>();
DomainModelInfo dmi = dm.DomainModelInfo;
ReadOnlyCollection<DomainClassInfo> domainClasses = dmi.DomainClasses;
ReadOnlyCollection<DomainRelationshipInfo> domainRelationships =
                                          dmi.DomainRelationships;
```

SUMMARY

In this chapter we talked about defining domain models for Domain-Specific Languages. These models are the foundation for language definition. By now you should have learned:

- How to build a basic domain model using the DSL designer
- What the DSL domain model notation means
- How to do basic programming against the DSL API to make a model

All of the other aspects of the language definition described by the next few chapters—notation, serialization, validation, code-generation, and user interface—are based on having a domain model that properly represents the concepts, properties, and relationships of the domain.

■ 4 ■
Presentation

Introduction

Chapter 2 introduced the different aspects of the definition of a DSL: the domain model; the presentation layer, including graphical notation, explorer, and properties window; creation, deletion, and update behavior; validation; and serialization. Chapter 3 described the first aspect, the domain model. This chapter describes how to define the presentation aspect, that is, how information encoded in the underlying model elements gets presented through the UI of the designer. There are three windows in the UI where information is presented: the design surface, the model explorer, and the properties window. Definition of the presentation aspect therefore involves the definition of the graphical notation used on the design surface, customization of the appearance of the explorer, and customization of the appearance of the properties window.

By far the most complex part is the definition of the graphical notation, so most of the chapter is set aside for explaining that aspect. The explorer and properties window are dealt with at the end.

The Issue State and Issue Project examples introduced in Chapter 2 and downloadable from www.domainspecificdevelopment.com are used to illustrate the concepts and are supplemented by designers built directly from the standard DSL templates shipped with the product. Four language templates have been shipped: Minimal Language, Class Diagrams, Component Models, and Task Flow. Together they exercise most of the graphical notation supported by the DSL Tools. We'll be careful to indicate which template we've used, where appropriate, and if you wish to try it out in the tools, all you need to do is create a test language using one of those templates.

■ TIP Creating a test language from a language template

As explained in Chapter 2, when you create a new DSL authoring solution using the DSL designer project template, you will be asked to choose a language template on which to base your new DSL. You can create a test language using this method if you want to try out the examples used to illustrate the text.

A couple of other samples, including a Circuit Diagrams DSL (for generating code from electronic circuit diagrams), are used to illustrate some of the code customizations. These are downloadable from the same location.

Graphical Notation—Overview

A graphical designer presents some elements of a model on a design surface through a graphical notation that uses shapes and connectors. Figure 4-1 shows an Issue State model where a number of issue states and one start element have been created, and where the "Start Element" property for the *Raised* issue state is set to be the start element **StartElement1**. All the elements were created through the default menus on the explorer, and the shapes were created on the diagram automatically, as was the connector when the "Start Element" property was set. In general, the creation of a model element automatically causes creation of the mapped presentation element (shape or connector).

The shapes on the diagram are mapped to the elements in the model, as shown in Figure 4-2. The connector maps to the link between the **Start-Element** instance and the **IssueState** instance with the name *Raised*.

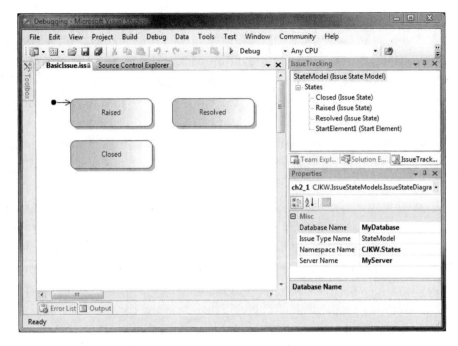

FIGURE 4-1: Issue State designer showing the presentation of a model

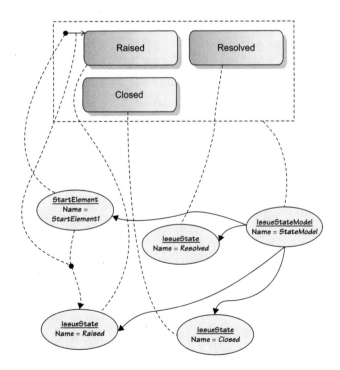

FIGURE 4-2: Maps between diagram elements and model elements

Shapes and connectors in the DSL definition have various properties that allow you to customize color and style, the initial size when the shape is first created, the geometry of the outline of the shape, and so on. You can also define text and icon decorators for shapes and connectors. A text decorator is used to show text, usually the value of some underlying domain property, within or adjacent to a shape; in this example, the **Name** domain property of each state is displayed as a text decorator in the middle of its shape. An icon decorator is used to display a small image whose visibility may be tied to the value of a domain property.

To enable model elements in your DSL to be visualized on the diagram surface, you need to define (a) the kind and appearance of shapes that will be used to present those elements, and (b) a mapping from the shape definition to the domain class of the elements, which dictates both the placement behavior of a shape and how the appearance of decorators is affected by data change. To enable links to be visualized on the diagram surface, you need to define (a) the appearance of the connector that will be used to present the links, and (b) a mapping from the connector definition to the domain relationship for the links, which dictates both the connection behavior of a connector and how the appearance of decorators is affected by data change.

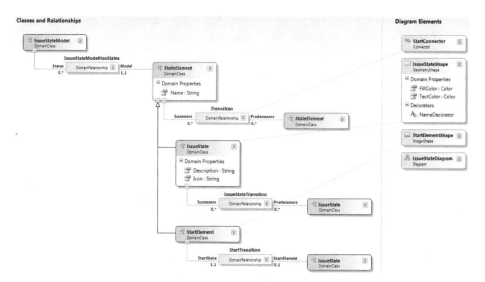

FIGURE 4-3: Definition of diagram elements and maps

Figure 4-3 shows the DSL definition for the Issue State language, created in Chapter 3, with two shape definitions and a connector definition added.

There are several categories of shape; this example uses geometry shapes and image shapes. An image shape displays a specific picture. A geometry shape displays a shape with a geometrical outline such as a rectangle, which the DSL user can resize. In the example, the shape definition called **IssueStateShape** defines a geometry shape that is mapped to the domain class **IssueState**. **StartElementShape** defines an image shape that is mapped to **StartElement**, and **TransitionConnector** defines a connector that is mapped to **Transition**. The effect of this definition on the behavior of the Issue State designer is that whenever an **IssueState** element is created in a model, an **IssueStateShape** representing that element, is created on the diagram. Similarly, for **StartElement**. And whenever a **Transition** link between states is created, a **TransitionConnector** connecting the shapes representing the source and target of the **Transition** link is created. There is also a "Diagram" diagram element (**IssueStateDiagram**), which represents the definition of the design surface itself. This must be mapped to the domain class at the root of the model, in this case, **StateModel**.

Diagram and Editor

The definition of the graphical notation is done in the context of a diagram, which in turn is referenced by the definition of the editor. This section describes these two aspects of a DSL Definition.

> ### ■ TIP Creating diagram and editor definitions
>
> The diagram and editor definitions appear as nodes in the DSL explorer. Both nodes in the DSL definition are created for you when you create a DSL authoring project using the DSL designer project template. If you happen to delete them, they can be recreated by clicking on the top level (Dsl) node in the DSL explorer and selecting "Add Diagram" or "Add Custom Editor"/"Add Designer" from the context menu.

Diagram

Primarily, the diagram definition is a container for the shape and connector maps. Figure 4-4 shows the definition of the diagram for the Issue State DSL.

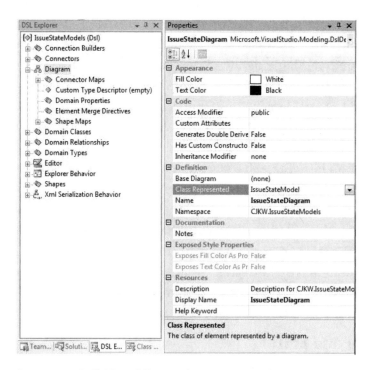

Figure 4-4: Definition of diagram for Issue State DSL

The window on the left shows sub-elements of the diagram definition in the DSL explorer, and the window on the right the properties of the diagram definition. The property settings are summarized in Table 4-1.

Table 4-1: Property Settings Categories for Diagram

Appearance	Settings that define the visual appearance of the diagram, such as background color.
Code	Settings that influence the form of the generated code for the diagram. All these settings are inherited from domain class, because a diagram definition is also a domain class.

Definition	These settings are similar to those for domain classes (name, namespace, base diagram), with the addition of a property to designate the class of element represented by a diagram.
Documentation	As with many other elements in a DSL definition, the documentation section defines a single property to contain notes about the design of the DSL.
Exposed Style Properties	These are all read-only properties and indicate whether or not a style setting in the appearances category, such as fill color, can be set by the user of the target designer in the properties window.
Resources	These properties provide text resources that are used within the UI of the target designer. Resources are generated into .resx files so that they can be localized for different cultures. A keyword to drive F1 Help in the target designer may also be provided.

▪ **TIP** Exposing style properties

To expose a style property, select the diagram definition in the diagram elements part of the DSL designer design surface and from the context menu choose "Add Exposed" followed by the style property you want to expose. The "Exposes XXX As Property" setting will then turn to true, and a new domain property with the name "XXX" will appear in the definition of the diagram.

When you build and run the generated designer, you'll find that you are able to change the value of the style setting, for example, the diagram fill color, through the properties window. This pattern applies to shapes and connectors also, and allows the DSL author to choose which style properties are an intrinsic part of the definition and which can be used by the users of the DSL for their own purposes, for example, to organize elements into categories of their own devising.

Apart from the shape and connector maps, the sub-elements of a diagram definition (specifically, custom type descriptor, domain properties, and element merge directives)[1] appear by virtue of the fact that a diagram definition is itself a special kind of domain class, as are shapes and connectors. This also explains the set of properties under the "Code" category, why a diagram can be related to other domain classes via domain relationships, and why a diagram can inherit from other diagrams. These facilities are not used often, if at all, for diagrams—it's a case of the underlying framework being exposed in the DSL. Nevertheless, there are occasions when these facilities are useful. For example, the ability to add domain properties and relate a diagram definition with other domain classes makes it possible to model information required by the diagram. An example of adding domain properties to a diagram definition is given as part of the "Variable Image" code customization discussed later. We also found a need for this in the DSL defining the DSL designer itself, where both these techniques are used to capture information on the diagram to drive its tree layout.

Localization

Localizing an application involves providing a set of resources, such as strings and images, that are specific to a particular culture. A culture may be region-neutral, such as French (fr), or region specific, such as French Canadian (fr-CA). These resources are compiled into a satellite assembly that is installed with the main assembly for the application. When the application is run on a machine set up for a particular culture, the resources in the satellite assembly for that culture are used instead of the resources in the main assembly.

The resources specified in the DSL definition are the resources for the main assembly of the designer, which are the resources for the default or neutral culture. Which culture this is can be set in the properties of the Dsl and DslPackage projects. To localize the designer for other cultures, you need to provide satellite assemblies containing appropriate resources for

---

1. Domain properties were explained in Chapter 3, the custom type descriptor is explained later in this chapter, and element merge directives are explained in the next chapter.

those cultures. A good article explaining localization in general, including how to create satellite assemblies, can be found at http://msdn. microsoft.com/msdnmag/issues/06/05/BasicInstincts/default.aspx.

Editor

There are two types of editor: a (graphical) designer and a custom editor. The definition of an editor appears under the "Editor" node in the DSL explorer. Data defined here is used to generate the implementation of the EditorFactory class, the toolbox, and any validation behavior. By default, when you create a DSL authoring project using the DSL designer project template, the DSL definition defines a designer as its editor.

The editor part of the DSL definition contains the definition of the toolbox (see Chapter 5) and validation behavior (see Chapter 7). The definition of the editor for the Issue State DSL is shown in Figure 4-5, where you will see the items mentioned above showing in the DSL explorer.

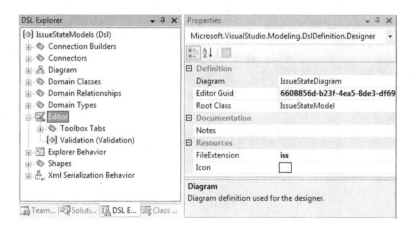

FIGURE 4-5: Definition of designer in Issue State DSL

The properties of the editor include a reference to the "Root Class" that gets associated with the designer (i.e., appears as the top element in the generated editor's explorer). The "Editor Guid" is used in the code for the generated EditorFactory class.

Under the "Resources" category, there are settings to define the extension of files used to store models for the DSL and to define the icon that is associated with those files, for example, in Windows Explorer or Visual Studio solution explorer.

Designer

When the editor is a designer, there is an entry under the definition category in the properties window that references the Diagram class to be used by the designer—**IssueStateDiagram**, in the example. The root class associated with the designer and the class that the referenced diagram represents must be the same. If they are not, a validation error in the DSL designer will result.

Custom Editor

It's also possible to define a custom editor, which is one without a diagram. You'd do this if a graphical design surface was not appropriate for presenting the information that you want to capture in your DSL. In this case, you must supply a Windows Forms control to provide your own custom presentation of data from the model. To do this, delete the designer that is playing the role of editor (select the editor node in the DSL explorer and press the delete key), and then add a custom editor (with the root node in the explorer selected, choose "Add Custom Editor") and set its properties as shown in Figure 4-6. (The starting point for this particular example was a new language created using the minimal language template.)

FIGURE 4-6: Properties of a custom editor definition

Regenerate and build the code. You'll get an error raised such as:

'CJKW.CJKWCustomEditor.CJKWCustomEditorDocView' does not implement inherited abstract member 'Microsoft.VisualStudio.Shell. WindowPane.Window.get'

> **▪ TIP** Click "Transform All Templates" after changing the DSL definition
>
> Just a reminder: Whenever you make a change to the DSL definition, click the "Transform All Templates" button in the header of the solution explorer. This recreates the contents of the GeneratedCode directories. Then use the F5 key to recompile the code and run the designer to see the effect of your changes.

Double-clicking on this error leads you to code with instructions on what you have to do:

```
internal partial class CJKWCustomEditorDocView : CJKWCustomEditorDocViewBase
{
  /// <summary>
  /// Constructs a new CJKWCustomEditorDocView.
  /// </summary>
  public CJKWCustomEditorDocView(DslShell::ModelingDocData docData,
                    global::System.IServiceProvider serviceProvider)
      : base(docData, serviceProvider)
  {
  }

  // This DSL defines a custom editor. Therefore, you must create a partial
  // class of CJKWCustomEditorDocView and override the Window property of
     this
  // class to specify the window that will be hosted as the editor.
  // In most cases this will be a class derived from
  // System.Windows.Forms.Control.
  // public override System.Windows.Forms.IWin32Window Window
  // {
  //   get
  //   {
  //   }
  // }
}
```

> **■TIP** **Let the compiler tell you what custom code you need**
>
> There are many places in the DSL definition where you can indicate that you want to supply some behavior through custom code. Examples include defining a custom editor or setting a custom flag to *True*. To find out exactly what is required, click the "Transform All Templates" button in the header of the solution explorer to recreate the content of the `GeneratedCode` directories from the DSL definition; then rebuild the code with Ctrl+Shift+B or the "Build Solution" menu item. In most cases, there will be error messages telling you about some missing code. Double-click on them and you'll see comments in the generated code telling you what you should supply.
>
> Define the missing methods in a separate file and in a separate folder. The methods will be in a partial class with the same name as the relevant generated class, and the file may need to use some of the same `using` statements.

Following these instructions, the partial class you need to write would be something like:

```
namespace CJKW.CJKWCustomEditor
{
  // Double-derived class to allow easier code customization.
  internal partial class CJKWCustomEditorDocView
        : CJKWCustomEditorDocViewBase
  {
    // The WinForms form that implements this view
    private ViewForm viewForm;

    public override System.Windows.Forms.IWin32Window Window
    {
      get
      {
        if (this.viewForm == null)
        {
          this.viewForm = new ViewForm(this);
        }
        return this.viewForm;
      }
    }
  }
}
```

The custom window class is `ViewForm`. In this case, we've defined a form with a list box called `elementList`, and two buttons called `addButton` and `updateButton`. `addButton` adds an element to the model in the store, and `updateButton` updates the `elementList` to show all the elements in the model. The custom code (as opposed to that generated from the Windows Forms designer) is:

```csharp
using System;
using System.Windows.Forms;
using Microsoft.VisualStudio.Modeling;

namespace CJKW.CJKWCustomEditor
{
  public partial class ViewForm : UserControl
  {
    private CJKWCustomEditorDocView docView;

    internal ViewForm(CJKWCustomEditorDocView docView)
    {
      this.docView = docView;
      InitializeComponent();
    }

    private void addButton_Click(object sender, EventArgs e)
    {
      if (!string.IsNullOrEmpty(this.nameTextBox.Text))
      {
        this.addElement(this.nameTextBox.Text);
      }
    }

    private void addElement(string name)
    {
      using (Transaction t = this.docView.DocData.Store.
            TransactionManager.BeginTransaction(
              Properties.Resources.Undo_AddElement))
      {
        ExampleElement newElement = new
          ExampleElement(this.docView.DocData.Store);
        newElement.Name = name;
        (this.docView.DocData.RootElement as
          ExampleModel).Elements.Add(newElement);
        t.Commit();
      }
    }

    private void updateButton_Click(object sender, EventArgs e)
    {
```

```
    this.SuspendLayout();
    this.elementList.Items.Clear();
    foreach (ExampleElement exampleElement in
        this.docView.DocData.Store.ElementDirectory.
            FindElements<ExampleElement>())
    {
      this.elementList.Items.Add(exampleElement.Name);
    }
    this.ResumeLayout();
  }
 }
}
```

The resulting editor looks like Figure 4-7.

FIGURE 4-7: Forms-based DSL editor

Shapes

Shapes are the nodes of a graphical notation and are used to visualize elements of a model. This section digs into the detail of defining shapes and shape maps.

Kinds of Shapes

There are five different kinds of shape: geometry shapes, compartment shapes, image shapes, ports, and swimlanes. The categories of settings that apply to all shapes are similar to those for Diagram, with the addition of a "Layout" category. They are summarized in Table 4-2.

TABLE 4-2: Property Settings Categories for Shapes

Appearance	Settings that define the visual appearance of the shape, such as color, line thickness, and so on.
Code	Settings that influence the form of the generated code for the shape. All these settings are inherited from domain class, because shape definitions are also domain classes.
Definition	These settings are similar to those for domain classes (name, namespace, base geometry shape), with the addition of a tooltip property that defines the behavior of tooltips when hovering over a shape in the target designer.
Documentation	As with many other elements in a DSL definition, the documentation section defines a single property to contain notes about the design of the DSL.
Exposed Style Properties	These are all read-only properties and indicate whether or not a style setting in the appearances category, such as fill color, can be set by the user of the target designer in the properties window. This was discussed earlier in the chapter in the section "Diagram."
Layout	These properties impact the layout and size of the shape.
Resources	These properties provide text and image resources that are used within the UI of the target designer. Resources are generated into .resx files so that they can be localized for different cultures.

Geometry Shapes

Figure 4-8 shows the anatomy of a geometry shape. With this information, it is fairly easy to determine what all the appearance settings on the shape are for. Descriptions are provided for each setting—just select the name of the setting and the description appears in the bottom pane of the properties window, as illustrated in Figure 4-9. Alternatively, you can press F1, and online or local help pages will appear with the full table of settings and their descriptions. Decorators are optional for all shapes and connectors, and are dealt with later.

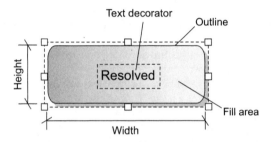

FIGURE 4-8: Anatomy of a geometry shape

FIGURE 4-9: Appearance settings for geometry shape

One appearance setting for a geometry shape is "Text Color," which is the color of the text that appears in any decorators associated with the shape. This may seem surprising—why not define this color as part of the decorator? The reason is that the color of text decorators positioned inside the shape needs to be compatible with the fill color for the shape, and a good way to achieve this compatibility is to define the two colors in the same place.

The layout settings define the default height and width of the shape when it is first created. As with a diagram definition, you can choose to expose some of the appearance (style) properties for changing by the user of your DSL. The method is exactly the same as that called out when discussing the diagram definition.

Compartment Shapes

A compartment shape is a geometry shape with compartments. A compartment is used to display a list of elements that are linked to the element mapped to a compartment shape instance. The list to be displayed is defined as part of the compartment shape map (see the section "Shape Maps" later in this chapter), together with the text that appears for each entry in the compartment. Figure 4-10 shows the anatomy of a compartment shape—the text decorator is optional, or there can be many such decorators.

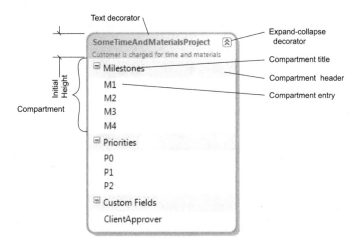

FIGURE 4-10: Anatomy of a compartment shape

The ability to have compartments restricts the outline geometry to only a rectangle or rounded rectangle, and there are two additional appearance settings: "Default Expand Collapse State" and "Is Single Compartment Header Visible." "Default Expand Collapse State" can be used to determine whether or not the shape is expanded or collapsed when it is first created. By default compartment headers are always shown in a compartment shape. When there is only a single compartment, it is not necessary to show the header to distinguish it from other compartments. "Is Single Compartment Header Visible" is a Boolean property that controls whether the header is shown in that case.

The height of a compartment shape is set automatically, taking into account the (fixed) height of the shape header and the (variable) height of the compartments. In this case, the value of the "Initial Height" property is used for the fixed height of the shape header.

A compartment shape may have more than one compartment. Compartments can be added to a compartment shape definition on the diagram surface of the DSL designer or in the explorer. Figure 4-11 shows the definition of the compartment shape in Figure 4-10, which is part of Issue Project DSL.

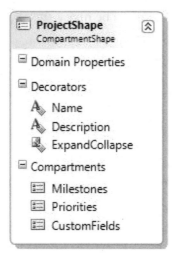

FIGURE 4-11: Definition of a compartment shape

Figure 4-12 shows the settings for one of these compartments, which should be self-explanatory given Figure 4-10.

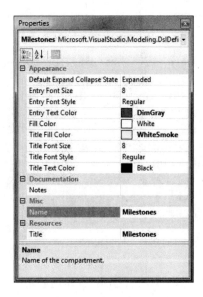

FIGURE 4-12: Settings for a compartment

Image Shapes

An image shape is a shape that displays an image rather than an outline. Figure 4-13 shows the anatomy of an image shape. As always, the decorator is optional, or there may be many decorators. This particular shape is defined in the Task Flow DSL template.

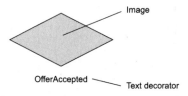

FIGURE 4-13: Anatomy of an image shape

Appearance settings associated with the outline or fill area have no impact on the appearance of an image shape. However, there are two settings that are very relevant to image shapes. The first is the "Image Resource," which determines what image is displayed.

> **■ TIP** Defining image and icon resources
>
> Any property used to reference an image or icon resource stores a file path relative to the location of the `.dsl` file in which the property is defined. The DSL designer provides a file picker for all such properties, which puts up a dialog that allows you to navigate the file system and pick a file. It filters the files available for selection by the type of image that is allowed for the property. In general, the DSL Tools support many kinds of standard image formats, but for certain properties only bitmaps, for example, are acceptable. The dialog also previews the image, and a thumbnail of the image is displayed along with the path string in the properties window itself.

The second is the "Has Default Connection Points" setting, which determines whether or not the shape has a set of North-South-East-West connection points. This can be very useful when the image shape needs to be connected to other image shapes, because it ensures that connectors connect at sensible points. For example, in a language created from the Task Flow template, if you change the "Has Default Connection Points" setting of **MergeBranchShape** to *True*, you'll find that however much you move around the merge branch shape, connectors will (nearly) always connect on the edges of the diamond image. However, if you set this property to *False*, connectors will connect anywhere along the (invisible) rectangular bounding box of the image. The two alternatives are shown in Figure 4-14.

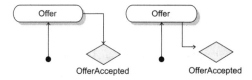

FIGURE 4-14: With default connection points and without

The "Initial Height" and "Initial Width" settings are also effective for an image shape. This is both good and bad. It is good if you want to enlarge or reduce the size of the image that you would otherwise get. It is bad if you want the image to be reproduced exactly. In that case, just copy the size of the image into these settings, remembering that the unit of measurement is inches.

Ports

A port is a shape attached to the outline of a shape that can only be moved around that outline, as illustrated in Figure 4-15. Other than that, its definition is no different than a geometry shape, including the ability to have decorators—the ports shown in Figure 4-15 each have an icon decorator. These particular ports are defined in the Component Models template.

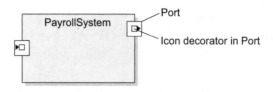

FIGURE 4-15: Geometry shape with ports attached

Swimlanes

Swimlanes are used to partition a diagram into either rows or columns. The anatomy of a vertical swimlane is shown in Figure 4-16, and a horizontal swimlane is shown in Figure 4-17. The swimlanes shown are defined in the Task Flow template.

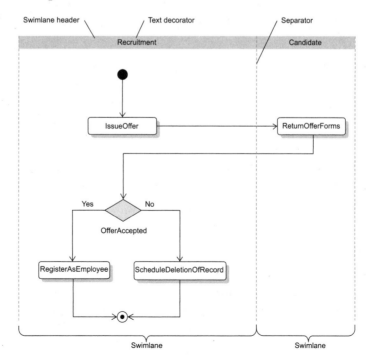

FIGURE 4-16: Anatomy of a vertical swimlane

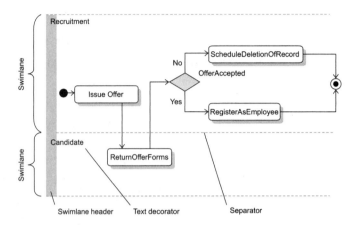

FIGURE 4-17: Anatomy of a horizontal swimlane

There are settings to change the appearance of the swimlane header and separator, as well as a "Layout" property that determines whether the swimlane partitions the diagram vertically or horizontally. The "Initial Height" of a horizontal swimlane definition determines the initial height of its instances, although any value below 1 is ignored—the smallest height is 1 inch. The initial width of a horizontal swimlane is ignored. For vertical swimlanes, the width is considered and the height ignored.

Shape Inheritance

Inheritance between shapes is supported, with the restriction that a shape of one kind (e.g., a compartment shape) can only inherit from a shape of the same kind. A sub-shape will inherit the decorators and compartments (if applicable) of the base shape but overrides the appearance, layout, and resource properties with its own data. The latter can be a little annoying, especially if you want most of them to be the same as the base shape—you just have to set them all again by hand.

Shape Maps

Shape maps are used to associate shape classes with the domain classes they represent. There are compartment shape maps for maps involving compartment shapes, swimlane maps for maps involving swimlanes, and shape maps for geometry, port, and image shapes.

> **■ TIP** Creating shape maps
>
> A shape map from a domain class to a shape is created using the "Diagram Element Map" tool in the DSL designer (look for the icon 🔲 in the toolbox), or by selecting the "Diagram" node in the DSL explorer and choosing from the context menu.

Once created, a shape map may be viewed and edited through the DSL details window by selecting it on the diagram surface or in the DSL explorer, under "Diagram/Shape Maps." The information that appears in that window and how it is interpreted depends on the kind of shape map and shape involved. We deal with each case in turn.

> **■ TIP** Making the DSL Details window visible
>
> If the DSL details window is not displayed, you can make it visible using the "View>Other Windows>DSL Details" command (from the main menu bar of Visual Studio).

Mapping Definition Common to All Shapes

Figure 4-18 shows the details of the mapping of the **IssueStateShape** in the Issue State language.

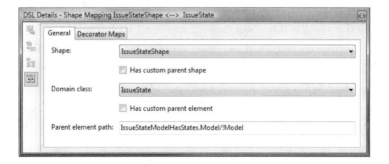

FIGURE 4-18: Mapping a geometry shape

The shape map identifies the kind of shapes used to represent instances of the referenced domain class and provides details of how a shape's decorators get mapped (discussed in a later section). The mapping in Figure 4-18 stipulates that instances of **IssueStateShape** are used to represent instances of **IssueState**. The "Parent element path" identifies the element, that is, the logical parent for the referenced domain class and on whose diagram element the shape should be parented.

Shape Parenting

In a running designer, all diagram elements, except the diagram itself, must be parented on another diagram element, which may be the diagram or a shape. Certain behaviors follow from being parented on a particular diagram element. The sections on ports and swimlanes below illustrate this. So in shape maps (and connector maps later) we must specify what diagram element a shape gets parented on when it is created.

The "Parent element path" uses a simple path syntax (see sidebar on page 157) for navigating across a structure of elements and links. In this case, it indicates that the element whose diagram element the shape should be parented on is the diagram element mapped to the element, which can be navigated to from the **IssueState** via the path IssueStateModelHasStates.Model/!Model. This returns an **IssueStateModel** element that is mapped to the diagram itself.

In addition, there are two Boolean flags, which when set to *True*, open up code customization points in the generated code, allowing you greater control over where a shape gets parented. Selecting "Has custom parent element" causes code to be generated that doesn't build. When you navigate to the source of the error, you'll find instructions on the custom code you need to write, as follows:

```
// Method:
// private Microsoft.VisualStudio.Modeling.ModelElement GetParentForIssue-
State(IssueState childElement)
// {
// }
// must be implemented in a partial class of
```

```
// CJKW.IssueStateModels.FixUpDiagram.  Given a child element,
// this method should return the parent model element that is
// associated with the shape or diagram that will be the parent
// of the shape created for this child.  If no shape should be created,
// the method should return null.
parentElement = GetParentForIssueState(
  (global::CJKW.IssueStateModels.IssueState)childElement);
```

Similar instructions are provided if you select "Has custom parent shape." In this case, you are asked to write a method in a partial class of the diagram class (**IssueStateDiagram** in this case), which is the method for creating the shape for **IssueState**. You'd use this if the parent shape is not mapped to a model element, for example, if it is an unmapped swimlane (see below).

Path Syntax

Path syntax is very simple, though it's rather verbose.

Let's look at a shape map example from the "Component Models" language template,[2] the one mapping InPortShape to InPort.

Open DslDefinition.dsl, and in the DSL explorer window, look under Diagram/ShapeMaps and select the shape map labeled "ComponentShape." There are some details in the normal Properties window, and more details in the DSL details window. (See earlier tip for bringing this into view.) The "Parent element path" shows in the "General" tab of the DSL details window when you have that shape map selected in the DSL explorer. The full path is given below:

```
ComponentHasPorts.Component/!Component
```

Each path has one or more segments separated by slashes.

Each segment is either a hop from an element to a link or from a link to an element. So they generally come in pairs: hop from element to link and then onto the element at the other end. (In most cases, a path goes link/element/link/element..., but in fact a link—that is, an instance of a

---

2. See the tip in the "Introduction" section for a reminder on how to create a test language from a language template.

relationship—can also be the target of a path, in which case the path would have an odd number of steps.)

Each segment starts with a relationship name. An element-to-link segment is written like this:

```
Relationship.Property
```

A link-to-element segment is written like this:

```
Relationship!Role
```

In the InPort shape map example, the parent element path begins like this:

```
ComponentHasPorts.Component
```

If you look at the DSL definition diagram in Figure 4-19, you'll see that **InPort** is a subclass of **ComponentPort** and has a relationship **ComponentHasPorts**, and the domain property is indeed called Component.

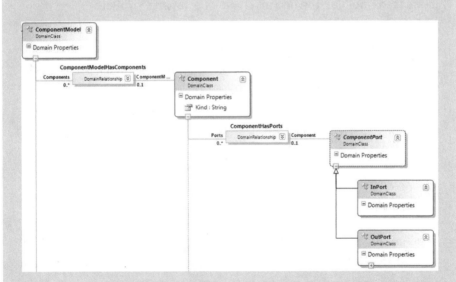

FIGURE 4-19: Fragment of domain model for Component Models language

When writing C# code against this model, you can jump across a link in one step using the property that the relationship generates on each of the classes it relates:

```
InPort port; ...  Component c = port.Component;
```

but in path syntax, you have to do both hops explicitly. This makes it easier to get at the intermediate link if you need to. So we complete the hop from the link to the **Component** like this::

```
ComponentHasPorts.Component/!Component
```

(You can omit the relationship name where it's the same as the previous segment.)

Notice that the name you use for the element-to-link hop is the **Property-Name** defined on the role—that's the name you see on the main diagram next to the corresponding line from the element's domain class. If you click on that role line, you'll see it in the properties window under "Property Name."

The name you use for the link-to-element hop is the "Name" of the role defined on the relationship for the destination end. So in the main diagram, if you click on the line on the other side of the relationship, you'll see it listed as that role's "Name" in the properties window. The "Property Name" and the "Name" of opposite roles are often the same.

As explained in Chapter 3, when programming, the "Property Name" is the name you use if you have an instance of a domain class and want to traverse the relationship, while the "Name" is the name you use if you have an instance of a relationship and you want the element at one end.

The facilities for editing paths in the DSL designer are a little rudimentary, so here are a few hints:

- You edit a path by typing a string. This means that it is a good idea to navigate to the relevant area of the domain model in the diagram before entering the path so that you have the information like relationship, role, and property names at hand.
- If you do have to navigate away from the path (sadly, this is often the case), remember to copy the text to the clipboard before you do so—if the string cannot be parsed on change of focus, it will be abandoned.

- If you are typing the path through the DSL details window, a popup appears as long as the string cannot be parsed into a valid path. However, you may still need to navigate away to find out information to enter.
- If you are typing the path through the properties window, ensure that you select the dropdown editor, otherwise you won't know that the path has errors until you try to confirm the change, which will be reported through a separate dialog.

Mapping Compartments

When mapping a compartment shape, it is also necessary to map compartments. The mapping of the project compartment shape in the Issue Project DSL is shown in Figure 4-20.

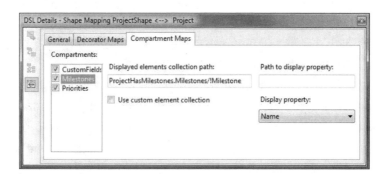

FIGURE 4-20: Mapping compartments

As this illustrates, an extra tab is provided in the DSL details window for mapping compartments. The compartments are listed on the left, and selecting each one reveals the definition of the mapping for that compartment.

There are two pieces of information one needs to provide for mapping a compartment. The first is the set of elements that will be used to create entries in the compartment. The second is the actual information that will be displayed for each element. The example shows the mapping of the **Milestones** compartment, and the set of elements used to populate the entries in this compartment are the milestones of the project, which are identified through the "Displayed elements collection path." The domain property used to provide the string that appears in each entry is **Name**. This is usually defined on the domain class of the element identified through the collection path, which is **Milestone** in this case. The "Path to display property" path can be used to further indirect from the domain class used for the list items to some other domain class on which to find the "Display property."

If you select the "Use custom element collection" box, then the generated code will not build, and the build error will take you to a place in the source code with instructions on how to proceed, as exemplified by the following code fragment:

```
////////
// CompartmentMap.UsesCustomFilter==true
// Please provide a method with the following signature to
// filter the list of elements to display in the compartment:
// global::System.Collections.IList
//    FilterElementsFromProjectForMilestones(
//        global::System.Collections.IEnumerable elements) {}
////////
return FilterElementsFromProjectForMilestones(result);
```

The method is added in a hand-coded partial class of the shape involved in the shape map, in this case **ProjectShape**. This is supplemental to the "Displayed elements collection path," which, if omitted, will cause validation errors.

Mapping Ports

Mapping ports is just like mapping geometry and image shapes, but in this case, the parent element path should identify an element that is mapped to a shape that can accept ports, that is, a geometry, compartment, or even another port shape (or "Has custom parent element" is set to *True*). If it is not, then you'll get a validation error like the following.

A Port may not be parented on a Diagram. In the ShapeMap mapping InPort to InPortShape, the parent element path leads to Component-Model, whose mapped shape is ComponentDiagram.

For example, in Figure 4-21, taken from the Component Models template, the parent element path refers to a component that is mapped to a geometry shape.

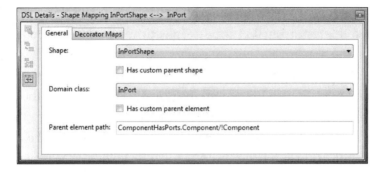

FIGURE 4-21: Mapping ports

Mapping Swimlanes

When mapping elements to shapes that should be contained in a swimlane, the parent path should identify the element mapped to the swimlane, as shown in Figure 4-22. This is taken from the Task Flow example, where the parent path for the **Task** shape mapping navigates to the **Actor** domain class that is mapped to a swimlane.

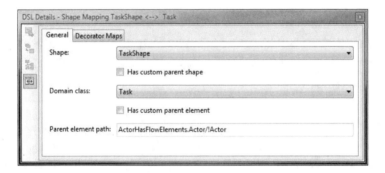

FIGURE 4-22: Definition of swimlane map in Task Flow example

Desirable behavior results by ensuring that the shapes are contained in the swimlane. If a shape is resized over the border of the swimlane, then the swimlane resizes with it. Similarly, if shapes are moved toward the border or slightly over it, the swimlane resizes in real time in that case. If a shape is moved from one swimlane to another, then the element mapped to the shape being moved becomes unmerged from the element mapped to the source of the move and merged into the element mapped to the swimlane that is the target of the move. Merging and unmerging are described in

Chapter 5, but the effect in the Task Flow example is that when a task shape is moved from one actor swimlane to another, the task is unlinked from the actor mapped to the swimlane at the source of the move and then linked to the actor mapped to the target of the move.

Note that it is still legitimate to have a parent element path in a non-swimlane shape map that navigates to the element mapped to the diagram when there are also swimlanes on the diagram. In that case, the shapes created for those elements are parented on the diagram and just appear in front of the swimlanes. However, they are not nested in the swimlanes and have no effect on the model when seemingly moved from one swimlane to another (because they are not nested in the swimlanes, all that is happening is the shape changing its position and appearing to move).

When mapping swimlanes, the parent path should identify the element mapped to the diagram ("Has custom parent element" is set to *True*). If it is not, then a validation error like the following will be raised:

> A SwimLane may not be parented on a GeometryShape. In the ShapeMap mapping DomainClass1 to SwimLane1, the parent element path leads to ExampleElement, whose mapped shape is ExampleShape.

You may define more than one mapped swimlane in a DSL, in which case you'll be able to add both kinds dynamically.

Unmapped Swimlanes

If a swimlane is unmapped, then the diagram will always contain exactly one instance of the swimlane. If there is more than one such swimlane, then it will contain one instance for each unmapped swimlane. If you then want to parent other shapes on the unmapped swimlane, you can then set the "Has custom parent shape" flag to *True* on the mappings for those shapes.

Advanced Shape Maps

It is possible to have shape maps between one domain class and many shapes, and between one shape and many domain classes. Also, inheritance between shapes and domain classes is taken into account in how a shape map behaves. The rules are summarized in Table 4-3, where **A**, **A1**, **A2** are domain classes and **S**, **S1**, **S2** are shapes.

TABLE 4-3: Advanced Rules for Shape Maps

A maps to **S**	The behavior is as described so far.
A maps to **S1**, **S2**, where **S1** may inherit from **S2**	The author will be required to write custom code that decides which kind of shape to create when an element of the domain class is created.
A1, **A2** map to **S**, where **A1** may inherit from **A2**	Elements of each domain class will cause the same kind of shape to be created.
A2 inherits from **A1**, **S2** inherits from **S1**, **A1** maps to **S1**, **A2** maps to **S2**	By the first rule, **A1** elements will be presented by **S1** shapes, and **A2** elements will be presented by **S2** shapes. However, any mappings between decorators and/or compartments specified in the mapping between **A1** and **S1** that are not remapped in the mapping between **A2** and **S2** will be used when using an **S2** shape to represent an **A2** element.

Connectors

In the same way that shapes define the appearance of nodes in a graphical notation, connectors define the appearance of links. And just as shape maps define how model elements are visualized by shapes, connector maps define how links are visualized by connectors. This section drills into the detail of defining connectors and connector maps.

Connector Anatomy and Appearance

The anatomy of a connector is shown in Figure 4-23. The particular connector used is defined in the Task Flow DSL template.

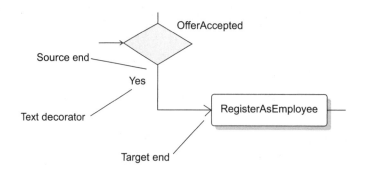

FIGURE 4-23: Anatomy of a connector

A connector is directional—it has a source end and a target end. The categories of settings that a connector can have are the same as for shapes, but under layout, instead of initial width and height, there is a routing style. You can choose either *Rectilinear* or *Straight*. The rectilinear style is illustrated in Figure 4-23—instead of going from point to point in a straight line, the connector takes a right-angled turn. When routed via the straight style, the connector takes the shortest possible route between two points.

The appearance settings impact the appearance of the line used to render the connector and allow source and target end styles to be defined, which determines whether symbols such as arrows appear. For example, the settings for the connector illustrated above are given in Figure 4-24.

FIGURE 4-24: Connector settings

Connectors and Inheritance

A connector can inherit from another connector, just like shapes can inherit from shapes. Decorators are inherited, and appearance, layout, and resource settings are overridden just like shapes.

Connector Maps

A connector map maps a connector to a domain relationship, not a domain class, and has no parent element path. Figure 4-25 shows the definition of the connector map for **FlowConnector**.

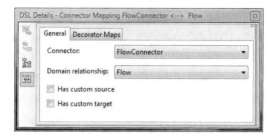

FIGURE 4-25: Definition of a connector map

The default behavior is that each link of the relationship is represented by a connector on the diagram that connects the shapes mapped to the source and target elements of that link.

This default behavior can be overridden in code. Select either "Has custom source," or "Has custom target," or both. This causes build errors in the generated code, and, as always, navigating to the source of those errors provides instructions on the custom code that needs to be written, which then determines the shapes actually connected by the connector.

Mapping connectors only to relationships may seem limiting. In many cases where it would seem desirable to map a connector to a domain class, it is possible and indeed sometimes preferable, to replace the domain class with a relationship, noting that (a) relationships can have domain properties, and (b) relationships can be derived from other relationships—that is, they behave very much like domain classes. If that is really unacceptable, then you can always map the connector to a relationship sourced or targeted on the domain class and provide custom source and/or target code to identify the source and/or target shape.

For example, suppose you were defining a concept modeling language and defined a domain class called **Specialization**, intended to capture a specialization or inheritance relationship between two concepts, and you wanted to depict this as an arrow from the specialist concept to the more general concept. You couldn't directly map a connector to a domain class, so one option would be to model specialization as a domain relationship instead of a domain class. However, the **Specialization** domain class would have two relationships to the **Concept** domain class, one called **SpecializationReferencesSpecialistConcept**, say, and the other called **SpecializationReferencesGeneralConcept**. So you could instead map the connector to one of these relationships, perhaps **SpecializationReferencesGeneralConcept**. The target of the relationship is the general concept, which is what the connector should target. However, the source is the **Specialization** element, so you need to provide custom code to navigate from that to the specialist concept, which can be done via the relationship **SpecializationReferencesSpecialistConcept**.

Advanced Connector Maps

It is possible to have connector maps between one domain relationship and many connectors, and between one connector and many domain relationships. Also, inheritance between connectors and domain relationships is taken into account in how a connector map behaves. The rules are summarized in Table 4-4, where **R**, **R1**, **R2** are domain relationships and **C**, **C1**, **C2** are connectors.

TABLE 4-4: Advanced Rules for Connector Maps

R maps to **C**	The behavior is as described so far.
R maps to **C1**, **C2**, where **C1** may inherit from **C2**	The author will be required to write custom code that decides which kind of connector to create when a link of the domain relationship is created.
R1, **R2** map to **S**, where **R1** may inherit from **R2**	Links of each domain relationship will cause the same kind of connector to be created.
R2 inherits from **R1**, **C2** inherits from **C1**, **R1** maps to **C1**, **R2** maps to **C2**	By the first rule, **R1** links will be presented by **C1** connectors, and **R2** elements will be presented by **C2** connectors. However, any mappings between decorators specified in the mapping between **R1** and **C1** that are not remapped in the mapping between **R2** and **C2** will be used when using a **C2** connector to represent an **R2** link.

Decorators

Decorators "decorate" shapes and connectors with text or images (icons). This section details the definition of decorators and decorator maps that determines how to use decorators to visualize data in the underlying model.

Kinds of Decorators

There are three kinds of decorator: text, icon, and expand collapse. Figure 4-26 shows the definition of **ProjectShape**, from the Issue Project DSL, which defines a text decorator and an expand collapse decorator, as well as the definition of **InPortShape**, from the component models language, which defines an icon decorator. Corresponding instances of those shapes, as they would appear in a running designer, are also shown.

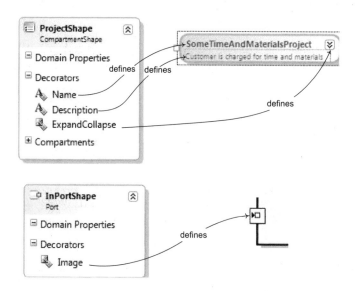

FIGURE 4-26: Different kinds of decorator

A text decorator is used to decorate a shape or connector with text, and an icon decorator is used to decorate a shape or connector with an image (icon). When defining a text decorator, it is necessary to define the "Default Text" resource, which is the text displayed, unless it is dynamically updated through a decorator map. When defining an icon decorator, it is necessary to define an "Image" resource that is the image displayed.

There is a range of settings that control the appearance of text displayed in a text decorator. These are self-explanatory, although the omission of a "Text Color" property might seem to be an oversight. In fact, the color of the text displayed in a decorator is determined by the "Text Color" property on the diagram element that defines the decorator, as we have seen earlier when discussing shapes. For example, setting the "Text Color" property of **IssueStateShape** to *Maroon* results in the text of the **NameDecorator**, defined by **IssueStateShape**, being rendered in maroon, as illustrated in Figure 4-27.

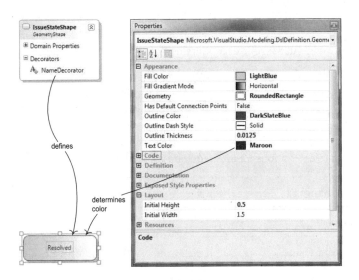

FIGURE 4-27: Definition of text color

All kinds of shapes and connectors can define text and icon decorators. However, an expand collapse decorator can only be added to compartment, geometry, or image shapes or ports. It has a predefined appearance and a special behavior when attached to compartment shapes—all the compartments can be hidden (when collapsed). Additional code customization must be undertaken to add behavior to this decorator for non-compartment shapes.

Positioning

Each decorator has a position with respect to the shape or connector it decorates. Figure 4-28 shows the full range of positions available for shapes and connectors, respectively, which may be further refined through offsets (expressed as inches). The positional information is set through the properties on the decorator.

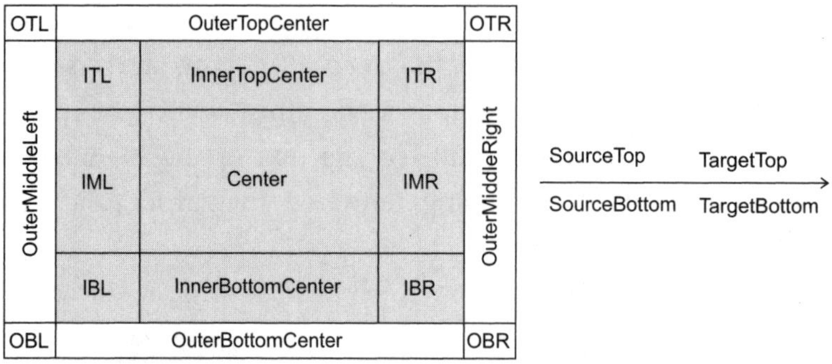

FIGURE 4-28: All possible decorator positions

Only a subset of the positions is supported for certain kinds of shape; the possibilities are summarized in Table 4-5.

TABLE 4-5: Decorator Positions for Different Kinds of Shapes

Geometry shape	All
Image shape	All
Compartment shape	All outer decorators, InnerTopLeft, InnerTopCenter, InnerTopRight
Port	All
Swimlane	InnerTopLeft, InnerTopCenter, InnerTopRight

Decorator Maps

The appearance of a decorator in any particular instance of a shape may change dynamically as the information in the model changes. This behavior is defined in decorator maps that are part of shape and connector maps. Figure 4-29 shows the decorator map for the **Name** decorator of the **ProjectShape** in the Issue Project DSL. There are two parts: the "Display property" and the "Visibility Filter."

If the decorator is a text decorator, then a "Display property" may be provided. This is a domain property of the domain class being mapped to the shape (**Project** in this case), or a domain property of the domain class of an element navigated to by the "Path to display property," if present.

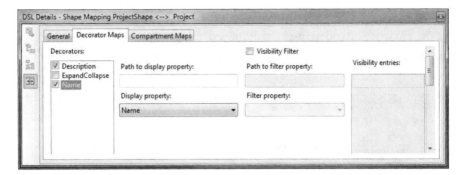

FIGURE 4-29: Definition of a decorator map

In order to understand the visibility filter, let's consider an alternative way of showing a start state in the Issue State example. Suppose that instead of having a separate start element connected to an issue state to indicate that the issue state is a start state, we define an icon decorator that should only appear in cases when the issue state is a start state. To indicate that fact, we'll add a Boolean flag to **IssueState** called **IsStartState**. That is, the definitions of **IssueState** and **IssueStateShape** are as shown in Figure 4-30.

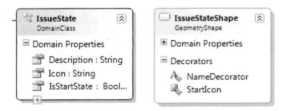

FIGURE 4-30: Definition of StartIcon and IsStartState

We can now define a visibility filter in the map for the decorator **StartIcon**, as shown in Figure 4-31. This says that the **StartIcon** will only be visible when the domain property **IsStartState** is true. The property can have any type—enumerated properties are particularly useful for this. By providing a path to the filter property, the property can be a domain property of another element navigable from the element mapped to the shape to which the decorator belongs. Text decorators can also be filtered—that is, you can set things up so that text appears only under certain circumstances. And if you want to base visibility on more sophisticated logic, then you can do this by introducing a calculated property and using that in the visibility filter.

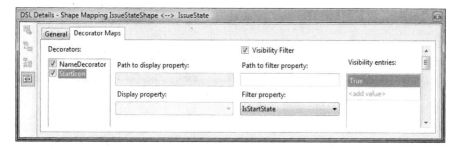

FIGURE 4-31: Decorator map showing visibility filter

The result in the generated designer is illustrated in Figure 4-32, where only the state *Raised* has the Boolean flag "Is Start State" set to *True*.

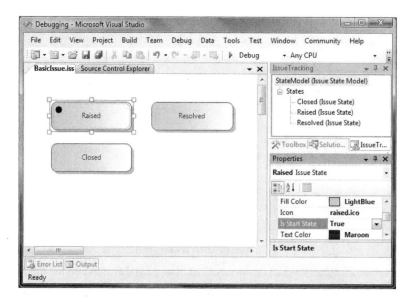

FIGURE 4-32: Result of using a visibility filter

Customizing the Graphical Notation in Code

We have already discussed the customization of shape and connector maps through code, as driven by the Boolean "HasCustomXxx" flags on shape maps. This section describes a range of other useful customizations.

Most of the code in this section requires the following using statements:

```
using Microsoft.VisualStudio.Modeling;
using Microsoft.VisualStudio.Modeling.Diagrams;
```

Multiline Text Decorators

There are occasions where you'd like the text in a text decorator to wrap across multiple lines. A common example is in the definition of a comment box that is used to add text comment boxes on the design surface.

The inner decorators of a shape are implemented as *shape fields*. By default, text shape fields only allow a single line of horizontal text. However, we can change that by setting the appropriate properties. To have the text wrap successfully within the containing shape, we also need to "anchor" the sides of the field to the sides of the shape (Figure 4-33).

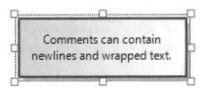

FIGURE 4-33: Wrapped text inside a
Comment Box

```
public partial class CommentBoxShape
{
  //Called once for each shape instance.
  protected override void InitializeDecorators
    (IList<ShapeField> shapeFields,
     IList<Decorator> decorators)
  {
    // Be sure to call the base method.
    base.InitializeDecorators(shapeFields, decorators);

    //Look up the shape field, which is called "Comment."
    TextField commentField =
          (TextField)ShapeElement.FindShapeField
                        (shapeFields, "Comment");
```

```
        // Allow multiple lines of text.
        commentField.DefaultMultipleLine = true;
        // Autosize not supported for multi-line fields.
        commentField.DefaultAutoSize = false;

        // Anchor the field slightly inside the container shape.
        commentField.AnchoringBehavior.Clear();
        commentField.AnchoringBehavior.
          SetLeftAnchor  (AnchoringBehavior.Edge.Left, 0.01);
        commentField.AnchoringBehavior.
          SetRightAnchor (AnchoringBehavior.Edge.Right, 0.01);
        commentField.AnchoringBehavior.
          SetTopAnchor   (AnchoringBehavior.Edge.Top, 0.01);
        commentField.AnchoringBehavior.
          SetBottomAnchor(AnchoringBehavior.Edge.Bottom, 0.01);
    }
}
```

Note that for this code to work, you must set "Generates Double Derived" to *True* for **CommentBoxShape** in the DSL definition.

Variable Image Shape

You can change the image displayed in an image decorator dependent upon data in the underlying model.

In the Circuit Diagrams DSL, the transistor shapes can have multiple orientations—eight in all (some of them are shown in Figure 4-34).

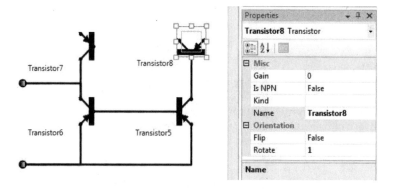

FIGURE 4-34: Transistor shapes have multiple orientations.

Rather than create a separate shape and toolbox tool for each orientation, we provide the user with one tool, one **TransistorShape**, and the ability to change the orientation of the image.

The eight images are selected depending on the value of two domain properties **Flip** and **Rotate**, which are on the **TransistorShape**. They would be inappropriate on the **Transistor** domain class, since they are only concerned with presentation. The wiring represented by the model would be the same no matter which way the components appear on the diagram.

We need to make our own custom `ImageField` class to perform the reorientation and then make sure that the field implementing the image decorator is an instance of this class. We'll call the new class `ComponentImageField`. It overrides `GetDisplayImage` and uses the standard image rotation facilities found in `System.Drawing` and caches the result to avoid computing every time.

```
public class ComponentImageField : ImageField
{
  public ComponentImageField(string tag) : base(tag) { }

  private RotateFlipType cachedRotateFlip =
                    RotateFlipType.RotateNoneFlipNone;
  private Image cachedImage = null;

  private static RotateFlipType[] rotateFlips =
                    new RotateFlipType[] {
                        RotateFlipType.RotateNoneFlipNone,
                        RotateFlipType.Rotate270FlipNone,
                        RotateFlipType.Rotate180FlipNone,
                        RotateFlipType.Rotate90FlipNone,
                        RotateFlipType.RotateNoneFlipX,
                        RotateFlipType.Rotate90FlipX,
                        RotateFlipType.RotateNoneFlipY,
                        RotateFlipType.Rotate90FlipY
                        };
  public override Image GetDisplayImage
                (ShapeElement parentShape)
  {
    ComponentShape componentShape =
                    parentShape as ComponentShape;
    RotateFlipType rotateFlip =
            rotateFlips[componentShape.RotateFlip];
    if (cachedImage == null || rotateFlip != cachedRotateFlip)
    {
      cachedImage = base.GetDisplayImage(parentShape);

      if (cachedImage != null &&
          rotateFlip != RotateFlipType.RotateNoneFlipNone)
      {
        cachedImage = (Image)cachedImage.Clone();
```

```
            cachedImage.RotateFlip(rotateFlip);
          }
          cachedRotateFlip = rotateFlip;
      }
      return cachedImage;
    }
}
```

Now we override `InitializeShapeFields` to supply an instance of this class instead of the default image field:

```
public partial class TransistorShape
{
  // Requires Generate Double Derived:
  protected override void InitializeShapeFields
                        (IList<ShapeField> shapeFields)
  {
    string decoratorName = "PNPImage"; // as in DSL Definition
    ComponentImageField field =
              new ComponentImageField(decoratorName);
    field.DefaultImage =
      ImageHelper.GetImage(
        CircuitsDomainModel.SingletonResourceManager.
        GetObject("TransistorShapePNPImageDefaultImage"));
    shapeFields.Add(field);
  }
}
```

The unrotated image `TransistorShapePNPImageDefaultImage` is the image resource for the decorator defined in the DSL definition. This is compiled into the set of resources for the designer via the `DomainModelResx.resx` file in the `Dsl` project, which is generated from the DSL definition. It can be in any of several formats, including JPEG, GIF, and BMP.

Set a Background Picture

It is possible to set a background picture for the diagram. To do this, you need to create an image resource and then create an image field on the diagram to act as the background field.

It is easiest to put the image resource in the project resources file:

- Include the image file (JPEG, GIF, BMP, etc.) in the `Resources` folder.
- Open the `Dsl` project properties, and open the `Resources` tab.

- Click the "Create Resource File" link if necessary.
- Drag the image file from the solution explorer into the resources window.

To create the image field in the diagram class, set the "Generates Double Derived" property in your diagram class in the DSL definition to *True*, and regenerate. Then write a partial class to create the background image field, as follows:

```
public partial class ComponentDiagram
{
  protected override void
        InitializeShapeFields(IList<ShapeField> shapeFields)
  {
    base.InitializeShapeFields(shapeFields);
    ImageField backgroundField = new ImageField("background",
        ImageHelper.GetImage(Properties.Resources.
                                    SampleBackgroundImage));

    // Make sure you can't do anything with it.
    backgroundField.DefaultFocusable = false;
    backgroundField.DefaultSelectable = false;
    backgroundField.DefaultVisibility = true;

    shapeFields.Add(backgroundField);

    // Make it center in the diagram.
    backgroundField.AnchoringBehavior.
          SetTopAnchor(AnchoringBehavior.Edge.Top, 0.01);
    backgroundField.AnchoringBehavior.
          SetLeftAnchor(AnchoringBehavior.Edge.Left, 0.01);
    backgroundField.AnchoringBehavior.
          SetRightAnchor(AnchoringBehavior.Edge.Right, 0.01);
    backgroundField.AnchoringBehavior.
          SetBottomAnchor(AnchoringBehavior.Edge.Bottom, 0.01);
  }
}
```

Set Custom Connection Points

The DSL Tools use a routing engine to route connectors between shapes. By default the routing engine will select any point on the bounding box of a shape as a connection point. For some shapes we might want to suggest specific connection points.

If you want just four connection points, one in the middle of each side of a shape, you can set the property "Has Default Connection Points" in the shape, as discussed earlier. To get a different pattern of connection points, you need to write custom code. In that case, you should *not* set "Has Default Connection Points" in the shape.

```
public partial class SyncBarShape
{
  public override bool HasConnectionPoints
  {
    get
    {
      return true;
    }
  }
  public override void EnsureConnectionPoints (LinkShape link)
  {
    // set connection points along the top and bottom,
    // to discourage connection to the sides
    foreach (double y in new double[]
          { AbsoluteBoundingBox.Top, AbsoluteBoundingBox.Bottom })
    {
      double spacing = AbsoluteBoundingBox.Width / 4.0;
      for (double x = spacing + AbsoluteBoundingBox.Left;
            x < AbsoluteBoundingBox.Right - spacing / 2;
            x += spacing)
      {
        this.CreateConnectionPoint(new PointD(x, y));
      }
    }
  }
}
```

The code only defines a preference—the user can move the end point of any line around the bounding box. `HasConnectionPoints` and `EnsureConnec-tionPoints` are called every time a link is made to a shape. Connection points can be set per instance shape. However, once set for a particular instance, connection points apply to all connections made to that instance. (Despite the `link` parameter to `EnsureConnectionPoint`, the connection point is not specific to a type of link.)

Change Routing Style of Connectors

Two routing styles for connectors are exposed in the DSL definition—straight and rectilinear. However, there is a wide range of other styles that you can choose, which can be done through custom code. For example, the Issue Project DSL uses a routing style for its connectors that is appropriate for presenting tree structures from top to bottom down the page, as illustrated in Figure 4-35.

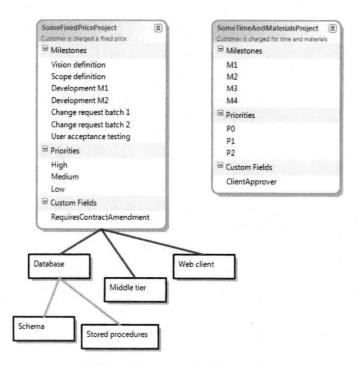

FIGURE 4-35: Illustration of North-South tree routing style

This is achieved by overriding the default routing style for the relevant connectors. Here's the code from the Issue Project DSL to do this.

```
namespace CJKW.IssueProject
{
    public partial class ProjectCategoryConnector
    {
        [CLSCompliant(false)]
        protected override Microsoft.VisualStudio.Modeling.Diagrams.
                          GraphObject.VGRoutingStyle DefaultRoutingStyle
        {
            get
            {
                return
                Microsoft.VisualStudio.Modeling.Diagrams.GraphObject.
                        VGRoutingStyle.VGRouteTreeNS;
```

```
          }
        }
      }

      public partial class CategoryTreeConnector
      {
        [CLSCompliant(false)]
        protected override Microsoft.VisualStudio.Modeling.Diagrams.GraphObject.
                        VGRoutingStyle DefaultRoutingStyle
        {
          get
          {
            return Microsoft.VisualStudio.Modeling.Diagrams.GraphObject.
                    VGRoutingStyle.VGRouteTreeNS;
          }
        }
      }
    }
```

In more sophisticated cases, changing the routing style of a particular connector may not be sufficient, which is one of the reasons that not all routing styles have been exposed in the DSL definition. Instead, you may need to write code that uses the facilities provided by `Microsoft.VisualStudio.Modeling.Diagrams.Diagram`. In particular, the method,

```
public void AutoLayoutShapeElements(
              System.Collections.ICollection
                shapeElementCollection,
              Microsoft.VisualStudio.Modeling.Diagrams.
                GraphObject.VGRoutingStyle routingStyle,
              Microsoft.VisualStudio.Modeling.Diagrams.
                GraphObject.PlacementValueStyle placementStyle,
              bool route)
```

may be useful for laying out either the whole diagram or particular parts of it.

Explorer

We've seen how information is presented through the graphical design surface. Now we turn our attention to the explorer, which appears in all designers by default.

Default Appearance

As mentioned in Chapter 3, the nodes in the explorer are derived from embedding relationships, and there is a set of behaviors that governs how nodes are displayed by default. Some of these rules can be overridden by adding data to the DSL definition; that will be discussed in subsequent sections. To illustrate the default rules, we'll look at the Issue Project DSL, whose domain model is shown in Figure 4-36. Figure 4-37 shows the model explorer for the Issue Project designer over a suitable populated model.

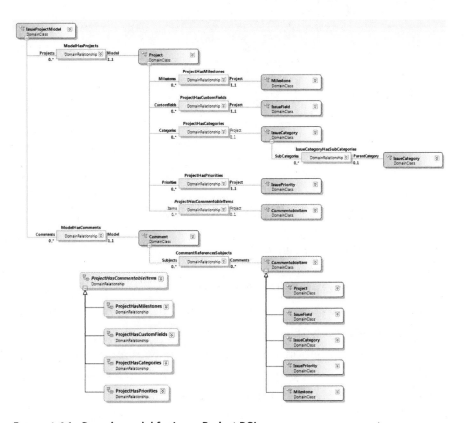

FIGURE 4-36: Domain model for Issue Project DSL

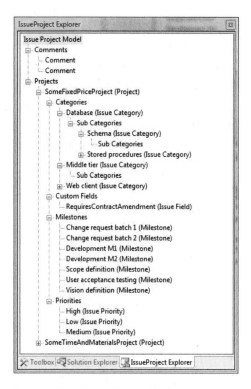

FIGURE 4-37: Issue Project Explorer over a populated model

The default behaviors are as follows:

- Every non-abstract embedding relationship is represented in the explorer by a collection node (or element node if the multiplicity of the source role of the relationship is 0..1 or 1..1).

- If an embedding relationship has source role with multiplicity 0..* or 1..*, then it is represented by a collection node (i.e., it has element nodes nested beneath it), and the "Property Name" of the source role is used to label the node. Examples in Figure 4-37 are Projects, Categories, Custom Fields, etc. Notice that there is no Items node beneath a project because the relationship **ProjectHas-CommentableItems** is abstract.

- If the multiplicity of the source role is 0..1 or 1..1, then the element node is not nested beneath the collection node but is conflated with it. The Issue Project example doesn't have any of these, but if you browse through the DSL explorer of the DSL designer on some DSL definition, you'll see some examples—"Custom Type Descriptor" on any domain class, or the "Validation" node under "Editor" (remember the DSL designer is itself developed using DSL Tools).

- Then there is an element node nested beneath the collection node for each embedded element, provided that the link to the element is not also a link of a derived relationship.[3] The information displayed for each element node is the value of the property providing the name of the element (if there is one) followed by the domain class of the element shown in brackets. If there is no property representing the name, then the domain class name is displayed instead. For example, the names of both projects are displayed, followed by their class (**IssueProject**). Notice, however, that only the class is displayed for both comments, because **Comment** has no name property.

- No reference relationships are shown in the explorer.

Changing the Window Icon and Label

The title of the explorer window, which then also appears in the tab when docked with the solution explorer, and in the view menu, can be changed through the "Title" property of the explorer behavior in the DSL definition, as illustrated in Figure 4-38.

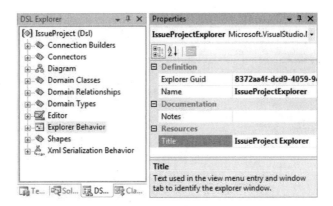

FIGURE 4-38: Changing the title of the explorer

---

3. This ensures that an element only appears once in the explorer and in a way that distinguishes between links that are also links of derived relationships from ones that are not.

The icon cannot be changed through the DSL definition but may be changed simply by substituting the `ModelExplorerToolWindowBitmaps.bmp` file in the `Resources` folder of the `DslPackage` project. This is because the `VSPackage.resx` file in the `DslPackage` project is not generated, unlike its counterpart in the `Dsl` project. Thus, unless you are prepared to hand-edit the `.resx` file, the filename for the icon used for the explorer window cannot be changed, so you just have to replace the file with another of the same name.

Customizing the Appearance of Nodes

The appearance of element nodes can be customized by adding custom explorer node settings to the "Explorer Behavior."

> **▪ TIP** Adding a custom explorer node setting
>
> Choose "Add ExplorerNodeSettings" from the context menu with explorer behavior selected. You can then identify the domain class of element the node represents, whether or not the display name for that class should be shown in brackets (the default is not), and the icon you wish to display. If you provide one or more custom node settings, icons get displayed on all nodes, with default icons used if no icon is provided.

This is illustrated in Figure 4-39, and the effect of the definitions on the appearance of the explorer is shown in Figure 4-40.

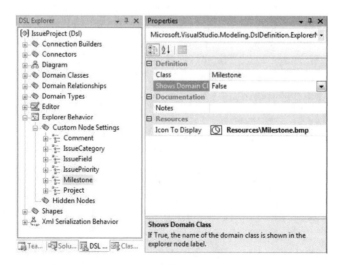

FIGURE 4-39: Defining custom node settings

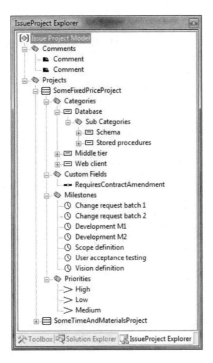

FIGURE 4-40: Result of defining custom node settings

You can also change the string that is displayed for each collection and element node. For a collection node, the string used is the value of "Property Display Name" (under the "Resources" category) on the source role of the relationship to which the collection node corresponds. By default this is just the property name with spaces inserted at word breaks.

For an element node, it is possible to choose the displayed string to be the value of a domain property from an element navigable via a path from the element that the node represents. This is done by adding a "Property Displayed" property path to the "Custom Node Settings" corresponding to the class of the element. Figure 4-41 shows an (unrealistic) example, highlighting the definition of a "Property Displayed" path in the custom settings for **Milestone**. The path instructs the explorer to navigate back from a **Milestone** element to the **Project** it belongs to, and then to use the **Name** domain property of that project for the display string. The effect of this definition is shown in Figure 4-42, where you will indeed see that all milestones are displayed using the name of the project. An example of where this is useful is provided by the DSL designer itself, indeed in exactly the area we are looking at now. Each custom node setting node in the DSL explorer displays the name of the class to which the custom node setting applies.

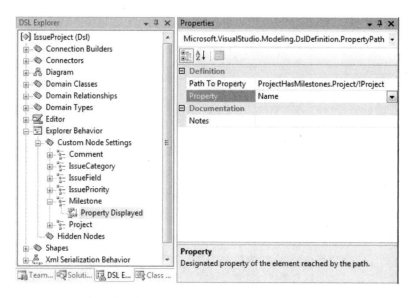

FIGURE 4-41: Changing the string displayed in an element node

---

▪ TIP Adding a property path

On the Custom node setting (Milestone), use the "Add New Property Path" contextual command. The subnode that was named "Property Displayed (empty)" changes to "Property Displayed," and you can change the "Path To Property" value to a path; when you have entered a correct path, you will be able to choose a domain property from the domain properties of the class of the element reached by the path (in this case, **Project**).

Hiding Nodes

It is also possible to hide collection nodes and all nodes beneath them from the explorer. To do that, you add domain paths under "Hidden Nodes." For example, to hide "Sub Categories" from the Issue Project explorer, add a new domain path under "Hidden Nodes" and then fill in the path in the "Content" field in the properties window.

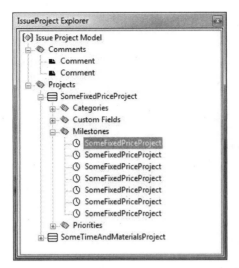

FIGURE 4-42: Result of changing the string displayed

> ■ **TIP** Adding a domain path
>
> The "Add Domain Path" context menu item is visible with the explorer behavior node selected, not the hidden nodes node. In general, to add an element beneath a collection node in the explorer, whether using the DSL designer or your own designer, you need to select the parent of the collection node.

All you need to provide is the name of the relationship and the role to navigate across, as shown in Figure 4-43. The effect in the generated designer is that all "Sub Categories" collection nodes, together with that part of the tree nested beneath them, will be hidden, as illustrated in Figure 4-44.

Customizing the Explorer through Code

If you want to change the presentation of the explorer through code, then you can, but not in a fine-grained way. If you look at the generated code (the ModelExplorer.cs file nested beneath ModelExplorer.tt in the GeneratedCode folder of the DslPackage project), you'll see that the creation and appearance of nodes is dependent on an ExplorerElementVisitor that is defined as part of the underlying framework in the Microsoft.VisualStudio.

`Modeling.Diagrams` namespace. You'll need to override the method that creates the element visitor with one that returns a visitor of your own devising. This is just a matter of adding a partial class, because the double-derived pattern (explained in Chapter 3) is used to generate the code for the explorer.

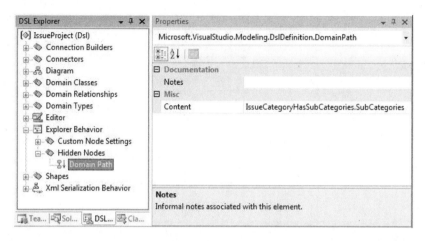

FIGURE 4-43: Hiding nodes

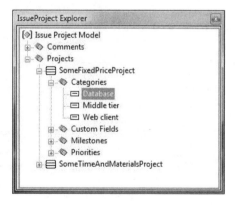

FIGURE 4-44: Result of hiding nodes

Properties Window

Default Appearance of Properties Window

By default the properties window shows the following properties of an element of a domain class when it is selected in the model explorer:

- Domain properties defined on the domain class
- Properties derived from roles whose roleplayer is that domain class and whose multiplicity is 0..1 or 1..1, and where the roleplayer of the opposite role has a domain property that acts as the element name (Is Element Name = true)
- Domain properties defined on the embedding relationship that targets the selected element

In the second case, the name used for the displayed property is the property name of the role. The value shown is the name of the element referenced, hence the constraint that it has a domain property that acts as the element name.

To illustrate the third case, imagine a domain model with domain class **A**, which has an embedding relationship **AHasB** to **B**, and where **AHasB** has a domain property **X** defined on it. Then, whenever a **B** element is selected, the property **X** will also appear in the properties window for that element. The motivation for this is that it is rare for embedding relationships to be mapped to connectors, so if this were not done, properties defined on embedding relationships could never be set, because links of those relationships could never be selected. This is an example of *forwarding* a property, which you can also do explicitly through the DSL definition, as explained in a later section.

If, instead of selecting an element via the model explorer, a *shape* representing an element is selected, then it will also show:

- Any domain properties explicitly defined for the shape, including browsable exposed style properties (such as fill color)
- Roles for which the shape is a roleplayer that satisfy the constraints just presented

> **■ TIP** Making style properties on shapes and connectors changeable programmatically
>
> Exposed style properties provide a way to expose certain style properties of shapes and connectors in the properties window so that they can be changed by the user of the designer. A style property is exposed by creating a domain property on the shape or connector definition.

> A side effect of exposing a style property in this way is that the property can also be set dynamically through the API. If that is all you want to do, then just change "Is Browsable" to *False* on the exposed domain property and that will hide it from the user in the properties window.

If a connector is selected, then it displays:

- Domain properties defined for the domain relationship it is mapped to
- Properties derived from appropriate roles for which the domain relationship is roleplayer (domain relationships may participate in other domain relationships—see Chapter 3)
- Domain properties explicitly defined for the connector, including browsable exposed style properties
- Appropriate domain roles for which the connector is roleplayer

Note that links of a relationship can only be selected via a connector.

By default, all properties appear in the "Misc" category, and their names and descriptions are derived from the name of the domain property (or property name, in the case of roles). See the next section for details on how to change this.

Categories, Names, and Descriptions

When a property is displayed in the properties window, it appears in a category, is identified through a display name, and has a description, as illustrated in Figure 4-45, which shows the properties of a **StartElement** element in the Issue State DSL.

All these are configurable in the DSL definition through property settings of domain properties and domain roles. Figure 4-46 shows the settings for the properties highlighted in Figure 4-45. The first is for the domain property **Name** on the **StartElement** domain class, and the second is for the **StartElement** role ("Display Name" is "Start State") played by **StartElement**.

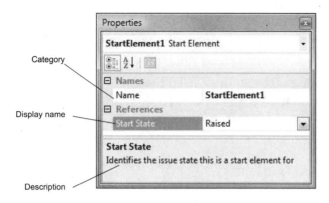

FIGURE 4-45: Anatomy of the presentation of a property

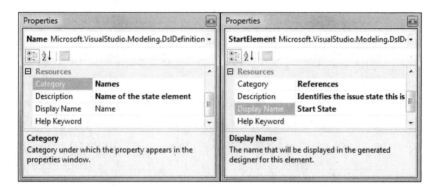

FIGURE 4-46: Settings on domain properties and roles governing their presentation

Note that, in the DSL designer, it is not possible to override the settings of a domain property already defined in a class in subclasses of that class. So, for example, it's not possible to change the description for **Name** to be "Name of the start element" in the **StartElement** class.

All the strings are generated as resources, which means they are localizable (see the section "Localization" earlier in this chapter). In particular, this means that it is possible to choose a different name to display in the properties window than the actual name of the property used in the DSL definition.

Note that exposing a style property on a diagram, shape, or connector introduces a domain property to represent it, which then behaves like any other domain property.

Hiding Properties and Making Them Read-Only

A property may be hidden from the properties window by setting "Is Browsable" to *False*, or it can be made read-only (the property is grayed out and its value can't be changed) by setting "Is UI Read Only" to *True*. These settings are available on both domain roles and domain properties.

Forwarding Properties

It was earlier explained how domain properties on embedding relationships get forwarded to the class that is the target of the relationship. It is also possible to do this for any property by making use of custom type descriptors on domain classes. Select a domain class in the explorer (or anything that can act like a domain class, such as a domain relationship, shape, etc.) and choose "Add New Domain Type Descriptor." This will create the custom type descriptor for the domain class. Then, to this you can add custom property descriptors, which can include a path to a property to be included in the type descriptor.

For example, suppose you wanted to display the **IssueTypeName** from an **IssueStateModel** as a read-only property in an **IssueState element**, for example, to remind you which **IssueType** element you were working on. You would define the pieces as shown in Figure 4-47 and get the result shown in Figure 4-48.

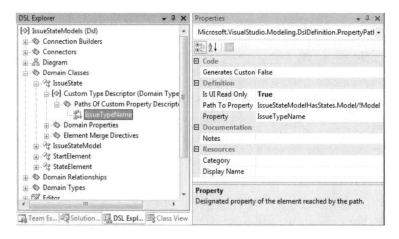

FIGURE 4-47: Definition of forwarded property

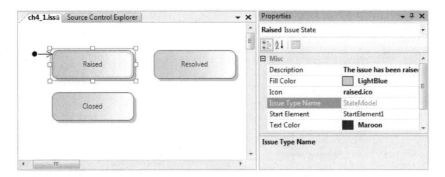

FIGURE 4-48: Forwarded property showing in generated designer

Customizing the Properties Window through Code

It is possible to customize the appearance and editing experience for individual properties in the properties window through code. The basic method is to attach a custom attribute to the domain property that identifies the custom handler to be used for that property. In Figure 4-49 we show how to attach a file picker to a domain property.

In the DSL definition, select the domain property for which the custom editor is required. Locate the "Custom Attributes" property in the properties window and click on the ellipsis (…) to open the attribute editor. Enter the attribute, as illustrated in Figure 4-49, and then save and regenerate the code. The .NET attribute `System.ComponentModel.EditorAttribute` is specifically used for identifying editors for .NET properties. The code generated from the definition just shown applies this attribute to the .NET property generated from the domain property **ExternalFileReference**. The first parameter of the attribute identifies the class defining the editor to be used, and the second identifies the base type for that class. In this case we have used a standard editor supplied as part of .NET, but you are at liberty to define your own.

In order to build the code, you'll need to add a reference to `System.Design` in the `Dsl` project. The resulting designer now provides a custom editor in the properties window for the designated domain property, as illustrated in Figure 4-50.

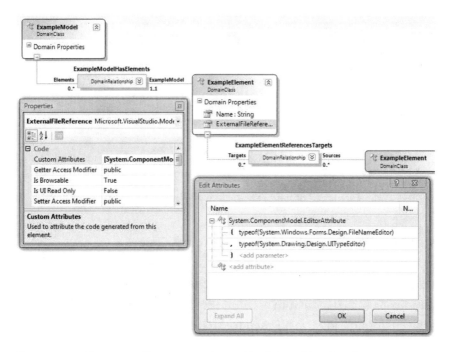

FIGURE 4-49: Custom attribute to associate a file picker with a domain property

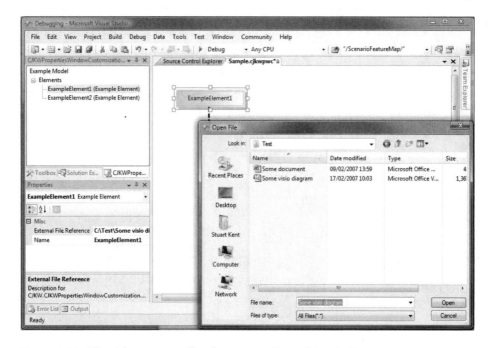

FIGURE 4-50: File picker custom editor for property in resulting designer

SUMMARY

This chapter has gone through most aspects of defining how information in a model for a DSL gets presented in the designer through the graphical design surface, the model explorer, and the properties window. It has explained the extensive facilities provided in a DSL definition to customize the way in which information is presented and has provided some examples of common refinements that can be made through custom code. More advanced examples, like how to do nested shapes, are covered in Chapter 10. Next comes Chapter 5, which looks at how you define creation, delete, and update behavior for a designer.

5

Creation, Deletion, and Update Behavior

Introduction

Chapter 2 introduced the different aspects of the definition of a DSL: the domain model; the presentation layer, including graphical notation, explorer, and properties window; creation, deletion, and update behavior; validation; and serialization. Chapter 3 described the first aspect, the domain model, and Chapter 4 described the presentation aspect. This chapter focuses on how to define update behavior, that is, creation of elements using the toolbox and explorer, editing of properties of elements through the properties window, and deletion of elements.

Element Creation

When a new element is created in the store, it must be linked into the embedding tree—that is, it must be the target of one embedding link, and there must be a path back through embedding links to the root element. It cannot otherwise be presented on the diagram or serialized.

When the user drags from an element tool onto the diagram, this gesture:

- Creates a new element of the class determined by the Tool definition (in the DSL explorer under "Editor\ToolboxTabs").

- Creates a link or links between the new element and the existing ones. This behavior is determined by the element merge directive of the target element—that is, the one the tool was dragged onto.

- Fires rules that update the diagram to show the new element. These are determined by the shape maps, as we saw in the previous chapter.

The last point is important. We rely on "fixup" rules to maintain, on the screen, a presentation of what is going on in the model. All the techniques in this chapter—and indeed much of the custom methods you might write—deal only with the domain classes and domain relationships. Once we've set up the shapes and their mappings to the domain model (as discussed in Chapter 4), we can just work with the domain model, leaving the diagrams to look after themselves.

The Toolbox

Tools are defined in the DSL explorer under "Editor\ToolboxTabs\ YourTab\Tools." You need to define a tool for each item you want to appear on the toolbox (Figure 5-1). The tab name is the heading that appears above each group of tools in the toolbox. By default, you have just one tab, named after your language, but you can add more tabs in the explorer if you wish.

FIGURE 5-1: The toolbox for the
Issue Tracking DSL

There are two kinds of tools: *element tools* and *connection tools*. At runtime, you operate an element tool by dragging it from the toolbox to the diagram; for a connection tool, you click it and then drag it between the two elements you want connected (or click them in succession). The most common scheme is to provide an element tool for each class that is mapped to a shape on the diagram and a connection tool for each relationship mapped to a connector.

Each tool has a name, caption, tooltip, toolbox icon, and help keyword; these are set in the properties window (Figure 5-2). In addition, an element tool can have a cursor icon that shows while you are dragging it, and a connection tool can have source and target cursor icons that show while waiting for you to select the source and target of the connection.

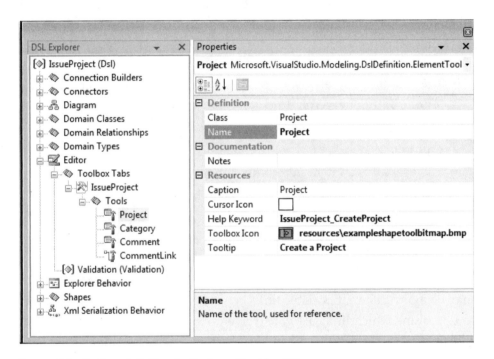

FIGURE 5-2: Toolbox definition for the Issue Tracking DSL

Each element tool is associated with a single domain class. Unless you write custom code, the tool creates a single element of this class each time the user drags from the tool to the drawing surface. The properties of the new element have their default values as specified in the DSL definition. The construction of relationships between the new element and the existing model is governed by an *element merge directive*, which we'll look at shortly.

Each connection tool invokes a specified *connection builder*, which governs what elements may be created and the result of creating them. You might expect that by analogy with the element tools, each connection tool would be defined to create instances of a particular domain relationship class; but no, a connection builder can be defined so as to instantiate any of several relationships, depending on the classes of the two elements the user wants to connect.

We'll come back to connection tools later in this chapter; first let's focus on creating elements.

Element Merge Directives

Element merge directives (EMDs) control what relationships are constructed when one element is *merged* into another. A merge happens when one of the following occurs:

- The user drags an element from the toolbox onto the design surface (or one of the shapes on it).
- The user creates an element using an "Add" menu in the DSL's explorer.
- The user adds an item in a compartment shape.
- The user moves an item from one swimlane to another.
- Your custom code invokes the merge directive, for example, to implement a paste operation (as described in Chapter 10).

In each of these cases, there are two elements to be connected, but there may be many different possible links between them. The job of the EMD is to determine which links are constructed. An EMD also has a disconnect function that is invoked when an element is to be moved between parents—for example, from one swimlane to another.

The simplest and most common case is when there is an embedding relationship between the two domain classes. In the Issue Tracking example, each **IssueProjectModel** element has projects and comments (Figure 5-3). An **IssueProjectModel** element is represented by the diagram, and the two others are each mapped to shapes.

When the user drags from the Project tool to the diagram, we want the new project to be embedded in the **IssueProjectModel** element using the **ModelHasProjects** relationship. This behavior is determined by an element merge directive, which can be found in the DSL explorer under "Domain Classes\IssueProjectModel." To see the full detail of the EMD, look in the DSL details window (Figure 5-4).

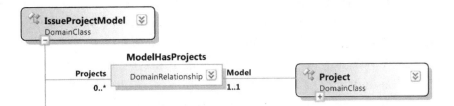

FIGURE 5-3: IssueProjectModel embeds Projects

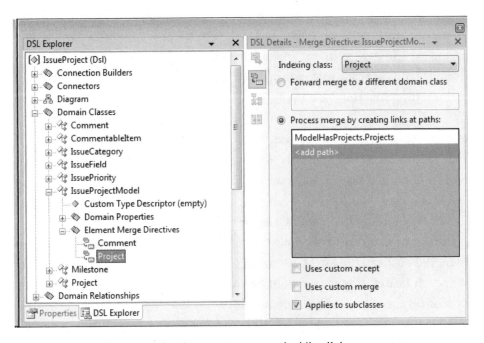

FIGURE 5-4: Element Merge Directive to create one embedding link

Notice that the EMD is defined under the target class—in this case, the **IssueProjectModel** element, because the user will drop the **Project** onto the diagram whose "Class Represented" is **IssueProjectModel**. The class of element being merged is called the "Indexing" class. Notice also that there are no shapes mentioned here—the EMD is defined in terms of the model classes and relationships.

This EMD says that (a) a **Project** can be merged into an **IssueProjectModel** element, and (b) when it is merged, a **ModelHasProjects** link will be created, adding the new **Project** to the **IssueProjectModel** element's **Projects** property.

The first part of this behavior is quite important, because it determines what the user is able to do. For example, if you drag a **Project** off the toolbox and hover over a **Comment**, you see the "not allowed" cursor. This is because **Comment** has no EMD for which **Project** is the "Indexing" class. Move the mouse over to the diagram and it changes back to "allowed," because **IssueProjectModel** has an EMD for **Project**.

Figure 5-4 shows the most common kind of EMD, in which a single embedding link is created. In fact, it is so common that whenever you add a new embedding relationship to the DSL definition, the DSL designer automatically creates an EMD under the source class, with the target class as index. (Be aware of this, because you might want to remove it, for example, if you want to create custom code that will be the only means of instantiating this relationship.)

Multiple Element Merge Directives

The root class is not the only owner of element merge directives, and more than one class can have an EMD for the same indexing class. In the Issue Tracking example, we want to be able to draw diagrams like that in Figure 5-5, where each **IssueCategory** element can either be owned by a project or can be a child of another **IssueCategory** element. We have chosen to model both relationships as embeddings—a convenient way of ensuring that each **IssueCategory** element has only one parent (Figure 5-6).

Each embedding relationship has its corresponding element merge directive, allowing the user to drag the "Category" tool onto either a **Project** or onto an existing **IssueCategory**. Each EMD of course instantiates its appropriate relationship, **ProjectHasCategories** or **IssueCategoryHasSubCategories**. There is no EMD under **IssueProjectModel** for **IssueCategory**, so the cursor shows "not allowed" as you drag from the "Category" tool over the diagram.

Element Merge Directives and Compartment Shapes

An element merge directive is usually needed for each class mapped to a compartment in a compartment shape. For example (Figure 5-7), milestones, priorities, and fields are displayed in a project shape; the domain classes **Milestone**, **IssuePriority**, and **IssueField** are embedded under **Project** and each has an EMD (which would have been created automatically by the DSL designer when the embeddings were defined).

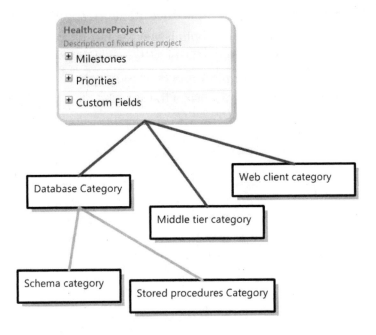

FIGURE 5-5: Elements with two alternative parent types

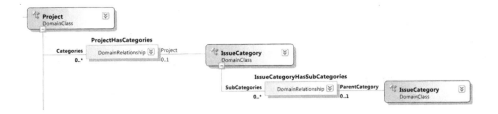

FIGURE 5-6: IssueCategory is the target of two alternative embeddings

Figure 5-8 shows the menu for adding items to a project shape. If we remove the element merge directive under **Project** for **Milestone**, that item would disappear from the menu. You could still have a **"Milestones"** compartment in **ProjectShape**, but you would have to write custom code to link **"Milestones"** to **Projects**.

Add Menu in the Explorer

The language explorer provides a tree view of the model. Embedded elements can be added using the context menu in the explorer as long as there is also an element merge directive. Figure 5-9 shows the "Add" menu for a project.

Notice that it can include every embedded item, irrespective of how it is represented on the diagram, so that both **IssueCategory** and **IssuePriority** are included. But in this example, the EMD for **Milestone** has been removed from the DSL definition, and so it does not appear on the menu—even though there is actually a **Milestone** in this instance of the model.

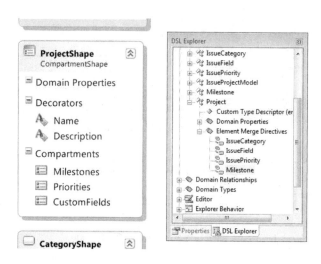

FIGURE 5-7: An EMD is usually needed for the class mapped to each compartment

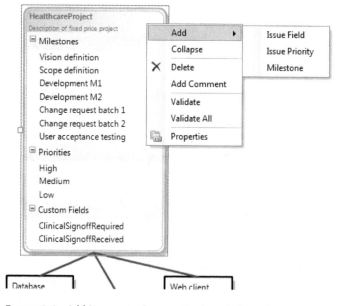

FIGURE 5-8: Add Item menu in a compartment shape is determined by compartments and EMDs

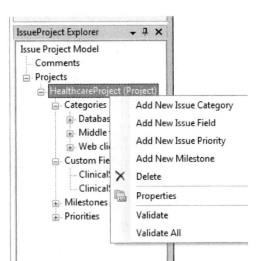

FIGURE 5-9: An Add command is generated in the explorer
for each embedded item with an EMD

Multiple Link Creation Paths in an EMD

The user's basic method of associating a **Comment** with a **Project** is to drag a **Comment** onto the diagram and then make a link from it to the **Project** (Figure 5-10).

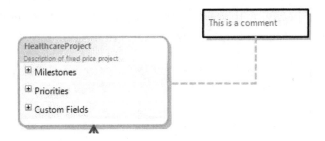

FIGURE 5-10: Comment attached to Project

We have defined **Comment** to be embedded in the **IssueProjectModel** so that **Comments** can stand on the diagram on their own, if required. The connector between the comment shape and its subject (the dashed line in Figure 5-10) is mapped to a reference relationship between **Comment** and **CommentableItem**, of which **Project** is a subclass (Figure 5-11).

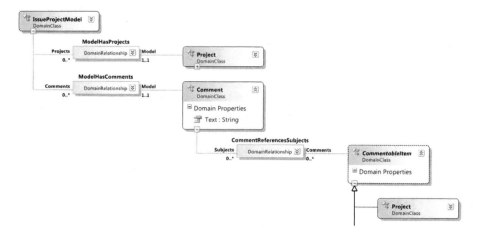

FIGURE 5-11: Comments and Projects

But suppose we want to provide an extra convenience for the user such as the ability to drag a **Comment** onto a **Project** and have the reference link made automatically. The EMD must create two links: the embedding in the **IssueProjectModel** and the reference to the **Project**.

Figure 5-12 shows the element merge directive we need. The index class is **Comment** and the EMD is owned by **Project** (because the user will drop the new comment onto a project). There are two link creation paths, both of which navigate from a project. The first creates the reference link from the project to the comment, specifying that we are creating a **CommentReferencesSubjects** link and adding it to the **Comments** property of the **Project**:

```
CommentReferencesSubjects.Comments
```

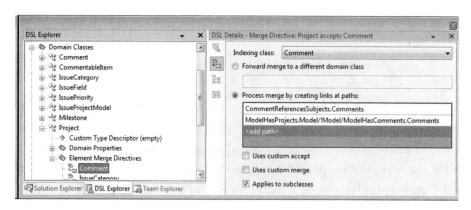

FIGURE 5-12: Element merge with multiple link creation paths

The second link directive creates the embedding link from the **Issue-ProjectModel** element to the **Comment**. But we're starting at a **Project** , so first we have to get to the **IssueProjectModel**:

```
ModelHasProjects.Model/!Model/ModelHasComments.Comments
```

In a link directive, the last segment defines the link to be created; any preceding segments are about getting to the right starting point. In this case:

- `ModelHasComments.Comments` instantiates the **ModelHasComments** relationship, adding the link to the **Comments** property of the model.
- `ModelHasProjects.Model/!Model` navigates from the project to the model in two steps: first onto the link between the two, and then onto the model itself.

Forwarding

The "Forward merge" option in an EMD simply sends the element to be merged onto a different target.

For an example, let's look at the Components sample that comes with the DSL Tools. In this model, each component can have a number of ports. On the diagram, each port appears as a box on the edge of its parent component's shape.

New ports can be created by dragging the "Port" tool onto a component. There is an element merge directive in **Component** for which **Port** is the indexing class.

A typical component may have several ports (see Figure 5-13). When the user drags yet another port onto the component shape, it is easy to mistakenly try to drop the new port onto an existing port shape. From the user's point of view, the ports are just part of the component. For the user's convenience, we can arrange that an existing port will accept a new one but deals with it just by passing the new element on to the parent component. There, one of the component's EMDs will process the new port. To set up the forwarding EMD on the **Port** class, we set its forwarding path to navigate from the **Port** element to its parent **Component** element:

```
ComponentHasPorts.Component/!Component
```

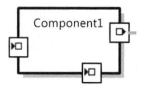

FIGURE 5-13: Component shape with ports

Notice that this path expression has two steps: from **Port** to the **ComponentHasPorts** link, and then on to the **Component** itself. (Without the second step, the forwarding would be to the intermediate link rather than the **Component** element.) A forwarding path can have several steps but must point to one specific element.

The target of a forwarding path must have an EMD that can deal with the class of element being forwarded. This is checked by the validation rules when you save your DSL definition.

> **TIP** **Dangling bits when you delete a domain class**
>
> If you delete a domain class from the DSL, the old element merge directives and toolbox entries must be removed explicitly. Validation errors will point you to them.

Custom Element Merge Directives

Custom Accept

The "Uses custom accept" flag allows you to write code to have extra control over whether a merge can be done.

For example, if you want to prevent the user from adding more than five issue categories to any project, set the "Uses custom accept" flag in the EMD for **IssueCategory** under **Project**. This signals your intention to write some custom code. As usual, the best way to remind yourself of the name of the method you are expected to write is to click "Transform All Templates" and rebuild. This will give you the error that `CanMergeIssueCategory()` is undefined.

The generated class for the **Project** domain class, if you wish to look at it, will be in the `GeneratedCode` folder of the `Dsl` Visual Studio project, inside the `DomainClasses.cs` file, which you will find hiding under the `DomainClasses.tt` template.

Write a partial class for `Project` containing the missing method `CanMergeIssueCategory()`. The file will look like this:

```
using System;
using System.Collections.Generic;
using System.Text;
using Microsoft.VisualStudio.Modeling;

namespace CJKW.IssueProject
{
  /// <summary>
  /// Additional code for the class generated from the
  /// Project domain class.
  /// </summary>
  public partial class Project
  {
    /// <summary>
    /// This method must be provided because we have set the
    /// Custom Accept flag in the Element Merge Directive
    /// for the Project class.
    /// Called by the Element Merge Directive to check whether a
    /// given element may be merged into a Project instance.
    /// </summary>
    /// <param name="rootElement"></param>
    /// <param name="elementGroupPrototype"></param>
    /// <returns></returns>
    private bool CanMergeIssueCategory
      (ProtoElementBase rootElement,
       ElementGroupPrototype elementGroupPrototype)
    {
      return this.Categories.Count < 5;
    }
  }
}
```

(The parameters are not very useful, because they merely identify the prototype from which the new element will be constructed: `this` has all the information we need.)

> **■ TIP** Custom accept code has to work fast
>
> Custom accept code is called whenever the mouse passes over the boundary of a potential target of this type—so don't have it doing something long and complicated.

Custom Merge

The "Uses custom merge" flag allows you to write code controlling how the merge is performed.

For example, we have already seen how an element merge directive can be designed to create and link a comment when the **Comment** tool is dropped onto a project; suppose we want to do the same for issue categories. Recall that the EMD has to create two links: a reference link from the comment to the target element and an embedding of the new comment into the model.

The embedding is more difficult, because it must first navigate from the drop target to the model. If the drop target is a **Project**, this just means navigating across the **ModelHasProjects** relation. But from **IssueCategory**, there is no fixed relationship to **Model**. An **IssueCategory** may be parented on other **IssueCategories**, and so there will be a variable number of steps up to the model. The path expression language does not include an iterative element.

Define an element merge directive under **IssueCategory** for **Comment** and set its "Uses custom merge" flag. In this case, you do not need to provide a path for link creation or forwarding. On transforming and building the code, you get errors that `MergeRelateComment` and `MergeDisconnectComment` are missing. Provide these in a partial class definition for `IssueCategory`:

```
using Microsoft.VisualStudio.Modeling;

namespace CJKW.IssueProject
{
  public partial class IssueCategory
  {
    /// <summary>
    /// The project that a category is ultimately parented by.
    /// </summary>
    public Project UltimateProject
    {
      get
```

```
        {
            if (this.Project == null)
                    return this.ParentCategory.Project;
            else
                    return this.Project;
        }
    }

    /// <summary>
    /// Connect a Comment into the model.
    /// </summary>
    protected void MergeRelateComment(
            ModelElement sourceElement, ElementGroup elementGroup)
    {
        Comment comment = sourceElement as Comment;
        this.UltimateProject.Model.Comments.Add(comment);
        this.Comments.Add(comment);
    }

    /// <summary>
    /// Disconnect a Comment from the model
    /// </summary>
    protected void MergeDisconnectComment(ModelElement sourceElement)
    {
        Comment comment = sourceElement as Comment;
        this.Comments.Remove(comment);
        this.UltimateProject.Model.Comments.Remove(comment);
    }
  }
}
```

> **■ TIP** Take care with namespaces in folders
>
> If the compiler persists in complaining that you have not supplied the
> required method, check both that you have its name correct and that
> the namespace in which you have declared it is correct. When you cre-
> ate a new file in a separate folder, Visual Studio creates a few lines of
> code for you, including a namespace that ends with the name of the
> folder: You need to delete that last part.

Re-Parenting with Element Merge Directives

In some cases, you need to move an element from one owner to another,
breaking its old links with its owning context and reforming them with the

new one. At the same time, we want to keep its other properties and links. In most cases, the link that has to be reformed is the single embedding link of which every element must be a target, but in some cases there may have been other links established by the element merge directive when the element was first created. For that reason, we can put an element merge directive into reverse, to do an "unmerge" or `MergeDisconnect`. Unmerging deletes those links that the EMD specifies (the same ones it normally creates). To move an element from one parent to another, first unmerge it from its existing context and then re-merge it into the new one.

An example occurs in the Task Flow example discussed in Chapter 4. Every **FlowElement** (task, start, stop, and so on) appears in the diagram on top of a swimlane, which represents an **Actor** (Figure 5-14).

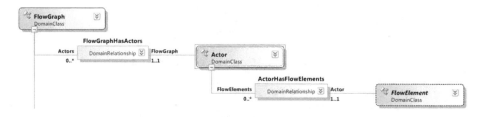

FIGURE 5-14: Part of the Task Flow model. FlowElements are owned by Actors

When the user moves a `FlowElement task1` from `actor1` to `actor2`, the framework calls

```
actor1.MergeDisconnect(task1); actor2.MergeRelate(task1);
```

Custom Element Tool Prototypes

Each element tool is initialized with a prototype of the element(s) that are created when the user drags the tool onto the diagram. The standard generated code creates a single element as a prototype for each element tool, but you can define a group of interlinked elements. When the tool is used, the whole group will be replicated and merge attempted.

Consider a type of component diagram where some components must be created with a fixed set of ports. Electronic diagrams are typically like this. For example, a transistor always has three distinct terminals to which connections can be made (see Figure 5-15). (This example DSL could be used to generate code simulating the circuit or analyzing its properties.)

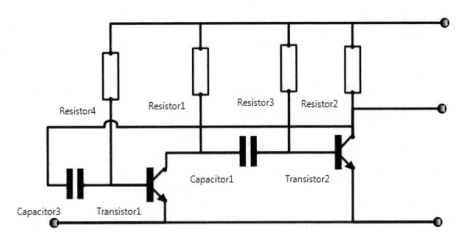

FIGURE 5-15: Transistors have three connections each

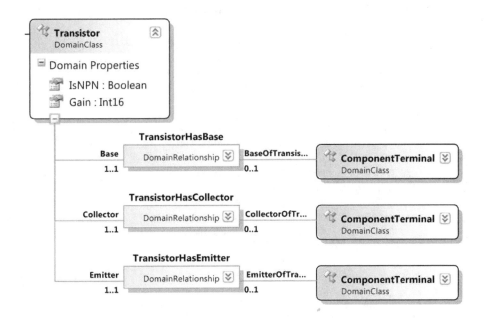

FIGURE 5-16: A component that must be created with three subsidiary elements

When the user drags a **Transistor** off the toolbox, we want a group of four elements to be created together: the transistor and its three component terminals, and the three links between them (see Figure 5-16). We therefore must override the initialization code that sets up the prototypes in the toolbox. This is in *YourLanguage*ToolboxHelper, which is always double derived (that is, all its methods are in a separate base class).

```csharp
using System;
using System.Collections.Generic;
using System.Text;
using Microsoft.VisualStudio.Modeling;

namespace Microsoft.Example.Circuits
{
  public partial class CircuitsToolboxHelper
  {
    protected override ElementGroupPrototype
        CreateElementToolPrototype(Store store, Guid domainClassId)
    {
      if (domainClassId == Transistor.DomainClassId)
      {
        // Set up the prototype elements and links.
        Transistor transistor = new Transistor (store);

        // Derived links must be set up in order of initialization
        transistor.Base = new ComponentTerminal(store);
        transistor.Collector = new ComponentTerminal(store);
        transistor.Emitter = new ComponentTerminal(store);

        transistor.Base.Name = "base";
        transistor.Collector.Name = "collector";
        transistor.Emitter.Name = "emitter";

        // Create a prototype for the Toolbox.
        ElementGroup elementGroup =
              new ElementGroup(store.DefaultPartition);
        elementGroup.AddGraph(transistor, true);
        // Don't need to add children and links explicitly
        // 'cos they're embedded.

        return elementGroup.CreatePrototype();
      }
      // Code for other multi-element components goes here
      else
      {
        // Default - single-element prototype - use generated code
        return base.CreateElementToolPrototype(store, domainClassId);
      }
    }
  }
}
```

This method is called once for each class on the toolbox when the DSL package is loaded. For classes that have standard single-element prototypes, we pass control to the base method. Where we want a multi-element prototype, we create an `ElementGroup` and construct a prototype from it.

Adding to an ElementGroup

You can add any number of elements and links to an `ElementGroup`. In this example, we have just included the embedding subtree (by using the `AddGraph()` method that does so automatically), but we could explicitly add other elements and reference links between elements in the same `ElementGroup`.

Instead of the `AddGraph()` method, you can use `elementGroup.Add` to add items individually to the group. `AddGraph()` automatically follows the embedding tree, while `Add` gives closer control.

Rather than writing out `Add(transistor.Emitter); Add(transistor.Collector)` and so on, this DSL has a common base relationship between all the components and their terminals, so that `TransistorHasEmitter` is derived from `ComponentHasComponentTerminal` (Figure 5-17), and all the `Component` subclasses have a property `ComponentTerminals`, which we can loop on:

```
Component component = element.ModelElement as Component;
elementGroup.Add(element.ModelElement);
elementGroup.MarkAsRoot(element.ModelElement);
foreach (ComponentTerminal terminal in component.ComponentTerminals)
{
    elementGroup.Add(terminal);
}
```

Notice that we must mark the root element of the tree.

The `Add()` method has the curious property of also adding any relationship links that exist between the element being added and the elements already in the group.

At the beginning of this chapter, we said that there are two kinds of tools on the user's toolbox: element tools and connection tools. We've now seen in detail how element tools create elements of a specific domain class and how they can be made to create groups of elements as well as how element merge directives control whether and how new elements can be merged into the existing model.

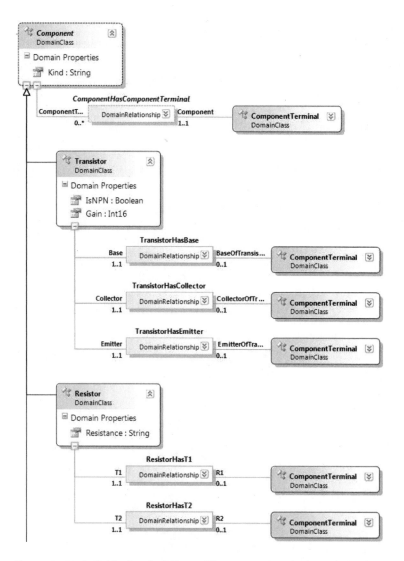

FIGURE 5-17: Individual embeddings of ComponentTerminal are derived
from ComponentHasTerminal.

Connection Builders

The connection tools on the user's toolbox work differently than the element tools. While an element tool creates elements of a specified class, a connection tool invokes a specific connection builder. This controls what elements the user may select to link and can generate a link of any of several different domain relationship classes, depending on the elements chosen. If you write custom code for it, you can make the user's connect-this-to-that gesture initiate any actions you like.

The connection builder is invoked as soon as its connection tool is clicked by the user. (And of course you can also invoke a connection builder in custom code.) The connection builder governs what elements may be connected and exactly what links are made. Connection builders are listed at the top level of the DSL explorer.

When you map a reference relationship to a connector in the DSL designer, it automatically creates a connection builder for you (though you may then opt to change or delete it). The Issue Tracking example contains one such default (Figure 5-18). It has a single link connect directive specifying that a **Comment** may be connected to a **CommentableItem** element using the **CommentReferencesSubjects** relationship.

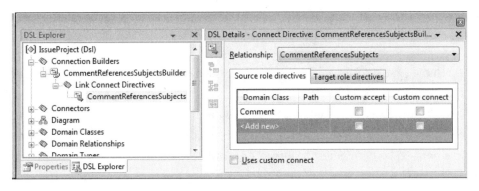

FIGURE 5-18: A connection builder

Notice once again the separation between diagrams and domain model. The connection builders deal only in domain relationships and their role-players. There is no mention of connectors or shapes. The connection builder creates a relationship, and then the connector mappings (which we saw in the previous chapter) do whatever is required, if anything, to display the relationship.

Multiple Source and Target Role Directives

One connection builder can be used to instantiate several different relationships. Let's look at the Task Flow example again (see Figure 5-19).

In this DSL several different types of element (**Task**, **MergeBranch**, **StartPoint**, and **EndPoint**) can be interconnected by **Flow** links. However, there are some restrictions; a **StartPoint** element cannot be the target of a **Flow** link, while an **EndPoint** element cannot be its source.

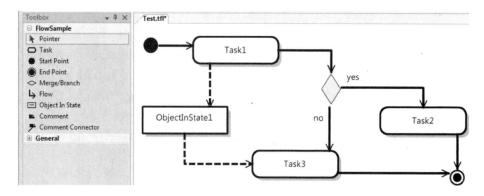

FIGURE 5-19: Task Flow DSL

In the DSL definition (Figure 5-20), all the above classes are subclasses of **FlowElement**, and the **Flow** reference relationship is defined as linking any two **FlowElements**. When we map **Flow** to its connector, the DSL designer helpfully creates a generic connection builder that will allow any **Flow-Element** to be connected to any other. But that's not what we want in this case. For example, we don't want an **EndPoint** to be an allowed source, and we don't want a **StartPoint** to be an allowed target. So we list explicitly what we want to allow for the source and the target (Figure 5-21). (Of course, it only makes sense to list subclasses of the source and target roleplayers.)

▪ TIP Adding a link connect directive

The user interface in the present version is slightly unintuitive. Scroll to the bottom of the list and click "<Add new>"; click the drop-down icon at the side and select the sole drop-down item—which also says "<Add new>"! This gives you a blank line. Now click on the blank domain class, and again click the drop-down icon. Usually it only makes sense to select the roleplayer class of that end of the relationship, or one of its derivatives—though this need not be the case if you write custom code to do some of the connect directive's job.

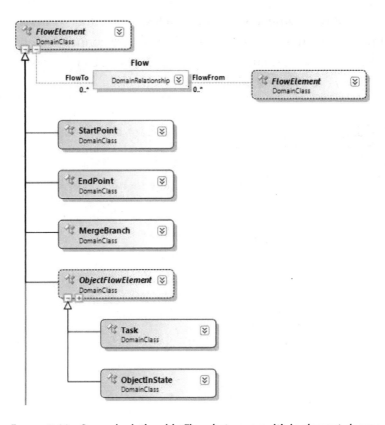

FIGURE 5-20: General relationship Flow, between multiple element classes

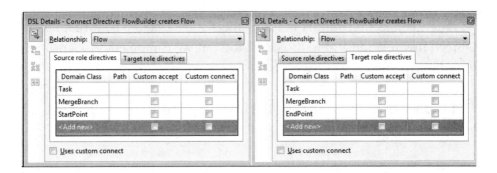

FIGURE 5-21: Connection builder listing restricted source and target sets

Multiple Link Connect Directives

An additional feature of this DSL is a domain class called **ObjectInState**. An element of this class can be connected to and from tasks but using a different relationship, **ObjectFlow** (Figure 5-22). **ObjectInState** instances can also be interconnected with **ObjectFlow** links, but tasks may not be interconnected with **ObjectFlow** links. By careful definition of the connection builder, we can implement these restrictions while using the same connection tool as the flows between the other elements.

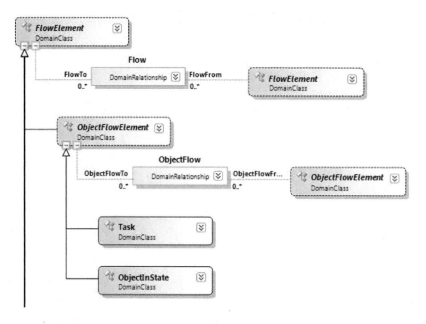

FIGURE 5-22: A second relationship, ObjectFlow

A new connection builder is automatically generated when we map the **ObjectFlow** relationship to its connector, but we can delete that. Instead, we add link connect directives to the existing **Flow** builder (Figure 5-23). This means that one tool can be used to create both types of relationship.

To summarize, we now have the following link connect directives all hanging off the Flow tool.

Relationship	Acceptable Sources	Acceptable Targets
Flow	Task, Merge, Start	Task, Merge, End
ObjectFlow	Task, ObjectInState	ObjectInState
ObjectFlow	ObjectInState	Task

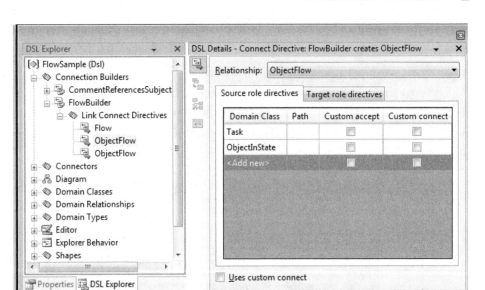

FIGURE 5-23: Additional link connect directives for the FlowBuilder connection builder

Where there are several sources and targets in the same link directive, they are not paired up; any combination of the listed sources and targets will work. However, the different link directives are separate; a user cannot connect an **ObjectFlow** from a task to a task.

Notice that after clicking the Flow tool, the user must click both a source and a target before it is clear whether a **Flow** or an **ObjectFlow** is to be created.

Sharing the one tool between several relationships is useful where they are similar; it reduces clutter on the toolbox and saves the user from remembering which tool to use. It is not recommended where the relationships are for different purposes—for example, connecting a comment to its subject should probably be a different tool.

Role Directive Path

A path can be specified for any source or target role in a link connect directive. This is to allow the user to click on one element while the link is actually made to another. The path navigates from the clicked element to the actual source or target.

Recalling the Components example, there is a relationship between **Components** called **Generalization**; the default connection builder lets the user drag from one component to another. But as we observed before, the user may naturally consider the ports around the edge to be part of a component, and therefore would expect to be able to drag to or from a port and have it work just the same as in the body of the component.

To allow this behavior, we define extra roles in the Link Connect Directive (Figure 5-24). The domain class listed is the one the user can click on; the path navigates from there to the actual start of the relationship being instantiated.

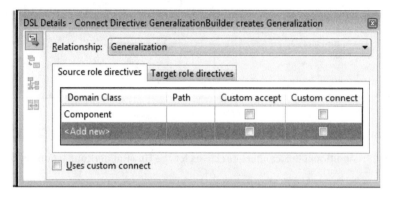

FIGURE 5-24: Link Connect Directive with Path to Roleplayer

> **■ TIP** Validate if you write custom connection builders
>
> Connection builders and element merge directives govern only how the user creates relationships from the toolbox. They do not place continuing constraints on the relationships, and so any code you write can circumvent their restrictions. If you provide other ways for the users to create relationships, you might therefore want to write appropriate validation code (see Chapter 7).

Custom Connection Builders

Multiple degrees of code customization are available for connection builders. There are several "custom" checkboxes:

- "Custom accept." Checking this box on a source or target role directive (see Figure 5-25) allows you to provide code that performs extra checks whenever the actual source or target belongs to that class.

- "Custom connect." Checking this box on a source or target role directive allows you to provide code that creates the connection in the case where the specified source or target class is the reason for activating the link connect directive.

- "Uses custom connect." This is the checkbox at the bottom of the connect directive (Figure 5-25); it also appears in the properties window when you select the link connect directive in the explorer. With this flag set, you provide code to deal with all cases when this link directive is activated.

- "Is Custom" property of each connection builder. This appears in the properties window when you select a connection builder in the DSL explorer. With this set, you provide code that takes over as soon as the user clicks the tool.

Let's look at these in greater detail.

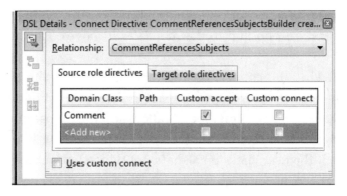

FIGURE 5-25: Custom accept on the target role

Custom Accept

Suppose we wish to prevent any comment (in, let's say, the Issue Project example) from being linked to more than three subjects. Recall from way back in Figure 5-11 that the relationship is **CommentReferencesSubjects**, with source **Comment** and target **CommentableItem** (from which most of the other domain classes in that model are derived). So to connect a comment to a subject, the user will click on the "Comment Link" tool, then click a comment, and then drag from there to a suitable subject. To apply this constraint, we can determine whether the link is allowed as soon as the user clicks on the source comment, by counting the number of links the comment already has. So we set "Custom accept" on the Source Role (Figure 5-25) to get the designer to incorporate our code.

After clicking "Transform All Templates" and a rebuild, we get errors that `CanAcceptCommentAsSource` and `CanAcceptCommentAndCommentable ItemAsSourceAndTarget` are undefined. In a separate file, we define

```
/// <summary>
/// Called repeatedly as the mouse moves over candidate sources.
/// </summary>
/// <param name="candidate">The element presented by the shape
///          the mouse is currently hovering over.</param>
/// <returns>Whether this is an acceptable source.</returns>
private static bool CanAcceptCommentAsSource(Comment comment)
{
   // Prohibit linking over 3 subjects to any comment using this directive.
   return comment.Subjects.Count < 3;
}
```

As with the custom accept on a merge directive, this code has to work reasonably fast, responding to the mouse as it moves over the different elements.

After clicking the connection tool, the user moves the mouse over various shapes on the diagram. As it crosses each boundary, your `CanAcceptXxxAsSource()` method is called, and the mouse cursor shows an encouraging or discouraging icon depending on the Boolean value you return. If the user clicks on a shape for which you return `true`, then that element becomes the selected source, and the user then goes on to choose the target.

(Notice that, as usual, the method deals entirely in domain elements— there is no mention of shapes.)

You also need to provide code for `CanAcceptXxxAsSourceAndTarget()`, which is called when the user is choosing the second roleplayer. In the example we described, once the comment has been chosen, any subject is acceptable, so it can just return `true`. But suppose we wanted to impose the same sort of limit the other way around, so that each subject can have no more than five comments:

```
/// <summary>
/// Called repeatedly while hovering over candidate
/// second roleplayers.
/// The first has already been chosen and accepted.
/// </summary>
/// <param name="sourceComment">Comment to be linked</param>
/// <param name="targetCommentableItem">Subject to be linked</param>
/// <returns>Whether it's OK to link these two.</returns>
private static bool
  CanAcceptCommentAndCommentableItemAsSourceAndTarget
    (Comment sourceComment, CommentableItem targetCommentableItem)
{
  return targetCommentableItem.Comments.Count < 5;
}
```

Notice that the … `AsSourceAndTarget()` method is passed by both roleplay-ers of the candidate link, so it can be used to apply more interesting constraints that involve the two ends. For example, in the Components sample, there is a generalization relationship between components; the user should not be able to create loops in which a **Component** could be among its own ancestors. To achieve this, we set the "Custom accept" flag in either the source or target role in the **Generalization** link directive, and add code:

```
private static bool CanAcceptComponentAndComponentAsSourceAndTarget
    (Component sourceComponent, Component targetComponent)
{
  if (sourceComponent == targetComponent) return false;
  if (targetComponent.Superclass == null) return true;
  else return CanAcceptComponentAndComponentAsSourceAndTarget
            (sourceComponent, targetComponent.Superclass);
}
```

There's a slight variation on the above if you have set the "Reverses Direc-tion" property of the connection tool (which appears in the properties win-dow on selecting the tool in the explorer). This flag allows the user to drag in the opposite direction, from the target to the source. In that case, you need to set "Custom accept" on the target role directive (instead of the source) and provide a method for `CanAcceptXxxAsTarget()`.

Notice that these custom methods only apply to the specific link directive for which you have set the "Custom accept" flag. The same connection builder may also be able to connect other combinations of elements with other directives.

> **■ TIP** Always set "Custom accept" on the source (unless you've reversed direction)
>
> Should you set "Custom accept" on the source or the target of the link directive? You might think it depends on whether you want to write code that filters on the source or the target of the link, but in fact you can normally do either or both of those by setting "Custom accept" on the source. You only need to set it on the target if you have set the "Reverses Direction" flag on the connection tool that uses this connection builder.

"Custom accept" is an example of a *hard constraint*—that is, a constraint imposed by the user interface. The alternative is a *soft constraint*, which allows the user to create any number of comment-subject links but shows an error message when the file is saved. To do this, you would write a validation method (as described in Chapter 7) instead of the "Custom accept."

However, as we remarked before, hard constraints only apply to a particular user operation, so if your customizations provide more than one method of creating this type of link, you must make sure that every method imposes the same constraint. For example, one of the variations above was designed to prevent more than a certain number of comments being linked to a single subject. Now suppose we have also implemented the neat element merge directive mentioned in the section "Multiple Link Creation Paths in an EMD" earlier in this chapter, in which you could create a comment and make a link to it at the same time just by dragging from the comment tool onto the required subject. In that case, the user can continue to connect up any number of new comments to one subject. The best approach to prevent this would be to add custom accept code to the merge directive, similar to what we've just written for the connect directive. (Just to be sure, we might also write a validation method to check the situation when the user saves the file.)

Custom Connect

Custom connect code is used to create a complex connection, for example, where the link is not between the source and target directly indicated by the user, but between some related items, or when there are actually several links to be created or perhaps some adjustment to be made to the properties of some of the elements.

If you set the "Custom connect" checkbox for a particular class in the "Connect Directive" details, then your code will be called just when the user's first click was on an element of that domain class. (As before, you would choose to set it in the "Source role directives" tab or the "Target role directives" tab, depending on whether you have set "Reverses Direction" on the tool that uses this connection builder.)

If you set the "Uses custom connect" checkbox for a whole link directive (see the bottom left of Figure 5-25) then your code will be called if some combination of source and target was accepted.

Alternatively, you can set the "Is Custom" flag on the whole connection builder, to determine everything that happens when the user selects the associated tool.

A typical customized connect creates additional links or elements. In the Components sample, the user must create ports on the components before linking them (Figure 5-26). To save the user some time, we can create a port if necessary. The user can drag the connect tool either between existing ports or from or to the main body of a component. In the latter case, a new port is constructed, and the connection is made to that.

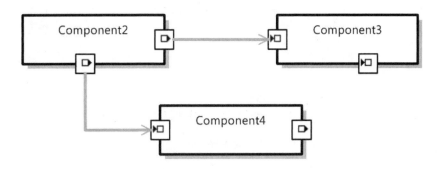

FIGURE 5-26: Components and ports

In this case, it is easiest to set the "Is Custom" flag on the whole connection builder. (Select the connection builder in the DSL explorer and set the flag in the properties window. As always, after modifying the DSL definition, click the "Transform All Templates" button to generate the code.) This generates a generic connection builder for which we have to provide three methods in a partial class.

```csharp
using System;
using System.Collections.Generic;
using System.Text;
using Microsoft.VisualStudio.Modeling;

namespace CJKW.CJKWComponentModels
{
    public static partial class ConnectionBuilder
    {
        ///<summary>
        /// Called to determine if we can drag from here.
        ///</summary>
        internal static bool CanAcceptSource
                    (ModelElement sourceElement)
        {
            return sourceElement is Component
                    || sourceElement is OutPort;
        }

        ///<summary>
        /// Called to determine if we can drag between these.
        ///</summary>
        internal static bool CanAcceptSourceAndTarget
            (ModelElement sourceElement, ModelElement targetElement)
        {
            return targetElement is Component
                    || targetElement is InPort;
            // CanAcceptSource already checked
        }

        ///<summary>
        /// Called to perform the connection.
        ///</summary>
        internal static void Connect
            (ModelElement sourceElement, ModelElement targetElement)
        {
            // Is the source a Component or a Port?
            OutPort outPort = sourceElement as OutPort;
            Component sourceComponent = sourceElement as Component;
            if (sourceComponent != null)
            {
                // A component - so we need to create a source port
                outPort = new OutPort(sourceComponent.Partition);
                outPort.Component = sourceComponent;
            }
            // Is the target a Component or a Port?
            InPort inPort = targetElement as InPort;
            Component targetComponent = targetElement as Component;
            if (targetComponent != null)
            {
```

```
                    // a component - so we need to create a target Port
                    inPort = new InPort(targetComponent.Partition);
                    inPort.Component = targetComponent;
                }

                // make the connection between the two ports
                outPort.Targets.Add(inPort);
                // easy, eh?
            }
        }
    }
```

Element Deletion

As the DSL is running in a designer or other application, instances can of course be both created and deleted. In a designer, the user can point to a shape or an element in the explorer and press delete, or code that you have written can call `Remove()` on the element. When an element is removed by any means, rules fire that seek to ensure the consistency of the store by removing any dependent elements.

One deletion rule is immutable: When any element is deleted, every link of which it is the source or target is deleted too. What happens next depends on the delete propagation rules for the links. Separate delete rules can be defined for each relationship. There is a default set of rules, so you only have to think about them when you want something special to happen.

Default Delete Propagation Rules

There are some default rules, but you can change them or add others.

- If the link belongs to an embedding relationship, then its target is also deleted. So deleting any element deletes its entire embedding subtree.
- The source of an embedding relationship is not deleted by default. If you want deleting a child to delete its parent automatically, you must add a delete propagation rule to the parenthood relationship.
- Deleting a reference link affects neither of its roleplayers.

For example, if you select the **Component** domain class in the Components sample and then click on the "Delete Behavior" tab of the DSL details window (Figure 5-27), you can see all of the domain relationships listed in which this class takes part. In fact, there is an entry for each role that the domain class plays, so that reflexive relationships like **Generalization** appear twice.

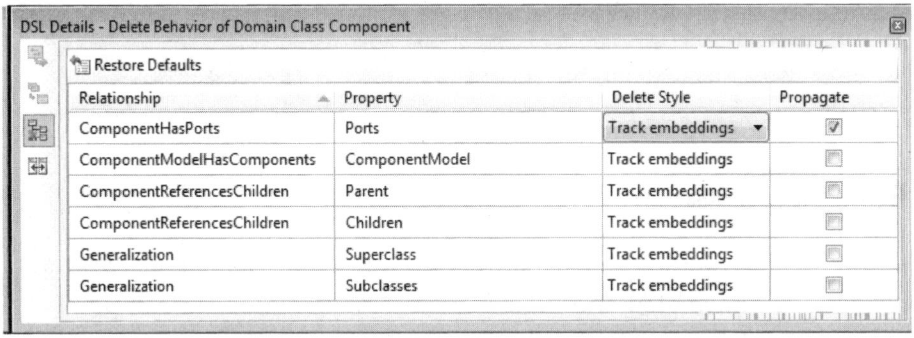

DSL Details - Delete Behavior of Domain Class Component			
Restore Defaults			
Relationship	Property	Delete Style	Propagate
ComponentHasPorts	Ports	Track embeddings ▾	☑
ComponentModelHasComponents	ComponentModel	Track embeddings	☐
ComponentReferencesChildren	Parent	Track embeddings	☐
ComponentReferencesChildren	Children	Track embeddings	☐
Generalization	Superclass	Track embeddings	☐
Generalization	Subclasses	Track embeddings	☐

FIGURE 5-27: Delete Behavior tab in the DSL Details window for the Component domain class

The Delete Style column indicates either "Track embeddings" or "User specified." "Track embeddings" means that the "Propagate" box is checked if this is the source of an embedding relationship, and unchecked otherwise.

It is mostly easy to test delete propagation. Set "Propagate" on the **Subclasses** property of **Generalization**, for example; click "Transform All Templates," build, and run; and draw some components and several generalization connectors between them. When you delete one component, you will see its subclasses in your diagram vanish too, along with all their subclasses. And of course any ports on the components also vanish because of the default setting of "Propagate" on the embedding relationship, **ComponentHasPorts**.

■ TIP Take care when disabling default delete propagation

Disabling propagation at the source of an embedding relationship means that if a parent instance is deleted (a component in this case), then any children (ports) are left lying around in the store without being in the embedding tree. This is a situation of dubious value, because displaying, serialization, and validation all depend on everything being in the tree. It is generally not wise to disable propagation on embedding relationships unless you have some custom code that will reassign the element to another part of the tree.

The effect of unchecking the "Propagate" flag on the source of an embedding relationship is less easy to detect. In this example, it still looks as though deleting a component appears to delete its ports—together with any connectors attached to them. However, the port shapes vanish because the view fixup rules (which implement the shape map) work down the tree and fail to find the associated model element. Removing the port shapes in turn removes their attached connectors from the diagram, because there is delete propagation from shapes to connectors.

Controlling Delete Propagation

In the Circuit Diagrams sample that we introduced earlier (Figure 5-15), each class of component is supposed to have a fixed set of ports—all transistors have three connections, all diodes two, and so on. But if the user selects any individual port and presses the delete key, the port will duly disappear. One way of avoiding this embarrassing inconsistency is to provide the convenient feature that deleting the port will delete the whole thing. This allows the user to click on the port—perhaps mistakenly intending to click its parent component—and still achieve the desired deletion. To make this happen, we first select the **ComponentTerminal** domain class and open the delete behavior tab in the DSL Details window. There are a lot of entries, because a component terminal can be attached to any of a number of different components by several relationships each. (See the model in Figure 5-17.) In fact, there is an abstract relationship from which all these are derived, and it would be nice if we could just check its box (**ComponentHasComponentTerminal**); in the current version of the DSL Tools, that doesn't happen, so we have to go through and check all of the boxes (Figure 5-28).

After clicking "Transform All Templates" and rebuilding, deleting any port now deletes the parent component and its other ports.

Delete Propagation and Constraints

Delete propagation is generally used to help enforce a hard constraint. For example, in the Task Flows sample, each instance of the **ObjectInState** domain class (see Figure 5-22) should always have one link to a source and one to a target task. Therefore, if a task is deleted, we want any linked **ObjectInState** instances to vanish too.

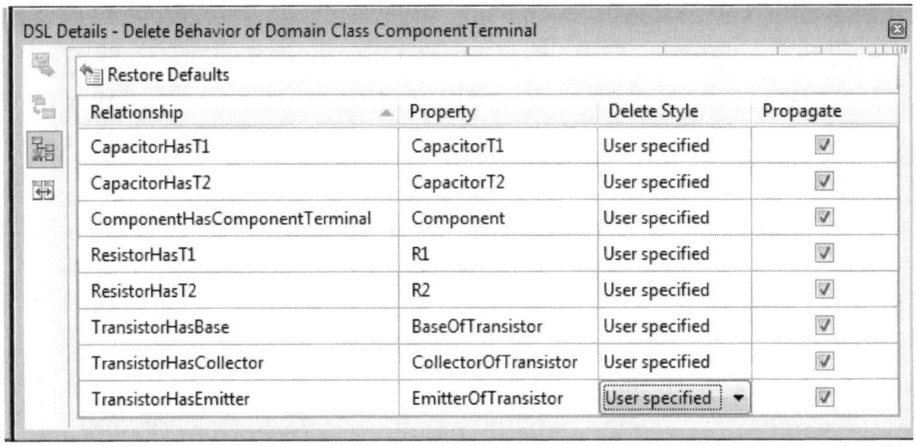

FIGURE 5-28: Delete Behavior tab for ComponentTerminal in the Circuit Diagrams sample

Once again, this feature does not guarantee a constraint by itself; you might in the same DSL provide the means for the user to create an unlinked **ObjectInState** element. To make sure a constraint is observed, you have to consider all the methods of creation and deletion that the user can access or that your custom code provides.

Customizing Delete Propagation

If you want more complex behavior, you can override parts of the XXXDeleteClosure class, which is generated from the Delete Behavior definition (where XXX is the name of your DSL). You will find the generated class in DomainModel.cs in the GeneratedCode folder of the Dsl project. There is only one class whose name ends with "DeleteClosure."

The ShouldVisitRolePlayer() method of this class is called every time any link is to be deleted, and its job is to decide whether each roleplayer (that is, the instance at the end of the link) should be deleted too. The default method just looks at the delete propagation flags in the DSL definition. But to get more dynamic behavior, we can override it. Because it is called for every link that is deleted, we must be careful to pass back control to the base method in the cases where we aren't interested in customizing the behavior.

For example, you might want to delete a **Component** element when, and only when, the last of its child ports have gone. To do this, you can write the following custom code.

```
// Replace "Components" in this class name with the name of your DSL.
public partial class ComponentsDeleteClosure
{
  /// <summary>
  /// Called when deleting a link, to decide whether to delete a
  /// roleplayer.
  /// </summary>
  public override VisitorFilterResult ShouldVisitRolePlayer
    (ElementWalker walker, ModelElement sourceElement,
     ElementLink elementLink, DomainRoleInfo targetDomainRole,
     ModelElement targetElement)
  {
    ComponentHasPorts portParentLink =
              elementLink as ComponentHasPorts;
    if (portParentLink != null)
    {
      // Delete if there is just one left in the *old* state.
      if (portParentLink.Component.Ports.Count == 1)
        return VisitorFilterResult.Yes;
      else
        return VisitorFilterResult.DoNotCare;
    }
    else
      return base.ShouldVisitRolePlayer(walker, sourceElement,
            elementLink, targetDomainRole, targetElement);
  }
}
```

■ **TIP** Customization with overrides

This customization is done just by overriding a method from the generated code. Unlike the previous examples in this chapter, it doesn't require you to set any "custom" flag in the DSL definition. Unlike the custom flags technique, it isn't always obvious what methods are good to override. We discuss more of them in the rest of this book, but you can always experiment. Write a partial class definition for any of the classes that occur in the generated code and type "override" within it. IntelliSense will give you a range of methods you can try overriding. Inefficient but fun.

The base method (which this one overrides) is called when any deletion is made to any element. There is just one such method in the DSL code (rather than, for example, one for each domain class). The method is called whenever a link is about to be deleted. The most useful parameters are elementLink, the link which is about to be deleted, and sourceElement and targetElement, the items at its two ends. Recall from Chapter 3 that the classes ElementLink and ModelElement are the ancestor classes of all domain relationship instances and all domain class instances.

The first thing we do is to try to cast the elementLink to the domain relationship class that we are interested in. This method will be called when any link is deleted, but we are only interested in the ComponentHasPorts relationship. If it isn't one of those, we just pass control back to the base method.

If this is indeed a link between components and ports, we can go ahead and decide whether the target should be deleted on the basis of our own requirements—in the case of this particular example, by counting the ports that the component still has. (Because this method is called before any changes are made, the condition we want is that there is just one port left—not zero!) This logic replaces the check to see whether the appropriate **PropagateDelete** flag is set in the DSL definition, which is what the base method would do.

The VisitorFilterResult values that we can return are

- Yes: The roleplayer should be deleted.
- Never: The roleplayer should not be deleted in this transaction.
- DoNotCare: The roleplayer should not be deleted, according to this rule. However, if another link targeting the same element causes its deletion, then that is OK.

SUMMARY

The main points made in this chapter were

- An element tool creates an instance of a specified domain class. You can customize it to create a group of instances, though there is always one principal element in such a group.
- As the user drags from an element tool onto the diagram or onto existing elements, the element merge directives of those elements (the root element, in the case of the diagram) determine whether the prototype from the tool is acceptable to be merged. By default, the

decision is made on the basis of classes, but you can write custom code to define more complex criteria.

- When an element tool is dropped onto the diagram or existing elements, a merge happens under the control of the element merge directive, which creates one or more links between existing and new elements. You can write code to handle more complex merge schemes.

- When the user clicks a connect tool, the associated connection builder is activated. This determines what elements may be linked together and what domain relationships will be instantiated to link them. In the DSL definition, you can specify which combinations of domain classes cause links of different domain relationships to be created. By writing custom code, you can make more complex choice schemes and create more than one link at a time.

- When an element is deleted, its neighboring links are deleted, too; they in turn may cause their other roleplayers to be deleted. Delete propagation is controlled by the DSL's `DeleteClosure` class, which normally uses the "Propagate" flags you have set in the DSL definition but whose code can be overridden to define more complex behavior.

6

Serialization

Introduction

This chapter looks at how the models and diagrams created using a DSL are saved to files so that they can be persisted and shared using a filing system or source control system. When a DSL is defined using the DSL Tools, a domain-specific serializer is automatically generated in the Dsl project that will save and load models in a domain-specific XML format. If the user wishes to modify this format, several customization options are available to do so, and these are explained in this chapter.

One of the goals of the DSL Tools is to enable the DSL user to understand these files directly and edit them by hand. For example, it's possible to create a DSL with just a domain model and no diagram, hand-edit files corresponding to that DSL, and use these files as input to templates that generate code and other artifacts. Another option is to transform the saved model to and from data formats used by other tools or electronic processes, using XSLT, for example. To make this easy, the domain-specific format of a DSL is designed to be human-friendly, with elements that correspond directly to the domain classes; a schema is generated that offers domain-specific IntelliSense to help the user to edit the XML file correctly, and the code that loads the file into the store is forgiving of errors and will provide helpful messages when errors are present.

Saving and Loading Models and Diagrams

This chapter uses for its examples the same Issue State model introduced and discussed previously in Chapters 2 and 3. Figure 6-1 shows the Visual Studio window open on a debugging solution that contains an Issue State model. In the solution explorer, notice the file `ch6_1.iss` and its dependent file `ch6_1.iss.diagram`. These are the files to which the Issue State model and diagram are saved, and from which they are loaded. The file extension `.iss` is part of the Issue State language definition, and when the language is deployed, this file extension is registered to launch the Issue State designer within Visual Studio. The associated diagram file has the additional extension `.diagram`, and is shown in the Visual Studio explorer as a dependent file. The model file is self-contained, and has no dependency on the diagram file. The diagram file contains only diagram layout information. If the diagram file is discarded, then the model file can still be opened; the diagram will then be automatically fixed up, and a new diagram file created when the model is saved.

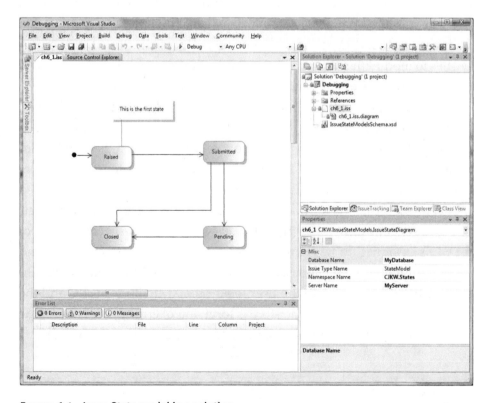

FIGURE 6-1: Issue State model in a solution

> **■ TIP** Deleting the diagram file will only lose the layout
>
> Discarding the diagram file can be useful in cases where the model file has been modified by hand, or because the domain model has changed, causing the diagram to be out of step.

Model XML File Format

Models and diagrams are saved by default as XML documents. We assume here that the reader already has a basic understanding of XML. If this is not so, there are many good books and online resources that explain it.

XML is a good choice for saving models and diagrams. because

- It is human-readable.
- It is a W3C (World Wide Web Consortium) standard.
- A large number of tools and libraries exist for processing it.
- Its nested structure corresponds well to the natural embedding structure of models and diagrams.
- XML documents can be validated by a schema.

Let's look at the XML in `ch6_1.iss` for the model shown in Figure 6-1.

```xml
<?xml version="1.0" encoding="utf-8"?>
<issueStateModel dslVersion="1.0.0.0"
      namespaceName="CJKW.States" issueTypeName="StateModel"
      serverName="MyServer" databaseName="MyDatabase"
      xmlns="http://schemas.cjkw.com/IssueStateModels">
  <comments>
    <comment Id="9f8bc7e9-579c-402a-a9a3-c854767161d1">
      <commentText>This is the first state</commentText>
      <subjects>
        <issueStateMoniker name="/CJKW.States/StateModel/Raised" />
      </subjects>
    </comment>
  </comments>
  <states>
    <issueState name="Raised" icon="raised.ico"
              description="The issue has been raised">
      <successors>
        <issueStateMoniker name="StateModel/Submitted" />
      </successors>
```

```
      </issueState>
      <issueState name="Submitted" icon="submitted.ico"
                  description="The issue has been submitted for assessment">
        <successors>
          <issueStateMoniker name="StateModel/Pending" />
          <issueStateMoniker name="StateModel/Closed" />
        </successors>
      </issueState>
      <issueState name="Pending" icon="pending.ico"
                  description="The issue is pending resolution">
        <successors>
          <issueStateMoniker name="StateModel/Closed" />
        </successors>
      </issueState>
      <issueState name="Closed" icon="closed.ico"
                  description="The issue is closed" />
      <startElement name="Start">
        <startState>
          <issueStateMoniker name="StateModel/Raised" />
        </startState>
      </startElement>
    </states>
  </issueStateModel>
```

The first line is the normal XML prolog, giving the XML version and encoding.

On the following line is the root element of the document, `<issueState Model>`. The definition of a DSL's editor identifies a single root domain class, which is mapped to the diagram and which serializes as the root element of the XML document. In this case, the root domain class is **IssueStateModel**, which is mapped to the XML element name `<issueStateModel>`. By default the DSL designer creates XML element names that are the same as corresponding domain classes, but with lowercase initial letters. The `<issueState Model>` element contains XML attributes to persist the domain properties of the **IssueStateModel** class, that is, **NamespaceName, IssueTypeName, ServerName,** and **DatabaseName**. Again, the initial letters have been defaulted to lowercase in the XML document. An attribute called `dslVersion` is used to save the version number of the language; we'll describe versioning later in the chapter. The final attribute of this element defines the default XML namespace for the root element (and thus the document); this is part of the DSL definition and can be customized by the DSL author.

There are two elements nested in the `<issueStateModel>` element: `<comments>` and `<states>`. These correspond to the two embedding relationships **IssueStateModelHasComments** and **IssueStateModelHasStates**, and their names are generated from the property names of the source roles of those relationships. This exemplifies the general pattern used to map models into XML documents: Embedding relationships map to nested XML elements.

Within the `<comments>` element is a single `<comment>` element. The `Id` attribute contains a .NET Guid (Globally Unique Identifier), which is used to refer uniquely to this element from elsewhere. Every referenced element must have some way to identify it uniquely, and the simplest technique is to use its `Id`, which every `ModelElement` has in the store, as introduced in Chapter 3. You might ask why it is necessary for this particular comment to have an identifier, because it isn't referred to from anywhere else in this file. It is, however, referred to from the diagram file, as we'll see later.

Embedded within the `<comments>` element is a nested `<commentText>` element, with the value of the comment's **CommentText** domain property as its content. Following that is a `<subjects>` element, representing the relationship **CommentsReferToIssueStates,** and embedded in that is the `<issueStateMoniker>` element that refers to the IssueState *Raised,* by its *fully qualified name* `/CJKW.States/StateModel/Raised`. We'll discuss the topic of *moniker elements* in more detail in the discussion of cross-references later in the chapter.

After the `<comments>` element is the `<states>` element, which contains four `<issueState>` elements and one `<startElement>` element. Each of the `<issueState>` elements represents an **IssueState** model element. Each of the domain properties of these MELs—**Name, Description, Icon**—is represented by an XML attribute: `name`, `description`, `icon`. The **IssueStateTransition** relationship is represented by the element `<successors>`, which contains one or more `<issueStateMoniker>` elements that refer to a succeeding **IssueState**, using a *locally qualified name* such as `StateModel/pending`. Finally, the `<startElement>` element is serialized with its name *Start* and the `<issueStateMoniker>` reference to the associated **IssueState**, which has the name *Raised.*

Elements and Properties

In this section and the following ones, we'll look systematically at each aspect of the serialization of a model in order to understand in more detail the defaults and the options available. As a starting point, note that every valid model consists of a tree of model elements (MELs), with a single root, that are linked together by links of the embedding relationships defined in the DSL. This tree maps directly into the nested structure of an XML document. Every MEL is mapped into an XML element, with the element name by default derived from the name of the domain class by changing the first character into lowercase in order to conform to XML conventions. You can override any of the elements, as we'll describe later in the section about customization.

The embedding relationship itself is, by default, represented by an element whose name is derived from the "PropertyName" of the source role of the relationship. In the example just presented, the source role of the **IssueStateModelHasComments** relationship has the "PropertyName" *Comments*, and with the first character changed to lowercase, this gives `<comments>`. By similar logic, the relationship **IssueStateModelHasStates** is represented by the element `<states>`. However, there are several other options for how to represent a relationship, as we'll see later.

Domain properties can be represented in one of two ways: as XML attributes, as exemplified by the **NamespaceName**, **IssueTypeName**, **ServerName,** and **DatabaseName** properties of the **IssueStateModel**, or as XML elements, as exemplified by the **CommentText** property of **Comment.** DSL authors can choose between these options depending on which they think is most readable. Properties are serialized as XML attributes by default.

If a domain property has its default value, it is not serialized unless a customization option is set that forces all domain properties to be serialized.

Where a domain class participates in an inheritance hierarchy, the elements and attributes defined highest in the hierarchy appear first in the XML element corresponding to a MEL of that class; see, for example, that `name` appears before `description` within an `<issueState>` element. Within a given domain class in the hierarchy, the relative order in which elements are serialized can be customized.

Relationships

We've seen that the default representation for a domain relationship is an XML element that derives its name from the "PropertyName" of the source role. This rule applies both for embedding and reference relationships; for embeddings, the embedded MEL's XML representation is nested within the relationship element, and for references, a *moniker* element is nested and contains a value that references the element whose actual contents are serialized elsewhere. We'll discuss moniker elements in the next section.

This simple default gives a nicely readable XML document, as we've seen in the example. However, with this format there is no explicit representation of the link itself. For example, let's say we alter the domain model for our language to give the **IssueStateTransition** relationship a property called **Action**, with an associated decorator. Figure 6-2 shows a model using this language as presented on the screen.

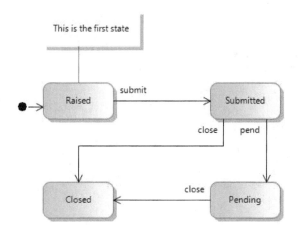

FIGURE 6-2: Transitions with actions

Let's look at the XML document for this model. The <comments> element has been left out because it is unchanged from the previous example.

```
<?xml version="1.0" encoding="utf-8"?>
<issueStateModel dslVersion="1.0.0.0"
     namespaceName="CJKW.States" issueTypeName="StateModel"
     serverName="MyServer" databaseName="MyDatabase"
     xmlns="http://schemas.cjkw.com/IssueStateModels">
  <comments>
```

```
      ...
    </comments>
    <states>
      <issueState name="Raised" icon="raised.ico"
                  description="The issue has been raised">
        <successors>
          <issueStateTransition action="submit">
            <issueStateMoniker name="StateModel/Submitted" />
          </issueStateTransition>
        </successors>
      </issueState>
      <issueState name="Submitted" icon="submitted.ico"
                  description="The issue has been submitted for assessment">
        <successors>
          <issueStateTransition action="pend">
            <"issueStateMoniker name="StateModel/Pending" />
          </issueStateTransition>
          <issueStateTransition action="close">
            <issueStateMoniker name="StateModel/Closed" />
          </issueStateTransition>
        </successors>
      </issueState>
      <issueState name="Pending" icon="pending.ico"
                  description="The issue is pending resolution">
        <successors>
          <issueStateTransition action="close">
            <issueStateMoniker name="StateModel/Closed" />
          </issueStateTransition>
        </successors>
      </issueState>
      <issueState name="Closed" icon="closed.ico"
                  description="The issue is closed" />
      <startElement name="Start">
        <startState>
          <issueStateMoniker name="StateModel/Raised" />
        </startState>
      </startElement>
    </states>
  </issueStateModel>
```

Notice that for each of the four **IssueStateTransition** links there is now an additional `<issueStateTransition>` element that acts as a container for the **Action** domain property of the link. When this additional element is included, we say that the relationship is serialized in "Full Form." This is necessary whenever the relationship has domain properties. The DSL author does not often have to think about the details of these options, though, because the DSL designer tool sets appropriate options by default and will give validation errors if the author chooses inconsistent options.

Relationship Derivation

Relationship derivation allows a link of a derived relationship to be considered as if it were a link of its base relationship. The effect of relationship derivation on serialization is quite straightforward. The basic rule is that it is necessary for the saved file to provide enough information to know which relationship a link instantiates.

In the current example, the relationship **Transition** is abstract. If it had been concrete, then the XML corresponding to Figure 6-1 would have been ambiguous, because it isn't possible to tell whether the `<issueStateMoniker>` element within the `<successors>` element for an **IssueState** corresponds to a link of the **Transition** relationship or the **IssueStateTransition** relationship. In such circumstances, it would be necessary to serialize the links in full form. Again, the DSL designer will validate your model to ensure that this is done correctly.

Cross-Referencing

Because a model is in general a graph, rather than a tree, it is necessary to represent cross-references, such as the transitions between **IssueStates** in our example, in the saved XML form. Cross-references can also be used when elements in one file refer to elements in another, for example, the references between a diagram and its associated model. The technique used in the DSL Tools to represent unresolved references in the In-Memory Store is called *monikers*. A `Moniker` is an object in the store that holds a string that can be used to identify the MEL that is the actual target of the relationship. A `Moniker` object can act as a roleplayer in a link, in which case it is a placeholder for the element that will eventually be the roleplayer. When the store contains the target MEL, the `Moniker` can be resolved, at which point the placeholder `Moniker` will be substituted by the actual target MEL to complete the graph.

Consider, for example, loading a file that contains forward references—such as the element

```
<issueStateMoniker name="StateModel/Submitted" />
```

in the XML file presented earlier. When this reference is encountered, a link of the relationship **IssueStateTransition** is created, with the **NextState** role played by a `Moniker` object holding the string `"StateModel/Submitted."` After the complete file has been read, all of the monikers are resolved, and this one will be replaced in the link by the **IssueState** MEL with the name *Submitted*, thus completing the graph.

There are many possible schemes for creating references to elements. The scheme described in this chapter is implemented by the DSL Tools through a class called `SimpleMonikerResolver`. This built-in scheme can be overridden for advanced scenarios if required but is actually quite sophisticated as it stands. The remainder of this section describes this scheme.

As already observed, any MEL that may be the target of a reference must be uniquely identifiable. We say that such an element must have a *key*. There are two kinds of keys: a Guid and a qualified name.

Using Guids as References

We saw in the example earlier that the Comment object is serialized with a Guid:

```
<comment Id="9f8bc7e9-579c-402a-a9a3-c854767161d1">
  <commentText>This is the first state</commentText>
  <subjects>
    <issueStateMoniker name="/CJKW.States/StateModel/Raised" />
  </subjects>
</comment>
```

We sometimes call such an element *definitional*, to distinguish it from a reference element. An element representing a reference to this looks like:

```
<commentMoniker Id="9f8bc7e9-579c-402a-a9a3-c854767161d1" />
```

By default, the element names for reference elements have the string `"Moniker"` appended to the element name of the definitional element, as in this case. These element names are customizable and can be any legal unique XML element name.

In order for an `Id` to be serialized for a MEL, its domain class must be marked with the metadata element "Serialize Id" = *True*. This property can be found under the "Xml Serialization Behavior" section of the DSL explorer, as shown in Figure 6-3.

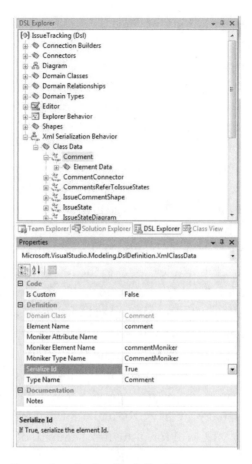

FIGURE 6-3: Setting "Serialize Id"

The result of this is that the Id used to identify the MEL in the store is automatically written out into the Id attribute of the corresponding XML element. The DSL designer will automatically set "Serialize Id" when it is needed, that is, when an element is the target of a reference and does not have any other kind of key.

> **TIP The DSL designer checks whether keys are properly defined**
>
> The user does not normally need to be concerned about whether domain classes define keys or not—the tool will ensure that there are keys, if necessary. If users override the options so that necessary keys are absent, they'll be warned through validation errors.

Using Qualified Names as References

Qualified names are names of the form `"/CJKW.States/StateModel/Raised"`. They consist of a sequence of strings separated by the "/" character. They occur in references either in full form or in short form. Qualified names are used when the DSL author specifies that a particular domain property—usually a *name* domain property—is to be used as a key.

A full-form qualified name for an object is constructed from the key property of the referenced object (`"Raised"` in the example), prepended by the values of key properties for its embedding ancestors (`"StateModel"` in the example). A full-form qualified name always starts with "/".

If keys were the only thing used to construct qualified names, every qualified name would start out with the key of the root element of the model, walking down the whole model to the referenced element, and this can be cumbersome for deeply nested models. To enable qualified names to be expressed more efficiently, the concept of a *qualifier* is introduced. A qualifier is much like a key but it has the special property of always starting the qualified name. In a particular domain model, certain domain classes are important containers that can have many embedded children. The DSL author identifies a property of that class that will be unique for every instance and defines that property to be a qualifier. Then the qualifier property of the container MEL will form the first segment of the fully qualified name for any of the embedded descendents of that MEL. The **Namespace-Name** property of the **IssueStateModel** has been marked to be a qualifier, so the fully qualified name of all of the **IssueState** MELs has this value as the first segment of the name.

Subsequent segments of the name are the key values found in the embedding hierarchy between the MEL that contains a qualifier and the MEL being referenced. In the example, the domain property **IssueTypeName** of the **IssueStateModel** domain class has been marked as a key, which produces the second segment of the fully qualified name.

A particular benefit of qualifiers is that they can be omitted whenever the qualifier value for the referring element and the referred-to element are the same. This produces the short form of the qualified name, which we see in the example. Notice that the short form of the name does not start with "/":

```
<issueStateMoniker name="StateModel/Submitted" />
```

For qualified names to work correctly, they clearly have to be unique. This happens as long as the key value for each element is unique within the scope of its nearest embedding ancestor that also has a key or qualifier. In general, it is up to the DSL author to ensure that this is the case; if a DSL author fails to do so, and a model ends up with non-unique keys, then it will fail to save. However, we saw in Chapter 3 that marking a property as a name ensures that it gets a unique value within the context of the MEL's parent when it is first created. This is such a useful pattern for keys that the "Named Domain Class" element on the toolbox, introduced in Chapter 3, automatically specifies that the name property is a key.

References to Links

It is relatively unusual for a DSL author to create models containing references to relationships that, when instantiated, will cause links between links. When this is done, the relationship at the target end of the reference must have either an Id or a key; the only difference between this situation and the normal configuration of links between MELs is that the container within which keys must be unique is the MEL at the source of the link rather than the embedding MEL.

However, it is extremely common to have links that associate connectors on diagrams with links in models. Using the basic scheme outlined so far, this would result in every link referred to by a connector having to carry a key value. Notice, though, that unless the link is marked with "Allows Duplicates" set, the identity of a link can be uniquely determined from its type and the identities of the MELs at its ends. Exploiting this, the diagram serialization scheme uses special case code to identify links associated with connectors and the links do not need to carry their own explicit key.

When "Allows Duplicates" is set, on the other hand, it is necessary for links associated with diagram connectors to carry a key. The model illustrated in Figure 6-4 is built from a domain model that has "Allows Duplicates" set on the relationship **IssueStateTransition**, as demonstrated by the existence of two links between the *Submitted* and *Pending* states.

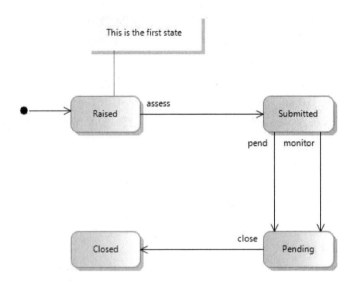

FIGURE 6-4: Multiple links between states

For this domain model, the domain property **Action** on the **IssueState-Transition** relationship is set to be both a name and a key. The latter is done in the DSL explorer through the "Xml Serialization Behavior," as shown in Figure 6-5.

The XML document for the model shown in Figure 6-4 is the same as for the previous example shown in Figure 6-2, except that instead of transitions coming from the *Submitted* state to the different successor states *Pending* and *Closed*, there are two outgoing transitions to the *Pending* state.

```
<issueState name="Submitted" icon="submitted.ico"
            description="The issue has been submitted for assessment">
  <successors>
    <issueStateTransition action="pend">
      <issueStateMoniker name="StateModel/Pending" />
    </issueStateTransition>
    <issueStateTransition action="monitor">
      <issueStateMoniker name="StateModel/Pending" />
    </issueStateTransition>
  </successors>
</issueState>
```

However, for this version it is possible to save references to the individual **IssueStateTransition** links. Since the **Action** property is a key for the link, the fully qualified name will end with the key for the link, which comes after the key for the source of the link, which itself comes after the key and qualifier for the model. Here is a moniker element using this scheme:

```
<issueStateTransitionMoniker
action="/CJKW.States/StateModel/Submitted/pend"/>
```

Such references would occur in the diagram file, so let's move on to that topic.

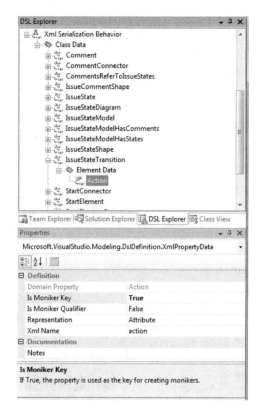

FIGURE 6-5: Setting the Action domain property to be a key

Diagram XML File Format

The diagram serialization uses the same techniques as the model serialization, and although it is built into the DSL Tools, it is in fact generated from a domain model in just the same way, with some minor customizations. For this reason, the format of the diagram file is straightforward and easy to understand. Unlike the model file, though, there are few options for the DSL author to customize the diagram file.

To help keep the discussion compact, we create a very small model, using the same domain model that we used for Figure 6-1, but with just two states. Figure 6-6 shows the diagram corresponding to this small model, as displayed on the screen.

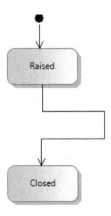

FIGURE 6-6: Simple Issue State diagram

Let's look at the contents of the diagram file that corresponds to the diagram shown in Figure 6-6.

```xml
<?xml version="1.0" encoding="utf-8"?>
<issueStateDiagram dslVersion="1.0.0.0"
                   absoluteBounds="0, 0, 11, 8.5"
                   name="ch6_1">
  <issueStateModelMoniker issueTypeName="/CJKW.States/StateModel" />
  <nestedChildShapes>
    <issueStateShape Id="8ced5d17-9c54-496c-8814-c979246c156b"
          absoluteBounds="1.375, 1.75, 1, 0.5">
      <issueStateMoniker name="/CJKW.States/StateModel/Raised" />
    </issueStateShape>
    <issueStateShape Id="64972ea6-400b-4188-ad55-bb5d22473d26"
          absoluteBounds="1.375, 3.375, 1, 0.5">
      <issueStateMoniker name="/CJKW.States/StateModel/Closed" />
    </issueStateShape>
    <startElementShape Id="b333c44b-5520-4478-81ca-5ba4fe73b651"
          absoluteBounds="1.75, 1.25, 0.1666666716337204,
          0.1666666716337204">
      <startElementMoniker name="/CJKW.States/StateModel/Start" />
    </startElementShape>
    <startConnector
```

```
        edgePoints="[(1.83333333581686 : 1.41666667163372);
                    (1.83333333581686 : 1.75)]"
        manuallyRouted="false" fixedFrom="NotFixed" fixedTo="NotFixed"
        TargetRelationshipDomainClassId="d82fc1a1-c67b-45ea-8aa1-
        a43c86f0a425">
        <nodes>
          <startElementShapeMoniker Id="b333c44b-5520-4478-81ca-5ba4fe73b651" />
          <issueStateShapeMoniker Id="8ced5d17-9c54-496c-8814-c979246c156b" />
        </nodes>
      </startConnector>
      <transitionConnector
        edgePoints="[(1.875 : 2.25);
                    (1.875 : 2.62125);
                    (2.75 : 2.62125);
                    (2.75 : 3.00375);
                    (1.85416666666667 : 3.00375);
                    (1.85416666666667 : 3.375)]"
        manuallyRouted="true" fixedFrom="NotFixed" fixedTo="NotFixed"
        TargetRelationshipDomainClassId="57f67bbc-668c-445a-af57-
        5fe3810f11da">
        <nodes>
          <issueStateShapeMoniker Id="8ced5d17-9c54-496c-8814-c979246c156b" />
          <issueStateShapeMoniker Id="64972ea6-400b-4188-ad55-bb5d22473d26" />
        </nodes>
      </transitionConnector>
    </nestedChildShapes>
  </issueStateDiagram>
```

The root element of the diagram file has the element `<issueStateDiagram>`. This can be customized using the DSL designer. It has three attributes. The `dslVersion` attribute gives the version of the diagram serializer. The `absoluteBounds` attribute exists for any shape including the diagram and specifies its position in world coordinates. It has the structure (x, y, *width*, *height*), where x and y are the coordinates of the upper left-hand corner of the rectangle bounding the shape. All coordinates and sizes are measured in inches. The `name` attribute contains the name of the diagram, which is initialized when the diagram is created.

For each DSL, the diagram refers to the root element of the model, which in this case is an instance of **IssueStateModel**. The next element in the diagram file is the cross-reference to that MEL, which uses its fully qualified name. The **IssueStateModel** MEL itself is serialized in the model file, of course, not the diagram file.

Following that is the `<nestedChildShapes>` element. This represents an embedding relationship—every shape that appears on the diagram is embedded in the diagram using this relationship. Nested in this element are all of the shapes and connectors on the diagram. Each shape is serialized with its attributes—in the case of the **IssueStateShape,** these are its `absoluteBounds` and its `Id`—and a cross-reference to the MEL that it represents.

Each connector is also serialized with its attributes. The `edgePoints` attribute gives the coordinates of the ends and kinks. The `manuallyRouted` attribute determines whether the connector has been routed by hand since creation. The `fixedFrom` and `fixedTo` attributes with the value of *NotFixed* determine that the place that the connector meets the shape can move.

Each connector is serialized within the child element `<nodes>` with references to the shapes at its ends. Together with the identity of the domain class of the relationship itself, this allows the associated link to be identified as long as duplicates are not allowed for the relationship. As noted earlier, this avoids the need for unique keys to be saved for every link and thus keeps the model file compact and easy to understand.

Versioning and Migration

A fundamental issue when working with DSLs is what happens to existing models when the DSL definition changes. DSL authors might decide to add, delete, or rename domain properties, domain classes, relationships, shapes, connectors, and so on. In such a situation, models corresponding to the original definition may contain valuable data that should not be discarded.

In order to help manage this situation, the saved file contains an attribute in the top-level element that records which version of the DSL was used to save the file:

```
<issueStateModel dslVersion="1.0.0.0" ÷ >
```

This version number can be set in the DSL designer through the properties of the DSL itself. Following .NET conventions, the version number has four components: {Major, Minor, Build, Revision}. Code is generated so that these values are saved in every model file from the generated designer, and the version is checked whenever a model file is loaded. If the version number does not match in every respect, then by default the model fails to load, and the user sees an error message that describes the problem.

This behavior can be overridden by custom code. It's possible, for example, to call a different serializer in cases where the version number does not match, thus providing for automatic migration for models created using older versions of the domain model.

The definition of a DSL can change for reasons other than deploying new versions. While the language is being developed, test and example models will be created in the debugging solution that is automatically created by the DSL Tools, and unless it is explicitly changed, all of these models will have the same version number. It would be frustrating if these models were invalidated for every change to the DSL definition. Fortunately, the file-reading code generated for a DSL is relatively forgiving and will do a good job of reading in models, even if the DSL definition has changed, and will issue warnings that indicate the steps it has taken. The file reader will take the following approaches when confronted with an incorrect file:

- Within the scope of a given domain class, elements (properties and relationships) may appear in any order. Elements defined in base classes must appear before elements from derived classes, though.
- Unexpected elements will be ignored, together with everything nested in them.
- Unexpected attributes will be ignored.
- Missing attributes and elements will cause the model to be populated using default values.

When such a file is encountered, warnings may be given to the user, because the file will fail its schema validation. Schemas are discussed in the next section of this chapter.

If, while reading in a model, monikers are encountered that cannot be resolved, file loading will fail. This is likely to happen when the DSL author changes the cross-referencing scheme for one or more relationships—for example, changing the key for a domain class from an Id to a name. In these cases, the model reader will open the file in the XML editor and will display errors in the error window that show which monikers have failed to resolve and on which lines of the file the corresponding cross-references appear. It such cases it is often easiest to edit the XML directly to change the moniker elements into the form that will successfully load. An example is illustrated in Figure 6-7, where the XML file has been edited so that line 12 contains the reference "StateModel/Opened"—for which there is no corresponding element. Double-clicking on the error message takes the user directly to the offending element.

In such a situation, the diagram file may also fail to load because its references into the model cannot be resolved.

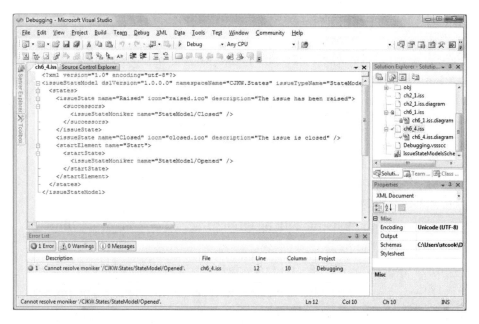

FIGURE 6-7: Error resulting from incorrect cross-reference in XML file

■ **TIP** Fix up a broken diagram file by editing the monikers, or delete the file

To recover from a situation where the diagram fails to load, the user may edit the moniker elements in the diagram file into a form that will resolve; alternatively, it may be simpler to delete the diagram file, because a new one will be automatically created by opening and saving the model file, and the only thing that will have been lost is the diagram layout. There is a tradeoff here between the effort needed to fix up the references by hand in the XML versus the effort needed to lay out the diagram.

The XML Schema

An XML Schema is a file that describes the structure of XML documents. The XML Schema definition is a standard from the W3C (World Wide Web Consortium). We won't give a detailed explanation of XML Schema here; there is a wealth of books as well as online resources and tutorials that describe its details.

Given a schema, XML documents can be validated to determine whether they are structured in accordance with it. In Visual Studio, if a schema is available, the XML editor will use it to offer IntelliSense: auto-completion, real-time error-checking, and interactive documentation via tooltips. This greatly enhances the user's experience in the XML editor.

When a language is defined using the DSL Tools, an XML Schema is generated that corresponds to the serialization options that have been selected. This schema can be used to enhance the XML editing experience. To augment this experience, the generated schema includes documentation elements that contain the descriptions for language elements defined by the DSL author, and these descriptions will be offered as tooltips in the XML editor if the user hovers over an element. Figure 6-8 shows an example, where the user is hovering over the <startElement> element in the XML model file for the model shown in Figure 6-6.

Additionally, the schema validation is invoked when a model file is loaded, and any errors produced from this validation are offered to the DSL user as warnings, as noted in the previous section. Schema validation does have limits though; most notably, the way it is used in DSL Tools offers no capability for checking the validity of cross-references. So although an XML file may be valid according to its schema, it may fail to load into the target DSL tool because its cross-references are incorrect.

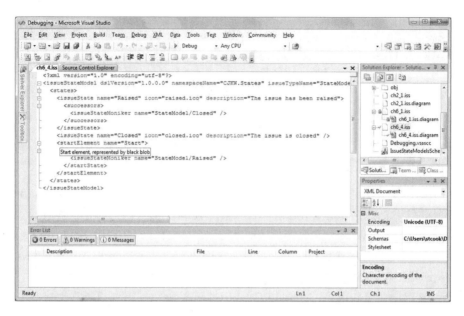

FIGURE 6-8: IntelliSense in the XML editor

Customization

Although as we have seen, the default serialization format for a model is quite easy to read, in some circumstances the DSL author may want to alter the way that models are serialized. There are several levels at which this can be done, ranging from simple settings in the DSL designer to replacing major components of the serialization infrastructure. This follows the principles that we set out in Chapter 1 for avoiding the "customization pit."

The serialization settings in the DSL designer are found in the DSL explorer window under the "Xml Serialization Behavior" node (see Figure 6-9). Selecting this node itself gives the opportunity to specify the root XML Schema namespace—and to specify that domain properties that have default values are to be explicitly written out.

▪ TIP Write out all domain properties when models are to be processed by other tools

There is no need to write out default values for domain properties if the model will be reloaded by a tool that knows the default values. This setting forces all of the domain property values to be saved, which enables processing by other tools.

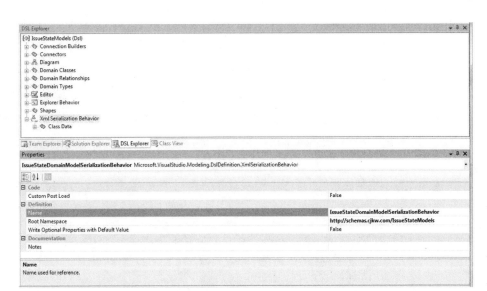

FIGURE 6-9: DSL explorer serialization settings

This node also offers the setting "Custom Post Load." If this is set to *True*, the loading code includes a call to methods called OnPostLoadModel() and OnPostLoadModelAndDiagram(). These methods are not implemented by the DSL Tools; the language author must implement them in a partial class to do post-load processing—for example, to create additional objects in the store that are not present in the file but need to be created in order to make a fully formed model.

Modifying XML Element Names

Beneath the "Xml Serialization Behavior" node are serialization data organized under Class Data, with a node for each domain class and domain relationship. Figure 6-10 shows the XML serialization data for the domain class **IssueState** selected in the DSL explorer and the property settings displayed in the properties window.

The simplest form of customization is to modify the names of the XML elements that correspond to a class. For example, changing the mapping so that an **IssueState** element is represented by the element <state> rather than <issueState>, and its moniker represented by <stateMoniker> rather than <issueStateMoniker>, is accomplished by setting "Element Name" and "Moniker Element Name" in the properties window, as shown in Figure 6-11. The consequence of this is that a serialized model appears as follows:

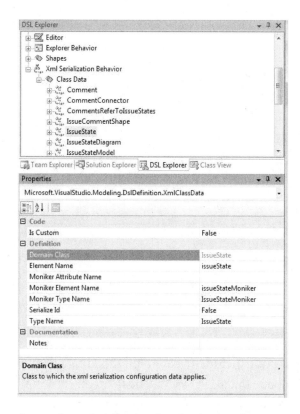

FIGURE 6-10: Serialization data for the domain class IssueState

```xml
<?xml version="1.0" encoding="utf-8"?>
<issueStateModel dslVersion="1.0.0.0"
      namespaceName="CJKW.States" issueTypeName="StateModel"
      xmlns="http://schemas.cjkw.com/IssueStateModels">
  <states>
    <state name="Start">
      <successors>
        <stateMoniker name="StateModel/Finish" />
      </successors>
    </state>
    <state name="Finish" />
  </states>
</issueStateModel>
```

Figure 6-11 also shows the "Serialize Id" property, which determines the serialization of the Guid of the element in order to enable cross-referencing, as explained earlier.

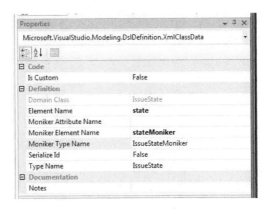

FIGURE 6-11: Customizing XML elements

The values for "Type Name" and "Moniker Type Name" determine the names of the types in the generated XML Schema corresponding to the language. Changing these names only has an effect on the details of the schema used to validate it, not on the serialized XML itself.

The moniker element is of this form:

```
<stateMoniker name="StateModel/Finish" />
```

The name of the attribute used to hold the moniker value, name in this case, is by default the attribute that corresponds to the key in the definitional element. If desired, a new attribute can be defined for this purpose by setting the "Moniker Attribute Name" to specify the desired attribute.

Element Data

Nested under each "Class Data" node is an "Element Data" node through which you can specify the structure of the XML element that represents the corresponding domain class. For example, Figure 6-12 shows the element data for the domain class **StateElement**, and in particular, has selected the element data for the domain property called **Name**. Here you can see that "Is Moniker Key" is set to *True*; this means that references to **StateElements** will be done via names, as explained earlier in this chapter. The "Representation" for a domain property gives the choice of *Attribute*, *Element*, or *Ignore.* Recall that any domain property can be serialized either as an XML attribute of the element corresponding to the domain class, or as a fully fledged nested XML element. A domain property can also be ignored altogether in the serialization—this is the default when the domain property is calculated. The "Xml Name" determines the name of the attribute or element used to serialize the domain property.

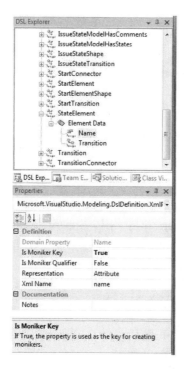

FIGURE 6-12: Element Data for StateElement

The "Element Data" node for a "Class Data" node also contains elements that govern the serialization of domain relationships that are sourced on the corresponding domain class. For example, Figure 6-12 also shows the element data for **Transition** nested under **StateElement**. This matches the fact that relationships are represented in the XML as elements nested in the element corresponding to the source of the relationship. A domain relationship also has its own "Class Data," but this only comes into play when the relationship is represented in its full form, for example, when it has properties.

To illustrate the effect of the element data for relationships, Figure 6-13 shows the data for **IssueStateModelHasComments**, as found under the "Element Data" node for **IssueStateModel**. The setting for "Role Element Name" determines the name of the XML element that represents the relationship, similarly to the settings for a domain class shown in Figure 6-11. The effect of the "Use Full Form" setting was discussed earlier in this chapter.

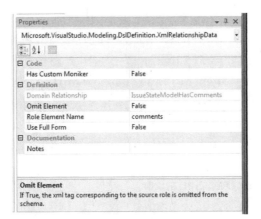

FIGURE 6-13: Domain relationship data for
IssueStateModelHas Comments

The effect of "Omit Element," if set to *True*, is to cause the containing `<comments>` element to be completely omitted from the serialized XML, as in this example:

```xml
<?xml version="1.0" encoding="utf-8"?>
<issueStateModel ÷>
  <comment Id="b6a8f11e-b806-4a0c-8f2c-511238ddb581">
    <commentText>Comment 1</commentText>
  </comment>
  <comment Id="1a9327e5-fefb-4b44-8eb7-133c002ed1f0">
    <commentText>Comment 2</commentText>
  </comment>
</issueStateModel>
```

This can be a useful way of making the XML simpler. By default, "Omit Element" is set to *False*.

> **■ TIP** Consider setting "Omit Element" to *True* if source multiplicity is *One* or *ZeroOne*
>
> If the source multiplicity of a domain relationship is *One* or *ZeroOne*, there will only ever be a single element targeted by the relationship. In such a case, the default serialization will contain a single element representing the relationship, containing a single element for the targeted element. Omitting the relationship element makes good sense here, unless the relationship is a derived or base relationship.

Figure 6-13 also shows a property for the domain relationship called "Has Custom Moniker." Setting this to *True* only affects reference relationships, and its effect is to require the DSL author to provide methods called `CustomSerializeReference()` and `CustomMonikerizeReference()` that will convert from a moniker to a string and vice-versa in order to customize the physical representation of the cross-reference in the file. You might do this, for example, to use a character different than "/" in qualified names.

Implementing Your Own Serializer

The customization options offered by the DSL Tools are principally designed so that a DSL author can improve the human-readability of the XML files used to store models. This can also assist with making these files amenable to processing by other tools. They do not give complete customization, though. If you have an existing file format that you want to interface with a DSL, then these options are likely to be insufficient. In such a case, there remains the possibility of implementing your own serializer. The entry points for this are the `Load()` and `Save()` methods in the `DocData` class, as described in the next section.

Further customizations are possible by implementing a customized `MonikerResolver` to replace the class `SimpleMonikerResolver` that is provided with the DSL Tools framework. This option is not for the faint-hearted, though, and requires an expert-level understanding of the DSL Tools.

Generated Serialization Code

Much of the code that implements the serialization behavior described in this chapter is generated from the DSL definition, in two files in the `Dsl` project called `Serializer.cs` and `SerializationHelper.cs`. The core of this code consists of a serialization class corresponding to every domain class (including relationships, shapes, diagram, connectors, and so on). For example, the domain class **IssueState** has a corresponding serialization class called `Issue-StateSerializer`. We will have a look at a simplified version of some of the methods of this class in order to get an understanding of how the serialization code is structured. You only need to understand this code if you need more customization than is provided by the settings described so far.

The starting points for serialization are the Load() and Save() methods in the IssueStateModelsDocDataBase class in the file DocData.cs generated in the DslPackage project. These methods are called by Visual Studio when the user opens or saves the file using the normal user interface. They deal with various interactions with Visual Studio, such as ensuring that the right files exist, locking them where necessary, and posting errors. At the heart of the Load() and Save() methods are calls to methods on a helper class called IssueStateModelsSerializationHelper, which is in the file SerializationHelper.cs in the Dsl project.

Loading the model, like any changes to the store, is done in a transaction. This is a special kind of transaction, called a *serializing transaction*, which allows links to exist in a partially instantiated state so that references can be fixed up at the end of the transaction.

The IssueStateModelsSerializationHelper class is paired, according to the double-derived pattern for customization introduced in Chapter 3 and discussed further in Chapter 10, with a class in the same file called IssueStateModelsSerializationHelperBase that introduces several overloads of the methods LoadModel(), LoadModelAndDiagram(), SaveModel(), and SaveModelAndDiagram(). Let's take a look at one of these:

```
public virtual IssueStateModel LoadModel(
                DslModeling::SerializationResult serializationResult,
                DslModeling::Partition partition,
                string fileName,
                DslModeling::ISchemaResolver schemaResolver,
                DslValidation::ValidationController validationController)
```

The first parameter, serializationResult, collects any warning messages that are encountered during serialization. The partition parameter specifies the partition, that is, the section of the store, where the deserialized model is to be created. The filename specifies the file to be loaded. The schemaResolver allows the loader to do XML schema validation on the model while it is being loaded and will cause any schema validation errors to be offered to the user as warnings. If this parameter is null, then loading will occur without XML schema validation. Similarly, if the validation-Controller is not null, then load-time constraint validation will occur on the model, as described in Chapter 7.

The LoadModel() method creates an XmlReader to acquire the content from the file. The XmlReader is one of several approaches that could have been chosen to load the file. It is flexible because it can read any well-formed XML content, and its performance is good. However, it does require the file to be processed sequentially, in contrast, say, to reading the entire file into a Document Object Model (DOM) before processing it. Having created the XmlReader, the method starts reading the file, and the first thing it does is create in the store an instance of the domain class that is mapped to the top-level element in the file. It then calls the ReadRootElement() method on the corresponding serializer class. This ReadRootElement() method is only generated for serializers that correspond to root domain classes and their subclasses, because these are the only elements that can appear as roots of a model file.

The ReadRootElement() method first checks the version of the file using the method CheckVersion(). This can be replaced if needed; to do so, the domain class **IssueStateModel** must have the "Generates Double Derived" property set to *True*, which will cause its serializer also to be generated using the double-derived pattern, so that methods such as CheckVersion() can be overridden. After checking the version, if passed a schemaResolver, the method sets up the XmlReader so that schema validation will occur while reading in the file. If not, it sets up the XmlReader to read the file without schema validation. Then it calls the Read() method, which exists for every serializer class.

Thus, the Read() method is called on the serializer for **IssueStateModel** when an instance of IssueState exists but none of its properties or embedded children have yet been deserialized. At this point, the deserializer will be looking at the point in the XML just after the <issueState> element has been recognized, as marked by the ▶ symbol in this fragment of XML:

```
<issueState ▶name="Raised"
            description="The issue has been raised"
            icon="raised.ico">
  <successors>
    <issueStateTransition action="submit">
      <issueStateMoniker name="StateModel/Submitted" />
    </issueStateTransition>
  </successors>
</issueState>
```

The method starts by calling `ReadPropertiesFromAttributes()`, which will deserialize the properties of this `IssueState` that have been saved as XML attributes. Then it calls `ReadElements()` to read the nested elements. It is possible that `ReadElements()` might fail because unexpected elements are encountered; in this case, `ReadElements()` is called repeatedly until there are no more nested elements to look at. Finally, the reader is advanced to the next element and control returns to the caller.

```
namespace CJKW.IssueStateModels
{
  public partial class IssueStateSerializer : StateElementSerializer
  {

    public override void Read(
      SerializationContext serializationContext,
      ModelElement element,
      System.Xml.XmlReader reader)
    {

      // Read properties serialized as XML attributes.
      ReadPropertiesFromAttributes(serializationContext, element, reader);

      // Read nested XML elements.
      if (!serializationContext.Result.Failed)
      {
        if (!reader.IsEmptyElement)
        {
          // Read to the start of the first child element.
          DslModeling::SerializationUtilities.SkipToFirstChild(reader);

          // Read nested XML elements, they can be either properties
          // serialized as XML elements, or child model elements.

          while (!serializationContext.Result.Failed &&
            !reader.EOF &&
            reader.NodeType == System.Xml.XmlNodeType.Element)
          {
            ReadElements(serializationContext, element, reader);
            if (!serializationContext.Result.Failed &&
              !reader.EOF &&
              reader.NodeType ==
                System.Xml.XmlNodeType.Element)
            {
              // Encountered one unknown XML element
              // skip it and keep reading.
IssueStateDomainModelSerializationBehaviorSerializationMessages.
                UnexpectedXmlElement(serializationContext, reader);
```

```
            DslModeling::SerializationUtilities.Skip(reader);
        }
      }
    }
  }

    // Advance the reader to the next element
    DslModeling::SerializationUtilities.Skip(reader);
```

The ReadPropertiesFromAttributes() method is generated from the knowledge that the domain class **IssueState** defines the properties **Icon** and **Description**. First it calls ReadPropertiesFromAttributes() on its base class—StateElementSerializer—which will read in the **Name**. It then proceeds to look for the value of the property **Icon**, serialized in the XML attribute called icon. If it fails to find it, this is not an error; leaving this attribute out simply means that it retains its default value. If it finds the attribute but it has a value that cannot be converted to the appropriate type, then a warning will be created that this attribute has been ignored. It continues to read in the value of **Description**, using the same pattern. The call to serializationContext.Result.Failed will only deliver *True* if a serious error occurs, such as the file not being well-formed XML; in other cases, any warning messages will be accumulated for the user and reading proceeds.

```
    protected override void ReadPropertiesFromAttributes(
      SerializationContext serializationContext,
      ModelElement element,
      System.Xml.XmlReader reader)
    {
      base.ReadPropertiesFromAttributes(serializationContext,
                    element, reader);

      IssueState instanceOfIssueState = element as IssueState;

      // Icon
      if (!serializationContext.Result.Failed)
      {
        string attribIcon = reader.GetAttribute("icon");
        if (attribIcon != null)
        {
          System.String valueOfIcon;
          if (SerializationUtilities.TryGetValue<System.String>(
                SerializationUtilities.UnescapeXmlString(attribIcon),
                out valueOfIcon))
          {
```

```
        instanceOfIssueState.Icon = valueOfIcon;
      }
      else
      {  // Invalid property value, ignored.
    IssueStateDomainModelSerializationBehaviorSerializationMessages.
      IgnoredPropertyValue(serializationContext, reader, "icon",
          typeof(System.String), attribIcon);
      }
    }
  }
  // Description
  if (!serializationContext.Result.Failed)
  {
    string attribDescription = reader.GetAttribute("description");
    if (attribDescription != null)
    {
      System.String valueOfDescription;
      ÷
    }
  }
}
```

The ReadElements() method starts by calling the base class ReadElements(). This means that, to be read successfully, elements defined in the base class must appear before elements defined in subclasses. Assuming that the reader is looking at an element as expected, this method continues by calling Read-ChildElements().

```
protected override void ReadElements(
  SerializationContext serializationContext,
  ModelElement element,
  System.Xml.XmlReader reader)
{
  base.ReadElements(serializationContext, element, reader);

  IssueState instanceOfIssueState = element as IssueState;

  // Read child model elements
  if (!serializationContext.Result.Failed &&
      !reader.EOF &&
      reader.NodeType == System.Xml.XmlNodeType.Element)
    ReadChildElements(serializationContext,
              instanceOfIssueState, reader);
}
```

The `ReadChildElements()` method looks for the `<successors>` element. If this is found, and it is not empty, then another method called `ReadIssueState-TransitionInstances()` is called to read in the instances of `IssueState-Transition`. This method, in turn, will call the `Read()` method of `Issue-StateTransition Serializer`, which continues using the same recursive pattern. Eventually, the `Read()` method of `IssueStateModel` completes, at which point the entire file has been read.

```
private static void ReadChildElements(
  SerializationContext serializationContext,
  IssueState element,
  System.Xml.XmlReader reader)
{
  if (!serializationContext.Result.Failed &&
      !reader.EOF &&
      reader.NodeType == System.Xml.XmlNodeType.Element)
  {
    if (string.Compare(reader.LocalName,
        "successors", System.StringComparison.CurrentCulture) == 0)
    {
      if (reader.IsEmptyElement)
      {  // No instance of this relationship, just skip
        SerializationUtilities.Skip(reader);
      }
      else
      {
        SerializationUtilities.SkipToFirstChild(reader);
          // Skip the open tag of <successors>
        ReadIssueStateTransitionInstances(serializationContext,
          element, reader);
        SerializationUtilities.Skip(reader);
          // Skip the close tag of </successors>
      }
    }
  }
}
```

The `Write()` methods are similarly structured, although rather more simply, because there is no need to check for errors.

In addition to the reading and writing code on each class, methods are also generated for calculating and resolving monikers. These methods can be customized using the "Has Custom Moniker" property described earlier.

Customized Serialization Code

There are some circumstances where the DSL author needs to customize the serialization more than is enabled by the use of the elements described so far. Let's say, for example, that a domain class called **Versioned** has four integer properties called **Major**, **Minor**, **Revision**, and **Build**, representing the different parts of a version number. The DSL author has decided that in the serialization, this should be represented as an element such as `<version>1.0.0.0</version>`. By default, the properties would be represented as attributes: `<versioned major="1" minor="0" revision="0" build="0" />`.

Referring back to Figure 6-11, each "Class Data" node has a property called "Is Custom." If this is set to *True*, then the generated serialization code calls methods on the serializer class such as `CustomRead()` and `CustomWrite()`, instead of the `Read()` and `Write()` methods described earlier. These methods are not implemented in the generated code and must be hand-coded. To make this simpler, the code that would have been generated for these methods is generated into another set of methods on the serializer class with names like `DefaultRead()` and `DefaultWrite()`, so that implementing the `CustomXXX()` methods by calls to the `DefaultXXX()` methods will give the original behavior. This gives a flexible customization scheme for implementing your own customization code by intermingling custom code with calls to the generated defaults.

To customize the serialization for the version number then involves writing code in a `CustomWritePropertiesAsElements()` method in a partial class as follows:

```
private static void CustomWritePropertiesAsElements(
                        SerializationContext serializationContext,
                        Versioned element,
                        XmlWriter writer)
{
  Versioned instance = element as Versioned;

  if (!serializationContext.Result.Failed && instance != null)
  {
    String[] parts = { instance.Major.ToString(),
                       instance.Minor.ToString(),
                       instance.Revision.ToString(),
                       instance.Build.ToString() };
```

```
    String dot = ".";
    writer.WriteElementString("version", String.Join(dot, parts));
  }
}
```

This method needs to be called from the `CustomWriteElements()` method, the remainder of which is copied verbatim from the `DefaultWriteElements()` method.

Complementary code must be written in the custom read methods to acquire the serialized string, split it into its constituents, and set the corresponding properties.

Impact of Customization on the Schema

Once the serialization for a domain class has "Is Custom" set to *True*, it is not possible to generate an effective XML schema to validate it. Instead, a flexible schema `complexType` is generated, as follows:

```
<xsd:complexType name="Versioned" mixed="true">
  <xsd:sequence>
    <xsd:any minOccurs="0" maxOccurs="unbounded" processContents="lax" />
  </xsd:sequence>
  <xsd:anyAttribute processContents="lax" />
</xsd:complexType>
```

This schema is usually sufficiently flexible to avoid warnings in the saved model file, although Visual Studio will offer informational messages that schema information cannot be found for the contents of the customized elements. This schema will, however, give warnings for unusual domain models when the domain class whose serialization is customized inherits from another domain class that is the target of an embedding relationship. In such cases, the flexible `complexType` shown above is not substitutable for the base class `complexType`, and schema validation errors will occur whenever instances of the customized domain class are embedded via this relationship. These will appear as warnings when the model file is loaded in the target designer. To avoid these warnings it is necessary to customize the schema by modifying its generation template or simply to write one by hand.

SUMMARY

In this chapter we explained how the models and diagrams created using a DSL are saved to files in domain-specific XML. This XML is designed to be easily readable by humans and consumable by other tools. We have seen how the serialization is carried out by generated code, which is fully accessible to the DSL author. We've discussed how the code that reads files is forgiving of errors and how versioning and migration work. We also explained several customization options for the XML and the generated schema, through serialization data properties and through writing additional code.

■ 7 ■
Constraints and Validation

Introduction

When you're programming with general purpose languages such as C# or Java, errors come in many flavors. You can mistype a keyword and get a lexical error, or you can get the order of a construct wrong and get a syntax error. These errors are the results of implicit constraints that the language imposes upon the stream of simple text that you pass to it. Strongly typed languages incorporate a type system into these constraints and produce errors at compile time, for example, when you try to set the value of a variable defined as an integer to a string value.

For many years now, good mainstream programming practice has suggested that assertions be used to impose further explicit constraints on what parameter values methods can be called with at debug time, for example, disallowing an empty string from being passed as a parameter. However, these constraints are not usually evaluated at compile time like those just mentioned; they require some context in which to be evaluated—and this context is typically provided by a running program.

Outside of commercial programming, there is a strong tradition of building facilities directly into programming or specification languages to express such user-definable explicit constraints as preconditions, postconditions, and invariants. Over the years, the academic community has done a significant amount of work on validating user-specified constraints at compile time rather than execution time, either by simulation or by logical proof.

In modeling, the situation is similar. Modeling languages have their own syntax that must be observed (e.g., transitions are always from one state to another). They typically can have a type system associated with them whose implicit constraints can be applied; for example, the `Width` and `Height` properties on a class representing a Door must be of type `float`. Modeling languages can then also have mechanisms or sub-languages for explicitly expressing user-defined constraints. User-defined constraints are generally thought of as expressions that can be evaluated against a model to produce a Boolean result that can be tested.

Examples of model constraints expressed in English might be:

- The `Height` property on `Firefighter` is always greater than 1.8 meters.
- `House` always has at least one `Door`.
- `ClassDefinition` does not directly or indirectly reference itself with its `BaseClass` property.

Constraints typically can be thought of as invariants, that is, they are always true throughout the life of the model, or as preconditions or post-conditions of some operation either at design-time (e.g., code generation, saving) or runtime (e.g., debiting a bank account). They can also be seen as a way for humans to evaluate the current state of a model with respect to some criteria; for example, whether all of the web server configurations are compliant with the corporate standards. You can see examples of this type of constraint in the Distributed System Designers that come with the Team Architect edition of Visual Studio 2005.

The DSL Tools do not provide explicit facilities for modeling runtime constraints, just as they do not attempt to say anything else specific about other aspects of the code or systems that their target designers are used to create models for. However, it is perfectly feasible that part of a DSL could itself be a model of a constraint system and that code generated by the target designer will complete a framework that supports runtime constraints of its own. For example, a logical UI design tool created with the DSL Tools might incorporate notation for defining constraints over the data that can be entered into text fields in the UI. The UI design tool could then generate code that completes a runtime data validation framework that is part of the UI platform being targeted.

The DSL Tools do, however, provide a full-featured framework for authoring constraints over a DSL as part of the language definition and for evaluating those constraints when a target designer is being used to create a model in the new DSL. The aim of this framework is to make it easier for end users of target designers to create models that are correct for use with respect to one or more targeted scenarios, such as code generation or conformance to some corporate standard. For example, a very typical constraint in a class design DSL might be to ensure that no inheritance relationships are created that have cycles in them.

Choosing Hard or Soft Constraints?

In the context of a visual designer or an API, constraints can be divided into two categories:

1. Hard constraints are constraints that the tool prevents the user from ever violating, for example, only allowing valid numbers in the "width" field of a shape element.
2. Soft constraints are constraints that the user is allowed to violate at some points in time but not at others, for example, all elements in a model having unique names.

Expressed like this, it seems that a user would never wish to make mistakes and would thus always need and prefer constraints to be expressed as hard constraints. However, in practice, the opposite is true more often than not, and it turns out that while this approach sounds desirable, it suffers from two practical problems:

1. Constraints in the large are often not computationally cheap.
2. Users don't actually want correct models all of the time.

When constraint languages are very expressive, it is a difficult problem to calculate the reach of the dependency graph of each constraint. Consequently, when a model changes, it is not cheap to calculate which constraints to rerun. Did the set of objects impacted by some constraint change because of a change to the value of a property on a model? Are newly introduced objects going to cause a size expression on a constraint of another object to fail? The approach typically taken is not to try and work out these problems but for a human to decide which set of constraints will be run at program creation time. Erring on the side of correctness, this decision is often evaluated as, "Run all constraints." If we want to encourage the proliferation of constraints to provide the end user with the best chance of building a correct model, then evaluating all constraints on every model change can severely drag down the practical performance of tools.

This performance problem can eventually be solved by clever technology and faster computers; however, there is a more fundamental problem—users work in differing ways. Some people like to build their models depth-first, building a slice through all layers present in a tool. Others like to set up all of one type of object before coming back to fill in all of another type. Is a model of a distributed system likely to be valid with only UI elements present? Probably not—and certainly not as valid as it would need to be to ensure successful generation of a working system. However, would it be reasonable to build the models in that order? Certainly it would—user-centered design proponents might even suggest it was the only good way to build it. If you were unable to add invalid elements to the model, then you'd be forced to build in the order that the designer author envisaged.

The next step might be to relax the constraint evaluation to allow invalid models to be created but to disallow saving or loading of a model that isn't valid. In this scenario, imagine a change to add a new property to a business object. That change is likely to ripple both up and down the tiers of a distributed system. Constraints might well be in place to make sure that every property in a business object is backed by one or more columns in a database table. However, what if you'd just made the change to the business object and noticed that it was 6:30 p.m. and past time to honor a promise to your spouse? You would likely be very unhappy if your modeling tool refused to save your work on the grounds that your constraints were breached.

The astute reader might at this point suggest that there is some kind of layered stack of constraints and that our examples are rather high up in that stack, being based on distributed system structure. Maybe there is more value in enforcing some lower level of constraint? What about something simpler, such as multiplicity in models? Imagine a domain model of a car's engine management system that contains a domain class **Limiter** with a multiplicity of *one* and no optionality. Surely it makes sense to prevent the one instance of **Limiter** from being deleted? After all, the domain model states that an engine must always have one and only one **Limiter**. Unfortunately, there is no easy, conclusive answer to this question; we are left with "sometimes." If **Limiter** is abstract and has two concrete derived types, **RoadLimiter** and **RacingLimiter,** then a user experience is needed to change the single instance from road to racing. There are several options. Either we can generate or hand-write special code to implement this experience, or we can simply allow an instance of **RoadLimiter** to be deleted and replaced at the user's convenience with a new instance of **RacingLimiter**. It is also possible to allow the **RacingLimiter** creation to occur before the **RoadLimiter** deletion, perhaps to facilitate copying property values between the instances. In these situations, for a transient period, this relationship with a defined multiplicity of one has either zero or two roleplayers. This type of thing can play havoc with code generation. You can imagine that the generated model code for this example has only allocated storage for a single roleplayer in the relationship and includes code to throw exceptions if it detects more than one. A useful compromise (and one that we've taken in several places in the DSL Tools) is to treat maximum multiplicity as a hard constraint but leave minimum as a soft one.

Let's take one final example and look at how it is treated by the DSL Tools. The DSL Tools enforce type-based constraints on property values as a hard constraint at the time of model change. This decision is primarily to enable type-safe data storage in the store implementation, which brings with it tremendous performance and robustness gains by removing many type conversions and explicit bounds checks. If a property is declared as being of type integer, then any attempt to put the string "hello" into it either via user interface or API will cause an immediate error. This decision does, however, have some disadvantages. Picture for a moment a designer for the early stages of the software lifecycle—perhaps a conceptual level design tool for relational databases. For the end user, at this time in the lifecycle, many decisions are not finalized. As well as an exact numeric value, it would be nice to allow a property such as the length of a string column to be specified as "20 or 24," "unknown" or "> 20." You might ask what place there is for such vagueness in a software development tool geared toward automation? If you automate processing this semi-vague model to extract elements where numeric literals are not specified correctly, then you have a powerful tool for reporting on the quantity of information that you *don't yet know*. Once all of the unknown items are eventually transformed into correct numbers, a further piece of automation could move the data into a more constrained model format.

> **■ TIP** Consider using weakly typed properties for analysis models
>
> When using the DSL Tools to model at the conceptual level, it can often prove useful to use strings as your basic property types and then apply a set of soft constraints to check that the values conform to some more rigorous type set.

Choices Made by the DSL Tools

The DSL Tools choose to enforce the following small set of hard constraints within generated designers at an API level.

- Maximum multiplicity of roles (one or many)
- Type-based constraints on roleplayers
- Type-based constraints on property values

These are all enforced both via both the weakly and strongly typed APIs and are also naturally exposed through the user interface in generated designers via the default design surface and model explorer.

Soft Constraints in the DSL Tools

Soft constraints are implemented in the DSL Tools by writing extra methods on domain classes. This decision to use simple .NET code rather than a specific constraint language came from the authors' experience with a constraint language called the Object Constraint Language (OCL), which is part of the UML. OCL is a textual language capable of providing testable constraints against any of the models defined within UML.

The authors' observation was that the skills required to write effectively in a rich constraint language such as OCL are actually very similar to those required to write C#, so long as the mechanism for evaluating the code is kept simple. Also the skills pool for C# is much wider than that of any current constraint language. There are many pros and cons to this approach, but we felt that the fact that it allowed for one or many constraint language systems to be added at a later date if necessary meant that it was a good bet. The fact that constraints are not stored in the model means that they are not as immediately visible to the casual observer. However, this also means that they are not edited with some compromised user experience but with the full power and ease of use of the built-in C# editor.

A further advantage of using C# is that it is trivially easy to reuse logic that is already available in any other class in either the .NET Framework or your own runtime domain libraries. For example, if you need to verify that a string property is a valid C# identifier, you do not need to write your own validation logic or create a regular expression; instead, you can use the `Microsoft.CSharp.CSharpCodeProvider` class and call its `IsValidIdentifier()` method.

One slight disadvantage in C# is that the current 2.0 version does not have clean ways to perform set-based operations over an object graph. However, these facilities have been announced as an extension to C# in its version 3.0 incarnation via the LINQ project.

The next thing to note about soft constraints in the DSL Tools is that they are wrapped into something called a *validation method*. The concept of validation expresses our observation that in a tool environment, writing a constraint expression solves only half of the problem and, in many cases, takes much less than half of the time spent. The remaining time goes to creating and parameterizing a high-quality warning or error message aimed at the end user to explain the often highly technical constraint in clear language at the correct level of abstraction.

The DSL Tools framework provides a mechanism for performing validation, both for designers and for custom tools running outside of the Visual Studio IDE. In both cases, it allows customization of how the validation is launched and where messages generated by the validation are directed.

Validation Methods

Validation methods can be added to any ModelElement-based class in the DSL Tools, including domain classes, domain relationships, shapes, and connectors. They are typically added by hand-writing a new partial class with a set of validation methods. It's worth noting that they can't be added to the shell aspects of the designer, such as DocData, DocView, or some diagram-related classes such as ConnectorAction, because they are not based on ModelElement or the store.

Here's a very simple example of a validation method applied to our Issue Tracking domain model. This method ensures that the names of IssueStates in the model are unique.

```
[ValidationState (ValidationState.Enabled)]
public partial class IssueStateModel
{
  [ValidationMethod(ValidationCategory.Menu)]
  private void ValidateStateNamesUnique(ValidationContext context)
  {
    Dictionary<string, IssueState> stateNames =
        new Dictionary<string, IssueState>();

    foreach (IssueStateElement element in this.Elements)
    {
      IssueState state = element as IssueState;
      if (state != null)
      {
        if (stateNames.ContainsKey(state.Name))
        {
          string description =
            String.Format(CultureInfo.CurrentCulture,
                        "State name '{0}' is used more than once.",
                        state.Name);
          context.LogError(description,
                        "Err 01",
                        state,
                        stateNames[state.Name]);
        }
        stateNames[state.Name] = state;
      }
    }
  }
}
```

First, a private method is declared in a partial class corresponding to one of the domain classes in our DSL.

> **▪▪ TIP** Use private methods for validation
>
> It is not strictly necessary to use a private method, but it saves the public API of your model from becoming overly cluttered with validation code.

This method simply takes a `ValidationContext`. It is the job of a validation method to use the context to log one or more errors, warnings, or informational messages if it finds something worth informing the user about.

The example method scans over the list of `IssueState` objects (via the base class `IssueStateElement`), storing their names in a `Dictionary`. If it finds a duplicate (the name is already in the `Dictionary`), then it reports an error. It does this by asking the context object to log the error for it. It could equally have asked for a warning or informational message. The context acts as a façade to the validation system so that different underlying error message objects can be used when running inside the Visual Studio IDE than are used in other environments. As well as an error message and a string code for the user to read and look up, `LogError` takes a list of `ModelElements`, which may be used to indicate to the end user where the error occurred, making it easier to fix the error at its source.

> **▪▪ TIP** Store validation messages in a resource file
>
> The code example presented here doesn't store the error message in a resource file because doing so makes the sample code harder to understand. However, in any production designer, such strings should always be externalized in a .NET resource file in order to make it possible to easily localize your designer.

You can imagine that the error code used here, `"Err 01"` could be part of a series, similar to the codes emitted from compilers. Unfortunately, these codes aren't visible anywhere in the error or output windows of Visual Studio after a validation has taken place, so they are only useful at present in scenarios with custom validation observers.

This method has been added to the `IssueStateModel` class, but it's actually validating a property (`Name`) of the `IssueState` class. This is a purely performance-driven choice. It would have been perfectly possible to place a validation method directly on `IssueState` and have it check that it had no peer instances with a clashing name. However, the scan of all `IssueStates` would then have been run as many times as there were instances, creating an algorithm with an $O(n^2)$ order. When you're writing code for a validation method, you are very focused on the individual element, and it's easy to forget that your code is part of a larger algorithm. This performance gain, however, like most of its kind, is a trade-off. Because this validation method is hosted on `IssueStateModel`, we can no longer choose to run validation across a subset of `IssueState` objects, for example, the set currently selected by the user. A good compromise is often to maintain central data structures holding data that can be referenced in validation methods and then to place the methods themselves on the individual model elements. In this case, this would involve maintaining a centralized dictionary of names of states and checking it from a validation method hosted on `IssueState`.

■ TIP Use efficient code in validation methods

Make validation method code efficient, especially for classes where there are likely to be a lot of instances in the model. This advice is especially relevant to validations marked as running on file open, because these will slow down the perceived startup time of your designer.

Enabling Validation

So how do validation methods get called? The DSL Tools validation framework includes a system that reflects over the methods on domain classes in the model looking for validation methods to call. It identifies these methods by combining two factors:

1. Each domain class that wishes to participate in validation must have the `ValidationState` custom attribute applied to it with the `Enabled` parameter.

```
[ValidationState(ValidationState.Enabled)]
partial class MyDomainClass
{
    ...
}
```

You can either add this attribute using the `CLRAttributes` property of a class in the DSL designer and have it generated into your code or, more simply, add it on the hand-written partial class that hosts the validation method.

2. Each validation method must be marked with a `ValidationMethod` custom attribute.

```
[ValidationMethod(ValidationCategory.Open|ValidationCategory.Save)]
```

In this case, you can see that the method is requesting that it is called at the time the designer opens model files and saves them.

This two-factor identification of methods is functionally redundant, because clearly all classes hosting validation methods can be identified when validation first occurs. However, to increase performance, especially on initial file open, this extra marker is used to reduce the set of classes that are scanned.

File open and file save are not the only times that a validation can be applied. Let's take a look at a further, richer example. When defining a state machine such as that for **Issues**, it can be useful to make sure that all of your **IssueStates** are reachable, that is, that they are either start states or they can be reached as the next state of some other state. This is quite easy to verify visually when the state diagram is small, but when things get complex, it can be easy to miss that a particular state only has outgoing rather than any incoming links. Here's the code for a validation method to do this:

```
[ValidationMethod(ValidationCategory.Menu)]
private void ValidateStatesReachable(ValidationContext context)
{
    List<IssueState> unvisitedStates = new List<IssueState>();
    // First locate the start state
    // Also make a complete set of states not yet visited
    IssueState startState = null;
    foreach (IssueState state in this.States)
    {
```

```
    if (state.Kind == StateKind.Start)
    {
      if (startState != null)
      {
        // Multiple start states is a different validation
        // and will confuse this rule.
        return;
      }
      startState = state;
    }

    unvisitedStates.Add(state);
  }
  if (startState == null)
  {
    context.LogError("Start state not specified.", "Err 02" );
    return;
  }

  // Beginning with the Start state, follow Next links.
  // At each state, add the Next links to the statesToVisit queue.
  // Remove every state we visit from unvisitedStates.
  // If we get to the end of the list and there are states
  // still unvisited, they must be unreachable.

  Queue<IssueState> statesToVisit = new Queue<IssueState>();
  statesToVisit.Enqueue(startState);

  while (statesToVisit.Count > 0)
  {
    IssueState visiting = statesToVisit.Dequeue();
    if (unvisitedStates.Contains(visiting))
    {
      unvisitedStates.Remove(visiting);
      foreach ( IssueState nextState in visiting.Next )
      {
        statesToVisit.Enqueue(nextState);
      }
    }
  }

  if (unvisitedStates.Count > 0)
  {
    IssueState[] unreachable = unvisitedStates.ToArray();
    context.LogWarning("States unreachable from start state",
                       "Err 03",
                       unreachable);
  }
}
```

You can see that this time, the attribute specifies a different time for the validation to run:

```
[ValidationMethod(ValidationCategory.Menu)]
```

Validations are put into categories that determine when they are evaluated. `ValidationCategory.Menu` indicates that the method should be run when a "Validate" context menu on the diagram surface or the model explorer is selected. The `ValidationCategory` enumeration literals can be combined using the logical OR operator to mix and match the times that a validation method is run. The `LogWarning()` method is used on the `ValidationContext` to provide a less urgent message to the end user.

The `ValidationContext` object provides the following public methods and properties:

```
public class ValidationContext
{
  public ValidationCategory Category { get; }

  public ReadOnlyCollection<string> CustomCategories { get; }

  public ReadOnlyCollection<ValidationMessage> CurrentViolations
                                              { get; }

  public ReadOnlyCollection<ModelElement> ValidationSubjects
                                              { get; }

  public ValidationMessage LogError(string description,
                          string code,
                          params ModelElement[] elements);

  public ValidationMessage LogMessage(string description,
                          string code,
                          params ModelElement[] elements);

  public ValidationMessage LogWarning(string description,
                          string code,
                          params ModelElement[] elements);
}
```

The `ValidationSubjects`, `Category`, and `CustomCategories` properties allow sophisticated validation methods to be written that vary their functionality based on the type of validation currently being requested and the exact set of elements being validated, for example, to check if the elements within a particular selection are uniquely named.

Invoking Validation

Having marked validation methods with the correct attribute, let's look in a little more detail at the mechanism by which they get called. A façade class called a `ValidatonController` is used to invoke validation methods. This façade is able to call the appropriate set of validation methods using the .NET reflection mechanism to look for the correct attributes and reflectively invoke the methods. We'll see more detail on the `ValidationController` shortly; however, in the typical case it is not necessary to use this class directly, because the DSL model and code generator will create a basic validation system for you.

In the DSL designer, under the Editor node of the DSL explorer window you'll find a "Validation" node, as shown in Figure 7-1.

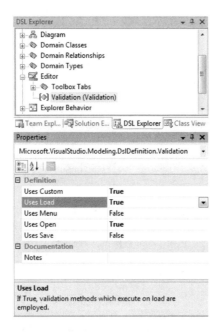

FIGURE 7-1: Setting values in the Validation node

This node controls generation of code to make calls to the validation framework in response to user actions, with each property causing validation methods with the matching `ValidationCategory` attribute to be called. The generated code is in the form of extra code in the file open and save mechanisms in the `DocData` class and an extra command in the `CommandSet` class to provide the "Validate" menu item. There is no requirement to use this facility to invoke validation in a designer; it is simply provided as a convenience. It's quite possible to set all of the properties of the "Validation" node in the DSL explorer to be *False* and then set up the validation infrastructure yourself. We'll see how to do that when we discuss using the infrastructure outside of the IDE a little later in the chapter.

Custom Validation Categories

You'll notice that there is a "Uses Custom" property on the "Validation" node. If Open, Save, or Menu are not suitable times to run your particular validation, then you might wish to run validation as part of some other custom code in your designer, perhaps as part of some larger custom command. The "Uses Custom" property is a marker to signal your intent to do this and generates just enough infrastructure code in your designer to make it easy.

Typically, you'd use custom validation categories when some set of validation functions are only true in the context of some specific operation. For example, imagine a database designer with a set of validations working at file open and save times and also checkable from a validate menu item. These validations check that the database model could generate a working database schema. However, perhaps this tool also has a second code generator to create a data access layer (DAL) targeting the schema. The DAL generator doesn't support arbitrary database schemas in its current version because it hasn't been coded to cope with large binary fields such as pictures, even though they form part of a perfectly valid database schema. Using custom validation groups, the tool authors can add a set of validation methods that disallow large binary fields. Then, when the DAL code generator is invoked, they can run both the regular validation methods and the custom set, ensuring that the model will generate a valid schema and a working DAL on top of it. However, users who never use the DAL generator aren't encumbered with validations that they have no interest in. If a tool had many different code generators (or other tool chains attached to it), it might have many sets of custom validation methods that might well overlap.

To see how to accomplish custom validation, let's take a look at the overall architecture of the validation framework in the DSL Tools in Figure 7-2. As you can see, the ValidationController is the main entry point for validation. To initiate validation, make a call to one of the overrides of either Validate() or ValidateCustom() on the controller. Validate() takes one of the ValidationCategory values, but ValidateCustom()takes one or more simple strings to denote a named grouping of validation methods, for instance, "MyValidations."

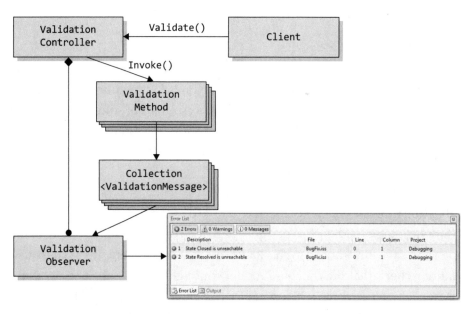

FIGURE 7-2: Architecture of the validation framework

Below you can see the set of overrides available for both types; the non-virtual methods are simply wrappers to call the matching virtual method. All methods return true if no validation messages have been logged.

```
public virtual bool Validate(IEnumerable<ModelElement> subjects,
                             ValidationCategory category);

public bool Validate(ModelElement subject, ValidationCategory category);

public bool Validate(Partition partition, ValidationCategory category);

public bool Validate(Store store, ValidationCategory category);

public virtual bool ValidateCustom(IEnumerable<ModelElement> subjects,
                                   params string[] customCategories);

public bool ValidateCustom(ModelElement subject,
                           params string[] customCategories);

public bool ValidateCustom(Partition partition,
                           params string[] customCategories);
```

```
public bool ValidateCustom(Store store,
                           params string[] customCategories);
```

You can choose to validate either a list or a single ModelElement, the entire content of a Partition or a complete Store.

When any of the properties of the validation node in the DSL explorer are set to true, a ValidationController object is generated as a member of your designer's DocData class along with a property called ValidationController used to access it.

Here, then, is an example of code in a custom command to initiate validation. Typically, you might manipulate the current UI selection to get a set of ModelElements to validate. In this example we've picked out any PresentationElements or ModelElements that are directly selected and asked for them to be validated using the two custom categories "Category1" and "Category2." Note how the standard CommandSet base class provides access to the current DocData and thus to the ValidationController in its CurrentData property:

```
internal partial class CommandSet
{
  internal void OnMenuCustomValidate(object sender, EventArgs e)
  {
    List<ModelElement> toValidate = new List<ModelElement>();
    foreach (object selected in this.CurrentSelection)
    {
      if (selected is PresentationElement)
      {
        toValidate.Add((selected as
                        PresentationElement).ModelElement);
      }
      else if (selected is ModelElement)
      {
        toValidate.Add(selected as ModelElement);
      }
    }
    if (toValidate.Count > 0)
    {
      this.CurrentData.ValidationController.ValidateCustom(
            toValidate,
            "Category1",
            "Category2");
    }
  }
}
```

We've already seen how to mark validation methods to run when a standard category is invoked using the ValidationMethod attribute. To mark them for invoking with a custom category, use the named parameter Custom on the ValidationMethod attribute:

```
[ValidationMethod(Custom="MyValidations")]
```

If needed, you can combine this with one or more of the standard categories:

```
[ValidationMethod(ValidationCategory.Menu, Custom="MyValidations")]
```

If you need to mark a validation method as being part of more than one custom category, then you can place multiple attributes on the method. It is worth noting that the reflective code for determining which methods are validation methods is set up to do efficient caching to minimize its performance impact, especially at designer startup time.

Inheriting Validation Behavior

By default, validation methods are inherited from their base classes when an inheritance hierarchy of domain classes is used in a model. This means that validation can be shared as common behavior, just as any other aspect of a base class. The behavior of the ValidationState attribute is, however, different. By default, it is not inherited and must be set as Enabled or Disabled on every class. It can, however, be forced to inherit its value using the special value Inherited.

```
[ValidationState (ValidationState.Inherited)]
public partial class SomeDerivedDomainClass
{
}
```

Validation Output

The output of validation is a collection of ValidationMessage objects that are sent to all of the ValidationObserver objects that the Validation-Controller knows about. By default, the generated designer code uses a Visual Studio–specific subclass, VsValidationController, and is set up with a single observer. The generated initialization code looks like this:

```
validationController =
    new VsValidationController(this.ServiceProvider);
errorListObserver =
    new ErrorListObserver(this.ServiceProvider);
validationController.AddObserver(this.errorListObserver);
```

You can add your own extra observers by deriving a class from `Validation-Observer` to send `ValidationMessages` to your own custom UI, logger, or database and then calling the `AddObserver()` method on the controller.

The `ErrorListObserver` class presents `ValidationMessages` that it receives in the Visual Studio error list window (Figure 7-3).

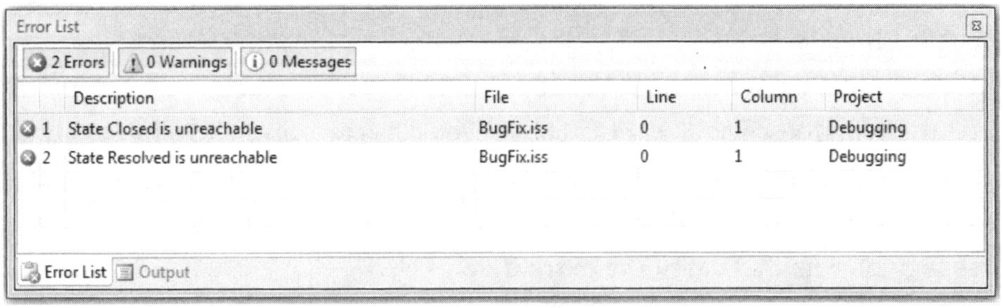

FIGURE 7-3: Validation messages displayed in the Visual Studio Error List Window

When the end user of the designer double-clicks on these messages, the selection in the designer is updated to reflect the `ModelElements` passed to the `LogError()` method, and the designer attempts to navigate its UI to make these elements visible.

Using Validation outside the IDE

It is very typical to want to use validation in a custom tool developed using the DSL Tools infrastructure. For example, in a command-line tool to transform model files, you might want to ensure that a model is well-formed before embarking on processing it. Happily, using validation in custom tools is very straightforward with the DSL Tools, although depending on your requirements you may need to write slightly more custom code than you do with validation in a designer.

The good news is that unless you have specifically hard-coded a dependency on Visual Studio, all of your validation methods should simply work both inside and outside of the IDE. However, you will have to set up the validation infrastructure of a `ValidationController`, associated `Validation-Context` and `ValidationObservers` yourself. Typically, you will simply instantiate and use the `ValidationController` base class. This will provide a basic `ValidationContext`, which creates simple `ValidationMessage` instances via its `LogError()` and related methods.

If, however, you need to pass richer information of some kind to your custom `ValidationObserver` when errors are raised, you'll need a custom `ValidationMessage` type and a way to construct it. Because the `Validation-Context` is a factory for `ValidationMessages`, a custom `ValidationContext` provides this facility. In turn, a `ValidationController` is a factory for `ValidationContext` objects, so you'll also need a custom `Validation-Controller`.

This is, in fact, what the `VsValidationController` that is used by default in designers does. The `ErrorListObserver` class requires extra information about the filename where the error was reported, so the controller creates a custom `VsValidationContext` to handle the creation of `TaskValidation-Message` objects that carry the extra data.

Validation Against External Data

Although the validation framework in the DSL Tools is tied to validating sets of `ModelElement`-derived objects as its subjects, it is also sometimes desirable to cross-validate these elements against external data sources.

For example, in the `IssueStateModel` designer, the connection to the external database is specified with the `ServerName` and `DatabaseName` properties on the `IssueStateModel` class. The following validation method checks that the connection is valid and available.

```
[ValidationMethod(ValidationCategory.Save | ValidationCategory.Menu)]
protected void ValidateDbConnection(ValidationContext context)
{
  bool ok = false;
  try
  {
    // IssueDBConnection is a specialized class
    // for talking to issue databases
    using (IssueDbConnection connection =
            new IssueDbConnection(this,
                this.ServerName,
                this.DatabaseName))
```

```
        {
           if (connection.Connection != null) ok = true;
        }
    }
    catch (System.Data.SqlClient.SqlException)
    {
    }
    if (!ok)
    {
        string description = String.Format(CultureInfo.CurrentCulture,
                "Failed to connect to database {0}/{1}.",
                this.ServerName,
                this.DatabaseName);
        context.LogError(description, "Err 04", this);
    }
}
```

This type of validation can be very valuable, especially before an operation that relies on external data, such as an import operation. However, it can also be troublesome. Here, the method is specified as running on load, save, and menu, which means that in order to save a model file when the database is unavailable, the user must wait for the network timeout of the database connection. In general, this type of validation is often best used from a custom command whose usage the end user expects to be coupled to the availability of the external data.

Hard Constraints in the DSL Tools

As we've seen by example, hard constraints are required less often than soft constraints. However, when author-specified hard constraints are required, they can be added by adding custom code to your designer. Because hard constraints are sometimes intimately connected to the user experience that would cause them to be broken, there is not a single standardized method to add them. Changes that would invalidate a hard constraint can often be disallowed at an API level by throwing an exception when some value changes in a model. We'll look at how to use one such change-handling mechanism, *rules*, shortly. Another store change-handling mechanism is to override the `OnXxxChanging()` method in the *value property handler* nested class for a given domain property. For example, if the string property `Name` on a domain class `NamedElement` can never have an empty value, the following code might be employed:

```csharp
/// <summary>
/// Add a hard constraint to NamedElement to prevent its
/// "Name" property from being empty.
/// </summary>
public partial class NamedElement
{
  /// <summary>
  /// Value handler for the NamedElement.Name domain property.
  /// </summary>
  internal sealed partial class NamePropertyHandler :
    DomainPropertyValueHandler<NamedElement,
                               global::System.String>
  {
    protected override void OnValueChanging(NamedElement element,
                                            string oldValue,
                                            string newValue)
    {
      if (!element.Store.InUndoRedoOrRollback)
      {
        if (string.IsNullOrEmpty(newValue))
        {
          throw new ArgumentOutOfRangeException("Name",
                  "Name cannot be empty or null.");
        }
      }
      base.OnValueChanging(element, oldValue, newValue);
    }
  }
}
```

Rules

Rules in the DSL Tools provide a versatile method of implementing behavior that is dependent on changes in a model; because they are based on model change, they can also be used as another method for implementing a type of constraint. A rule can be used either to raise an exception, disallowing an attempted change, or to propagate a change through the model, forcing other parts to conform to the change.

A rule can be associated with any domain class (including relationships and diagram elements). If any instance of that class changes, the rule executes, usually during the commit of the transaction in which the change occurred. Rules can be set to fire when a domain property changes, when an instance is added or deleted, and on several other conditions.

Let's look at a real-world example of a hard constraint and see how we would implement it with a rule.

Using the Class Design template supplied with the DSL Tools, it is quite straightforward to add a rule as a hard constraint to prevent cycles in generalization (or inheritance) from being created. Figure 7-4 is a snippet of the domain model for class design that shows the reflexive `Generalization` relationship on `ModelClass`.

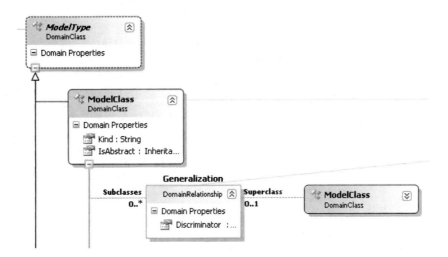

FIGURE 7-4: Snippet OF CLASS DESIGN domain model

The code to prevent creation of cyclical inheritance is an add rule on the domain relationship:

```
[RuleOn(typeof(Generalization), FireTime = TimeToFire.TopLevelCommit)]
internal sealed class CyclicInheritanceAddRule : AddRule
{
  public override void ElementAdded(ElementAddedEventArgs e)
  {
    string message = string.Empty;
    Generalization g = e.ModelElement as Generalization;
    if (g != null)
    {
      if (!CyclicInheritanceAddRule.
            TestValidInheritance(g.Subclass,
                                 g.Superclass,
                                 ref message))
      {
        throw new InvalidOperationException(message);
      }
```

```
      }
      base.ElementAdded(e);
  }

  internal static bool TestValidInheritance(
                          ModelClass sourceClass,
                          ModelClass targetClass,
                          ref string errorMessage)
  {
    if (sourceClass != null && targetClass != null)
    {
      if (object.Equals(sourceClass, targetClass))
      {
        errorMessage = "Reflexive inheritance detected.";
        return false;
      }

      ModelClass current = targetClass.Superclass;

      // Repeat until we detect an existing loop
      // or the root of the hierarchy.
      while (current != null && current != targetClass)
      {
        if (object.Equals(current, sourceClass))
        {
          errorMessage = "Inheritance loop detected.";
          return false;
        }
        current = current.Superclass;
      }
    }
    return true;
  }
}
```

This rule will cause attempts to add an invalid link instance to the model to fail. Note that we've broken out the logic of the test into a helper method to make clear which part is DSL infrastructure and which is core logic.

Remember that you need to register your rules in the DomainModel class:

```
public partial class ClassDiagramsDomainModel
{
  protected override Type[] GetCustomDomainModelTypes()
  {
    return new System.Type[] { typeof(CyclicInheritanceAddRule) };
  }
}
```

Putting Together Hard and Soft Constraints

When hard constraints are necessary in a designer, implementing them on their own using the techniques just described can lead to a suboptimal user experience that rather jarringly prevents users from performing an erroneous action rather than guiding them to perform a correct action. Let's continue the cyclic inheritance example and see how we can add some custom code to get a great user experience. You can find this complete worked example in the code download for Chapter 7 in a project called NoLoopClass.

First, let's think about what happens when the CyclicInheritanceAddRule raises its exception.

Attempts to create such links could be originated from several sources. Because inheritance is a relationship with multiplicity 0..1 at one end, code generation automatically provides an editing experience on that roleplayer type (ModelClass) in the properties window in the form of a drop-down selector. More typically, however, inheritance is set up using an inheritance connector tool on the toolbox that is driven from a ConnectionBuilder class and an associated ConnectAction-derived class. Finally, of course, links may be created as part of loading a model. Let's explore the experience for each of these in turn.

Selecting a ModelClass and clicking the drop-down button in its SuperClass property shows a list of all the other ModelClass elements in the store. Elements that would be invalid are presented in this list alongside all of the valid choices because there is no prescreening. If an element is chosen that fails the rule, an error dialog similar to the one shown in Figure 7-5 will be shown.

FIGURE 7-5: A basic error dialog from the
properties window

In itself, the message is not very informative, but clicking the "Details" button reveals the true error message, shown in Figure 7-6.

FIGURE 7-6: An expanded error dialog from the properties window

While this isn't a superb user experience, it does share a comon look and feel with other validation errors for properties, so we'll accept that and move on.

A similar experience is presented if you use the toolbox inheritance connector to create a looped inheritance. The cursor indicates that the choice is valid, but when the target is selected, the dialog shown in Figure 7-7 is presented.

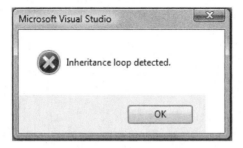

FIGURE 7-7: Drag-drop error dialog

At least this time the error message is presented directly; however, in the case of a drag-drop tool, it seems much more jarring. The typical experience for such tools is that they present a "No entry" sign for invalid choices when they are simply hovered over, before the user has even made a selection. This allows a much more exploratory style of user interaction. You'll see this type of interaction automatically supplied by the generated code for multiplicity constraints on relationships, so let's see how to improve the experience for our cyclical rule in this case.

A nested partial class has to be added to the designer:

```
public partial class GeneralizationConnectAction : ConnectAction
{
  private partial class GeneralizationConnectionType :
                          GeneralizationConnectionTypeBase
  {
    /// <summary>
    /// Helper method to skip from compartment
    /// shapes up to their parents
    /// </summary>
    /// <param name="shape"></param>
    /// <returns></returns>
    private static ShapeElement RemovePassThroughShapes
                              (ShapeElement shape)
    {
      if (shape is Compartment)
      {
        return shape.ParentShape;
      }
      SwimlaneShape swimlane = shape as SwimlaneShape;
      if (swimlane != null && swimlane.ForwardDragDropToParent)
      {
        return shape.ParentShape;
      }
      return shape;
    }

    /// <summary>
    /// Only allow connections that don't
    /// create a cycle in the inheritance chain.
    /// </summary>
    /// <param name="sourceShapeElement"></param>
    /// <param name="targetShapeElement"></param>
    /// <param name="connectionWarning"></param>
    /// <returns></returns>
    public override bool CanCreateConnection
            (ShapeElement sourceShapeElement,
             ShapeElement targetShapeElement,
             ref string connectionWarning)
    {
      ShapeElement sourceShape =
```

```
                        RemovePassThroughShapes(sourceShapeElement);
        ShapeElement targetShape =
                        RemovePassThroughShapes(targetShapeElement);

        if (sourceShape != null && targetShape != null)
        {
          ModelClass sourceClass = sourceShape.Subject
                              as ModelClass;
          ModelClass targetClass = targetShape.Subject
                              as ModelClass;
          if (!CyclicInheritanceAddRule.
              TestValidInheritance(sourceClass,
                              targetClass,
                              ref connectionWarning))
          {
            return false;
          }
        }
        // Fall through to the base test if
        // we haven't detected a cycle.
        return base.CanCreateConnection(sourceShapeElement,
                    targetShapeElement,
                    ref connectionWarning);
      }
    }
  }
```

This code overrides the CanCreateConnection() method in the double-derived GeneralizationConnectionType nested class within the GeneralizationConnectAction class. This method is called repeatedly as the mouse is moved over the design surface when the inheritance connection tool is selected. The ConnectAction-derived type effectively forms the handler for the modal interaction and the method allows or disallows potential connections for any pair of shapes. This code deals in the world of Shapes rather than raw ModelElements, but once the top-level shapes have been identified and their underlying model elements retrieved, it can make use of the same TestValidInheritance() method that the previously described rule uses, ensuring that the logic isn't duplicated. If the test fails, then the method simply returns false to indicate that the "No entry" message should be shown over the element currently under the mouse cursor. Additionally, if the reference parameter connectionWarning is set, then a tooltip will be shown that makes it very clear why this particular connection would not be acceptable.

The final case to examine is loading a model that already contains an instance of cyclical inheritance. Perhaps this model came from an earlier version of the tool that didn't have validation rules, or perhaps the XML was supplied from some other tool in a tool chain or was hand-edited. Whatever its source, the tool needs to decide on a strategy for handling such files. As the code stands, when an attempt is made to load an erroneous file, the rule will fire in the load transaction and the load will then fail, causing an error message similar to the one shown in Figure 7-8.

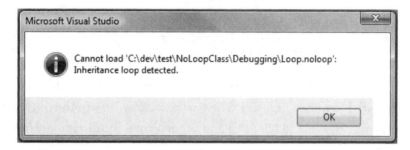

FIGURE 7-8: Error message shown when a load fails

This message presents the problem to the user but doesn't indicate any good way to fix the problem. They have no option but to choose "OK," at which point they will be returned to Visual Studio as though they had never asked to open the file. What's generally required is to point the user in the direction of fixing the problem; here, a decision has to be made. Can this violation be fixed using the modeling tool itself, or is it serious enough that the XML must be edited by hand to fix the problem? Typically, this comes down to one of two possibilities. First, is the presentation model of the designer capable of rendering the malformed model? In this case, the presentation doesn't care about cyclical loops, so the answer is yes. Second, does any of the other custom code in the designer make assumptions that this rule is an invariant? As you add code to your designer, it's very easy to start to assume that your own rules will not be broken. Indeed, if you are fairly confident that the rules are unlikely to change much, this may be a good, pragmatic approach to keeping your code free from reams of unnecessary precondition checks. However, it does tend to mean that you will have to intercept problems in malformed XML files before your designer is launched; custom code will likely crash otherwise. For example, you may have custom code in several places that walks the inheritance class hierarchy using a simple loop. If a file is loaded that contains a cycle, then this code will be stuck in an endless loop.

The starting point for handling either of these situations more gracefully is to make the rule class previously described initially disabled and only turn it on once the designer is fully running. This will allow you to handle the error yourself at a time of your choosing. To do this, modify the `RuleOn` attribute on the rule by adding the `InitiallyDisabled` parameter:

```
[RuleOn(typeof(Generalization),
        FireTime = TimeToFire.TopLevelCommit,
        InitiallyDisabled=true)]
```

You'll also then need to create a partial `DocData` class to switch the rule on after the initial load has finished. The `DocData` class lives in the `DslPackage` project. Typically, we add `DocData` and other Visual Studio integration customizations in new partial class files under a directory called `Shell` in the `DslPackage` project.

```
internal partial class NoLoopClassDocData : NoLoopClassDocDataBase
{
  protected override void Load(string fileName, bool isReload)
  {
    base.Load(fileName, isReload);
    RuleManager ruleManager = this.Store.RuleManager;
    ruleManager.EnableRule(
      typeof(CJKW.Examples.NoLoopClass.CyclicInheritanceAddRule));
  }
}
```

■ TIP Make DslPackage project a friend of Dsl project

You'll notice that this code in the `DslPackage` project is referring to the rule that is defined as being internal to the `Dsl` project. This wouldn't normally be allowed, but in order for the two packages to work together as one while still presenting an uncluttered public API, it is typical to make the `DslPackage` project a "friend" of the `Dsl` project. To do this, add an attribute like the following to your `Dsl` project's Properties\AssemblyInfo.cs file:

```
[assembly:
InternalsVisibleTo("CJKW.Examples.NoLoopClass.
DslPackage,
PublicKey=00240000048000009400000006020000002400005253413100
040000010001009b498f24fcd75c6a243ae1831202e2da959d2c51662c94
8c0491e96bb4e924522f583e5149366919102d3c7b2b64fe6e70c282b065
a99cd0a79f30ad02a12e266aa2375b0d912408ec11ea924c1c617d1cd7f0
1e8cf56943fef1227c6d02568767b21a669e12de23f89c350faf638c04fa
a20131e7b4436d9ffc31ccd0c0fe9d")]
```

You can retrieve the very unwieldy `PublicKey` entry for this attribute by using the `sn -Tp <assembly>` command on your designer's assemblies from a Visual Studio command prompt.

This code now lets diagrams containing cycles load happily, allowing them to be corrected using the modeling tool itself. However, there is now no indication that there is any problem to correct, so we need to introduce yet another mechanism to detect this error on loading—a validation method will prove very effective:

```
[ValidationState(ValidationState.Enabled)]
public partial class Generalization
{
  [ValidationMethod(ValidationCategories.Open)]
  private void ValidateNonCyclical(ValidationContext context)
  {
    string message=string.Empty;
    if (!CyclicInheritanceAddRule.
          TestValidInheritance(
              this.Subclass,
              this.Superclass,
              ref message))
    {
      context.LogError(message, "Err01", this);
    }
  }
}
```

Note again that this method reuses the same validation logic test, so only infrastructure has to be added. We now have a designer that does not allow cycles to be created via the properties window, does not allow them to be created via the toolbox, and provides a nice experience to prevent it. It also allows any cycles introduced in XML files to be easily corrected by raising errors that when double-clicked on take you directly to the erroneous link so you can delete it with the UI shown in the error list and on the design surface in Figure 7-9.

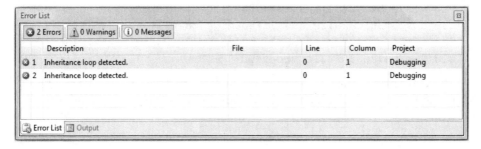

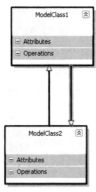

FIGURE 7-9: Validation errors exposed both in the error list and via selection on the diagram surface

What if we do have custom code in our designer that assumes that no cycles exist? We can switch the validation from using the "Open" category to the "Load" category instead. This will impose validation after the model file is loaded but before the diagram file is loaded. If that validation fails, then it will load the model file in the XML editor. It isn't a perfect user experience, because there is no way to relate the validations back to the exact failing line in the XML, but it is much nicer than the unfriendly experience we were originally given. Now the experience is as shown in Figure 7-10.

When "OK" is clicked, the XML editor opens (Figure 7-11).

In this example, we've seen how hard and soft constraints can be used together, driven by a single piece of easily maintainable constraint logic,

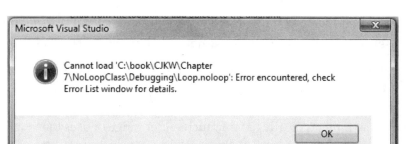

FIGURE 7-10: Initial error message when Load category validations fail

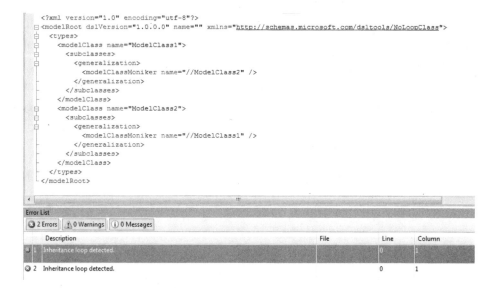

FIGURE 7-11: XML editor showing location of Load category validation failures

and how, when combined with some simple UI customizations, they can be used to craft a relatively sophisticated user experience.

SUMMARY

Constraints are a highly useful mechanism that allow the author of a designer to extend correctness-checking of their models far beyond the abstract and concrete syntax of their modeling language and into complex interrelationships between model data in much the same way that asserts can go beyond syntax checking in procedural code.

- Hard constraints are invariants across the model that prevent the user from ever getting into a situation where they are invalid.
- Soft constraints are checks against the model that can be evaluated for correctness at a point in time.

Soft constraints typically have a much wider range of uses than hard constraints due to the needs of end users to use designers in a flexible manner.

The DSL Tools include a validation framework; validation is the process of evaluating a soft constraint, and if it is invalid, creating a useful message for the user of the designer.

The DSL Tools automatically support performing validation on file open, file save, and by selecting a context menu. Custom invocation of constraints is also supported.

The DSL Tools support hard constraints, but typically a greater amount of custom code writing is required to provide a satisfactory user experience.

Hard and soft constraints can be combined using only a single piece of reusable logic to provide relatively sophisticated user experiences.

▪8▪

Generating Artifacts

Introduction

As we saw in Chapter 2, a key task that domain-specific languages can be used for is to generate code and other artifacts. In this chapter, we'll review styles of artifact generation that can be used with DSLs and then look at a specific worked example of using the default artifact generation system supplied with the DSL Tools. Then we'll review in detail the syntax used by that system. Finally, for those interested in deeply customizing the artifact generation system, we'll look at its implementation architecture and three customization examples.

Historically, artifact generation has typically been spoken of simply as code generation. The analogy is often drawn between the move from assembly code to high-level third-generation languages and the move from those languages to domain-specific languages. However, the current reality is a world where software-intensive systems are composed of a much more diverse group of artifacts than ever before, only some of which would traditionally be recognized as source code. Others might be configuration files, either for packaged applications or middleware, and others might be the content of databases, both schema and raw data.

Consequently, although DSLs can be seen as a more abstract form of source code in a compiler-like tool chain for custom code in a solution, they can also be used to configure applications and middleware as well as to initialize and populate databases. The benefits of using DSLs in these situations are also varied. In some cases, raising the level of abstraction is an adequate benefit itself. In others, complex relationships must be maintained, and a graphical DSL brings order and visual understanding to data that would otherwise need more expert interpretation even if the abstraction level is only minimally affected.

Nonetheless, it is still true that software systems are principally developed in a world where the simple text file dominates. Whether to store source code, or to persist a scripted means of setting up the data in some more complex piece of software or database, the ability for a set of text files to be managed together in a single version control system means that this style of working is unlikely to disappear for some time; indeed, the rise of XML as the de facto standard structured data representation language has probably ensured the endurance of this approach for the foreseeable future.

Consequently, the single most important transformation that can be applied to a DSL is to produce another artifact as a simple text file, whether that is source code, database script, or the persisted representation of a different DSL.

We can see this clearly at work in our example from Chapter 2. If we examine the scenarios around the `IssueProject` DSL, we can see that there are two primary pieces of artifact generation applied to it. First, code is generated to improve the domain-specific API for manipulating `Issue` data within the database. We'll look much more deeply at how that is achieved in this chapter. Second, scripts can be generated from this DSL to populate a production SQL Server Issues database with the settings described by a particular instance document. This is an interesting case, because the DSL also has custom code added to it to allow a database to be configured directly from the tool. Why would a DSL provide two such apparently redundant methods of working? The answer is that although the direct database connection-based tools are convenient for running a quick test or updating a staging version of a database, it is unlikely that the user of a DSL would have such direct access to a production server. It would also not be sensible for an organization to operate without a scripted install for a database that was important to its working practices in order to be able to build servers from scratch. The generation of such scripts for administrators thus complements convenience tools aimed more at developers, and is a useful pattern.

Artifact Generation Styles

Before looking in detail at the code generation associated with the Issue-Project DSL from Chapter 2, we'll review a range of techniques that can be used to generate artifacts and discuss their pros and cons.

Extensible Stylesheet Language Transformations

One method is to simply transform the persisted representation of a DSL directly to the desired artifact. Given that DSLs are typically persisted as XML, the natural tool for this task is XSLT. Here's a fragment of a class design DSL:

```
<class namespace="Foo" name="Bar" access="family">
  <property name="Height" type="System.String" access="public"
            modifier="sealed" />
</class>
```

Here's a matching XSLT stylesheet to transform the class design DSL into C# code:

```
<?xml version="1.0" encoding="UTF-8" ?>
<xsl:stylesheet version="1.0" xmlns:xsl="http://www.w3.org/1999/XSL/
Transform">
  <xsl:output method="text" />
  <xsl:template match="class">
    namespace <xsl:value-of select="@namespace"/>
    {
      <xsl:apply-templates select="@access"/> partial class
         <xsl:value-of select="@name"/>
      {
        <xsl:apply-templates select="property"/>
      }
    }
  </xsl:template>
  <xsl:template match="property" xml:space="preserve">
      private <xsl:value-of select="@type"/> _<xsl:value-of
select="translate(@name,
         'ABCDEFGHIGKLMNOPQRSTUVWXYZ',
         'abcdefghijklmnopqrstuvwxyz')"/>;
      <xsl:apply-templates select="@access"/> <xsl:value-of
select="@type"/> <xsl:value-of select="@name"/>
      {
        get
        {
          return _<xsl:value-of select="translate(@name,
          'ABCDEFGHIGKLMNOPQRSTUVWXYZ',
```

```
                  'abcdefghijklmnopqrstuvwxyz')"/>;
              }
              set
              {
                _<xsl:value-of select="translate(@name,
                 'ABCDEFGHIGKLMNOPQRSTUVWXYZ',
                 'abcdefghijklmnopqrstuvwxyz')"/> = value;
              }
          }
      </xsl:template>
      <xsl:template match="@access">
        <xsl:choose>
          <xsl:when xml:space="preserve"
  test="./parent::*[@access='public']">public</xsl:when>
          <xsl:when xml:space="preserve"
  test="./parent::*[@access='family']">protected</xsl:when>
          <xsl:when xml:space="preserve"
  test="./parent::*[@access='private']">private</xsl:when>
          <xsl:when xml:space="preserve"
  test="./parent::*[@access='assembly']">internal</xsl:when>
          <xsl:when xml:space="preserve"
  test="./parent::*[@access='familyandassembly']">protected internal</xsl:when>
        </xsl:choose>
      </xsl:template>
  </xsl:style>
```

And now here's the output generated from applying the stylesheet to the DSL fragment above:

```
namespace Foo
{
  internal partial class Bar
  {

    private System.String _height;
    public System.String Height
    {
      get
      {
        return _height;
      }
      set
      {
        _height = value;
      }
    }

  }
}
```

An important aspect of the DSL Tools is that the default serialization mechanism uses XML formats that are simply specified and as natural a match as possible to the domain model. The details of model serialization were discussed in Chapter 6. However, while these domain-specific, simple XML formats mean that XSLT-based transforms are certainly possible with the DSL Tools, there are several issues that make them far from ideal.

The first thing to note is that there's quite a lot more code generated than the terse DSL serialization syntax; this code generator has some decisions baked into it:

- It provides backing store for all properties using a field with the property name prefixed with an underscore and transformed to lowercase (we'd have liked to use camel-case[1] to follow .NET conventions, but the XSLT for camel-case is rather extensive for an example).
- It generates partial classes—a sensible extensibility plan for any C# code generator.
- It provides both a getter and a setter for each property.

The generator also has to transform from the language-agnostic accessibility level "assembly" in the DSL to the matching C# term "internal."

Even for this tiny fragment, it can be seen that the XSLT is nontrivial—largely because artifact generation tends to require rich string-manipulation features such as the lowercase function (and in a more realistic example, a camel-casing function). The XSLT template can be somewhat simplified using the Microsoft XSLT engine's ability to inject custom functions into a transform. If the type of the property were expressed in the XML as a cross-reference (especially one that doesn't use XML's rather weak built-in IDREF mechanism), or the DSL is spread across multiple files, the XSLT code rather quickly becomes relatively hard to create and maintain. One distinct advantage of XSLT transforms, however, is that they are extremely quick to run. The latest version of Visual Studio contains an XSLT debugger that can

---

1. Camel-casing is the practice of forming a compound word by joining a set of individual words together with each member except the first having its initial letter capitalized, for example, "thisIsTheHouseThatJackBuilt." In .NET coding, this casing style is typically used for method parameter names, local variables, and private member fields.

make working with such transforms much less of a chore than it used to be, although the pattern-matching style of design required to create XSLTs is not to every developer's taste.

> **■ TIP Use XSLT for model file migration**
>
> One use of XSLT that we've found very useful is migrating model files from one version of a DSL to another—typically, a lot of the XML hasn't changed, so you can make use of the identify transform mechanism in XSLT and simply specify transformations for the modified elements.

Making Use of the Domain-Specific API

When we create a language with the DSL Tools, we are automatically provided with a domain-specific API for manipulating instances of that language in memory. For example, in the `IssueProject` DSL, we are provided with an API that has a `ProjectDefinition` class, which has an `IssueDefiniton` sub-object and a `Milestones` collection where the details of individual `Milestones` can be accessed and manipulated.

Let's see how we can use that API as another way to generate artifacts.

First, we'd need to use the API to load the model into memory. As we saw in Chapter 3, model instances live inside a `Store` instance, so we need to initialize a store and then load the model. Here's some example code to do just that:

```
Store store = new Store(typeof(ProjectDefinitionDomainModel));
using (Transaction t =
        store.TransactionManager.BeginTransaction("Deserialize", true)
{
  ProjectDefinition def =
        ProjectDefinitionSerializationHelper.LoadModel(
          store,
          "MyProjectDefinition.pdef",
          null,
          null);
  t.Commit();
}
```

First, a `Store` object is initialized using the type of the `DomainModel` object that we want the store to be able to hold. A `Transaction` is then started in which to perform the load, because we will necessarily be modifying the `Store` as part of loading it with elements in the file. This is a transaction specifically for deserializing a model file, so we'll pass `true` to the `isSerializing` parameter. Finally, the static `ProjectDefinitionSerializationHelper` class is used to read the file according to the serialization scheme defined along with the language. This helper class is also generated as part of the API to a model in the `SerializationHelper.cs` file.

All well and good; we now hold a `ProjectDefinition` reference called "`def`," which we can use to examine the model we've loaded. Let's start by producing code for accessing specific issues in the issues database. In the database, the data representing an individual issue is normalized heavily, as is usual in a relational database application supporting online transactions. One of the key features supported by this normalization is the ability for an issue to have values for one or more custom fields defined on a per-project basis. This gives a degree of flexibility for customers of the database without the need to modify the database schema itself and is a common technique. The tables that support this are shown in Figure 8-1. The `Projects` table holds a row for every project that has been instantiated, and there is then a row in the `ProjectCustomFields` table for each custom field defined for that project. Each issue created (with its own row in the `Issues` table) can then have a set of rows in the `ProjectCustomFieldValues` table that specifies a value for each custom field.

This structure is efficient and flexible, but doesn't make for pleasant client programming. For example, to create an issue with values for all of its properties, both normal and custom, a record must be created in the `Issues` table, and then a further set of records must be created in the `CustomProperty Values` table, one for each custom value that is defined for the project.

If you are a developer trying to produce a program to manipulate `Issues` in the context of a specific project with a defined set of custom fields, then all of this database complexity is really implementation detail that you may well have little interest in. A rather basic example of an API that would be more productive for such a developer wishing to create an issue without regard to its implementation details might look like the following:

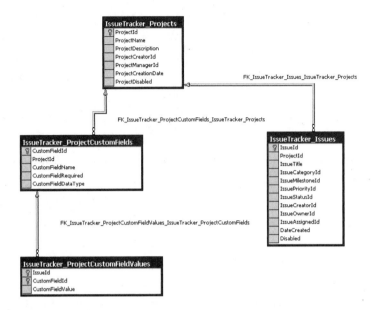

FIGURE 8-1: Database tables for an issue and its custom fields

```
public IssueId CreateIssue(ProjectMilestone issueMilestone,
    ProjectUser creator, ProjectUser initialOwner,
    string someCustomProperty, bool anotherCustomProperty)
{
    // Some implementation
}
```

To generate such a domain-specific API, we need to do two things.

- Write out code for the standardized part of the method that is tied to the fixed part of the database schema for Issue.
- Write out code for the part of the issue that is custom for this project.

To do the first of these, we'll effectively just be outputting a standard piece of text. For the second, we'll need to traverse the set of custom fields in the IssueDefinition part of the ProjectDefinition model. It's worth noting that to execute this task, the DSL author is focusing on two domain-specific APIs at the same time—first, there's the domain-specific API she is trying to generate code for that will be incorporated into some aspect of the running Issue Tracking application (or tools that interoperate with it); second, there's the domain-specific API onto the IssueProject DSL that she's using to read the model file. It is often the case, as it is here, that both these levels of modeling share many concepts (issues, in this small example) and consequently it's equally common to find yourself thinking about the wrong level from time to time. The need for tool authors to manage this mental complexity (which only expands when programs are part of an even longer tool chain across more levels of abstraction) seems to be inherent in the domain-specific development approach.

Here's some code that emits both the standardized and custom parts of the method for the `CreateIssue ( )` method just proposed, given a `ProjectDefinition`.

```
using System;
using StringHelpers;

public void GenerateCreateIssue(ProjectDefinition definition)
{
  Console.WriteLine("public IssueId CreateIssue(ProjectMilestone
issueMilestone,");
  Console.WriteLine("ProjectUser creator, ProjectUser initialOwner");
  foreach (CustomField field in
            definition.IssueDefinition.CustomFields)
  {
    Console.Write(", " + field.Type.FullName +
                  " " + StringHelper.ToCamelCase(field.Name));
  }
  Console.WriteLine(")");
  Console.WriteLine("{");
  Console.WriteLine("    // Some implementation");
  Console.WriteLine("};");
}
```

Thanks in large part to the model's domain-specific API, this is pretty straightforward code. It makes the assumption that the code generation output is going to be written to the console, but it could have equally been coded to direct the output to another device or direct it to some user-specified place. The structure of the code is very simple, and there is an easy-to-read match between collections in the data structures of the domain-specific API and iteration in the control logic. First the standard code is written out, and then one extra comma-preceded method parameter is written for each `CustomField` in the model. Finally, the standard close bracket and method body are written; of course, in reality, the method body would also be custom. Because this is just standard .NET code, it is trivial to invoke custom methods such as the helper to convert a string to its camel-cased equivalent. We've chosen to present this code in C#, but of course it would be very similarly expressed in any procedural language.

However, it does have some flaws. The code to be generated is hard-coded in individual strings. Where this is in large blocks, it's quite easy to read, as in the first two lines of the sample just presented. However, looking at the line inside the `foreach` loop, it is less easy to pick out what the shape of the generated code will be. Experience has shown that when editing a large volume of such code, the visual noise of the `Console.WriteLine` (or equivalent) statements, and especially the extra quotation marks and brackets, is very distracting and often leads to small errors. This is particularly the case when strings with quotation marks of their own are being generated, because a lot of character escaping may be necessary.

In normal coding projects, it would be a best practice to move strings into resource files, but in the case of code generation, it would actually detract seriously from the maintainability of the code. Generated code is not usually localized, and even well-chosen resource identifiers would make divining the code to be generated more troublesome from an inspection of the code. More importantly, when the code to be generated needs to change slightly, it is very frequently the case that the logic surrounding it must change as well. For example, if it was decided to switch the custom parameters to a `params` array of some standard `Parameter` type, then the logic in the line of code inside the `foreach` loop would be entirely incorrect; simply changing a resource would not be sufficient. Consequently, if this approach is taken to code generation, it is usually necessary to ship the source code of the generator in order to allow for small modifications to both logic and strings.

A variation on this approach is to use the *CodeDOM* instead of writing out the generated code directly. The CodeDOM is a standard facility of the .NET framework that allows an abstract syntax tree for languages to be created and then transformed into a variety of procedural language syntaxes. Here's a snippet of CodeDOM code to create the abstract syntax for a property definition:

```
CodeMemberProperty rootElement = new CodeMemberProperty();
rootElement.Name = "Height";
rootElement.Type = CodeTypeReference(typeof(float)));
```

```
rootElement.Attributes = MemberAttributes.Private;
rootElement.HasSet = false;
rootElement.HasGet = true;
rootElement.GetStatements.Add(
  new CodeMethodReturnStatement(
    new CodeFieldReferenceExpression(
      new CodeThisReferenceExpression(),
      "height")));
```

If translated to C#, this snippet would generate the following code:

```
private float Height
{
  get
  {
    return this.height;
  }
}
```

As you can see, this is extremely verbose code for such a simple piece of output. It has one great advantage—it can be transformed into C#, Visual Basic, or any other language for which a CodeDOM is implemented. However, that advantage is usually greatly outweighed by the fact that the code to create the abstract syntax tree is so far removed from the generated code that small modifications become relatively major pieces of work. While libraries can be built up to simplify this code, in practice we've found that the CodeDOM is only suitable for generating small quantities of code.

A Template-Based Approach

You'll notice that the way we worked out the preceding code generation schemes followed a simple process. We gave an example of the desired code to be generated and then worked out an algorithm to generate it. It turns out that there is a well-known pattern for code generation that supports this process more explicitly while still making best use of the domain-specific API—parameterized template-based generation. Here's a fragment of a parameterized template for generating the `CreateIssue` sample from the previous section:

```
public IssueId CreateIssue(ProjectMilestone issueMilestone,
 ProjectUser creator, ProjectUser initialOwner
<#
  foreach (CustomField field in
```

```
                    definition.IssueDefinition.CustomFields)
  {
#>,<#=field.Type.FullName#> <#=StringHelper.ToCamelCase(field.Name)#>
<# } #>
  )
  {
  // Some implementation
  }
```

The key to this technique is that the elements outside of the control markers (<# and #>) are rendered directly to the output file, whereas code within the markers is evaluated and used to add structure and dynamic behavior. Where control structures such as the foreach loop above surround non control areas, the enclosed non-control area is subject to the control structure, in this case repeating it once for each iteration of the loop.

This technique has been used very successfully in a wide range of products, perhaps most widely in Microsoft's dynamic website rendering technology, *Active Server Pages*. It is the principal artifact-generation technology used by the DSL Tools, and we refer to it as *text templating*.

You can see from the preceding example that the template is based on a copy of the expected output. Points of variability based on the underlying model are then analyzed, and control code is inserted at those points. Where the text is not dependent on the model, it is simply left as a copy of the desired code to be generated and so is very readable.

A great advantage of this technique is that it can be a gradual process. Minimal parameterization can occur to prove a generation strategy and then the fine detail can be parameterized later. For example, in the preceding code, all parameters could initially be given the generic type object as a first step on the way to parameterization.

The readability of this template is not perfect, but it is a lot closer to the desired output than any other methods we've looked at. Its readability can also be enhanced greatly by some judicious code colorization in an editor to separate the control code from the literal text.

■ TIP Get a template editor

You can download colorizing code editors for the DSL Tools' text templates from various third-party community sites.

Complex Relationships and Round-Tripping

The techniques for managing the transformation from a model to an artifact described so far all have one thing in common—they presuppose that the transformation is one of taking a model in a given state and producing the matching artifact. But what if a developer modifies the artifact after generation? Should the model synchronize to the changes in the generated artifact? What if a whole new version of the artifact is retrieved from source code control? What if the model is generative of two artifacts and one is changed in a way that clashes with the other? What if a part of an artifact that has no representation in a model is changed, such as a comment? These problems are often grouped together under the heading *round-tripping*.

The DSL Tools do not currently provide direct support for round-tripping, because the complexities typically outweigh the benefits for all but a small subset of DSLs. For the majority of DSLs, we've found that text templating is a more productive solution.

It is, however, possible to layer such round-tripping facilities on top of the domain-specific APIs that the DSL Tools provide if there is a requirement to do so. Indeed, the class designer and distributed system designers included in Visual Studio 2005 include just these types of features. Detailing exactly how to go about implementing similar facilities is well beyond the scope of this book, but let's look at what needs to be taken into account in order to assess the level of complexity for anyone wishing to tackle such a project.

Dealing with complex relationships between models and their artifacts typically involves further new techniques for artifact generation. The two key complexities we've identified here are

- Data loss—Models typically don't represent every detail of the generated artifact, as we've seen, with much of the fine detail being stored as boilerplate. If this boilerplate is changed in the artifacts, then the changes need to be preserved in some way.

- Ripple effects—When an artifact is changed, propagating that change to a model can make it necessary to regenerate other artifacts. It is very common for artifacts to support a much wider set of valid edits than would ever be generable from the model. If the changes in the original artifact didn't respect the exact schema of the model-artifact mapping, then the manually edited artifact and the newly generated ones may well clash.

Because there is a clear outcome, the artifact generation techniques presented previously can generally be initiated by a simple user command. The model is not changed, but the artifact is changed. However, complex generation typically requires more complex trigger points because the consequences of changes to models and artifacts can have ripple effects on others. This can mean reacting to changes in models and artifact files. There are standard .NET and Visual Studio SDK techniques for noticing changes in artifact files. Reacting to changes in models can be accomplished via the DSL Tools' APIs using a combination of *rules* and *events*. We'll look at both of these concepts and how they can be used in Chapter 10.

Regardless of the way in which the synchronization process is triggered, being able to react in detail to changes in artifacts requires that some kind of parser for each artifact type involved is available. This need not be a formal parser in all cases, because only some aspects of the artifact may be interesting to the tool chain. For example, perhaps a regular expression to pick out the names of C# classes and methods might be adequate for populating certain DSLs.

Once an artifact has been parsed, what kind of transformation should be performed and what other actions should be taken? In our previous example techniques, the one-way mapping between model and artifact has been specified using relatively simple code, either in XSLT or control structures in regular C# or in a template. Complex mappings between several models and artifacts are hard to specify in this manner unless there is no data loss allowed, which is rarely possible if artifact editing is permitted. Unfortunately, specifying two simple mappings, one for each direction, does not typically work well, because there is nowhere in the models to store the parts of the artifacts that were generated from boilerplate. The one-way techniques are a formal description of how to produce the desired output, given a set of input; for two-way mappings, a formal description of the *relationships* between the model and artifacts is more useful. This relationship description can then be processed to decide what actions to take when a change occurs at either end. To be successful with processing when it is an artifact that changes, it would generally be necessary to have a complete parse of the artifact.

A secondary question then arises: Should the artifact side of such a relationship description (or relationship model) be directly expressed in terms of the syntax of the artifact? This would entail the relationship model describing a transformation not just between two types of model, but between two modeling technologies as well—the parse trees of the artifact and the DSL model. Instead, it might be preferable to create a DSL model of the parse tree of the artifact and then describe the relationships using only model technology. However, creating such a model for every artifact type (as well as the parser) is an extra cost that must be borne.

In the wider modeling field, various approaches to transformation have been proposed, including the Query View Transformation (QVT) initiative from the Object Management Group. However, designing a workable transformation algorithm is unfortunately not the entirety of the problem. When such complex transformations are triggered in the context of a modern IDE, the issue of managing the end user's experience of the transformation must also be tackled.

If the effects of a transformation ripple out to artifacts that the user hasn't yet edited, it may be necessary to invoke source code control mechanisms to make the change. If the source code control operation is unsuccessful (perhaps another user has the file in question locked), then decisions must be taken. Should the artifact be left in an inconsistent state with the model and potentially other artifacts, or should the entire set of changes be abandoned? It seems we must implement an overarching transactional mechanism to handle such failure states gracefully and to enforce that synchronizations work as atomic operations.

We've seen that in many useful transformations, a lot of unchanging boilerplate code must be generated that is not affected by the content of models. Consequently, any transformation scheme has to be able to store and produce this type of output in artifacts. A synchronization scheme also needs to decide what happens when an end user makes a change in a part of an artifact that was generated from boilerplate rather than from a transform of a piece of model data. For example, imagine a template that generates C# classes but does not add the partial keyword to those classes. A user needs to add an extra piece to the class and so adds the partial keyword in to the generated class definition. The generative model has no place to store this extra information—it has no concept of classes being either partial or not. But the boilerplate in the transformation has not changed, and the next time the synchronization happens the user's change will be lost. If this type of change to generated files is to be respected, then there is a need to delineate the editing of boilerplate from the model-generated aspects. This can be achieved either by only allowing boilerplate to be edited inside a template that is part of the generation mechanism or by marking the output file with separate areas for generated code and user-editable boilerplate.

From this discussion, we can see that complex relationships will necessarily be significantly more costly to implement than one-way generation. What would be indicators that such an investment might be worthwhile in your DSL project? The Class Designer DSL that is part of Visual Studio 2005 was deemed to be such a case. Here the visual language is very, very close to the textual language. The two are so close, in fact, that they can almost be viewed as different syntaxes to the same parse trees (though one is a subset of the other, because class designer does not concern itself with method bodies). In fact, in the class designer, the two models are close enough that the class structure data itself is never persisted in model format. Instead, only the diagram layout is persisted and everything else is derived directly from the actual code every time the diagram is opened.

In similar cases where models and artifacts are either isomorphic or very close to being so, some of the issues outlined here become less problematic because there is either no data loss or a very well-defined loss between the two sides.

Given that we believe that the majority of DSLs are a significant abstraction over their generated artifacts, as opposed to being close to them, simple text templating is a natural choice as a default generation mechanism for the DSL Tools. As with most features of Visual Studio, a significant aim of the tool is to support high-productivity ways of working. We've found that template-based generation ideally supports such productivity through an iterative development process based on a gradual transition from static artifacts to parameterized templates.

We'll look in detail at the syntax for text templates a little later, but first let's investigate this development process from the standpoint of our CJKW developer, Devika, and see how she goes about iteratively developing generated code that meshes with the predominantly manually written code of the Issue Tracker application.

The Templatization Process

The last project that Devika worked on used the CJKW Issue Tracking system in the healthcare domain, installing a system to help a local hospital management authority manage bugs in its IT projects. On that project, Devika spent a good deal of time writing reports and utilities to work with the particular project customization scheme that the health authority used. This scheme added two custom fields to issues.

- `ClinicalSignoffRequired`—Whether this issue must be approved by the clinical supervision team before it is closed.
- `ClinicalSignoffReceived`—Whether this issue has received clinical supervision sign-off.

Because the authority was particularly concerned with the quality of clinical systems, an extra stage in the bug management process of all of the authority's IT projects existed. The project manager reviewed all incoming bugs and decided whether they needed sign-off from a team of clinicians assigned to consult on new IT projects. If they did, he set the `Clinical-Sign-offRequired` flag. If this flag was set, then the `ClinicalSignoff-Received` flag also had to be set before an issue could be closed. The authority found that this process brought user acceptance much closer to their development process and caught many problems before systems were deployed. They wanted a bug-tracking system to support this process and were delighted that CJKW's system could adapt so easily.

Consequently, while on the project, Devika added hand-customized extras to the Issue Tracker application's standard business logic and data access layer code to manipulate issues with these two extra fields seamlessly using the same code techniques that the application used to manage issues with the standard set of properties. This saved her lots of repetitive coding; as we've seen, in Issue Tracker, custom fields must normally be manipulated separately from the `Issues` they are associated with.

In the Issue Tracker business logic layer, classes are provided for each of the principal database entities. The classes allow instances of entities to be managed in memory. The data access layer provides methods to query for and retrieve collections of these entities. The entities can then be modified in memory and changes updated back to the database. In some cases, this is achieved using a Save() method on an entity class; in other cases, a specific data access layer method must be called to perform the update.

For example, here's the minimal code needed to create a new issue and its associated custom fields, and to save them to the database:

```
public static void
  CreateNewHealthIssue(string title,
                       int categoryId,
                       int milestoneId,
                       int priorityId,
                       int statusId,
                       int assignedUserId,
                       int ownerUserId,
                       string creatorName,
                       bool clinicalSignoffRequired)
{
  Issue newIssue = new Issue(0,
                             HealthProjectId,
                             title,
                             categoryId,
                             milestoneId,
                             priorityId,
                             statusId,
                             assignedUserId,
                             ownerUserId,
                             creatorName);
  newIssue.Save();
  CustomFieldCollection fields =
    CustomField.GetCustomFieldsByProjectId(HealthProjectId);

  foreach (CustomField field in fields)
  {
    if (field.Name == "ClinicalSignoffRequired")
    {
      field.Value = clinicalSignoffRequired.ToString();
    }
  }
  CustomField.SaveCustomFieldValues(newIssue.Id, fields);
}
```

In this code, a regular issue is being created, and then the clinical-Sign-OffRequired parameter's value is set. The data access layer provides methods to get the project's collection of CustomFields and then to set them back with actual values on a per Issue basis. The clinicalSignoff Received flag is ignored here, because it never makes sense to set it to anything but its default when an Issue is created. We'll see later how this different treatment of the two custom fields has consequences for code generation.

We've omitted the database transaction-handling code from this method in order to keep the size down, but clearly, because two database operations are being used to create a single logical item, it is important that either both succeed or that neither succeed.

Rather than just having a library of methods like the preceding code to manipulate `Issue` objects and their `CustomFields` together, Devika packaged up functionality similar to this in a custom derived `HealthIssue` class. This enabled her and her team to simply create and work with `HealthIssue` objects in exactly the same way that they would normally work with `Issue` objects and made the two custom fields indistinguishable from the other fields on `Issue`. Figure 8-2 shows these classes.

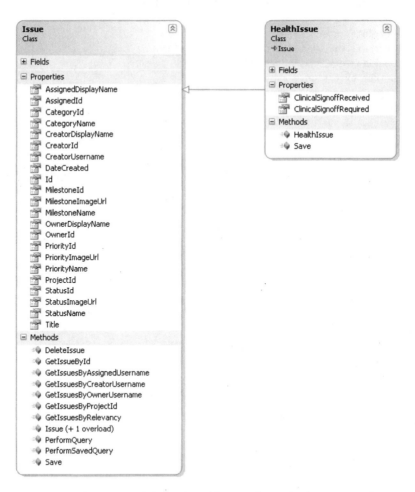

FIGURE 8-2: The Issue and derived HealthIssue classes in the Issue Tracker business logic layer

Now, as she works with Archie, Devika thinks that she can generalize the approach of creating custom derived entity classes for any deployment of the Issue Tracker application using some code generation from the domain-specific languages they are building.

The First Cut Template

Devika examines the code in her derived HealthIssue class and starts to think about parameterizing it. She'll obviously need to change the name— she can probably derive that from the name of the project that it's being used in. She'll need fields and matching properties to represent every custom field defined. That looks like everything to her, at first examination, so she goes ahead and creates her first text template:

```
<#@ template inherits=
  "Microsoft.VisualStudio.TextTemplating.VSHost.
    ModelingTextTransformation"#>
<#@ output extension=".cs" #>
<#@ issueProjectModel processor="IssueProjectsDirectiveProcessor"
  requires="fileName='HealthProject.issueProj'"
  provides="IssueProjectModel=IssueProjectModel" #>
using System;
using System.Collections.Generic;
using System.Text;

<#
foreach (Project project in this.IssueProjectModel.Projects)
{
#>
namespace <#= project.CodeGenNamespace #>
{
  public class <#= project.Name #>Issue :
    ASPNET.StarterKit.IssueTracker.BusinessLogicLayer.Issue
  {
<#
  // Generate member fields for custom fields
  foreach ( IssueField customField in project.CustomFields )
  {
#>
    private <#= FieldTypeToType(customField.Type) #>
      _<#=customField.Name.ToLower() #>;
<#
  }
#>

<#
  // Generate Properties for custom fields
```

```
   foreach ( IssueField customField in project.CustomFields )
   {
#>
   public <#= FieldTypeToType(customField.Type) #>
     <#= customField.Name #>
   {
     get { return _<#= customField.Name.ToLower() #>; }
     set { _<#= customField.Name.ToLower() #> = value; }
   }
<#
   }
#>
<#
}
#>
   }
}
<#+

#region Helper methods for code generation
private static string FieldTypeToType (FieldType modelType)
{
  switch (modelType)
  {
    case FieldType.Boolean : return "bool";
    case FieldType.String: return "string";
    case FieldType.Float: return "float";
    case FieldType.Double: return "double";
    case FieldType.Int32: return "int";
    case FieldType.Int16: return "short";
    default: return "string";
  }
}
#endregion

#>
```

This template starts with some directives; these are the three lines beginning with the delimiter "<#@." Directives provide processing instructions to the underlying engine that executes text templates, and this template uses three.

```
<#@ template inherits=
  "Microsoft.VisualStudio.TextTemplating.VSHost.
  ModelingTextTransformation"#>
```

The template directive specifies general processing options for a text template. An individual template can broadly be thought of as a class with the usual .NET characteristics of properties, fields, and methods, and this directive is used here to specify that this template inherits from a standard class provided by the DSL Tools for building text templates that access model files.

```
<#@ output extension=".cs" #>
```

The output directive specifies the type of file that the text template will produce—here, it's producing a C# file.

```
<#@ issueProjectModel processor="IssueProjectsDirectiveProcessor"
  requires="fileName='HealthProject.issueProj'"
  provides="IssueProjectModel=IssueProjectModel" #>
```

The issueProjectModel directive is specific to templates that work with the model files produced by the IssueProject designer. Here, it specifies that the "HealthProject.issueProj" model should be loaded into the member variable "IssueProjectModel" within this template.

One point to note here is that this use of the directive ties the template file to a particular model instance. We'll see techniques later in the chapter to allow the logic of a template to be split into multiple files to avoid this pitfall.

Next come some using statements taken directly from the example code, followed by the following control statement:

```
<#
foreach (Project project in this.IssueProjectModel.Projects)
{
#>
```

The "<# ... #>" delimiters denote a control block whose content is used to control the flow of processing of the template rather than being written as output of the template. In this case, a foreach loop is being initiated. Everything in the template following this block will be repeated for each iteration of the loop until a matching control block with the closing brace of the loop is encountered, thus:

```
<#
}
#>
```

Here the loop is being controlled by the set of `Projects` read in from the model file and exposed via the property `IssueProjectModel,` which was added with the `issueProjectModel` directive described earlier. The local variable "`project`" is now available to all control code nested within this structure, just as if all of the control code had been written in a single method in a regular piece of C# code.

> ### ■. TIP Use C# or Visual Basic in templates
>
> Template logic isn't tied to C#; if you're more comfortable with Visual Basic, then you can use that for the control logic in your templates.

Next, the `namespace` for the generated code is written out, followed by a class declaration for the new custom derived `Issue` type. The name of the class is generated using another type of control block called an expression block, delimited with "`<#= … #>.`" This type of control block evaluates the expression it contains and converts the result to a string that it writes directly to the output of the template. Here, the name of the `Project` being processed is being catenated with the word "Issue."

To generate both a C# field and a matching property for each defined custom field of the project, the same nested loop is then used twice in succession within control blocks to loop over the `CustomFields` collection on the `Project`. To calculate the C# type that must be used for each of the values of the `FieldType` enumeration used in the model, a switch statement is the obvious choice. However, repeating this switch statement every time it is needed would be cumbersome. What is needed is to encapsulate this small piece of reusable code within a method. The expression block

```
<#= FieldTypeToType(customField.Type) #>
```

is used in several places to emit the correct type into the template output. This method is defined at the end of the template file in a further kind of block called a *class feature block*.

A class feature block is delimited with "`<#+ … #>.`" Class feature blocks can best be explained by saying that they allow you to add extra methods to the template, just as if the template were a C# class. In fact, it allows any valid .NET class members to be added to the template, such as fields, properties, or even nested classes.

```
<#+
#region Helper methods for code generation
private static string FieldTypeToType (FieldType modelType)
{
    ...
}
#endregion

#>
```

Devika saves the template and sets the "Custom Tool" property on the template file to be "TextTemplatingFileGenerator."

This custom tool is provided with the DSL Tools and instructs Visual Studio to process the template file using the text templating engine, adding the template output as a subordinate file nested under the template itself.

Devika then picks "Run Custom Tool" from the context menu on the template and observes the results. A new node appears in the solution explorer underneath the template containing the template output.

Looking at the code, Devika realizes she can generate more than a simple derived class with fields and properties. She needs a custom constructor and a version of the Save() method that actually updates the database with her custom fields. She also wants to allow custom fields that have their AlwaysRequired flag set to *False* to be represented by C# 2.0 nullable[2] values so there is always a value available to represent "unspecified." She updates her template to be as follows:

```
<#@ template inherits="Microsoft.VisualStudio.TextTemplating.VSHost.
  ModelingTextTransformation" debug="true"#>
<#@ output extension=".cs" #>
<#@ IssueProject processor="IssueProjectDirectiveProcessor"
  requires="fileName='Ch8.1.issueproj'" #>
using System;
using System.Collections.Generic;
using System.Text;

<#
```

---

2. Nullable types are a facility provided in the C# 2.0 language that allows scalar value types to additionally hold the special value NULL as well as their natural set of values. For example, a Nullable <short> can contain the value NULL as well as -32768 to 32767.

```
foreach (Project project in this.IssueProjectModel.Projects)
{
#>
namespace <#= project.CodeGenNamespace #>
{
  public class <#= project.Name #>Issue :
    ASPNET.StarterKit.IssueTracker.BusinessLogicLayer.Issue
  {
<#
  // Generate member fields for custom fields
  foreach ( IssueField customField in project.CustomFields )
  {
#>
    private <#= GetFieldType(customField) #>
           _<#=customField.Name.ToLower() #>;
<#
  }
#>


<#
  // Generate Properties for custom fields
  foreach ( IssueField customField in project.CustomFields )
  {
#>
    public <#= GetFieldType(customField) #> <#= customField.Name #>
    {
      get { return _<#= customField.Name.ToLower() #>; }
      set { _<#= customField.Name.ToLower() #> = value; }
    }
<#
  }
#>

    public new bool Save()
    {
      // Save the standard Issue part
      base.Save();

      // Save the custom fields for the issue.
      CustomFieldCollection fields =
        CustomField.GetCustomFieldsByProjectId(ProjectId);

      foreach (CustomField field in fields)
      {
<#
  foreach ( IssueField customField in project.CustomFields )
  {
#>
        if (StringComparer.Ordinal.Compare(field.Name,
            "<#= customField.Name #>") == 0)
```

```
            {
<#
      if (!customField.AlwaysRequired ||
            customField.Type == FieldType.String)
      {
#>
            if (this.<#= customField.Name #> != null)
             {
<#
      this.PushIndent("        ");
      }
#>
                field.Value = this.<#= customField.Name #>;
                continue;
             }
<#
      if (!customField.AlwaysRequired ||
            customField.Type == FieldType.String)
      {
        this.PopIndent();
#>
         }
<#
      }
    }
#>
        }
        CustomField.SaveCustomFieldValues(this.Id, fields);

    }

    public <#= project.Name #>Issue( int id,
                                     int projectId,
                                     string title,
                                     int categoryId,
                                     int milestoneId,
                                     int priorityId,
                                     int statusId,
                                     int assignedId,
                                     int ownerId,
                                     string creatorUsername<#
    // Add extra parameters
    foreach ( IssueField customField in project.CustomFields )
    {
#>,
                                     <#= FieldTypeToType(customField.Type) #>
                                       <#= customField.Name.ToLower() #><#
    }
#>
                                   )
```

```
        : base(id, projectId, title, categoryId, milestoneId,
             priorityId, statusId, assignedId, ownerId, creatorUsername)
    {
<#
  // Populate member fields
  foreach ( IssueField customField in project.CustomFields )
  {
#>
      _<#= customField.Name.ToLower() #> =
        <#= customField.Name.ToLower() #>;
<#
  }
#>
    }


<#
  // Close the class and namespace
#>
  }
}
<#
}
#>


<#+
#region Helper methods for code generation
private static string FieldTypeToType (FieldType modelType)
{
  switch (modelType)
  {
    case FieldType.Boolean : return "bool";
    case FieldType.String: return "string";
    case FieldType.Float: return "float";
    case FieldType.Double: return "double";
    case FieldType.Int32: return "int";
    case FieldType.Int16: return "short";
    default: return "string";
  }
}

private static string GetFieldType(IssueField field)
{
  return FieldTypeToType(field.Type) +
          ((field.AlwaysRequired ||
              field.Type == FieldType.String) ? string.Empty : "?");
}
#endregion
#>
```

Note: We've again taken the liberty of omitting database transaction code for the sake of brevity.

Devika now has a template that adds a custom constructor and `Save()` method to her specialized `Issue` class. She regenerates the template output once more with the Health model and inspects the code. Here's the output:

```
using System;
using System.Collections.Generic;
using System.Text;

namespace Healthcare.IssueTracker.BusinessLogicLayer
{
  public class HealthcareProjectIssue :
                ASPNET.StarterKit.IssueTracker.BusinessLogicLayer.Issue
  {
    private bool _clinicalsignoffrequired;
    private bool? _clinicalsignoffreceived;

    public bool ClinicalSignoffRequired
    {
      get { return _clinicalsignoffrequired; }
      set { _clinicalsignoffrequired = value; }
    }
    public bool? ClinicalSignoffReceived
    {
      get { return _clinicalsignoffreceived; }
      set { _clinicalsignoffreceived = value; }
    }

    public new bool Save()
    {
      // Save the standard Issue part
      base.Save();

      // Save the custom fields for the issue.
      CustomFieldCollection fields =
        CustomField.GetCustomFieldsByProjectId(ProjectId);

      foreach (CustomField field in fields)
      {
        if (StringComparer.Ordinal.Compare(field.Name,
            "ClinicalSignoffRequired") == 0)
        {
          field.Value = this.ClinicalSignoffRequired;
          continue;
        }

        if (StringComparer.Ordinal.Compare(field.Name,
```

```
                "ClinicalSignoffReceived") == 0)
    {
      if (this.ClinicalSignoffReceived != null)
      {
        field.Value = this.ClinicalSignoffReceived;
        continue;
      }
    }
  }
  CustomField.SaveCustomFieldValues(this.Id, fields);

}

public HealthcareProjectIssue (int id,
                               int projectId,
                               string title,
                               int categoryId,
                               int milestoneId,
                               int priorityId,
                               int statusId,
                               int assignedId,
                               int ownerId,
                               string creatorUsername,
                               bool clinicalsignoffrequired,
                               bool clinicalsignoffreceived
                               )
      : base(id, projectId, title, categoryId, milestoneId,
             priorityId, statusId, assignedId, ownerId,
             creatorUsername)
  {
    _clinicalsignoffrequired = clinicalsignoffrequired;
    _clinicalsignoffreceived = clinicalsignoffreceived;
  }
 }
}
```

Note that the optional ClinicalSignoffReceived field is now stored using a Nullable<bool> using the bool? syntax. This has been accomplished by adding a richer utility method for property type creation. Also, in the Save() method, the optional field's value is only written to the database if it is non-null.

There also is an extra level of indenting here for the optional field's database transfer. This is accomplished using the PushIndent()/PopIndent() template methods in the case where the extra if statement is generated.

Devika now takes a moment to compare her generated code with the code she'd previously hand-written.

Generation-Specific Model Data

Apart from a few coding standards and commenting issues that she makes a mental note to address later, Devika finds two main functional differences.

- In the hand-written code, the second custom field, `Clinical-SignoffReceived,` is not a parameter to the constructor. Its initial value is always `false` because sign-off is never received until an issue has been in existence for some time.
- The first custom field, `ClinicalSignoffRequired` is initialized to the database in the `Save()` method even if its value is `false`, which the database would return as a default in any case. This is creating an unnecessary round-trip to the database in many cases.

Devika decides that the second issue can wait until they have some performance data from the application, because she doesn't want to optimize prematurely. However, she knows that the first problem is more serious, because it could lead to bugs where developers construct an issue that is instantly signed off and thus misses out an important stage in the client's workflow. She goes to talk to her architect, Archie, and together they realize that they need to add some code generation-specific data to the `IssueProject` model to denote whether custom fields should be initialized in constructors. Archie and Devika are discovering a common pattern here. When you want to generate real artifacts that are complete and don't require amending by humans to be put into production, you often need to add rather detailed model information that is specific to your code generation scenario. In this case, Archie and Devika agree to just add an `IsConstructorParameter` to the `IssueField` domain class.

> ■ **TIP** Consider separating domain data from artifact generation data
>
> There's a balance to be struck here. If too much code generation-specific information is visible front and center in the model, it can make it harder for domain experts to digest and work with models. At the opposite extreme, a specific, separate code generation model

> can be created that merely references the "pure" domain model. In the typical case where only one set of artifacts is being generated from a model, we've found that a separate model is overkill, although we have sometimes moved code generation data into child domain classes of the ones that hold the "pure" domain model.

Now that Devika has more data to work with, she amends the constructor generation part of her template:

```
public <#= project.Name #>Issue (int id,
                                 int projectId,
                                 string title,
                                 int categoryId,
                                 int milestoneId,
                                 int priorityId,
                                 int statusId,
                                 int assignedId,
                                 int ownerId,
                                 string creatorUsername<#
    // Add extra parameters
    foreach ( IssueField customField in project.CustomFields )
    {
      if (customField.IsConstructorParameter)
      {
#>,
                                 <#= FieldTypeToType(customField.Type) #>
                                   <#= customField.Name.ToLower() #><#
      }
    }
#>
                                )
        : base(id, projectId, title, categoryId, milestoneId,
                priorityId, statusId, assignedId,
                ownerId, creatorUsername)
    {
<#
  // Populate member fields
  foreach ( IssueField customField in project.CustomFields )
  {
    if (customField.IsConstructorParameter)
    {
#>
  _<#= customField.Name.ToLower() #> =
    <#= customField.Name.ToLower() #>;
<#
    }
```

```
        else // Is not a constructor parameter, use the default.
        {
#>
    _<#= customField.Name.ToLower() #> =
        <#= customField.InitialValue #>;
<#
        }
    }
#>
    }
```

Devika flips the **IsConstructorParameter** property of the **Clinical-SignoffReceived IssueField** in her Health model, regenerates the template output, and gets code that is functionally identical to her hand-written code.

You can see that Devika's process of iterating on the template is enabling her to gradually move from a minimal generation experience to a richer, more mature one. In practice, such iterations may also be staged across releases into production of a DSL, gradually adding further parameterization to make using the model more valuable and requiring less extra code to be hand-written.

Starting to Build a Library

To start testing her template code more thoroughly, Devika runs it against a whole batch of `IssueProject` model files that she and Archie have been working on. She notices that she's copying and changing her template every time she uses a different model file, which doesn't seem right to her. She has a look at some of the DSL Tools' standard templates and sees that they typically use just a short template that simply specifies the model file to be loaded and then use an `include` directive to pull in the standard part of the template. She reworks her template into two files and checks the standard part into the `IssueProject` Visual Studio project. Here's what her header template now looks like:

```
<#@ issueProjectModel processor="IssueProjectsDirectiveProcessor"
    requires="fileName='HealthProject.issueProj'"
    provides="IssueProjectModel=IssueProjectModel" #>
<#@ include file="GenCustomIssue.tt" #>
```

The `include` directive simply inserts the contents of another template file at the point where it is located in the file. Devika's included template,

"GenCustomIssue.tt," is simply a copy of her previous template with the issueProjectModel directive removed—everything else is standard, regardless of the model used. It does occur to Devika that if she needs to reuse her FieldTypeToType() method from another template that also deals with custom fields, then she could split the class feature block it lives in into its own include file and gradually start to build up a library of useful functions. All in all, Devika feels she's done a good day's work.

In this section, we've seen Devika starting from an existing artifact, adding some parameterization, and getting a working template. She then added more control structures to the IssueProject DSL definition and data to drive those structures in order to get a more refined artifact that more closely matched her needs. She ended up generating code that was every bit as clean and usable as hand-written code. Finally, she turned her code into a reusable library piece that could be included in any Visual Studio project using the IssueProject DSL.

Syntax of a Text Template

In the previous example, we watched Devika use several of the features of the text templating system; let's look at the whole feature set a bit more closely.

Directives

Directives have the following syntax:

```
<#@ directiveName parameter="Value" parameter2="Value2" #>
```

Directives provide instructions to the templating engine and come in two flavors, built-in and custom. The built-in directive types are described next.

Template Directive

```
<#@ template inherits="MyNamespace.MyBaseClass" language="C#"
  culture="en-US" debug="false" hostspecific="false" #>
```

The template directive specifies general transformation options for this text template.

The `inherits` parameter specifies the base class to use for the class representing the template. The default is `Microsoft.VisualStudio.Text Templating.TextTransformation`. A custom base class `Microsoft.Visual-Studio.TextTemplating.VSHost.ModelingTextTransformation` is provided with the DSL Tools that works together with custom directives to make it easy to read in and process model files. Custom base classes must themselves ultimately be derived from `Microsoft.VisualStudio.TextTemplating.TextTransformation`.

The `language` parameter specifies which programming language is used in code inside control blocks. The supported languages are `"VB"` and `"C#"`, where `"VB"` denotes Visual Basic.NET. The default is `"C#"`. It's important to note that the language used in control blocks has no impact whatsoever on the language of any code generated by the template. Visual Basic control code can be used to generate C# (or indeed any) output and vice versa.

The `culture` parameter specifies which .NET culture is used to format the values evaluated from expression control blocks. The standard .NET "xx-XX" specifier must be used, for example, "en-GB" for British English.

The `debug` parameter allows text templates to be debugged while under development. Under the covers, the code within the control blocks is consolidated into a class that is compiled and executed. The debug parameter places the generated code in a file on disk rather than working wholly in memory. We'll see more of the execution architecture of the text templating engine later on.

■ TIP Debug code can fill up your temp directory

This debug code can be found in the logged-in user's temporary directory and will not be deleted by the text templating system. When the debug flag is used repeatedly on a large set of templates, the `temp` directory can quickly fill up with these files; this can slow down some operations in Windows.

The `hostspecific` parameter causes the template to have a `Host` property added to it that can be accessed from template control code. This `Host` property is a reference back to the application hosting the text transformation engine and is used in specialist scenarios where the engine itself is being reused. We'll look at the architecture of the text transformation system at the end of the chapter. In typical uses of the DSL Tools, this parameter would never be set to true.

Output Directive

```
<#@ output extension=".cs" encoding="utf-8"#>
```

The output directive specifies the style of output of the template. Both the file extension (including its "." prefix) and the character encoding of the output file can be specified. Specifying the character encoding in the output directive will guarantee the encoding of the output over and above any other factors that might otherwise influence it, such as the encoding of processed model files. The default encoding is UTF-16.

Assembly Directive

```
<#@ assembly name="System.Drawing.dll" #>
```

The assembly directive allows control code in a template to use classes from another assembly. It is the direct equivalent of adding a reference to an assembly to a Visual Studio project. For example, if you wanted to construct a bitmap on the fly and then emit a base 64 encoded representation of that bitmap into a resource file, then you'd need to add an assembly reference to System.Drawing. The assemblies System.dll and mscorlib.dll are implicitly included by the engine and never need to be specified.

Import Directive

```
<#@ import namespace="System.Collections.Generic" #>
```

The import directive allows control code in a template to reference types without fully qualifying their names. It is the direct equivalent of a using statement in C# or an import statement in Visual Basic. This shouldn't be confused with simply adding using statements to the boiler-plate of the template if you happen to be generating C# code, as in our example.

Include Directive

```
<#@ include file="FileToInclude.tt" #>
```

The include directive allows a text template to be broken down into multiple files. The content of the included file is inserted into the template exactly at the same point in the template file where the directive is itself located. The search path for include files starts next to the top-level template that is being transformed. From then on, the path depends on the file extension of the template. The registry key HKEY_LOCAL_MACHINE\SOFTWARE\Microsoft\ VisualStudio\8.0\TextTemplating\IncludeFolders\ <FileExtension> contains a list of text values named Include0 to Include<N> that specify the paths to search when templates are run inside Visual Studio.

Custom Directives

Custom directives are the route for DSL authors to add their own code into the text templating process. They typically add .NET members to the template, often to enable the template code to access external data such as model files. In the DSL Tools, custom directives are usually associated with a particular DSL designer. Their supporting code is called a directive processor, which is created as part of the DSL solution. Directive processors are small code plug-ins that specify a named set of directives that they handle and the parameters that they can process. Here's an example of a custom directive:

```
<#@ issueProjectModel processor="IssueProjectsDirectiveProcessor"
   requires="fileName='HealthProject.issueProj'"
   provides=IssueProjectModel=IssueProjectModel" #>
```

This custom directive causes the template to load the "HealthProject. issueProj" model file and emits a .NET property into the template called IssueProjectModel that references the root of that model file in memory.

This directive uses a special pattern of syntax called the *Requires/Provides* pattern. It's a rather clumsy syntax, but it allows a lot of richness to be packed into a single line directive. Let's examine this directive piece by piece.

```
<#@ issueProjectModel processor="IssueProjectsDirectiveProcessor"
```

The text templating engine finds a directive processor as specified by the `processor` argument and enquires if it supports the named directive. Directive processors are free to support as many named directives as they choose, and directive names only have to be unique within a particular directive processor. Directive processors are registered with Visual Studio using the registry, and we'll see more of them later in the chapter.

```
requires="fileName='HealthProject.issueProjects'"
```

The `requires` parameter specifies a list of named sub-parameters that this processor requires to complete its processing, and optionally, their values. The list is semicolon-separated within the double-quotation marks of the whole `requires` parameter, and sub-parameter values are enclosed by single quotation marks. Here's a more complex example:

```
requires="subParam1;subParam2='Value2';subparam3='Value3'"
```

If, as in the first sub-parameter of this second example, the value of the parameter is not specified, then Visual Studio (or whatever process is hosting the text templating engine) is asked to try to find an appropriate value for the parameter for this specific instance of the directive. Unfortunately, Visual Studio does not currently have a general mechanism for supplying such values, so this facility is of very limited use.

```
provides="IssueProjectModel=IssueProjectModel"
```

The `provides` parameter specifies a list of named sub-parameters that the directive processor will emit as named elements into the template for use by control code. Once again, this is a semicolon-delimited list, but in this case the values of the sub-parameters are not enclosed in single quotes. The sub-parameter names specify default names for elements emitted into the template by the directive processor, and their optional values specify that the template author would like to substitute a different name instead of that default. In fact, the entire `provides` parameter is entirely optional, because defaults will be used if it is not supplied. However, it is often included in templates purely as documentation to readers of templates about the elements they can expect to find added to the template. In this example, a .NET property named `IssueProjectModel` is being added to the template. If, instead, the `provides` parameter had been specified as

```
provides="IssueProjectModel=Model"
```

then a property named `Model` would have been added to the template.

This facility is key in allowing multiple directive processors to be used in the same template that would otherwise cause a clash. This allows templates to be written that combine multiple model files or compare model files to give a representation of difference. Here's an example of this in practice:

```
<#@ issueProjectModel processor="IssueProjectsDirectiveProcessor"
  requires="fileName='HealthProject.issueProjects'"
  provides="IssueProjectModel=Model" #>
<#@ issueProjectModel processor="IssueProjectsDirectiveProcessor"
  requires="fileName='HealthSubProject.issueProjects'"
  provides="IssueProjectModel=SubModel" #>
```

These two directives will cause the template to have both a `Model` and a `SubModel` property, allowing data from the two to be combined in the template output.

Control Block Types

Apart from directives and boilerplate text that is copied directly to the template output, the remainder of template files consists of control blocks. We saw all three types of control blocks used in our scenario with Devika, but it's worth pointing out a few extra details.

As a reminder, the three types of control blocks are discussed below.

Standard Control Block

```
<# ... #>
```

A standard control block introduces control statements into a template. All of the code inside all of the control blocks in a single template (including the code added to the template with any `include` directives used) forms the content of a single method added to the template. This means that any variables declared inside standard control blocks must be uniquely named across the entire template. If you're building up a library of template fragments to be included in other templates, this can lead to surprising errors. One technique that can be used to combat this in library templates is to catenate a standard string (perhaps the name of the template `include` file) to all variable declarations within each template file to avoid clashes. However, the best way to avoid such clashes is to put most repetitive code either inside class feature control blocks or to create your own template base class derived from `ModelingTextTransformation` to contain this code.

As well as properties and other members added by custom directive processors, the template has a small set of utility methods provided on its base class, `TextTransformation`, which can be used in control blocks.

`Write()` and `WriteLine()` methods are provided to allow code to be emitted directly to the template output. There are variants of both these methods taking a simple string and a standard .NET format string and `params` argument array pair. Generally, use of these methods is a poor substitute for using boilerplate text in a template and hinders readability. However, if the template's control logic is dense with a very small piece of text output needed in the middle of it, then a judicious call to `WriteLine()` can avoid the visual clutter of toggling in and out of a control block. These methods are also useful for porting across code from legacy code generators.

`Error()` and `Warning()` methods are provided so that control logic can flag errors to the template user. There's a set of indentation management methods which we'll discuss shortly and finally, the `GenerationEnvironment-StringBuilder` property allows direct access to the intermediate value of the template output as it is being built.

A key point to note is that the DSL Tools also provide a more specific derived template base class, `ModelingTextTransformation`, which provides a `Store` property. This allows access to a single shared modeling store that all model files used within a template are loaded into. Templates that wish to manipulate the models they load, for example, to merge two model files, can start a transaction against this store in the normal way without fear of impacting the models on disk or any models that are currently open in designers.

Class Feature Control Block

```
<#+ ... #>
```

A class feature control block adds methods, properties, fields, or nested classes to the template. This is the best way to add reusable pieces of template, because they can be embedded within parameterized methods and thus any local variables they declare won't clash with other templates; however, it is still advisable to use very explicit method names to avoid clashes. Class feature control blocks must be placed at the end of each template file, and after the first such block is introduced, no further standard control blocks may be used. This restriction allows boilerplate text to be embedded within a method in a class feature block unambiguously, like this:

```
<#+
public void GenerateEmptyClass(string name)
{
#>
public partial class <#= name #>
{
// Some class content
}
<#+
}
#>
```

This code allows you to call GenerateEmptyClass from any other control block anytime you want to generate a class. However, the class, as specified, will always be emitted with the same level of indentation in the generated code. If you're trying to generate an embedded class, for example, this may not be what you want. We've found that a best practice is to format generated code exactly as you would format hand-written code, wherever that is possible, because it greatly aids debugging. To help with that, the TextTransformation class provides three methods and a property to manage indentation.

```
public void PushIndent(string indent);
public string PopIndent();
public void ClearIndent();
public string CurrentIndent { get; }
```

The class manages a string buffer that every output line is prefixed with. This buffer is managed as a stack, so, for example, successive calls to

```
PushIndent("\t");
```

will gradually indent lines further and further to the right using a tab character with PopIndent() doing the opposite.

Expression Control Block

```
<#= ... #>
```

An expression control block simply evaluates the expression it contains and then calls the standard .NET method ToString() on the result. If the type of the result supports a ToString() overload that takes an IFormatProvider interface, then that version is used, supplying the culture of the template as an argument; if not, the vanilla version is used. An instance-based method is used to make this decision, meaning that expression control blocks can't be used inside static methods declared in a class feature block. Hence it is a good idea to only use instance methods in class feature blocks.

Problems of Large-Scale, Real-World Artifact Generation

Generation from large models using large and complex sets of templates brings with it complexities that need to be managed.

The options available to the DSL author for controlling this complexity depend on what facilities are available in the artifact's native format for division across multiple files. In the case of C#, the partial keyword can be used to great effect. If such a solution is available, then to avoid creating huge output files, it is usually advisable to run multiple smaller templates against the same model file. A suitable scheme for dividing up these templates must then be found. For example, the DSL Tools themselves use many templates to generate a large number of files. Its templates are divided up functionally, with design surface code separate from domain model code and the latter separate from IDE integration code.

Large models also typically have complex domain models underlying them. These domain models will typically be optimized either for ease of understanding in the model explorer of their designer or for ease of mapping to their visual representation. Neither of these schemes may be ideal for artifact generation. One slight disadvantage of the template scheme is that it is inherently linear in nature. If the model structure is mismatched with the internal structure of artifacts that must be generated, then the control blocks and expression blocks in templates can very often be filled with complex expressions to retrieve the data required from the model.

■ TIP Create a data structure optimized for code generation at the beginning of a template

We've found that the best mitigation for this problem is to take the trouble to produce a reorganized data structure at the top of a template. This new data structure uses standard .NET collections and structures, and consolidates the job of gathering together and aggregating dispersed data from across the model in a manner optimized for the job of traversing it to produce template output.

Very often this data structure can itself be reused across a range of similar templates. This produces a template organized into a data-gathering phase and an output phase that is then relatively simple because it traverses the pre-prepared data structures with simple expressions.

When output formats for artifacts do not natively support being constructed from multiple files, a two-stage approach can provide another solution. Let's take the example of the web.config file for our Issue Tracker system. web.config files are simple XML files and don't support any standard mechanism for inclusion. However, we can create a master text template that stitches together the output of several other templates to produce a consolidated file. Here's an example of such a master template:

```
<#@ output extension=".config" #>
<configuration>
<#@include file="AppSettings.config" #>
<#@include file="System.Web.Config" #>
<#@include file="Locations.config" #>
</configuration>
```

Any of the three included component .config files could be either the generated output of another template or a simple text file. In the case of a simple text file, that part of the file is then free to be manually edited, thus combining manual editing with code generation in the same output file. One further problem remains, however, with this approach—the template transformations must be executed in the correct order to produce the correct output. The DSL Tools V1 do not have a pre-canned solution to this problem, providing only the "Transform All Templates" button inside Visual Studio. When there are only a few files involved that are not often changed, the manual approach of running the templates in the correct order may suffice, but when the problem grows and this becomes unmanageable, a custom solution must be developed. A custom command can be developed as part of a DSL designer that invokes the text templating engine in the correct sequence; we'll see how to do this shortly.

The master template approach just outlined brings many further file types into the realm of the generable, but it is not suitable for all file types. Where a file is a complex and perhaps unpredictable mixture of manually editable sections and sections that it would be desirable to code generate, then the current version of the text templating engine does not have a clear answer. In those cases, there may be no alternative but building a full parser for the artifact and coupling that to your designer using the Visual Studio SDK in order to be able to watch changes to the artifact and merge generated sections and hand-edited ones. This is not a trivial undertaking, and it may be that using generated code only as a one-shot starting point for manual editing of this kind of file is the best that can be achieved with a practical amount of investment for most projects.

Advanced Customizations

If you find you need to tailor the artifact generation system to your exact needs, there are a variety of customization points available:

- The text templating system can be embedded into other tools outside of Visual Studio that you ship with your DSL using a mechanism called custom hosting.
- Custom data can be imported into a text template for processing using a custom directive processor.
- The text templating system can easily be invoked inside Visual Studio to build a custom orchestration system.

We'll look at these three extensibility points in turn but first, in order to understand how they fit into the bigger picture, let's take a tour through the implementation architecture of the text templating system.

Text Templating Architecture

The text templating *engine* (`Microsoft.VisualStudio.TextTemplating.dll`) is the heart of the text templating system. It is in charge of processing the contents of a text template and producing appropriate output. The engine is designed to be a passive component existing within a *host* environment; the host must provide it with the template text and do something with the output that the engine produces. Any other information the engine needs, such as how to find any files that get included into a template, must also be provided to it by the host. This information is provided by way of a callback mechanism implemented by the host, which we'll see described in detail when we look at custom hosting.

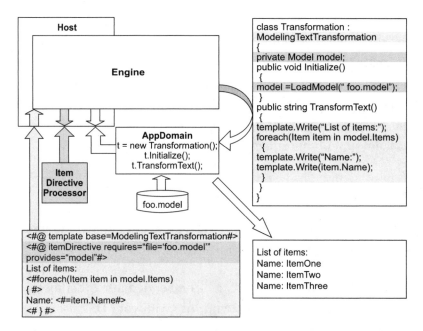

FIGURE 8-3: The implementation architecture of the text templating system

A typical text template execution sequence can be seen in Figure 8-3 and looks like this:

- The host reads in a template file from disk.
- The host instantiates a template engine.
- The host passes the template text to the engine along with a callback pointer to itself.

- The engine parses the template, finding standard and custom directives and control blocks. In this case, the template directive specifies a base class and there is a single custom directive, `itemDirective`.

- The engine asks the host to load the directive processors for any custom directives it has found. In this case, the Item Directive Processor is loaded.

- The engine produces in memory the code for the skeleton of a `Transformation` class, derived ultimately from `TextTransformation`. This template has specified the derived `ModelingTextTransformation`.

- The engine gives directive processors a chance to contribute code to the `Transformation` class for both class members and to run in the body of the `Initialize()` method. The item directive processor has added a single member, `model`, to store some root MEL of type `Model`. It has also added code in the `Initialize()` method to set up that member variable using the `LoadModel()` method. Note that the filename is hard-coded as a literal in the contributed code because it comes from the item directive's `requires` parameter.

- The engine adds the content of class feature blocks as members to the `Transformation` class, thus appearing to allow methods and properties to be "added to the template." There are none specified in this template.

- The engine adds boilerplate inside `Write` statements and the contents of other standard control blocks to the `TransformText()` method. This template has a simple `for` loop controlling how often the "Name: " boilerplate is written.

- The engine compiles the `Transformation` class into a temporary .NET assembly.

- The engine asks the host to provide an `AppDomain` in which to run the compiled code.

- The engine instantiates the `Transformation` class in the new `AppDomain` and calls the `Initialize()` and `TransformText()` methods on it via .NET *remoting*.[3]

---

3. An Application Domain is an isolated and unloadable environment in which an assembly can be executed. .NET remoting is a mechanism for invoking methods across AppDomain or machine boundaries.

- The `Initialize()` method uses code contributed by directive processors to load data specified by the custom directives into the new `AppDomain`. In this case, the `LoadModel()` method loads "`foo.model`" into a store and returns the root element to populate the `model` member.

- The `TransformText()` method writes boilerplate text to its output string, interspersed with control code from regular control blocks and the values of expression control blocks. Here the "List of items" header is first written out, followed by the `foreach` statement from the control block. The loop contains the "Name: " boilerplate followed by the value obtained by evaluating the expression block `item.Name`.

- The output string is returned via the engine to the host, which commits the generated output to disk.

Now we'll look at how this overall architecture impacts three kinds of customization.

Custom Hosting

The text templating engine is deliberately designed to be hosted in a variety of processes. Clearly, Visual Studio is its natural home, but it takes no dependencies on Visual Studio or indeed the modeling components of the DSL Tools. It achieves this by having no understanding of its outside environment, instead relying on its host to provide it with all of the information it needs to do its job. This allows it to be integrated into other tools in a tool chain that works with your DSL designer, for example, an advanced UI application for configuring how templates are applied to models in a large-scale development scenario. This technique is called custom hosting.

As well as the host that is integrated into Visual Studio, the DSL Tools supply one custom host out of the box, the command-line text templating tool `TextTransform.exe`, which can be found in the directory `<%Program-Files%>\Common Files\Microsoft Shared\TextTemplating\1.1`. This tool allows text template transformation to be easily incorporated into automated scripts and processes such as software build systems. It has options for specifying all of the important configuration information needed to successfully run a text template, such as paths to find included sub-templates, referenced assemblies, and directive processors.

▪ TIP Use DslTextTransform for transforming .dsl models

Because the set of parameters to `TextTransform.exe` can be somewhat intimidating, the DSL Tools provide a small wrapper script, `DslText-Transform.cmd`, to set them up for you. It's also a good idea to provide a similar script for use with your own DSLs. You can find `DslText-Transform.cmd` in the `<%Program Files%>\Visual Studio 2005 SDK\2006.09\VisualStudioIntegration\Tools\Bin` directory.

If `TextTransform.exe` proves insufficient, you can host the template processor in your own application by simply instantiating the class `Microsoft.VisualStudio.TextTemplating.Engine` and calling its single method:

```
public string ProcessTemplate(string content,
                              ITextTemplatingEngineHost host);
```

As you can see from this method, the template engine really has no notion of the external environment it is living in. It simply takes a text string containing the template contents and processes it to return another text string containing the processed output. It is entirely the responsibility of the host to decide which template files to process, from where, and what to do with the output once received. Of course, it is not possible to process a template without finding out interesting things about the hosting environment, for example, where to retrieve a file that has been included with a `<@# include #>` directive. The host must also provide this type of information via the `ITextTemplatingEngineHost` callback interface:

```
public interface ITextTemplatingEngineHost
{
  // Methods
  object GetHostOption(string optionName);
  bool LoadIncludeText(string requestFileName,
                       out string content,
                       out string location);
  void LogErrors(CompilerErrorCollection errors);
```

```
    AppDomain ProvideTemplatingAppDomain(string content);
    string ResolveAssemblyReference(string assemblyReference);
    Type ResolveDirectiveProcessor(string processorName);
    string ResolveParameterValue(string directiveId,
                                 string processorName,
                                 string parameterName);
    string ResolvePath(string path);
    void SetFileExtension(string extension);
    void SetOutputEncoding(Encoding encoding, bool fromOutputDirective);

    // Properties
    IList<string> StandardAssemblyReferences { get; }
    IList<string> StandardImports { get; }
    string TemplateFile { get; }
}
```

This interface provides included files, paths for referenced assemblies, general paths, and the location of assemblies implementing specific directive processors. It also allows the host to provide any arguments for directive processors not already provided inline in the template. It also allows hints in a template on what file extension and file encoding to use for output to be passed out to the host and allows the host to inject standard assembly references and import statements into the processing pipeline. It further allows the host to provide a mechanism for the template processing engine to log errors and warnings it encounters during its processing and to supply values for any standard configuration options that the engine requires.

Most importantly, this interface allows the host to specify the .NET AppDomain that should be used as the execution context for the template transformation class.

.NET is not by nature a scripting or interpretive environment, so to make this process work, the transformation class has to be run through the C# or VB.NET compiler (depending on the language used in the control code). This compilation process produces a standard .NET assembly that must be loaded; then the transformation class can be instantiated and the method called. The AppDomain forms the environment in which to load the generated assembly and run the method. The text templating host that is built into Visual Studio with the DSL Tools chooses to use a separate AppDomain from that used by the rest of Visual Studio in order to provide a measure of isolation of this compiled-on-the-fly code and to allow the AppDomain to be conveniently discarded. Discarding the AppDomain is occasionally necessary, because .NET does not allow the unloading of assemblies before `AppDomain` termination; consequently, with each new compiled template (and thus new assembly), a small amount of system memory is used up that cannot otherwise be recovered. Any custom text templating host must decide on a strategy for dealing with this gradual accumulation of memory.

The text templating engine provides a helper class `AssemblyCache` that can be instantiated remotely inside any `AppDomains` you create to help you monitor how many transformation assemblies are present and how old they are.

▪ TIP Use the walkthroughs

The DSL Tools documentation has a very comprehensive walkthrough of building your own custom host in the section entitled "Walkthrough: Creating a Custom Text Template Host."

Custom Directive Processor

Earlier in the chapter, we discussed how the directive processor generated as a standard part of a DSL can be used with a custom directive in a template to read in model files and add .NET properties to the template to access the root of that model file, for example:

```
<#@ issueProjectModel processor="IssueProjectsDirectiveProcessor"
   requires="fileName='HealthProject.issueProjects'"
   provides="IssueProjectModel=IssueProjectModel" #>
```

If you need to process other kinds of data within a template, for example, to combine model data with an XML file that you don't have a DSL for, you can add further custom directive processors to bring that data into the environment of the template for processing.

As we've seen in the architecture section, a text template is converted into a .NET class ultimately derived from the abstract class `TextTransformation`, called the *transformation class*. This class is compiled and run in the host-supplied `AppDomain` via an override of the following methods:

```
public abstract void Initialize();
public abstract string TransformText();
```

It is this latter method that returns the string text that forms the output of the processing engine.

Now that we know the mechanism by which templates run in the engine, we can deal with how to load data into them. The canonical behavior for a directive processor is to add a property to the transformation class that transparently allows code in the template to access the data. To realize this, directive processors are given an opportunity to inject code into the transformation class. The principal task when creating a custom directive processor is to decide what this code should be and to parameterize it with the parameters supplied by the custom directive that invokes the directive processor. As discussed, this code may likely be running in a clean `AppDomain` and so cannot directly rely on the current in-memory data held by the rest of Visual Studio; instead, it must be able to initialize the data from scratch. There are a couple of strategies for achieving this.

- Inject code that contains a call to data-loading code using a parameter such as a filename taken from the custom directive.
- Use the parameters from the custom directive to acquire the data and then serialize it into a blob; inject code that contains the blob and a call to deserialize it.

Either of these strategies can be augmented by various caching techniques or special code to communicate between `AppDomains` to retrieve data. These techniques are beyond the scope of this book, but in any case, they can only be a backup to the fundamental requirement to be able to load the data in a clean `AppDomain`.

Again, the DSL Tools documentation is helpful in this area, and the walkthrough "Creating a Custom Directive Processor" explains in detail the process for creating a directive processor that uses the first strategy just mentioned to load an XML file and provide its DOM as a parameter.

It's worth noting that if you are only concerned with running your templates inside one particular host, you can set the `hostSpecific` parameter on your `<#@template #>` directive and acquire a reference in the template's

AppDomain to the instance of the host object in the original AppDomain. This can make data acquisition a little easier. For example, a template that is coupled to the Visual Studio host supplied with the DSL Tools can use this mechanism to acquire the Visual Studio DTE object in the template and thus write templates that interact with the project system and the many other objects available via DTE. Here's an example:

```
<#@ template debug="true" hostspecific="true" #>
<#@ output extension=".txt" #>
<#@ assembly name="EnvDTE" #>
<#@ import namespace="EnvDTE" #>
Get the names of the projects in the Debugging solution from Dte
<#
  DTE dte = ((IServiceProvider)this.Host).GetService(typeof(DTE))
                      as DTE;
  if (dte != null)
  {
    foreach (Project project in dte.Solution.Projects)
    {
#>
    Project: <#= project.Name #>
<#
    }
  }
#>
```

The preceding simple template produces the following output when run in a typical DSL Tools Debugging project:

```
Get the names of the projects in the Debugging solution from Dte
    Project: Debugging
```

Remember that use of this mechanism will couple your templates to a particular host and preclude their use, for example, with the command-line TextTransform.exe tool.

Custom Orchestration

The final area of customization we'll examine is in many ways the simplest conceptually, but it requires quite a lot of custom code. It's quite a common scenario to want to invoke a text template to create a file at a different level of granularity than that provided by the DSL Tools in Visual Studio. The default mechanism by which text templating is invoked in the IDE is by setting the "Custom Tool" property in the IDE on a template file to

"TextTemplatingFileGenerator" as we saw Devika do earlier in the chapter. This causes the output of the template to be added to the project as a dependent file nested beneath the template file in a 1-1 relationship. This is a very easy way to quickly add templates to a solution and have issues such as source control handled automatically for the new file, but the single template/single generated file restriction can be quite limiting. For example, if you have a class design DSL, it would probably be a best practice to generate one C# class file for each class defined in your model. This can't be achieved using the default mechanism and requires custom code. This scenario doesn't require a custom host, because you'd typically run it from inside Visual Studio. You can find a complete worked example of this approach in the project called "GenClass" in the "Chapter 8" folder of the web code download.

In this example, we're adding a custom menu command to generate one class file for each class in a model, which is based on the standard class design template supplied with the DSL Tools. You could also couple this type of code to the save event on a DSL model using DTE's event model.

The details of how to set up a custom command are covered in Chapter 10, but the upshot is that when the menu item for the command is selected, a method in the CommandSet class is called. Here's a very basic implementation of such a method:

```
internal virtual void OnMenuGenerateClasses(object sender, EventArgs e)
{
  DTE dte = this.ServiceProvider.GetService(typeof(DTE)) as DTE;
  if (dte == null)
  {
    throw new InvalidOperationException("Failed to retrieve DTE.");
  }
  Project project = dte.ActiveDocument.ProjectItem.ContainingProject;
  if (project == null)
  {
    throw new InvalidOperationException("Failed to retrieve project.");
  }
  ITextTemplating templatingService =
    this.ServiceProvider.GetService(typeof(STextTemplating))
        as ITextTemplating;
  if ( templatingService == null)
  {
    throw new InvalidOperationException(
        "Failed to retrieve Text Templating service.");
  }
```

```
// Retrieve the text of the template from a resource.
// The template could alternatively be loaded from disk.
string baseTemplate = VSPackage.GenIndividualClass;

if (!string.IsNullOrEmpty(baseTemplate))
{
  // If the generated code directory doesn't exist then create it
  string genCodeDir = Path.Combine(
    Path.GetDirectoryName(project.FullName), "GeneratedCode");
  if (!Directory.Exists(genCodeDir))
  {
    Directory.CreateDirectory(genCodeDir);
  }

  if (!Directory.Exists(genCodeDir))
  {
    throw new InvalidOperationException(
            "Failed to create generated code directory.");
  }

  templatingService.BeginErrorSession(); // Avoid duplicate errors
  if (this.CurrentDocData != null)
  {
    foreach (ModelClass eachClass in this.CurrentDocData.Store.
                      ElementDirectory.FindElements<ModelClass>())
    {
      // Replace the marker text in the template with the name
      // of the class to generate and the model file to load
      string specificTemplate = baseTemplate.Replace(
                                "@@CLASSNAME@@",
                                eachClass.Name);
      specificTemplate = specificTemplate.Replace(
                                "@@MODELFILE@@",
                                dte.ActiveDocument.FullName);

      string output = templatingService.ProcessTemplate(
                      "", specificTemplate, null, null);
      string filePath = Path.Combine(genCodeDir,
                                  eachClass.Name + ".cs");
      using (StreamWriter writer = new StreamWriter(filePath))
      {
          writer.Write(output);
          writer.Flush();
      }

      // If this is a new file then add it to the project
      try
      {
          project.ProjectItems.AddFromFile(filePath);
      }
```

```
        catch // Ignore add failures
        {
        }
      }
    }
    templatingService.EndErrorSession(); // Avoid duplicate errors
  }
}
```

First, the services necessary to run the command are set up using Visual Studio's standard service provider mechanism.

The built-in Visual Studio host exposes a service containing a simple API to call the template engine on demand via the service identifier STextTemplating. Note that the service is immediately cast to its interface when it is returned.

```
public interface ITextTemplating
{
  string ProcessTemplate(string inputFile,
                         string content,
                         ITextTemplatingCallback callback,
                         IVsHierarchy hierarchy);
      void BeginErrorSession();
      bool EndErrorSession();
}
```

The ProcessTemplate() method runs the text template provided in its content parameter and returns its output. There are three optional parameters to this method:

- inputFile—Provide the file path of the template to allow it to be shown in error messages generated by processing the template.
- hierarchy—Provide a Visual Studio SDK hierarchy object to cause any referenced assemblies in the template to be resolved using the Visual Studio project system's standard assembly reference mechanism.
- callback—Provide this to be notified of errors and any file extension or encoding options requested by the template.

Errors and warnings will be raised to the Visual Studio errors window automatically. If you're going to make multiple calls to the Process-Template() method, you can bracket them with calls to BeginErrorSession()

and EndErrorSession(), and any non-unique error messages will be
skipped; this is a very handy feature, because errors in repeatedly applied
templates tend to lead to a lot of confusing duplicate messages.

In this example, the text for the template is being stored in a .resx
resource file and is retrieved using Visual Studio's strongly typed resource
wrapper mechanism. It could equally be stored on disk somewhere under
your DSL's installation directory and loaded as required.

The template being loaded here has the following content:

```
<#@ template inherits="Microsoft.VisualStudio.TextTemplating.VSHost.

  ModelingTextTransformation" debug="true"#>
<#@ output extension=".cs" #>
<#@ GenClass processor="GenClassDirectiveProcessor"
  requires="fileName='@@MODELFILE@@';name='@@CLASSNAME@@'" #>

namespace ClassGen.Output
{
  public class <#= this.ModelClass.Name #>
    <#= this.ModelClass.Superclass != null ?
          " : " + this.ModelClass.Superclass.Name :
          "" #>
  {
    #region Members
<#
  foreach (ModelAttribute attribute in this.ModelClass.Attributes)
  {
#>
    private <#= attribute.Type #> <#=attribute.Name #>;
<#
  }
#>
    #endregion

    #region Operations
<#
  foreach (ClassOperation operation in this.ModelClass.Operations)
  {
#>
    public void <#=operation.Name #> (<#= operation.Signature #>)
    {
    }
<#
  }
#>
    #endregion
  }
}
```

This is a fairly standard text template that simply writes out a basic skeleton for a C# class making the assumption that it has the reference to the class as a member of the template in its ModelClass property. The item to note is the GenClass custom directive, which has two requires parameters with odd-looking tokens supplied as values.

Going back to the command code, the next actions are to create a directory to generate code into, start an error session to avoid duplicate errors, and loop over each **ModelClass** found in the model of the current document.

Having got an individual **ModelClass,** the code then replaces the tokens in a copy of the template text with the filename of the current document and the name of the **ModelClass**. The templating service is then called to process this individualized template, and the output is written to an appropriate file. Finally, the file is added to the Visual Studio project; in a more complete implementation, the DTE API should be used to ensure that source code control is integrated into this scenario, checking out the file if necessary before generation.

The trick of doing a token replacement on the template text has provided an individual directive specifying a **ModelClass** by name for each call to the templating service, but one final piece is still needed to connect that up to the ModelClass property on the template.

To achieve this, the custom directive processor in the solution is amended to take an extra requires parameter, "name" and to provide the ModelClass property. The implementation for the extra code contributed by this directive processor simply searches the loaded model for a **ModelClass** instance whose **Name** domain property matches the passed-in name parameter and sets the backing store for the property accordingly. Here's the code that declares the property and its backing store:

```
protected override void GenerateTransformCode(
                    string directiveName,
                    StringBuilder codeBuffer,
                    CodeDomProvider languageProvider,
                    IDictionary<string, string> requiresArguments,
                    IDictionary<string, string> providesArguments)
{
  base.GenerateTransformCode(directiveName,
                    codeBuffer,
                    languageProvider,
                    requiresArguments,
                    providesArguments);
```

```
    // TODO: This would be better done using CodeDOM in a production
    // designer in order to support Visual Basic.

    // Add ModelClass property's backing store
    codeBuffer.AppendLine("private ModelClass _" +
                         providesArguments["ModelClass"] + ";");

    // Add ModelClass property
    codeBuffer.AppendLine("public ModelClass " +
                   providesArguments["ModelClass"] + "{ get { return _" +
                   providesArguments["ModelClass"] + " ; } }");
}
```

Although this isn't the easiest code to read, you can see that the provides-
Arguments dictionary is being used to specify the name of both the property
and its backing store. This allows the directive to be used more than once in
a single template without name clashes.

Finally, here's the code that initializes the backing store:

```
protected override void GeneratePostInitializationCode(
                         string directiveName,
                         StringBuilder codeBuffer,
                         CodeDomProvider languageProvider,
                         IDictionary<string, string> requiresArguments,
                         IDictionary<string, string> providesArguments)
{
    base.GeneratePostInitializationCode(directiveName,
                                        codeBuffer,
                                        languageProvider,
                                        requiresArguments,
                                        providesArguments);

    // Initialize the ModelClass property
    codeBuffer.AppendLine(@"foreach (ModelClass eachClass in
            this.Store.ElementDirectory.FindElements<ModelClass>())");
    codeBuffer.AppendLine(@"{");
    codeBuffer.AppendLine(@"  if (StringComparer.Ordinal.
               Compare(eachClass.Name,
                       """ + requiresArguments["name"] + @""") == 0)");
    codeBuffer.AppendLine(@"  {");
    codeBuffer.AppendLine(@"    this._" +
                            providesArguments["ModelClass"] +
                            " = eachClass;");
    codeBuffer.AppendLine(@"    break;");
    codeBuffer.AppendLine(@"  }");
    codeBuffer.AppendLine(@"}");
}
```

This code is placed in an override of `GeneratePostInitializationCode()`, because by this time the store will have been initialized and the model file loaded by the base class.

The `requiresArguments` dictionary is used to acquire the `name` parameter that was replaced in the template with the name of the current class being processed. All of the instances of **ModelClass** in the store are then searched to find one element matching this name, and the field is initialized.

■ **TIP** Use the CodeDOM to emit code in custom directive processors

It's interesting to note that we're using one of our other styles of code generation here inside the directive processor customization, namely, simply writing out code as strings using `AppendLine()` methods. In this case, (which is slightly mind-boggling because it is a piece of code generation used inside the infrastructure of a larger piece of code generation!), the CodeDOM would actually be the best approach, because the amount of code needed is quite small and there is a strong requirement to support C# and Visual Basic so that this processor can be used with templates that use either as their control language.

This example adds the useful facility of writing out one file per class in the model, but it's also easy to see how this technique could be expanded to support generation of files that have dependencies in their generation order—or perhaps to support scenarios where text templates are constructed on the fly from a selection of common template fragments.

SUMMARY

In this chapter, we saw that textual artifact generation is a key task required in domain-specific development.

We then reviewed approaches to artifact generation—at the level of the relationship between the model and the artifacts as well as at the level of the mechanics of performing the transformation.

We then looked at DSL Tools V1's template-based, forward-only approach to generation and worked through an example of the incremental templatization process that it enables.

Next, we reviewed the text templating constructs and syntax in detail, looking particularly at the importance of directives and the types of control block.

We reviewed some of the issues raised by working with large models, large sets of templates, and diverse artifact output types.

Finally, we investigated three areas of code customization for the text templating system: custom hosting, custom directive processors, and orchestration, using the simple Visual Studio hosted API to the text templating system.

■9 ■
Deploying a DSL

Introduction

So far, using a DSL has meant launching the generated designer as part of a debugging session in the experimental version of Visual Studio. This is suitable for the DSL author while building the designer, but is not an appropriate experience for users of the designer. Users will expect to launch the designer from within Visual Studio just like the XML or C# editor or the WinForms designer, after going through a familiar installation process. To enable that, DSL authors need to be able to build a Windows installer package (`.msi` file) for their designer. The DSL Tools make this really easy by providing a DSL Setup project template, which is used to create a setup project in the DSL authoring solution. Building the setup project produces the `.msi` and associated files. This chapter describes this process in greater detail, and explains how you can customize the setup project to include additional components, such as DLLs, that your designer may depend on. In particular, it covers

- A description of files needed to install a designer
- A description of how to create a setup project
- An explanation of the contents of the setup project
- A description of the process for refreshing the installation files when changes have been made to the designer

- The difference between deploying a designer with and without a package load key
- A description of the format of the `.dslsetup` file, and an explanation of how to customize the installation files that get generated by changing this file

Files Needed to Install a Designer

Formally, a designer built using the DSL Tools is a *Visual Studio Package*. Installing a Visual Studio Package is nontrivial; files have to be placed in various locations, and Windows registry settings must be updated.

Windows Registry

The Windows registry is the place where some applications, including Visual Studio, store any configuration settings they may need; settings can be per user or per machine. The contents of the registry, which is essentially a tree of keyed values, can be browsed by invoking the `regedit.exe` command from Start >Run. This brings up the registry editor, which is illustrated in Figure 9-1.

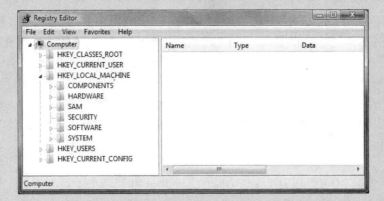

FIGURE 9-1: The Windows registry editor

Care should be taken not to change the settings, because doing so could cause applications or Windows itself to stop working or behave erratically.

The location of all these files and the registry settings made must be remembered so that when the application is uninstalled, the state of the system can be reset. So building an installer is not a simple affair. Many organizations make do with hacked-together scripts that do not work with every machine configuration and that do not work with corporate systems for deploying purchased package software. This leads to brittleness in the installation process and incurs cost in setting up an additional, often manual and inferior, one-off deployment process.

Producing a robust installer is typically the preserve of companies that produce packaged software, where the return justifies the investment. The same used to be said for building graphical designers, but the DSL Tools reduce the cost to the point where producing a domain-specific graphical designer for internal use becomes a viable option for an organization. So it would be disappointing if this saving was compromised by not making it just as easy to produce a robust installer for DSL designers.

A common and safe way to install a Windows application is via a Windows installer package that is realized as a `.msi` file. A `.msi` file contains all the components and registry settings for installing a piece of software. Often it is accompanied by a few other files external to it, and which it may reference, such as a Readme file; but that is an option, not a necessity. When a `.msi` file is launched, the built-in Windows installer infrastructure takes over, processing the file and overseeing the installation process. The Windows Installer takes care of adding entries to the Add/Remove Programs dialog in the control panel, and for keeping a record of all changes that were made to the system during installation, so that the system can be put back to its original state when the software is uninstalled. If multiple `.msi` files are to be installed in a single step, then a `setup.exe` file is also provided to launch all the `.msi`'s in the correct order.

Windows Installer XML (WiX)

Some progress has been made to make it easier to create `.msi` files. In particular, WiX (Windows Installer XML) is an open source set of tools for building Windows installation packages. With WiX, you write an XML script declaring all the components that need to be included in the `.msi`, and providing configuration settings for the installation wizard that appears when you run a `.msi`. The WiX tools then compile this script into a `.msi` file. More information on WiX can be found at http://wix.sf.net.

To install a designer built using the DSL Tools, you need the following files:

- A `.msi` file for installing the designer itself
- A `.msi` file that installs the *DSL Tools Redistributable*, which contains a set of binaries which all designers are dependent upon
- A `setup.exe` file, which chains the installation of the DSL Tools Redistributable and the designer `.msi` files, installing the former only if it hasn't already been installed
- Additional files, such as a Readme and license agreement, at the designer author's discretion

Of these, only the DSL Tools Redistributable `.msi` is independent of the designer being installed, although the `setup.exe` file can be made independent by using a configuration file that identifies the `.msi` for the designer to be installed. Using WiX (see sidebar) would certainly simplify the job of creating the first `.msi` file, but that still requires in-depth knowledge of the domain of Windows installation, because it needs to be flexible enough to produce an installation package for any piece of Windows software. The requirements for the DSL Tools are far more focused: Create Windows installation packages for the installation of designers and associated components, such as the text templates introduced in Chapter 8. These requirements can be met by a simpler, more specific language than WiX, whose focus is the domain of installing designers and associated components in Visual Studio. The DSL Tools Installer Definition language, realized as `.dslsetup` files, is such a language. About 30 lines of XML are required to specify the information required to install a designer, and from this about 800 lines of WiX are generated. The WiX tools are then used to generate the Windows installer package. But it doesn't stop there. The DSL Tools also provide the DSL Setup Visual Studio project template, which adds a setup project to the DSL authoring solution. When created using this template, the setup project is configured with an initial complete version of the installer definition specific to the DSL being authored, the WiX generation templates, and build rules to process the generated WiX files to create the Windows installer package.

The remainder of this chapter describes the use of the DSL Setup project and the DSL Tools Installer Definition language.

Getting Started—Creating a Setup Project

To recap, a DSL author works in a Visual Studio solution, which has two projects: the `DslPackage` project and the `Dsl` project. When F5 is pressed, the projects are built and a debugging session is launched in which the generated designer can be exercised in an instance of the experimental version of Visual Studio. In order to generate the installation files for deploying the designer, it is necessary to create a third project. This is created using the Domain-Specific Language Setup Visual Studio project template. Select the solution node in the solution explorer and select "Add New Project" from the context menu. Choose the "Domain-Specific Language Setup" template, which can be found under the "Extensibility" category, and give the project a name, as illustrated in Figure 9-2.

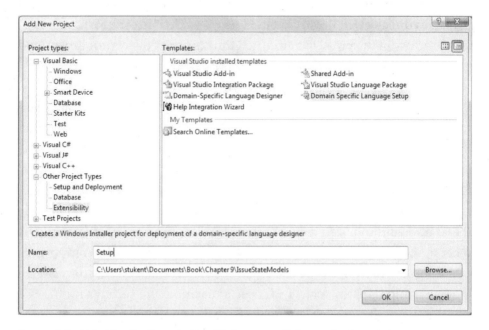

FIGURE 9-2: Selecting the Domain-Specific Language Setup project template

Click "OK," and after a short delay a setup project will have been added to the solution, with contents such as those illustrated in Figure 9-3.

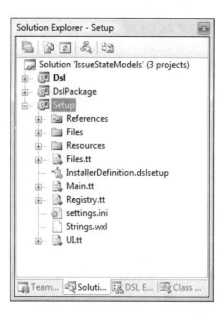

FIGURE 9-3: Contents of the DSL Setup project

Building this solution results in a set of installation files being generated in the bin directory, as illustrated in Figure 9-4. The bin directory is the output directory of the project (configured through the project properties), and is where the project build action places all the files it creates.

There are two Microsoft Installer (.msi) files. The DSLToolsRedist.msi is the DSL Tools Redistributable, which is common to all designers and contains all the components required for a designer to run on a machine with Visual Studio Standard or later installed (see, however, the section "Package Load Key"). The redistributable components include the DSL Tools' DLLs, on which the designer depends, and the components required to execute text transformations. The DSL Tools Redistributable does not include the components required for authoring DSLs, such as the DSL designer. The other .msi (IssueStateModels.msi, in this case) contains all the components of the specific designer to be installed. The setup.exe file is used to launch the installation process on a DSL user's machine, the settings.ini file is a configuration file used by setup.exe, and Readme.htm is an optional Readme file that accompanies all the other installation files.

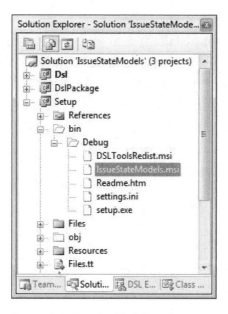

FIGURE 9-4: Result of building the setup project

Copying the installation files onto another machine and launching `setup.exe` will cause the DSLToolsRedist to install, if it has not been installed already. Then an installation wizard is launched for installing the designer, as illustrated in Figure 9-5.

FIGURE 9-5: Installation wizard

If the prerequisites for the designer installation are not met, for example, if Visual Studio is not installed, then an error message is raised and the designer is not installed. If this doesn't occur, once the wizard has been completed, the designer is installed and entries for both the DSL Tools Redistributable and the designer appear in the "Control Panel>Add or Remove Programs" dialog.

Setup Project Contents

The setup project contains:

- A `.dslsetup` file
- A set of text templates, all with extension `.tt`
- A `settings.ini` file
- A `Strings.wxl` file
- A folder `Files`, containing ancillary installation files, such as `Readme.htm` and license agreement
- A folder `Resources`, containing resources used by the installation wizard UI

The `.dslsetup` file contains information about the components to be installed. It is specific to the installation of DSL designers; it is not a format for creating the installation files for any Windows application. The text templates take information from this file and generate WiX files—WiX was introduced earlier.

The information contained in the `.dslsetup` file generated by application of the DSL Setup project template is specific to the DSL being authored. This book is not the place to go into the details of project template authoring in Visual Studio, but at a high level the template contains custom code that scours the solution to which it is being added to find the `.dsl` file in the `Dsl` project and use the information contained there to prime the `.dslsetup`, `setup.ini`, and `Strings.wxl` files that it generates.

When the setup project is built, the WiX files generated from the `.dslsetup` file are processed by the WiX tools, which generate the `.msi` file for installing the designer. This is copied to the output directory, together with `DSLToolsRedist.msi` and `setup.exe`, both of which are copied onto the DSL author's machine as part of the DSL Tools installation. The `settings.ini` file is also copied to the output directory, together with any supporting files, such as `Readme.htm`, as specified in the `.dslsetup` file.

Customizing Setup

Before releasing the final version of the installation files to users, it is likely that the DSL author will need to customize the setup project. In many cases, only changes to the supporting files, specifically `Readme.htm` and the license agreement (EULA), will be required. Further customizations can be made through the `InstallerDefinition.dsletup`, `settings.ini`, `Strings.wxl`, and `Product.ico` files.

Customizing InstallerDefinition.dslsetup

If additional installation components are required, for example, a project template, additional DLLs, or other documentation files, then the author will need to edit the `.dslsetup` file to include references to these components and, of course, supply the components themselves. A detailed description of the `.dslsetup` format is given in the next section. An example of including additional components, which requires changes to `InstallerDefinition.dsl setup`, is provided as part of the section "Deploying Text Templates for Code Generation."

Customizing settings.ini

The file `settings.ini` contains configuration data for `setup.exe`, which is generic to the installation of all designers. It identifies the particular `.msi` file for installing the designer together with the product name, as illustrated in the contents of the `settings.ini` for the setup project of the Issue State designer:

```
[Bootstrap]
Msi=IssueStateDesigner.msi
ProductName=IssueStateModels
```

> **■ TIP** When to edit settings.ini
>
> `settings.ini` should only need to be edited if the name of the product, as recorded in the DSL definition in the `Dsl` project, changes.

Customizing Strings.wxl

`Strings.wxl` allows the UI of the wizard, which is launched when installing a `.msi` file, to be localized. This file will need to be edited in order to localize the wizard for different languages. Outside of localization, an author will need to change the second, third, and fourth entries if any of this information changes after the setup project has been created:

```xml
<?xml version="1.0" encoding="utf-8" ?>
<WixLocalization xmlns="http://schemas.microsoft.com/wix/2003/11/
localization">
  <!-- Following strings will commonly need to be edited in this file. -->
  <String Id="LANG">1033</String>
  <String Id="Manufacturer">CJKW</String>
  <String Id="ProductName">IssueStateModels</String>
  <String Id="FileDescription">IssueStateModels File</String>

  <!- Following strings can generally be left as-is. ->
  …
</ WixLocalization>
```

Customizing Product.ico

The author may wish to change the `Product.ico` file in the Resources folder, which is the product icon that appears in the list of programs under the "Control Panel>Add or Remove Programs" dialog.

The .dslsetup Format

The `.dslsetup` file defines information about the designer and other components to be installed when the DSL is deployed. It can be edited to add or remove components and change the way existing components are installed. A default `.dslsetup` file is created when a DSL Setup project is created, reflecting the state of the DSL designer solution at the time of creation. This is illustrated in the `.dslsetup` file created for the Issue State designer, which is repeated in full here.

```xml
<installerDefinition xmlns="http://schemas.microsoft.com/VisualStudio/2005/
                DslTools/InstallerDefinitionModel"
        productUrl="InsertProductUrlHere"
        defaultDirectoryName="IssueStateModels"
        productVersion="1.0.0"
        requiresCSharp="true"
```

```
                         requiresVisualBasic="true"
                         productCode="416b3e59-485f-478c-87da-ad13df7952f3"
                         upgradeCode="f3653e49-fd1d-4568-b97b-4a2a78b4d7a7"
                         localeId="1033">
        <dslPackage name="IssueStateModels" project="DslPackage"
                    assemblyPath="CJKW.IssueStateModels.DslPackage.dll"
                    registryRoot="Software\Microsoft\VisualStudio\8.0">
          <fileExtensions>
            <fileExtension name="iss" extension="iss"
                           descriptionKey="FileDescription"
                           hasIcon="true" iconId="0"/>
          </fileExtensions>
            <supportingAssemblies>
              <supportingAssembly name="Dsl" project="Dsl"
                             assemblyPath="CJKW.IssueStateModels.Dsl.dll"/>
            </supportingAssemblies>
        </dslPackage>
        <licenseAgreement filePath="Files\EULA.rtf" isEmbedded="true" />
        <supportingFiles>
          <supportingFile name="Readme" filePath="Files\Readme.htm"
                          installShortcut="true"
                          shortcutIconPath="Resources\ReadmeShortcut.ico"
                          openAfterInstall="true" />
        </supportingFiles>
        <vsItemTemplates>
          <vsItemTemplate localeId="1033" targetDirectories="CSharp"
                          project="DslPackage"
                          templatePath="CSharp\1033\IssueStateModels.zip"/>
          <vsItemTemplate localeId="1033" targetDirectories="VisualBasic"
                          project="DslPackage"
                          templatePath="VisualBasic\1033\IssueStateModels.zip"/>
        </vsItemTemplates>
        <dslSchemas>
          <dslSchema project="Dsl"
                     filePath="GeneratedCode\IssueStateModelsSchema.xsd"/>
        </dslSchemas>
      </installerDefinition>
```

Let's look at this piece by piece. The top level element is `<installer-Definition>`. A number of attributes apply to this, which are explained in Table 9-1.

The `<installerDefinition>` element must have a single `<dslPackage>` child element, and the following optional child elements: `<licenseAgreement>`, `<supportingFiles>`, `<vsItemTemplates>`, `<dslSchemas>`, `<vsProjectTemplates>`, `<mergeModules>` and `<textTemplates>`. Each is considered in turn in the sections that follow.

TABLE 9-1: Attributes of <installerDefinition>

defaultDirectoryName	The name used as the default installation directory during the install process.
productUrl	URL that appears in the "Add or Remove Programs" entry for the product.
productVersion	Version of the product being installed.
requiresCSharp	Used to indicate that the C# language is a prerequisite for your DSL. If true, the installer will verify that C# is installed before installing the DSL.
requiresVisualBasic	Used to indicate that the Visual Basic language is a prerequisite for your DSL.
requiresCPlusPlus	Used to indicate that the C++ language is a prerequisite for your DSL.
requiresJSharp	Used to indicate that the J# language is a prerequisite for your DSL.
upgradeCode	MSI upgrade code. This value generally should not be changed. See the Windows Installer documentation for more details.
productCode	MSI product code. This value generally should not be changed. See the Windows Installer documentation for more details.
customFragmentIds	A semicolon-delimited list of WiX fragment identifiers. This can be used to include hand-written WiX files in the installer. Files containing the WiX fragments must be added to the project, and must have the "BuildAction" property set to "Compile." See the WiX schema documentation(http://wix.sourceforge.net/manual-wix2/wix_xsd_index.htm) for more about using fragments.

<dslPackage>

The <dslPackage> element defines all the information required to install the DSL designer. The project and assemblyPath attributes identify the location of the DLL in which the Visual Studio package implementing the DSL designer resides. This is the DLL resulting from building the DslPackage project. If the project attribute is omitted, then the path is interpreted relative to the location of the .dslsetup file. The registryRoot attribute provides the path to the location in the Windows registry in which registry entries extracted from the DslPackage DLL will be placed. These entries ensure that Visual Studio recognizes the installed package and is configured to open the designer when files of the registered extension are opened. The name attribute, like all name attributes in the .dslsetup format, is used as a unique identifier in the generated WiX.

Child elements of <dslPackage> are <fileExtensions> and <supporting-Assemblies>. The first lists file extensions that need to be registered as part of the installation. The attributes of the <fileExtension> element are explained in Table 9-2.

TABLE 9-2: Attributes of <fileExtension>

name	Used as a unique identifier in the generated WiX.
extension	The file extension string, such as .iss (the initial '.' is optional).
descriptionKey	Key into the Strings.wxl in the DSL Setup project that identifies a description string for the file extension. This is optional.
hasIcon	Indicates whether the extension is identified with its own icon.
iconId	Used to locate the icon associated with the file extension in the DSL package assembly. It is a 0-based index into the set of Win32 icon resources stored in the assembly.

<supportingAssemblies> lists all other assemblies to be installed with the DslPackage. Each assembly is identified through project and assemblyPath attributes, which are interpreted in exactly the same way as for <dslPackage> itself. In many cases, this is just the assembly resulting from building the Dsl project.

\<licenseAgreement\>

The \<licenseAgreement\> element specifies the path to the file that acts as the license agreement. The embed flag indicates whether or not the license agreement file should be embedded within the MSI or exist alongside it. If a license agreement is included, then it will be shown as part of the installation wizard, which will then not continue without the user accepting its terms.

\<supportingFiles\>

Supporting files are any other files that need to be installed along with the other components. In the Issue State example, there is one supporting file, which is the Readme.htm file. The attributes of the \<supportingFile\> element are described in Table 9-3.

TABLE 9-3: Attributes of \<supportingFile\>

name	Used as a unique identifier in the generated WiX.
project	With the filePath, locates the file to be included.
filePath	Used to locate the file to be included. It is interpreted relative to the location of the .dslsetup file or the project output directory if the project attribute is used.
openAfterInstall	Boolean value, which indicates whether the file should be opened after installation has finished.
installShortcut	Boolean value, which indicates whether a shortcut to the file should be installed to the "All Programs" menu.
embed	Boolean value, which indicates whether the file should be embedded in the MSI or exist alongside it.
shortcutIconPath	If installShortcut is true, this may be used to specify a custom icon for the shortcut. It should be a path to an icon (.ico) file, relative to the location of the InstallerDefinition.dslsetup file or the project output directory if the project attribute is used.

Readme.htm is not embedded, so it is one of the installation files alongside the MSI, and a shortcut to the Readme is also installed with its own icon. The file is also opened after installation has completed.

```
<supportingFiles>
  <supportingFile name="Readme" filePath="Files\Readme.htm"
                  installShortcut="true"
                  shortcutIconPath="Resources\ReadmeShortcut.ico"
                  openAfterInstall="true" />
</supportingFiles>
```

\<vsItemTemplates\>

VS Item Templates are the templates that appear in the "Add New Item" dialog in Visual Studio. This section allows the author to specify which Item Templates should be installed alongside the designer. Typically, this will refer to the two item templates (a VB and C# one) created as part of building the DslPackage project. The attributes of a \<vsItemTemplate\> are explained in Table 9-4.

TABLE 9-4: \<vsItemTemplate\> attributes

project	With the filePath, locates the file to be included.
localeId	The locale to which the item template applies (e.g., 1033).
targetDirectories	A semicolon-delimited list that identifies the target directories, relative to the Visual Studio item template directory, where the template should be installed. This determines the locations in the "Add New Item" dialog where the template will appear.
templatePath	The path to the .zip file containing the item template. It is interpreted relative to the location of the .dslsetup file or the project output directory if the project attribute is used.

In the Issue State example, the two item templates listed are the two resulting from building the DslPackage project:

```
<vsItemTemplates>
  <vsItemTemplate localeId="1033" targetDirectories="CSharp"
```

```
                    project="DslPackage"
                    templatePath="CSharp\1033\IssueState_CS.zip"/>
    <vsItemTemplate localeId="1033" targetDirectories="VisualBasic"
                    project="DslPackage"
                    templatePath="VisualBasic\1033\IssueState_VB.zip"/>
  </vsItemTemplates>
```

\<dslSchemas\>

This element lists XML schemas that need to be installed with the designer. Typically, there is only one, the schema generated from the DSL definition. One may have thought that these could be installed simply as supporting files, but including them in this section ensures that they are installed to a location that is recognized by Visual Studio for finding schemas to validate XML files from within the XML editor.

As elsewhere, the location of the file to be installed is determined through project and path attributes.

\<vsProjectTemplates\>

VS project templates are the templates that appear in the "Add New Project" dialog in Visual Studio, which appears when you select "File>New Project," and the information required to identify them in the .dslsetup file is similar to that required to identify VS Item Templates.

It is common to include a VS project template when the DSL provides input to code generators, because text templates are required to exist alongside models expressed using the DSL in a VS project, and the VS project will likely need to be configured in a particular way for the generated code to build. There is a section at the end of this chapter that walks through an example typifying the deployment of text templates and a VS project template for code generation.

\<mergeModules\>

This section lists Windows Installer Merge Modules (MSMs) that need to be included as part of the install. A merge module is similar in structure to a Windows Installer .msi file. However, a merge module cannot be installed alone; it must be merged into an installation package first. When a merge module is merged into the .msi file of an application, all the information and resources required to install the components delivered by the merge module are incorporated into the application's .msi file. The merge module is then no longer required to install these components and the merge module does not need to be accessible to a user. For more details about Windows Installer Merge Modules, see the MSDN platform SDK help documentation.[1]

In a DSL Tools context, merge modules might be used to package up companion tools that consume models produced by the designer but have been built in separate Visual Studio solutions; WiX could be used to create the merge module. The ability to include merge modules within the designer `.msi` file means that the designer and companion tools can be installed together in a single step.

The only information required in the `.dslsetup` file to include a merge module is a name, which is used as a unique identifier in the generated WiX, and the path to the `.msm` file, which should be relative to the location of the `.dslsetup` file.

\<textTemplates\>

Finally, a list of text templates may be provided. These are text template `include` files that get installed into the `TextTemplates` subdirectory of the target installation directory. This location is also added to the `include` files search path of the text templating Visual Studio host, which ensures that they are found when referenced from text templates in any VS project.

As elsewhere, the location of the file to be installed is determined through `project` and `path` attributes.

The deployment of text templates is illustrated in an example described in the section "Deploying Text Templates for Code Generation" later in this chapter.

The .dslsetup format as a little DSL

The DSL Setup format is a good example of a non-graphical domain-specific language that was itself created using the DSL Tools.

It is a narrowly focused language whose sole purpose is to abstract out the essential information required to generate the WiX files that can be processed to build an MSI for installing the designer and its associated components. Its use simplifies the process of creating the MSI by releasing

---

1. At the time of writing, http://msdn2.microsoft.com/en-us/library/aa369820.aspx.

the DSL author from having to understand MSIs, or the WiX used to create MSIs, and having to hand-write boilerplate WiX that would be common to the deployment of all DSLs. It is such a simple language that it is barely worth the effort of creating a designer to edit it, at least not a graphical designer. Editing the XML is sufficient.

The domain model used to define this format is illustrated in Figure 9-6. The usual text templates, as discussed in Chapters 3 and 6, were applied to generate the implementation of domain classes and relationships, and to generate the XML serialization code. A set of validation methods were written in partial classes according the scheme discussed in Chapter 7. Text templates were written to generate WiX from .dslsetup files, calling out to the validation methods before starting the generation, following the approach discussed in Chapter 8. The directive processor used in those templates is a customized version of the one generated from the domain model. It is customized to look through the VS solution and resolve file paths for components identified through a project and path.

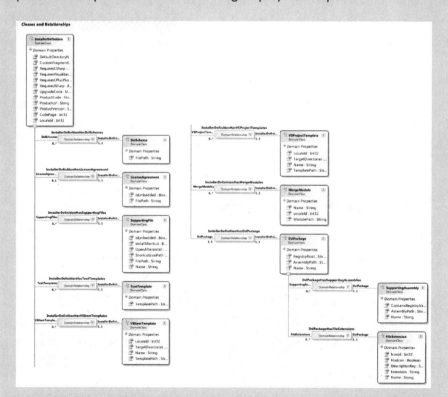

FIGURE 9-6: DSL Definition for .dslsetup format

> A similar approach could be used to develop similar languages for installing other kinds of applications.

Refreshing the Installation Files

A sequence of steps is required to refresh a set of installation files after changes have been made to the designer. It's not enough just to rebuild the setup project, which only causes the `.msi` file for the designer to be regenerated from the already generated WiX files. It may be necessary to regenerate the WiX files themselves first. The `.msi` file is built from the WiX packages together with the components that implement the designer, such as the DLLs that result from building the `DslPackage` project and the `Dsl` project in the designer solution. The text templates that generate the WiX files from the `.dslsetup` file access the VS solution structure to resolve file path names specified in the `.dslsetup` file to locate the components, such as DLLs, that need to be installed. They also reflect on some of these components to extract information that is then injected into the WiX files that are generated. This information may change whenever the designer is rebuilt.

This means that in order to refresh the installation files, the following steps must be performed in the order specified:

1. Rebuild the `DslPackage` and `Dsl` projects.
2. Regenerate the WiX files, by transforming all the templates in the `DslSetup` project.
3. Rebuild the setup project.

The result of executing the text templates in the setup project is also influenced by the current solution configuration being used on build, typically Debug or Release. The solution configuration influences the location of the build output directory. So if the configuration is set to Release from Debug, then the location of the DLLs built from the `DslPackage` and `Dsl` directories switches from `bin\Debug` to `bin\Release` under each project. This change of location is picked up by the text templates in the setup project when they are reapplied, and the installation files are also generated to `bin\Release` in the setup project.

Package Load Key

You'll find that if you try to install and run a DSL designer on a machine without the Visual Studio SDK installed, it won't work. When you start Visual Studio you'll get a package load error, where the package causing the error is your designer. This is because a designer built using the DSL Tools is implemented as a Visual Studio package, and in order for it to load on a machine that does not have the Visual Studio SDK installed (but does have Visual Studio Standard Edition or later installed), it must have been given a package load key (PLK). A PLK is a string comprising a long sequence of capital letters and numbers. A specimen example is given below:

```
P2R2E3I1HTRJH3DJIEKKDPRMD3JEECIHRHQ8C3EZZRMRAZC1AAK2KZA9RJDJKKKPZ3A3HMHJPKI-
IMIHKC2C3EQE3KHKTM3HPQPIHADPKRIQ8JQDHPMQIRJIPIHABCDEF
```

A PLK can be obtained by filling in a form online at the Visual Studio extensibility website,[2] where a package author provides details about the product and package the load key is for. More detailed instructions are available from the MSDN help pages at http://msdn2.microsoft.com/en-us/library/bb165395(VS.80).aspx. If this link does not work, then go to http://msdn2.microsoft.com/ and search for "How to obtain a PLK." Once the details about the product have been submitted, the key is emailed to the author.

> ■ **TIP** Points to note when applying for a PLK
>
> There are two cases: either you are already registered as a VSIP partner or you are not. If you are not, you must associate your .NET Passport or Windows Live account to a VSIP account. If you don't have a passport account, you can create one.
>
> Registering as a VSIP Partner is free, but care should be taken when providing the Company Name, because it cannot be changed afterwards and is associated with your .NET passport / Windows Live account. The company name must also match the company name you used when authoring the designer to be registered.
>
> Requesting a PLK is free, but the registration for the product cannot be removed once created.

---

2. The Visual Studio 2005 Extensibility Center can be found at http://msdn.microsoft.com/vstudio/extend/. You can sign in to register your product and obtain a PLK at http://affiliate.vsipmembers.com/affiliate/default.aspx.

Once the author has the key, he needs to do some work in the `DslPackage` solution to ensure that it is included with the package. Specifically, he needs to apply the `ProvidePackageLoadKey` attribute to the `Package` class. This can be done by uncommenting the `[VSShell::ProvideLoadKey(...)]` lines in the following fragment of `Shell\Package.tt`:

```
...
/// <remarks>
/// A package load key is required to allow this package to load
/// when the Visual Studio SDK is not installed.
/// Package load keys may be obtained from
/// http://msdn.microsoft.com/vstudio/extend.
/// Consult the Visual Studio SDK documentation for more information.
/// [VSShell::ProvideLoadKey("Standard", Constants.ProductVersion,
///      Constants.ProductName, Constants.CompanyName, 1)]
/// </remarks>
...
internal sealed partial class <#= dslName #>Package :
      <#= dslName #>PackageBase
{
}
...
```

The combination of the first four parameters to this attribute (minimum edition, product version, product name, and company name) are encoded in the PLK. The author will be asked to provide these values when requesting the PLK; the values are provided in properties on the `Dsl` node in the explorer when viewing the DSL definition through the DSL designer. The author will also be asked to provide the package GUID, which can be found in the same place. Be aware that the components of the version are not in the right order in the properties window (`Build` number is first, and then `MajorVersion`, `MinorVersion`, and `Revision`) so be sure to provide the right version number. In case of doubt, look in the `Constants.cs` generated file, where you are certain to find the right values.

The last parameter to the `ProvideLoadKey` attribute indicates the key into the entry in `VSPackage.resx`, found in the `DslPackage` project, which holds the PLK string. For example, given the preceding code, the PLK resource would have key "1." The `VSPackage.resx` file must be edited to add a string entry with this key, giving it the value of the PLK obtained via the VS SDK website, as illustrated in Figure 9-7.

Name	▲ Value	Comment
101	IssueStateModels	
102	Adds a IssueStateModels file to the project.	
103	IssueStateModels	
1	P2R2E3I1HTRJH3DJIEKKDPRMD3JEECIHRHQ8C3EZZRN	
*		

FIGURE 9-7: View of VSPackage.resx in the .resx editor, showing the entry with the PLK

Once this is all done, the steps in the previous section should be followed to refresh the installation files, and once the designer is installed there should no longer be a package load error when Visual Studio is launched.

> **TIP** To test that the PLK is working, run devenv with /NoVSIP switch
>
> Install the designer on your machine using the install files generated from the setup project. Open the Visual Studio 2005 command prompt, from "Start>All Programs>Microsoft Visual Studio 2005>Visual Studio Tools." In the command window type "devenv /NoVSIP". In the copy of Visual Studio that opens, use "Add>New Item..." within a suitable project to create a new model in your designer.

Deploying Text Templates for Code Generation

Chapter 8 described how to generate code and other text artifacts from a model, and it showed how to do this for the Issue Project DSL.

Recall that text templates were developed inline in the debugging solution, where they could be run against test models. One constraint on the way in which templates are invoked in the DSL Tools V1 (i.e., by using the "Transform All Templates" button at the top of the solution explorer), is that they must appear in the same solution as the model files that provide input to the templates, and each of them must have a directive at the top that identifies the specific model file that is providing input.[3]

Creating a Project Template from the Debugging Project

This means that if you want to deploy the text templates together with the DSL, you need to package them up in some way. Fortunately, Visual Studio

---

3. Unless you orchestrate code generation from the menu item on the designer, as discussed in Chapter 8.

allows you to export a project as a project template, and this mechanism can be used to package up the templates. As explained earlier, a project template can be included in the `.dslsetup` file for inclusion in the `.msi`. The steps are as follows.

1. Clean up the `Debugging` project of your DSL authoring solution so it is suitable as the basis of a project template. A project containing a blank model file, plus the text templates, would make a suitable basis.

2. With the project selected in the solution explorer, run the "File>Export Template" command. This will create the project template.

3. Copy the created project template into the setup project of the DSL authoring solution. After this step, you should see something like Figure 9-8.

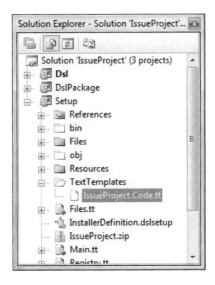

FIGURE 9-8: VS project template added to setup project

4. Add a line to the `.dslsetup` file to include the project template— something like the following:

```
<vsProjectTemplates>
  <vsProjectTemplate localeId="1033"
                     targetDirectories="CSharp"
                     templatePath="IssueProject.zip"/>
</vsProjectTemplates>
```

5. Rerun the text templates in the DSL authoring solution, which will then regenerate the WiX files from the `.dslsetup` file.

6. Rebuild the setup project to create the `.msi`.

Using a Text Template Include File

A further refinement you can make is to change the text templates in the Debugging project so that they only include two lines: a directive identifying the input model file, and a directive for including another text template file that contains the main body of the template. The included text template should be kept in the same directory as the including text template. Once tested, a copy of the included template can then be placed in the setup project for inclusion in the `.msi` file. This refinement means that users of the DSL can easily create new text templates for each new model file, because all they have to do is create a template containing two lines. They also don't need to mess with the code generators themselves, or, at least, not without going to look for the place where it has been installed.

For example, if we want to apply this refinement to the Issue Project DSL, change the text template created in Chapter 8 to have something like the following two lines:

```
<#@ include file="IssueProject.Code.tt" #>
<#@ IssueProject processor="IssueProjectDirectiveProcessor" requires="file-
Name='Ch8.1.issueproj'" #>
```

where the included file, `IssueProject.Code.tt`, now contains the main body of the template:

```
<#@ template
  inherits="Microsoft.VisualStudio.TextTemplating.VSHost.ModelingTextTransformation"
  debug="true"#>
<#@ output extension=".cs" #>
using System;
using System.Collections.Generic;
using System.Text;

<#
etc.
```

Do not include the include file in the project (otherwise it will be executed with all the others and fail). However, when you execute the original template, you should find that it still works (template execution looks first in the same folder as the template being executed for include files). Once you've checked that it works, create a copy of the include file and put it in the setup project as illustrated in Figure 9-9. Again, don't include it in the project itself, or it will be executed every time the templates in the authoring solution are executed.

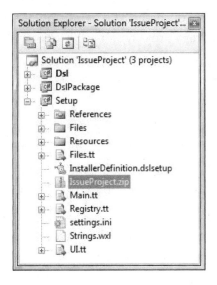

FIGURE 9-9: Setup project showing .tt include file

Finally, add the following lines to the `.dslsetup` file, rerun the text templates, and build the setup project, as before.

```
<textTemplates>
  <textTemplate templatePath="TextTemplates\IssueProject.Code.tt"/>
</textTemplates>
```

When the resulting `.msi` is executed to install the DSL, it will install the text templates identified in the `.dslsetup` file into the TextTemplates subdirectory of the target installation directory, a location that is registered with the text templating execution engine, as explained earlier.

Including Text Templates in the VS Item Template

If the instructions so far have been followed, a user of the DSL will be able to unfold the project template, create a model file using "Add New Item," add a text template containing only two lines—the two directives mentioned in the previous section, and then use this to generate code from the model. The last refinement is to automate the step of adding the text template containing the two lines, which would otherwise have to be done manually for every model file created.

This step is automated by making a change to the project item template that is installed with the designer. The definition of the item templates can be found in the DslPackage project, under the ProjectItemTemplates folder. We'll show how to make changes to the CSharp template; the VisualBasic template can be altered in a similar way.

First, create a file in that folder containing just the two directives identified in the previous section, replacing the name of the file in the requires clause for the second directive to $safeitemname$, as follows:

```
<#@ include file="IssueProject.Code.tt" #>
<#@ IssueProject processor="IssueProjectDirectiveProcessor" requires="file-
Name='$safeitemname$'" #>
```

Save the file as issueproj.ttfile, where issueproj is the file extension being used for the Issue Project DSL (you'll use your own file extension for your own DSL).

> **⬛ TIP Why not use a .tt extension?**
>
> Using a .tt extension would automatically cause the file to be associated with the TextTemplatingFileGenerator, which will be executed every time the "Transform All Templates" button is used in the authoring solution. Using the .tt file extension avoids this.

This provides the text of the new file to be created alongside the model file. $safeitemname$ will be substituted for the item name entered in the "Add New Item" dialog on item template expansion.

Now we need to reference this file from the item template definition. Open CSharp.tt in the same folder and edit it to add an entry in the <TemplateContent> section, as follows (the entry is shown in *bold italics*):

```
<#@ template
inherits="Microsoft.VisualStudio.TextTemplating.VSHost.ModelingTextTransformation"
  debug="true"#>
<#@ output extension=".vstemplate" #>
<#@ Dsl processor="DslDirectiveProcessor"
requires="fileName='..\..\Dsl\DslDefinition.dsl'" #>
<!--DSL Tools Language Template-->
<VSTemplate Version="2.0.0" Type="Item"
xmlns="http://schemas.microsoft.com/developer/vstemplate/2005"
xmlns:xsi="http://www.w3.org/2001/XMLSchema-instance">
  <TemplateData>
    <Name Package="{<#= this.Dsl.PackageGuid #>}" ID="103"/>
    <Description Package="{<#= this.Dsl.PackageGuid #>}" ID="102"/>
    <Icon Package="{<#= this.Dsl.PackageGuid #>}" ID="201" />
    <ProjectType>CSharp</ProjectType>
    <SortOrder>360</SortOrder>
    <DefaultName>
      <#=this.Dsl.Name#>.<#=this.Dsl.Editor.FileExtension#>
    </DefaultName>
    <AppendDefaultFileExtension>true</AppendDefaultFileExtension>
  </TemplateData>
  <TemplateContent>
    <ProjectItem TargetFileName="
        $fileinputname$.<#=this.Dsl.Editor.FileExtension#>">
      <#=this.Dsl.Editor.FileExtension#>.<#=this.Dsl.Editor.FileExtension#>
    </ProjectItem>
    <ProjectItem TargetFileName="
        $fileinputname$.<#=this.Dsl.Editor.FileExtension#>.diagram">
      <#=this.Dsl.Editor.FileExtension#>.diagram
    </ProjectItem>
    <ProjectItem ReplaceParameters="true"
            TargetFileName="$fileinputname$.tt">
      <#=this.Dsl.Editor.FileExtension#>.ttfile
    </ProjectItem>
  </TemplateContent>
</VSTemplate>
```

This new entry ensures that when this item template is used to add a file, not only does it add the model and corresponding diagram file, but it also adds a correspondingly named .tt file based on the .ttfile item template created in the first step. If you regenerate, rebuild, and relaunch the debugging solution, and then use "Add New Item" to create a new model for your designer, you'll see that the .tt file now gets added automatically. You don't need to make any changes to the setup project, because it picks up only the built project item templates, which will incorporate these changes when you build the DslPackage project.

SUMMARY

This chapter described how to create a setup project in a DSL authoring solution and use this to build installation files for deploying a DSL designer and associated components. It explained the contents of the setup project, in particular, the format of the `.dslsetup` file. The `.dslsetup` file is the main focus of change when customizing or adding to the installation files generated. The chapter also explained the process for refreshing the installation files whenever the designer and/or other components are changed, and concluded with an example of deploying a set of text templates for code generation, which involved the creation of a project template, customization of the `.dslsetup` file to include this and supporting text templates, and extension of item templates to add a `.tt` file whenever a new model file is created by the user of the DSL.

10

Advanced DSL Customization

Introduction

You can design a good range of graphical languages just by editing the DSL definition. As we've seen in previous chapters, you can go beyond that, writing code to define validation checks (Chapter 7), to generate material from your users' models (Chapter 8), and to customize the fine detail of the language features (Chapters 3–5). These extra facilities can be picked up progressively—the gradual steps upward that allow you broader and broader scope, as we illustrated in Chapter 1.

This chapter brings together the level of customization that involves writing code. Many of the topics have been touched on in earlier chapters, but here our intention is to go into customization techniques in more detail.

Tools for Customization

There are a number of basic mechanisms we use to enable us to integrate custom and generated code.

Partial Classes

Partial classes are the feature of .NET languages that allows the methods of one class to be compiled from several different files. All the generated classes are partial, allowing you not only to add methods of your own to a class in a separate file, but also to add overrides of methods defined in the framework base classes. Never change the content of the generated code—add material in separate files.

You can override and add methods to the generated code in your partial class. But if you add a private variable in a partial class, it won't be kept in the store, and so (a) events and rules can't be used to observe it, (b) any undo that the user performs won't apply to it, and (c) it won't be persisted and reloaded when the user saves the model. Generally, therefore, you should not declare member variables in custom code (even if you don't need them to be persisted); declare properties in the DSL definition.

Double Derived—The Generation Gap

If you look at the generated code, for example, for any shape in Dsl\ GeneratedCode\Shapes.cs, you'll see that there are a variety of methods that it might be interesting to modify such as HasBackgroundGradient(), which always returns a fixed value (depending on how you have set the **FillGradient** domain property of the shape in the DSL definition). But perhaps you would like to make it variable at runtime so that the existence of the gradient can give some indication of state, and so you would like to override the method. Unfortunately, that is not how partial classes work; your custom code is in the same class as the generated material.

The solution is to select the domain class, relationship, or shape in the DSL definition and set to true the "Generates Double Derived" flag in the properties window. Now when you regenerate the code (by clicking "Transform All Templates" in the header of the solution explorer), the generator creates two classes, one derived from the other. All the generated methods and properties are placed into the base class, leaving only constructors in the derived class. It is always the derived class that is instantiated. In your custom code, you can now override any methods defined (or overridden) by the generated code (Figure 10-1).

This is a use of the "Generation Gap" design pattern described by John Vlissides (in his book *Pattern Hatching* [Addison-Wesley, 1998]). It is an important technique wherever code is generated, enabling you to preserve the generated material and regenerate it when required without losing your customizations.

Double derived is useful for diagrams, shapes, and connectors. It is less useful for the generated code of domain classes and relationships because they just contain accessors for properties and relationships.

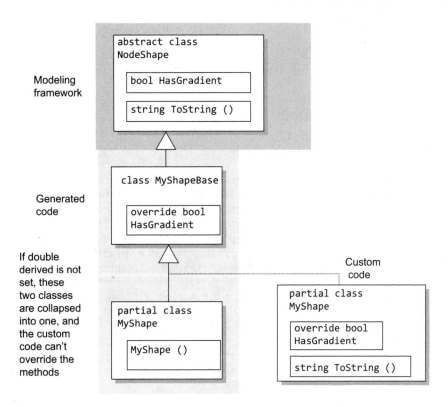

FIGURE 10-1: Double derived classes

Some classes not directly defined in the DSL definition, such as Toolbox-Helper, are double derived by default.

Custom Constructors

Double derivation doesn't work for constructors—the constructors have to be in the class they're constructing, of course. If you want to override a constructor, therefore, you need to tell the generators not to create one. To do this, set the flag "Has Custom Constructor" in the domain class properties. The resulting generated code will not compile until you provide the constructor.

Customization Switches

Customization switches are Boolean properties in the DSL definition that cause the generated code to invoke a method that must be supplied by you. For example, if you set "Is Custom" in a connection builder, the solution will not build until you have supplied the missing code, in a partial class.

Comments near the resulting errors in the generated code give brief guidance on what you need to provide.

Table 10-1 lists the most commonly used customization switches.

TABLE 10-1: Customization Switches

To provide code to do this	Set this
Derive the value of a property from others.	**DomainProperty.Kind** = *Calculated* for a read-only property; *CustomStorage* to provide both setter and getter.
Variable tooltip.	**TooltipType** = *Variable* on the mapped shape. Code can be provided in an abstract base shape, but the setting itself is not inherited.
Determine what element tools can be dragged onto a class, and what happens when dragged.	**UsesCustomAccept** and **UsesCustomMerge** in the element merge directive of the receiving domain class.
Determine the parent shape of a new shape.	**HasCustomParentElement** in the **ShapeMap** for the shape.
Determine the list of displayed elements in a Compartment Shape.	**UseCustomElement** in the **CompartmentShape** Map.
Determine what may be connected by a connection tool, and what happens when the connection is made.	**CustomAccept** and **CustomConnect** in the Source and Target Role Directives in a **Link-ConnectDirective.**
	LinkConnectDirective.UsesCustomConnect and **ConnectionBuilder. IsCustom** provide for customization of more of the behavior.
Define how a class is serialized to file.	**IsCustom** in the XML Class Data for the domain class.
	HasCustomMoniker in the XML Property Data for a property allows you to customize the physical representation of a moniker in a serialized file.
Additional processing after a model is loaded from file.	**CustomPostLoad** in XML Serialization Behavior.

Custom Overrides

A great many methods can be overridden to change the behavior of the designer, especially in shape, connector, and diagram classes. The complete set can be seen by writing a partial class and typing "override"—the Visual Studio IntelliSense system will prompt you with the possibilities.

Some useful overrides are listed in Table 10-2.

TABLE 10-2: Custom Overrides

Class group	Methods	Used for
Domain classes	OnDeleted(), OnDeleting(), OnCopy()	
Property handlers MyClass. MyProperty- Handler	OnValueChanged(), OnValueChanging()	Propagating changes to display states or external applications, and to update calculated properties. You can also disallow a value by throwing an InvalidOperation exception.
Shapes	CanFocus	Can receive keyboard input and mouse clicks.
	CanMerge()	Allows a paste operation.
	CanMove	Can be moved.
	CanSelect	Can be added to the current selection.
	HasShadow	Set false to lose the default shadow effect.
	OnDoubleClick()	Intercept mouse actions—one of many.
	OnBoundsFixup()	Use to place a new shape when its domain element is first created.

Continues

TABLE 10-2: *Continued*

Class group	Methods	Used for
	`Initialize Resources()`	Set the fill and outline colors and styles. Called once per class.
	`OnInitialize()`	Called once per shape.
Connectors	`CanManuallyRoute`	Set false to prevent the user rerouting.
	`DefaultRoutingStyle`	A wider set than available in the DSL definition.
Diagram	`DefaultGridSize`	Return smaller values to allow finer positioning.
	`RequiresWatermark,` `WatermarkText`	Sets the text that appears in a blank diagram.
ToolboxHelper	`CreateElementToolPrototype`	Create multi-object prototypes on the toolbox.
DocData	`OnDocumentLoaded`	Initialize non-persisted data from the model.

Responding to Changes

Much of the custom code you need to write within a designer is about responding to changes initiated by the user, or in some cases preventing certain changes. This section brings together all the techniques for doing that. Some of them we have discussed before, but here we try to compare and contrast so that you can see which technique to apply.

As a rough guide, consider the techniques in the order of presentation here.

Property Handlers "On Value Changed/Changing"

Each domain class has an internal handler class for each property. This has methods you can override: in particular, `OnValueChanging()` and

OnValueChanged(), called immediately before and immediately after the changes.

For example, if a domain class **IssueProject** has a string domain property **Sort**, we can add a partial class like this:

```
public partial class IssueProject
{
  internal sealed partial class SortPropertyHandler
  {
    protected override void OnValueChanged(State element,
                            string oldValue, string newValue)
    {
      if (!this.Store.InUndoRedoOrRollback)
      {
        // propagate in-Store changes here...
      }
      // propagate external changes here...

      // And always call the base method!
      base.OnValueChanged(element, oldValue, newValue);
    }
  }
}
```

The handlers are only called if the new and old values are not the same; they don't get called just because an assignment has happened.

Use OnValueChanged to propagate changes either inside or outside the store.

One use of OnValueChanging is to throw an exception if you don't like the value that is about to be set.

These handlers are not available for built-in properties such as the bounds of a shape.

Undo, Redo, and Property Handlers

If the user invokes "undo," all of the changes made to the store in the most recent top-level transaction are undone. The undo mechanism essentially works by keeping a trail of previous values of every property, instance, link, and shape in the store. Undo replaces every value with its old one, while redo just winds the tape forward again.

This means that methods and rules that only propagate changes around the store should not operate when an undo or redo is happening. If a method's job is to keep one store value in line with another, then it only needs to calculate a new value when we're really going forward.

For this reason, the above code uses `Store.InUndoRedoOrRollback` to guard the part of the code that deals with in-store content, that is, anything that sets any domain property, or creates or deletes an instance of a domain class or relationship, or a shape, connector, or diagram.

However, let's suppose that this domain property's purpose is to be the proxy for some external state: a database entry, a piece of user interface, or even a chunk of hardware. In that case, the handler should certainly keep the external state in step with undos and redos, and that part of its code would be outside the guard.

Calculated Domain Properties

A calculated domain property is not stored but always computed using a getter you supply.

Calculated properties are good for any case where the property should be a determined function of either external state, or other parts of the model—for example, a sum of other values, a count of relationships, or a composition of other strings.

There is an example of a calculated property in the Class Diagrams sample that can be found in the Visual Studio SDK Samples. Each **Model-Attribute** displayed in a **ModelClass** has two domain properties called **name** and **type**, which the user can see and alter in the properties window in the usual way. But on the diagram, each **ModelAttribute**'s name and type appear in a single line: "name : Type". This is useful because each model attribute appears as one line of a compartment shape (Figure 10-2).

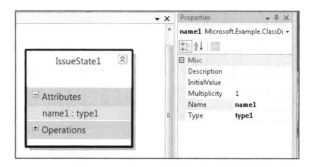

FIGURE 10-2: Two property values displayed on one line
in a compartment shape

To get this effect, we create a domain property called **NameAndType** in the **ModelAttribute** domain class, and set its "Kind" to *Calculated* in the properties window. "Transform All Templates" and an attempt at building produce the error message that we have not defined a method in the `Model-Attribute` class, and following the error takes us to a helpful comment in the generated code that tells us what's expected: in this case, a getter method for `NameAndType`.

The expected method for a calculated domain property is always called `GetXXXValue()`, where `XXX` is the name of the domain property. In a separate custom code file, we provide the required code. It just combines the values from the two other domain properties:

```
public partial class ModelAttribute
{
    public string GetNameAndTypeValue()
    {
        return this.Name.Trim() + " : " + this.Type.Trim();
    }
}
```

To avoid confusing the user, we set the "Is Browsable" flag of this domain property to `false`, so that it does not appear in the properties window at runtime. (You could alternatively set "Is UI Read Only" to `true`, which allows the user to see it in the properties window without modifying it there.)

You can use any source data for the calculation—they don't have to be in the store. For example, you might use the value to determine the orientation of an image, or perhaps to set the content of a file.

Custom Storage Domain Properties

A *CustomStorage* domain property is one where you provide both setter and getter. You save the value however you like—for example, in the state of some external application or just by setting the values of other properties in the store.

In the Name and Type example, rather than insist that values be entered through separate lines in the properties window, we can let the user set both name and type properties by typing into the display field, separating the name and type with a colon (":").

Set the **NameAndType** property's "Kind" to *CustomStorage*, transform, and rebuild in the usual way. The build error tells us we need another method:

```
public partial class ModelAttribute
{
  public void SetNameAndTypeValue(string newValue)
  {
    if (!this.Store.InUndoRedoOrRollback)
    {
      // in-Store changes
      string[] separated = newValue.Split(new char[] { ':' });
      if (separated.Length > 0) this.Name = separated[0].Trim();
      if (separated.Length > 1) this.Type = separated[1].Trim();
    }

    // Handle here any propagation outside the Store.

  }
}
```

Notice that this method guards changes it makes within the store with `InUndoRedoOrRollback`, in the same way as `OnValueChanged()`; and if there are any changes to be made outside the store, they should happen anyway.

If you really want to ensure that your custom storage domain property works just like a real one, then you should

- Do nothing if the old and new values are equal.
- Call `ValueChanging()` and `ValueChanged()` before and after your update; these in turn call `OnValueChanging/ed()` and ensure that any rules defined on the property work properly.

The extended result looks like this:

```
public partial class ModelAttribute
{
  public void SetNameAndTypeValue(string newValue)
  {
    string oldValue = this.GetNameAndTypeValue();
    if (oldValue != newValue)
    {
      ValueChanging(this, newValue, oldValue);
      if (!this.Store.InUndoRedoOrRollback)
      {
```

```
        // in-Store changes
        string[] separated = newValue.Split(new char[] { ':' });
        if (separated.Length > 0) this.Name = separated[0].Trim();
        if (separated.Length > 1) this.Type = separated[1].Trim();
      }

      // Handle here any propagation outside the Store.
      // ...

      ValueChanged(this, newValue, oldValue);
    }
  }
}
```

> **■ TIP** Calculated properties, Custom Storage, and value handlers
>
> Use **Calculated** properties where you want a value to depend completely on others, and want it to be read-only. Use **Custom Storage** properties when you also want to write back to the places from which the value is derived. If those other values can't represent all of its state, use an ordinary property but propagate its value with `OnValueChanged ()`.

Notify Value Change

If you tried the Calculated Value example, you may have noticed that when you change, say, the **Type** property, the display of the calculated **Name-AndType** does not immediately change. You have to reselect the diagram or cause a redisplay in some other way to see the change.

By themselves, custom and calculated values don't automatically propagate changes to their observers. They will recalculate the value when asked, but unlike ordinary domain properties, have no inbuilt mechanism for telling interested parties when the calculated value might have changed. We have to do this for them, by observing each of the source values in some way—for example, by overriding a property handler—and calling `Notify-ValueChange()` on the calculated or custom domain property. That call will propagate changes to observers by firing rules and events just as a change in a normal property does.

```
public partial class ModelAttribute
{
  internal sealed partial class TypePropertyHandler
```

```
  {
    protected override void OnValueChanged(ModelAttribute element,
                                  string oldValue, string newValue)
    {
      base.OnValueChanged(element, oldValue, newValue);
      element.Store.DomainDataDirectory.
        GetDomainProperty(ModelAttribute.NameAndTypeDomainPropertyId)
            .NotifyValueChange(element);
    }
  }
}
```

Notice the method is actually on the **DomainPropertyInfo** class, whose instance represents the definition of the **NameAndType** domain property within the **ModelAttribute** class. (This is one of the metadata classes from which you can get information at runtime about the DSL definition.)

Propagating Change from Model to Shape: OnAssociatedPropertyChanged

As we know from Chapter 4, the shape map is the principal method of defining how model elements and links are presented using shapes and connectors. The visibility of the shapes' decorators and the text presented in the shapes can be controlled by the domain properties of the presented model elements.

The mechanism we look at here provides a complementary and more customizable method that allows change to propagate along the same conduit: the PresentationViewsSubject relationship between model elements and their presentation elements.

As an example, consider the class diagrams standard template that comes with the DSL Tools. Running it, you see that it allows you to draw classes that can be interconnected by several different kinds of association. Unfortunately, once you have created a particular sort of association, you cannot change it to any other, and the several different sorts make a long list in the toolbox (Figure 10-3).

We can make a substantial improvement on this. (And there is an implementation of this solution in the class diagrams sample that comes with the Visual Studio SDK—look in the sample browser.)

Let's just have a single type of **Association** (a relationship between the model classes), and let's give it an enumerated property **Sort**. We want the user to be able to change the sort of an existing association simply by selecting it and changing its "Sort" in the properties window. In response, the ends of the connector should change to show various combinations of diamonds, arrowheads, and plain ends.

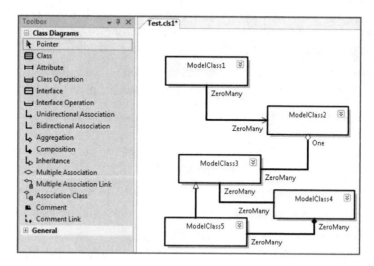

FIGURE 10-3: Standard Class Diagrams template has several separate types of association.

First, features such as connector ends, line thicknesses, colors, and so on are not governed by the shape maps, so we need to use custom code to change them.

For `OnAssociatedPropertyChanged()` to work, we must first set it up by calling a static method of the connector. We only need to do this once for the class—it isn't necessary to set up an observer relationship separately for each instance. We set it up like this:

```
public partial class AssociationConnector
{
  protected override void InitializeResources (StyleSet classStyleSet)
  {
    base.InitializeResources(classStyleSet); // don't forget!

    AssociationConnector.AssociateValueWith(this.Store,
                           Association.SortDomainPropertyId);
  }
}
```

> **■ TIP Override InitializeResources to set up per-class relationships involving shapes or connectors**
>
> Even though this is an instance method, it is called once for each shape or connector class when the package is loaded. It's better to perform setups here than in a class initializer, because at this point all the required initializations will have been done.
>
> In some cases it is necessary to set the "Generates Double Derived" flag for the shape or connector in the DSL definition.

In this DSL definition, `AssociationConnector` is the connector that will present Association relationships on the screen. The argument `Association.SortDomainPropertyId` identifies the **Sort** domain property of the relationship to which the connector is mapped. Each property has a `XXXDomainPropertyId`.

Once this setup has been performed, `OnAssociatedPropertyChanged()` will be called whenever this domain property's value changes. We write it in the same class:

```
protected override void OnAssociatedPropertyChanged
                                      (PropertyChangedEventArgs e)
{
  // Called for a change in any property, so we must discriminate:
  if ("Sort".Equals(e.PropertyName))
  {
    // OK; we know the type of domain property "Sort" from DSL Defn:
    switch ((AssociationSort)e.NewValue)
    {
      // Set the arrowheads depending on the sort of association:
      case AssociationSort.Aggregation:
        this.DecoratorTo = null;
        this.DecoratorFrom = LinkDecorator.DecoratorEmptyDiamond;
        break;
      // and so on for other values and other properties…
    }
  }
  base.OnAssociatedPropertyChanged(e);
}
```

This method will be called on an instance of the connector whenever any associated property changes on the mapped domain relationship instance.

It is essential to begin by checking which property has changed, because the generated code may have registered the class to observe several other properties. The event arguments contain the name of the changed property and its old and new values. The old and new values will always be of the appropriate type for the property (possibly including null).

The arrowheads, colors, line thickness, visibility, and other visual properties of a shape or connector are *not* domain properties, persisted in the store—although the shapes and connectors themselves are. These properties should therefore be handled as we've described for external state, so there is no check to see whether we are InUndoRedoOrRollback. (It is possible to define domain properties on shapes, and you could use On-AssociatedPropertyChanged() to update them from the model element properties. In that case, you would avoid updating them in an Undo.)

Always call the overridden method in base; in this case, we do so at the end, because it will take care of redisplaying the connector.

> ■**TIP** Use OnAssociatedPropertyChanged to link shape features to domain properties
>
> This is the easiest way to make the color, line thickness, and other features of a shape depend on domain properties.

Why don't we use some other method to perform this function? For example, could we define an OnValueChanged() in the **Sort** domain property, and make that update the arrowheads? Well, yes, but (a) it would be necessary to navigate explicitly the PresentationViewsSubject link between the model element and the connector, (b) to future-proof that, we should allow for the possibility of different views on the same model, and (c) putting the display logic in the main part of the model doesn't feel like good separation of concerns. The OnAssociatedPropertyChanged() method provides you with a convenient way to add relationships between presentation and model, augmenting the basic facilities of the shape maps.

Rules

Rules are the most general purpose mechanism for propagating and responding to change within the store. Rules are triggered by changes in the store such as property value changes, or the creation or deletion of an object or link, shape, or connector.

In the usual case, the rule executes during the `Commit()` operation of the outermost transaction in which the triggering change occurred. A rule can trigger further firings, which are added to the end of the queue. The transaction is completed when the rule firing queue is empty. It is of course possible for badly organized rules to cause a transaction never to complete, until the firing queue runs out of space.

> **■ TIP** **Consider other mechanisms before rules**
>
> Because rules can execute in a difficult-to-control order, a large set of rules can be difficult to debug. So although rules are a powerful and general mechanism, it's good to look first for other ways of achieving the result you want.

Here is the code of a rule. This rule responds to the change of any shape's absolute bounds (that is, if it moves or changes shape).

```
[RuleOn(typeof(NodeShape), FireTime = TimeToFire.TopLevelCommit)]
public sealed class ContainerShapeChangesRule : ChangeRule
{
  public override void ElementPropertyChanged
                              (ElementPropertyChangedEventArgs e)
  {
    NodeShape stateShape = e.ModelElement as NodeShape;
    if (stateShape == null) return;
    if (stateShape.Store.TransactionManager.
                CurrentTransaction.IsSerializing)) return;

    if (e.DomainProperty.Id == NodeShape.AbsoluteBoundsDomainPropertyId)
    {
      RectangleD oldBounds = (RectangleD)e.OldValue;
      RectangleD newBounds = stateShape.AbsoluteBoundingBox;

      HandleAbsoluteBoundsChange(stateShape, oldBounds, newBounds);
} }
```

Notice:

- The RuleOn attribute marks this class as a rule.
- The rule class can be called anything you like, but must inherit from one of a fixed set of abstract rules.
- The rule is defined on a class (NodeShape, in this case); it does not have to be separately registered for each instance.
- The code of the rule is entirely separate from the code of the class it observes.

The RuleOn Attribute

```
[RuleOn(typeof(NodeShape), FireTime = TimeToFire.TopLevelCommit)]
```

The attribute specifies the observed class, which may be any domain class, relationship, shape, connector, or diagram. You cannot specify that a rule observes a particular property of a class, nor that it observes specific instances. You must specify the class to which the property you are interested in belongs. In this case, we specify NodeShape so that we can look at the AbsoluteBounds properties of the shapes.

NodeShape is the common base class of all shapes. To catch all connectors, use BinaryLinkShape; all connectors or shapes, ShapeElement; all relationships, ElementLink. ModelElement is the superclass of everything.

You can apply as many rules as you like to the same class. Changes in any instance of the class (and its subclasses) will trigger all the applied rules.

TopLevelCommit is the usual FireTime, but you can also specify Local-Commit, which means that the rule executes at the end of the innermost transaction; or you can specify InLine, which means that the rule executes as soon as possible after the triggering change.

You can also set a Priority integer. The problem with using priorities is that you pretty soon get to devising some big table of all the relative priorities of your rules and start depending on them firing in that order, with one rule depending on another having set something up. Pretty soon after that, you're into rule spaghetti, finding it impossible to debug heaps of rules that fire in the wrong order. So on the whole, it's easier to leave the priority at the default and write your rules not to assume any particular order of execution.

You can set `InitiallyDisabled` = `true` in the `RuleOn` attribute, and rules can be turned on and off using the store's RuleManager. In Chapter 7, we saw an example where the rule was turned off until the model had loaded.

```
store.RuleManager.EnableRule(typeof(ContainerShapeChangesRule));
```

Rule Types

Each rule must be a subclass of one of a fixed set of base classes. These provide the means to observe different categories of events. Rule base classes are listed in Table 10-3.

TABLE 10-3: Rule Types

Rule base class	Fires when
AddRule	An element is created. Consider whether you want to apply this to the element or the shape that presents it. If you need to guarantee to fire after the shape and the element have been connected, apply an `AddRule` to `PresentationViewsSubject`.
DeleteRule	An element has been deleted.
DeletingRule	An element is about to be deleted.
ChangeRule	A property has been changed. This applies to ordinary domain properties. It doesn't apply to the role properties of the class at each end of a relationship; if you want to observe a link being created, set Add and Delete rules on the relationship.
RolePlayerChangeRule	The roleplayer of a link changes.
RolePlayerPositionChangedRule	The ordering of links sourced at a particular object is changed.
MoveRule	An object has been moved from one store partition to another.

Rule base class	Fires when
`TransactionBeginningRule`	Start of a transaction.
`TransactionCommittingRule`	Successful end of a transaction.
`TransactionRollingBackRule`	Rolled back transaction.

Rule Body

The name of the method you override and its parameter type vary between rule types. Type "override" and let IntelliSense do the rest! For a ChangeRule, you get the model element that has changed, the Id of the property that has changed, together with its old and new values.

Remember to test the domain property **Id**, because the method will be called for every property of the class. Every domain property has a domain property **Id**, that is a static constant of its declaring class. In addition to the domain properties you have declared in your DSL, there is a small selection of predefined properties on the base classes. NodeShape has two such properties—**AbsoluteBounds** and **IsExpanded**—which in the method arguments are identified by their **Ids** AbsoluteBoundsDomainPropertyId and IsExpandedDomainPropertyId.

This example responds to changes in the location of a shape.

```
public override void ElementPropertyChanged
                              (ElementPropertyChangedEventArgs e)
{
  NodeShape stateShape = e.ModelElement as NodeShape;
  if (stateShape == null) return;
  if (stateShape.Store.TransactionManager.
                  CurrentTransaction.IsSerializing)) return;

  if (e.DomainProperty.Id == NodeShape.AbsoluteBoundsDomainPropertyId)
  {
    RectangleD oldBounds = (RectangleD)e.OldValue;
    RectangleD newBounds = stateShape.AbsoluteBoundingBox;

    HandleBoundsChange(stateShape, oldBounds, newBounds);
} }
```

Rules and Calculated and Custom Storage Domain Properties

Store rules and events cannot be set on calculated or custom storage properties. Instead, you need to set rules on the sources of the values.

Rules and Transactions

Every rule fires within the transaction that triggered it. This means that from the user's point of view, the effects of the rules are all part of the same change as their trigger. In this example, moving a shape moves all those contained within it. If the user clicks the "Undo" button, all the shapes move back to their original places.

An alternative approach would have been to use the `OnAbsoluteBounds-Changed` event. This works after the original transaction has completed—to make any changes to the store (such as shape locations), you have to open another transaction. This means that if the user then clicks "Undo," the contained shapes would be shifted back but the original move of the container shape would not. If this is the effect you want, don't use a rule.

Rules are not called as a result of changes in an undo or redo, or when a transaction is being rolled back. The assumption is that all the changes you make in a rule are to other values within the store; the undo manager will reset these to their former values, so there should be no need to call any rules.

For this reason, you should not use rules to change values that are outside the store. This would be other values in your application such as file contents or some of the purely graphical properties of the shapes such as color or line thickness.

Transaction Context

Rules are a very powerful facility, but one of the difficulties working with rules is in passing information between rules, and between the triggering events and the rules. For this reason, each transaction carries a general dictionary to which you can attach information. Transactions can be nested, so it's best always to make sure you've got hold of the outer one:

```
stateShape.Store.TransactionManager.
        CurrentTransaction.TopLevelTransaction.Context.ContextInfo
```

You can get to the transaction from any domain class instance through the store. You may need to check that there is a current transaction first! The

`ContextInfo` is a `Dictionary <object, object>`. In simpler cases, you might just use the top-level transaction name to check the reason your rule has been triggered.

Registering a Rule

To ensure a rule runs, you need to register it with your domain model class. (Check in the generated `DomainModel.cs` for its name.)

```
public partial class StateChartsDomainModel
{
    protected override Type[] GetCustomDomainModelTypes()
    {
        return new System.Type[] { typeof(ContainerShapeChangesRule) };
    }
}
```

If you have a lot of rules, you can cook up a reflexive mechanism that returns all the rule types so that you don't have to add them all to this array manually.

Store Events

Store events are similar to rules, but are called after the completion of the originating transaction and are called on any subsequent undo or redo.

■ **TIP**

Unlike rules, store events are good for keeping non-store values in line with the objects and properties in the store

---

Like rules, store events are defined on a per-class basis. You don't have to register the observer with each object it is observing, and you don't have to modify the class you are observing.

In this example, we set up a change handler to deal with changes in any domain properties of the `State` domain class. Notice that we put this in the `DocData` class, which manages the loading of the document.

```
public partial class DocData
{
    // Called once on loading.
```

```
protected override void OnDocumentLoaded(EventArgs e)
{
  base.OnDocumentLoaded(e);
  Store store = this.Store;

  DomainClassInfo observedClassInfo =
      this.Store.DomainDataDirectory.FindDomainClass(typeof(State));

  this.Store.EventManagerDirectory.ElementPropertyChanged.Add
    (observedClassInfo,
     new EventHandler<ElementPropertyChangedEventArgs>
                                (StateChangeHandler));
}

private static void StateChangeHandler
          (object sender, ElementPropertyChangedEventArgs e)
{
    State changedElement = e.ModelElement as State;
    if (e.DomainProperty.Id == State.NameDomainPropertyId)
    {
       // Do stuff to things outside store.
    }
} }
```

Substitute for `ElementPropertyChanged` and `ElementPropertyChanged-EventArgs` to listen for different events. The flavors of events that can be handled are:

- `ElementAdded`
- `ElementDeleted`
- `ElementMoved`
- `ElementPropertyChanged`
- `RolePlayerChanged`
- `RolePlayerOrderChanged`
- `ElementEventsBegun`
- `ElementEventsEnded`
- `TransactionBegun`
- `TransactionCommitted`
- `TransactionRolledBack`

The corresponding argument types are called "*<event name>*EventArgs."

Generally, if you want to respond to the same event with some work both on external and on in-store elements and their properties, then it's best to set up a separate rule for the in-store material. However, if you do want to work on the store elements from the event, bear in mind that you must create a transaction to do it in, and you should not perform those actions if the event is called as a result of an undo or redo:

```
// Do things in Store, but not in Undo
if (!changedElement.Store.InUndoRedoOrRollback)
{
  using (Transaction t =
   this.Store.TransactionManager.BeginTransaction("event x"))
  {
    // Do things here to domain elements and shapes.
    // ...
    t.Commit();
} }
```

.NET Event Handlers

There are a number of .NET events that you can use, particularly in the shape classes. They mostly report user interface events like mouse and keyboard actions. They all happen outside any transaction, so if you want to use them to change a property, element, or link, you need to open a transaction. This kind of event will not normally be called on undo, since it originates outside the store, so we don't need to guard against UndoRedoOrRollback.

```
public partial class StateShape
{
 protected override void InitializeInstanceResources()
  {
    base.InitializeInstanceResources();
    this.DoubleClick += StateShape_DoubleClick;
  }
  void StateShape_DoubleClick(object sender, DiagramPointEventArgs e)
  {
    StateShape shape = sender as StateShape;

    // Do things here to non-store objects, outside transaction.
    // ...

    using (Transaction t =
        this.Store.TransactionManager.BeginTransaction("double click"))
```

```
    {
        // Do things here to domain elements and shapes.
        // ...
        t.Commit();
    }
  }
}
```

Although in this example, the listener is the object itself, an advantage of an event handler is that you can set it up from any object to listen to any other object without changing the observed object's code. However, the event listener has to be set up separately for each instance.

Events are available on shapes, connectors, and diagrams for AbsoluteBoundsChanged, Click, DoubleClick, KeyDown, KeyPress, KeyUp, MouseDown, MouseMove, MouseUp, and MouseWheel.

Event Overrides

A simpler approach in cases where the listening code can be in the subject class is to override the event-raising method. For each event, there is a corresponding On<*event name*> method. In addition, there are some others, including BoundsFixup, Begin/EndEdit, ChildConfigured/ing, ShapeInserted/Removed, and a variety of drag, mouse, keyboard, and painting events.

Always be sure to call the base method.

```
public override void OnDoubleClick(DiagramPointEventArgs e)
{
        base.OnDoubleClick(e);
        Diagram d = e.DiagramClientView.Diagram;
        // respond to event ...
}
```

Bounds Rules

A bounds rule is used to constrain the location or dimensions of a shape in response to a user gesture. It is very specific to this function, providing feedback in the "rubber band" as the user drags a corner to alter the shape. (As such it is rather different from the other change propagation mechanisms in this section, but we include it here because if we didn't, you might think some of the other types of rules look like a reasonable way to achieve the effect!)

For example, in the Task Flow DSL, there is an object called "synchronization bar." (It represents where a flow splits into concurrent threads or where they join again.) The shape is ideally a solid bar of fixed dimensions, but it can be used either horizontally or vertically (Figure 10-4).

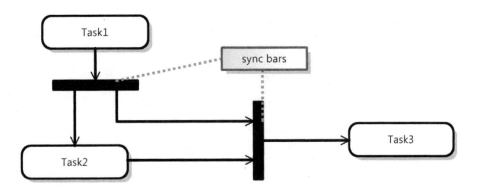

FIGURE 10-4: Synchronization bars can be horizontal or vertical.

In the template that comes with the DSL Tools, the shape is represented by a rectangular geometry shape (with shadow and shading turned off). Unfortunately, the user can change the shape to any size or shape—we would prefer only to allow two alternatives, the horizontal and vertical. By adding a bounds rule, we can ensure that the user can only achieve two shapes (Figure 10-5).

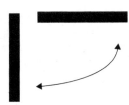

FIGURE 10-5: This bounds rule constrains the shape to two alternatives.

A bounds rule is represented by a class. To attach it to a class, override the **BoundsRules** property of the Shape class.

```
public partial class SyncBarShape
{
    /// <summary>
    /// Provide a specialized rule that constrains the shape and/or
    /// location of an element.
    /// </summary>
public override BoundsRules BoundsRules
{
  get
```

```
      {
          return new SyncBarBoundsRule();
      }
    }
  }
}
```

The rule class itself has one method, `GetCompliantBounds()`:

```csharp
/// <summary>
/// Rule invoked when a shape changes its bounds.
/// Provides real-time mouse rubber-band feedback, so must work fast.
/// </summary>
public class SyncBarBoundsRule : BoundsRules
{
  public override RectangleD GetCompliantBounds(ShapeElement shape,
                           RectangleD proposedBounds)
  {
    double thickness = 0.1;
    if (proposedBounds.Height > proposedBounds.Width)
    {
      // There is a minimum width for a shape; the width will
      // actually be set to the greater of thickness and that minimum.
      return new RectangleD(proposedBounds.Location,
                new SizeD(thickness, proposedBounds.Height));
    }
    else
    {
      // There is a minimum height for a shape; the height will
      // actually be set to the greater of thickness and that minimum.
      return new RectangleD(proposedBounds.Location,
            new SizeD(proposedBounds.Width, thickness));
    }
  }
}
```

When you run the code, you'll find that the shape is constrained while you drag the corners; it doesn't go wherever you drag it and then snap to shape afterwards. The rule is being invoked repeatedly as you drag the corner. For this reason, it's a good idea to make the code perform pretty snappily!

While this rule constrains the size or relative lengths of the shape, you could equally write a bounds rule that constrains the location of the shape. For example, you could anchor a shape to part of a container or neighbor. In the case where the user drags the whole shape, the rule is only executed once, when they let go.

Notice that there are two distinct cases—either users move the whole shape, or they drag a corner or a side to alter the lengths of its boundaries. In the case of a whole-shape move, the bounds rule is invoked once, and the lengths of the sides will not have changed. In the case of a side-length adjustment, the bounds rule is invoked repeatedly, and the side lengths vary. Within the rule, you can work out which case is happening by comparing the old and new side lengths; but remember that, as with any values of double or float types, it can be unreliable to compare for equality without some rounding.

Bounds Rules on Ports

You can apply a bounds rule to a port, for example, to fix or constrain it to a particular location on the parent shape. Your rule overrides the normal port positioning constraints.

Notice the following:

- The property **ParentShape** navigates from the port shape to its parent. It may be null when the child shape is first created.
- The location of the port shape that you should return is relative to the location of the parent.

This also applies to other kinds of child shape, although you can't create these without custom code in the present version of the DSL Tools. This example comes from the Components sample that comes with the DSL Tools:

```
public class InPortBoundsRules : BoundsRules
{
  public override RectangleD GetCompliantBounds
          (ShapeElement shape, RectangleD proposedBounds)
  {
    InPortShape portShape = shape as InPortShape;
    ComponentShape parentShape =
          portShape.ParentShape as ComponentShape;
    // on initial creation, there is no parent shape
    if (parentShape == null) return proposedBounds;

    double x = Math.Min(
        Math.Max(proposedBounds.Left, proposedBounds.Width * 0.5),
        parentShape.AbsoluteBoundingBox.Width
                - proposedBounds.Width * 1.5);
    double y = parentShape.AbsoluteBoundingBox.Height
                - proposedBounds.Height * 0.5;
    return new RectangleD(x, y,
        proposedBounds.Width, proposedBounds.Height);
  }
}
```

Undoable Changes

You'll be familiar with the way Microsoft Word adjusts your quotation marks or indenting as you type. Sometimes you really did want what you typed in the first place, so you can undo the (sometimes irritating!) adjustment. You may want to provide the same facility in your DSL. The user moves the shape; you shift it to an "approved" place; then the user may press Ctrl+Z to undo your adjustment—she really does want it where she put it, thank you.

To do this, override `OnAbsoluteBoundsChanged` in your `Shape` class. This method is called after the close of the transaction in which the user's move happened. Therefore, you must make your adjustment inside a new transaction. This means that if the user calls undo afterwards, the first undo will apply only to your adjustment, and another will undo the original move.

```
public override void
   OnAbsoluteBoundsChanged(AbsoluteBoundsChangedEventArgs e)
{
  base.OnAbsoluteBoundsChanged(e);

  // Decide whether to adjust
  if (e.NewAbsoluteBounds.Height > e.OldAbsoluteBounds.Width)
  {
    // Now outside the original transaction; so open another.
    using (Transaction t =
      this.Store.TransactionManager.BeginTransaction
          ("adjust shape"))
    {
      // Make adjustment
      // ...

      t.Commit(); // Don't forget to commit
      // - notice BoundsRules will be called again here
    }
  }
}
```

Summary of Change Propagation and Constraint Techniques

Table 10-4 summarizes the techniques we have discussed for propagating changes and applying hard constraints.

TABLE 10-4: Change Propagation and Constraint Techniques

Technique	Need to modify observed class	Runs in originating transaction	Good for	Not so good for
Calculated properties	*	Yes	Plain property values.	
Custom Storage	*	Yes	Plain property values.	
OnValueChanged()	Yes—override	Yes	Domain properties.	Not predefined properties like shape bounds.
OnAssociated-PropertyChanged()	No	Yes	Shapes and connectors monitor MEL.	
Rules	No	Yes	Change within the store.	Changes outside the store; changes that should be undoable separately from the original action.
Store Event handlers	No	No	Change outside the store.	Changes inside the store.
.NET events	No	No	UI—mouse and keyboard events.	Must register per instance.
OnXXX()	Yes—override	No	Changes after the transaction.	
Bounds Rules	Yes—initialize	yes	Shape bounds constraints.	Change propagation.

* Calculated and Custom Storage properties don't by themselves require modification of the observed class, but you usually need to supply some means of calling NotifyValueChange() to propagate changes. This could be done with a non-modifying rule, or it could be done using OnValueChanged(), as we illustrated earlier.

The next few customizations aren't limited to your DSL definition and its diagram; they're more strongly tied to the way your DSL is integrated into the Visual Studio environment. To this end, it's helpful before going further to have a better understanding of what a DSL actually is from the point of view of the IDE and its extensibility mechanisms.

DSL Shell Architecture

Visual Studio is a highly extensible tool platform. The product feels like a single integrated tool when you use it out of the box, but actually it's based on a core IDE shell and a set of extensibility plug-ins called *packages* that provide most of the functionality, such as the C# code editor and project system, the Windows Forms GUI builder, and the RAD database tools.

A Visual Studio package is simply a DLL that contains classes that implement a well-defined set of interfaces to enable them to integrate into the IDE. Packages can be used to add or extend almost any kind of functionality within the IDE, such as new editors, programming languages, tool windows, debuggers, and so on. The Visual Studio SDK that the DSL Tools is contained in is primarily concerned with providing facilities to make this task easier. You can find much more information in the SDK's included documentation and also online at the Visual Studio 2005 Extensibility Center at http://msdn2.microsoft.com/en-us/vstudio/aa700819.aspx.

The DSL Tools add a new editor for your DSL by creating a Visual Studio Package. You can find this in the `DslPackage/GeneratedCode/Package.cs` file of your DSL solution. We generally refer to the way the DSL is integrated into the IDE as the *shell*, because the IDE is providing an outer shell for your language. You'll find the base classes for code in this area in the `Microsoft.VisualStudio.Modeling.SDK.Shell.dll`.

The key elements of a package declaration look like this:

```
[DefaultRegistryRoot("Software\\Microsoft\\VisualStudio\\8.0")]
[PackageRegistration(RegisterUsing = RegistrationMethod.Assembly,
  UseManagedResourcesOnly = true)]
[ProvideToolWindow(typeof(MyDSLExplorerToolWindow),
  MultiInstances = false,
  Style = VsDockStyle.Tabbed,
  Orientation = ToolWindowOrientation.Right,
```

```
    Window = "{3AE79031-E1BC-11D0-8F78-00A0C9110057}")]
[ProvideToolWindowVisibility(typeof(MyDSLExplorerToolWindow),
  Constants.MyDSLEditorFactoryId)]
[ProvideEditorFactory(typeof(MyDSLEditorFactory), 103,
  TrustLevel = __VSEDITORTRUSTLEVEL.ETL_AlwaysTrusted)]
[ProvideEditorExtension(typeof(MyDSLEditorFactory),
  "." + Constants.DesignerFileExtension, 32)]
[RegisterAsDslToolsEditor]
[ComVisible(true)]
internal abstract partial class MyDSLPackageBase : ModelingPackage
{
  protected override void Initialize()
  {
    base.Initialize();

    // Register the editor factory used to create the DSL editor.
    this.RegisterEditorFactory(new MyDSLEditorFactory(this));

    // Create the command set that handles menu commands
    // provided by this package.
    MyDSLCommandSet commandSet = new MyDSLCommandSet(this);
    commandSet.Initialize();

    // Register the model explorer tool window for this DSL.
    this.AddToolWindow(typeof(MyDSLExplorerToolWindow));

    ...
  }
  ...
}
```

You can see that the package class has a lot of custom .NET attributes
applied to it. The way Visual Studio is told about the existence and facilities
of packages is primarily by creating a set of registry entries under the
HKEY_LOCAL_MACHINE\SOFTWARE\Microsoft\VisualStudio\8.0 key. This
activity is known as package registration. These attributes (derived from
the base class RegistrationAttribute) provide a handy way of defining
those registry entries in a relatively human-readable and easily maintainable fashion. They enable the DSL Tools to build infrastructure to
extract the data and create the registry entries. This is done on the fly during
a build in the IDE and also as part of creating a setup program for your DSL
tool.

The package is the entry point into Visual Studio for your DSL and you
can see from the preceding code that it has registry attributes declaring the

existence of several other interesting items that are then created in the `Initialize()` method:

- `EditorFactory`—Creates instances of your DSL editor via the `DocData` and `DocView` classes
- `CommandSet`—Implements menu commands in your DSL
- `ToolWindow`—Adds extra non-editor windows (in this case, your DSL explorer)

Figure 10-6 shows how these pieces fit together.

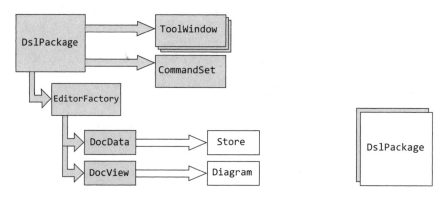

FIGURE 10-6: Shell architecture of a typical DSL tool

As we've seen, the package class registers the editor factory, tool windows, and command set. Visual Studio instantiates your package class as a singleton and also hooks it into the standard `IServiceProvider` mechanism to allow it to access other Visual Studio facilities (and provide its own services for use by other parts of Visual Studio, if desired). The package creates instances of the `EditorFactory` and `CommandSet` directly, but any tool windows are actually instantiated by Visual Studio; the package simply tells the system about their type.

The `EditorFactory` class is rather simple since it is, as its name implies, just a factory for your custom DSL editor. The editor itself comes in two parts, a `DocData` and a `DocView`.

The `DocData` class is your DSL's backing store manager. It provides the entry points for loading and saving model and diagram files and manages the instance of the in-memory store in which your MELs live.

The `DocView` class represents the open window in Visual Studio, visualizing your diagram. It typically has a 1-1 relationship with the diagram instance within your store.

How to Add a Menu Command

The examples in this section are taken from the Class Diagrams sample that comes with the Visual Studio SDK (and can be found in the Samples Browser). This sample extends the plain Class Diagrams template solution in several ways.

Class diagrams have several sorts of association: aggregations, compositions, unidirectional, and bidirectional. In the template solution (that is, the one you get if you choose "Class Diagrams" in the wizard when you create a new DSL), each of these four sorts is separately implemented, with its own toolbox entry, its own domain relationship, and its own connector. The drawback of this arrangement is that if you want to change the sort of an association, all you can do is delete it and draw another one.

So in the Class Diagrams sample, there is a single class of association, but the sort is represented by an enumeration property. The user can change it either in the properties window, or by choosing the sort from a context menu. When the sort is changed, the line-ends (diamonds or arrows) change automatically.

The menu items appear when at least one association is selected (see Figure 10-7), and the change is applied to all associations selected.

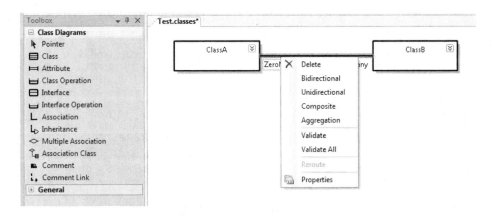

FIGURE 10-7: Class diagrams example, with context menu on association

Add a Command Id for Each Command

In `DslPackage\CtcComponents\Commands.ctc`, under the `#include` directives, add a line for each new command that looks like the following. The integer must be unique for commands in your DSL:

```
#define AssociationSortBidirectional 1
```

The Class Diagrams sample defines four commands in this way.

In the same file, add under "BUTTONS" an entry for each command like this:

```
guidCmdSet:AssociationSortBidirectional,
        guidCmdSet:grpidContextMain,
        0x0200,
        OI_NOID,
        BUTTON,
        DIS_DEF,
        "Set to Bidirectional" ;   # Menu text
```

Notice that most of the content in this file (including the definitions of the constants) comes from the inclusion of `GeneratedCode\GeneratedCmd.h` and

```
<VS SDK>\VisualStudioIntegration\Common\inc\DSLToolsCmdId.h.
```

Compare your entry with other lines in these files.

The first item on each line identifies the command. The prefix `guidCmdSet` qualifies it with a Guid unique to this DSL, and is defined in `Dsl\GeneratedCode\GeneratedCmd.h`. The last item is the text that will appear on the menu.

More information about the Command Table Configuration (CTC) file (`.ctc`) can be found in the online MSDN Library (http://msdn.microsoft.com) under Development Tools and Languages>Visual Studio>Visual Studio SDK>Visual Studio Integration>Menu and Toolbar Commands. You can also install these help files locally with the Visual Studio SDK.

Increment Menu Resource Index

Whenever you change the CTC file, it is necessary to increment the second integer in this line in `DslPackage\GeneratedCode\Package.tt`. (You do not need to do this when you are changing the code in the handlers of a command you have already defined.)

```
[VSShell::ProvideMenuResource(1000, /* Increment this: */ 5)]
```

This causes the Visual Studio menu cache to be reset when the package builds or installs.

As we mentioned earlier, "Provide…" attributes on the package are executed by `regpkg` during a build. The `ProvideMenuResource` attribute runs the compiled version of the CTC file. This places the commands into the Visual Studio command cache. The cache persists between runs of VS; this is because some packages require their commands to be visible even before the package is loaded so that a command can load and start its package. Because executing the cache update can be a lengthy operation, the `ProvideMenuResource` attribute doesn't bother unless it notices a change of version. Running `devenv/setup` has the effect of rerunning all the command attributes for all the known packages.

Add Commands to Command Set

Add a new class file to `CtcComponents`. Ensure the namespace ends with `DslPackage`. (Delete the `.CtcComponents` that will have automatically been generated when you created the file.) Add `using` statements as shown here.

```
namespace Microsoft.Example.ClassDiagrams.DslPackage
{
  using System;
  using System.Collections.Generic;
  using System.Text;
  using System.ComponentModel.Design;
  using Microsoft.VisualStudio.Modeling;
  using Microsoft.VisualStudio.Modeling.Shell;
```

Create a partial class definition for `YourLanguageCommandSet`, marking it `internal`. (The other part of the definition is in `GeneratedCode\Command-Set.cs`). In this class, define a constant that has the same name and value as you defined in the CTC file for each command.

Override `GetMenuCommands()`. This method is called once when the designer starts and registers handlers for each command. First get the command list from the base method, and then add your own command.

```
internal partial class ClassDiagramsCommandSet
{
  private const int AssociationSortBidirectional = 1;
  protected override IList<MenuCommand> GetMenuCommands()
  {
    // Get command list from base method.
```

```
IList<MenuCommand> commands = base.GetMenuCommands();

// Add my own menu item.
commands.Add(new DynamicStatusMenuCommand(
    new EventHandler(OnStatusChangeAssociationSort),
    new EventHandler(OnMenuChangeAssociationSort),
    new CommandID(new Guid(Constants.ClassDiagramsCommandSetId),
            AssociationSortBidirectional)));

// For each separate menu item, add a new command here….
}
```

Notice that the actual `CommandID` is created from the Guid shared by all the commands in your DSL, and the integer you have assigned to the command. This makes it unique in the system.

To use this program code, you need to replace `AssociationSort-Bidirectional` with a name for your own command, `ClassDiagrams` with the name of your language, and `OnStatusChangeAssociationSort` and `OnMenuChangeAssociationSort` with handler names appropriate to your commands. In the Class Diagrams sample, there are four menu items registered in `GetMenuCommands`, with four separate command Ids. Typically, you would create a separate pair of handlers for each command, but in this example it is convenient for them to share the same code.

Define the Command Handlers

Define the command handlers in the same class. If your commands are complex, you may prefer to move the bulk of the code into a separate class.

You need an `OnStatus…` and an `OnMenu…` handler for each command; the first determines whether the command should be listed when the user clicks the right mouse button, and the second performs the command when the user clicks the menu item.

The `OnStatus…` handler should query the current selection to see whether the command is applicable, based on the selection's type and current state. Decide whether the menu item should be visible and enabled (that is, not greyed out) and set the appropriate flags like this:

```
/// <summary>
/// Called by the framework command handler to ask if this menu item
/// should be displayed.
/// This method was registered in GetMenuCommands.
/// </summary>
```

```
internal void OnStatusChangeAssociationSort(object sender, EventArgs e)
{
  MenuCommand command = sender as MenuCommand;
  command.Visible = false; // Default not visible.
  // Alternatively, we could leave it always visible, but:
  command.Enabled = false; // Default greyed out.

  foreach (object selectedObject in this.CurrentSelection)
  {
    // We'll get a mixed bag of connectors and shapes –
    // just deal with the ones we're interested in.
    AssociationConnector associationConnector =
        selectedObject as AssociationConnector;
    if (associationConnector != null)
    {
      // We could do more checks on its state here.

      command.Visible = command.Enabled = true;
      break;  // Found one -- that's all we need!
    }
  }
  // Visible and Enabled flags passed back to menu.
}
```

The OnMenu... handler should perform the command on each applicable member of the current selection. (There may be other items selected at the same time.)

Note that any change to a model item must be done within a transaction.

The selection is a set of shapes and connectors, but you normally want to operate on a shape or connector's subject—in this case, the Association rather than the AssociationConnector.

```
///<summary>
/// Called to execute a command when the user selects the menu item.
/// This method is registered in GetMenuCommands.
///</summary>
internal void OnMenuChangeAssociationSort(object sender, EventArgs e)
{
  MenuCommand command = sender as MenuCommand;

  // All changes must be done within a Transaction
  using (Transaction transaction =
      this.CurrentClassDiagramsDocData.Store.TransactionManager.
          BeginTransaction("Change Association Sort menu command"))
  {
    // There may be a mixed bag of shapes and connectors.
    foreach (object selectedObject in this.CurrentSelection)
```

```
    {
      // Filter the ones we're interested in.
      AssociationConnector connector =
                        selectedObject as AssociationConnector;
      if (connector != null)
      {
        // Navigate to the Association that this Connector presents.
        Association association = connector.Subject as Association;
        if (association != null) // Just in case....
        {
          // This same handler is registered for several commands.
          // What we want to do now depends on which command.
          switch (command.CommandID.ID)
          {
            case AssociationSortBidirectional:
              association.Sort = AssociationSort.Bidirectional;
              break;
            // ... code for the other cases here ...
          }
        }
        // else ignore other types in the selection
      }
    } // Change every applicable object in the selection.

    transaction.Commit();  // Don't forget this!
  }
}
```

Good Practices for Command Handlers

- Make changes inside a transaction. Give it a descriptive name.

- Make changes only to the model (the domain class and domain relationship instances), not their presentation on screen. There should be separate rules or event handlers that keep the presentation up to date with the model, and they will be applied when the transaction closes.

- In the Class Diagrams sample, this causes the line-ends to change, because of the custom `OnAssociatedPropertyChanged` handler in `AssociationConnector`.

- Generally, define a separate pair of handlers for each menu command. Share the handlers between menu items (as in the example) only if there is little of the code that varies.

- If the handlers are big and complex, move them into a different class and put the code in a custom code file.

- Don't forget that the current selection may include multiple shapes and connectors of different types.

Build and Run

The command should appear in the diagram's context menu (right-click) whenever the OnStatus...() method sets the flags to true. (In the Class Diagram sample, this is whenever an **Association** is selected.)

Normally, clicking the right mouse button selects the single object underneath the arrow. But you can select multiple items by pressing the control key at the same time.

Providing Handlers for Standard Commands

Each command has a Guid and an index number; the combination must be unique. The Guid identifies a series, and the index number is any short integer. For your own DSL commands, a Guid is assigned and defined as CircuitsCommandSetId in Constants.cs in the generated code of DslPackage, and also as guidCmdSet in GeneratedCmd.h. (It's important that the two are the same.) In the CTC file, we used that Guid to define our own command.

But in Chapter 5, we implemented the Copy and Paste commands, and called them from the standard Edit menu, or by pressing the usual key combinations. To do this, you don't need to add anything to the CTC file—the commands already exist. You just need to add the OnStatus and OnMenu handlers to your CommandSet.

But you do need to know the Guid and index for the commands you want to implement. The commands are all listed in Program Files\Visual Studio-2005 SDK*\VisualStudioIntegration\Common\Inc. The two files of interest there are stdidcmd.h, which contains the Windows standard command Ids, and vsshlids.h, which identifies the standard Visual Studio commands.

Building the DSL Diagram into Another Interface

You can embed your DSL diagram inside a standard Windows control, which displays as a Visual Studio document.

First make a User Control file inside your DslPackage project. In solution explorer, right click on DslPackage, click the "Add menu" item, and choose the "User Control template." Using the usual WinForms editor, add your buttons, menus, and so on, and a panel into which the DSL window will appear.

Add a public property into the User Control to let you get and set the content of the panel, or put it in a constructor. While you're there, add a property to let you keep a reference to a `DiagramDocView`.

The extra code looks like this:

```
public partial class MyContainerControl : UserControl
{
  public MyContainerControl()
  {
    InitializeComponent();
  }
  // Start of my extras
  private DiagramDocView docView;
  public DiagramDocView { get { return docView; } }

  public MyContainerControl(DiagramDocView docView, Control content)
                    : this()
  {
    this.docView = docView;
    panel1.Controls.Add(content);
  }
}
```

Now add a partial class definition for your `DocView` class, and override `Window`. It should return your `ContainerControl`. If the control doesn't exist yet, it should create it and put the `base.Window` inside it.

```
internal partial class WinformDSL1DocView
{
  private ContainerControl container;
  /// <summary>
  /// Return a User Control instead of the DSL window.
  /// The user control will contain the DSL window.
  /// </summary>
  public override System.Windows.Forms.IWin32Window Window
  {
    get
    {
      if (container == null)
      {
          // Put the normal DSL Window inside our control
          container = new ContainerControl(this,
              (System.Windows.Forms.Control) base.Window);
      }
        return container;
    } } }
```

At this point, the DSL should display nicely inside the form.

Now you'll probably want to access the store contents from buttons and so on, on the form:

```
private void button1_Click(object sender, EventArgs e)
{
  ExampleModel modelRoot =
        this.docView.CurrentDiagram.ModelElement as ExampleModel;
  foreach (ExampleElement element in modelRoot.Elements)
  {
    listBox1.Items.Add(element.Name);
  }
}
```

Implementing Copy and Paste

To make cut, copy, and paste work on your DSL, you need to do the following:

- Write a copy and/or cut handler to push serialized elements onto the clipboard.
- Write a paste handler to get things from the clipboard.
- Register the menu handlers.

The handlers should be added as custom code to the DslPackage project.

The Copy Method

Copy and paste work by storing an element group prototype (EGP) on the clipboard. We met EGPs in the discussion of custom tools, where an EGP containing several objects can be placed in the toolbox, and the Copy() method is very similar to toolbox initialization (see Chapter 5).

Let's first look at what the methods do, and then discuss where to put them and how they are invoked.

The Copy() method looks through all the items in the current selection and picks out those that present items of interest. Of course, the selection contains shapes and connectors, so we need to look at the corresponding ModelElements. This example is drawn from the circuit diagrams example we looked at earlier in which the transistors, resistors, and so on all have Component as their common base class. The AddGraph() method automatically adds embedded children (ComponentTerminals in this case), together with the links to them. (Recall also the Add() method that can be used to add elements one by one.) Once an ElementGroup has been constructed, it is turned into a Prototype and serialized onto the clipboard.

The Cut() method (which you might like to try!) will do essentially the same as Copy(), but is followed by deleting the selection. The most general way of doing this is to apply the MergeDisconnect() method that we discussed earlier.

```
internal partial class CircuitsCommandSet
{
  internal void OnMenuCopy(object sender, EventArgs e)
  {
    Diagram diagram = this.CurrentDocView.CurrentDiagram;
    bool foundSome = false;
    ElementGroup elementGroup = new ElementGroup(diagram.Partition);
    foreach (object o in this.CurrentSelection)
    {
      // Pick out shapes representing Component model elements.
      ShapeElement element  = o as ShapeElement;
      if (element != null && element.ModelElement != null
                    && element.ModelElement is Component)
      {
        // add the element and its embedded children to the group
        elementGroup.AddGraph(element.ModelElement, true);
        foundSome = true;
      }
    }
    if (!foundSome) return;

    // A DataObject carries a serialized version.
    System.Windows.Forms.IDataObject data =
              new System.Windows.Forms.DataObject();
    data.SetData(elementGroup.CreatePrototype());
    System.Windows.Forms.Clipboard.SetDataObject
          (data,    // serialized clones of our selected model elements
           false,   // we don't want to export outside this application
           10,      // retry 10 times on failure
           50);     // waiting 50ms between retries
  }
}
```

The Paste Method

The Paste() method extracts the data from the clipboard, tests whether it can be merged, and if so, merges it within a transaction.

```
internal void OnMenuPaste(object sender, EventArgs e)
{
  Diagram diagram = this.CurrentDocView.CurrentDiagram;
  if (diagram == null) return;

  System.Windows.Forms.IDataObject data =
               System.Windows.Forms.Clipboard.GetDataObject();
  DesignSurfaceElementOperations op = diagram.ElementOperations;
  if (op.CanMerge(diagram, data))
  {
    // Find a suitable place to position the new shape.
    PointD place = new PointD(0,0);
    foreach (object item in this.CurrentSelection)
    {
      ShapeElement shape = item as ShapeElement;
      if (shape != null)
      {
        place = shape.AbsoluteBoundingBox.Center;
        break;
      }
    }
    using (Transaction t = diagram.Store.
                TransactionManager.BeginTransaction("paste"))
    {
      // Do the business.
      op.Merge(diagram, data, PointD.ToPointF(place));
      t.Commit();
} } }
```

There are a couple of surprises here. First, we are merging into the diagram—not the model root—even though it was model elements that we saved to the clipboard rather than shapes. The second surprise is that this works!

The reason we want to merge into the diagram is that it gives us some control over where the new shapes will appear. In this example, we place the new shape's top left corner over the center of the current selection.

The reason it works is that we are using the utility class `Design-SurfaceElementOperations` to supervise the merge. It knows about the `PresentationViewsSubject` relationship and the view fixup rule, and can locate the shapes created from the model elements. It can also handle merging into the model root if we prefer, and in that case would find some spare space on the diagram to put the new shapes. It also ensures that the new elements have new names (because our DSL definition marks the **Name** property with the "Is Element Name" flag).

(OK, that's a bit glib. Of course the new shapes are not created until the view fixup rule fires inside the transaction `Commit()`. So what the `merge` operation does is to hang some context information off the transaction. Transactions have a dictionary called `Context`, which is a miscellaneous hook for transferring information between rules. When the fixup rule fires and creates a new shape for the new model element, it looks for the context information and, if found, uses it to place the new shape. If you run in debug, break just on the `Commit()` and look at the transaction `Context`, you'll find the paste location under `DropTargetContext`.)

Registering the Menu Handlers

Our Copy() and Paste() methods must be registered as implementors of the standard copy and paste commands. To register the handlers, we need to know the Guid of the command group to which the Copy and Paste commands belong and their individual identity numbers within that group. This information can be found within your installation of `Visual Studio-2005 SDK\200*.*\Visual StudioIntegration\Common\Inc\stdidcmd.h`.

Our methods need to be added to the `XXXCommandSet` (where `XXX` is the DSL name, `Circuits`, in this example) within the `DSLPackage` project. Create a partial definition of this class in a new file in that project.

In that class, we override the `GetMenuCommands()` method. The job of this method is to accumulate a list of handlers for menu commands. After getting the list inherited from the base method, we add our own. There is a pair of handlers for each command: `OnStatusX` and `OnMenuX`.

```
// In DSL Package project
using System;
using System.Collections.Generic;
using System.ComponentModel.Design;
using Microsoft.VisualStudio.Modeling;
using Microsoft.VisualStudio.Modeling.Diagrams;
using Microsoft.VisualStudio.Modeling.Shell;
internal partial class CircuitsCommandSet
{
  // From VSSDK\*\VisualStudioIntegration\Common\inc\stdidcmd.h
  private const string guidVSStd97 =
                "5efc7975-14bc-11cf-9b2b-00aa00573819";
  private const int cmdidCopy = 15;
  private const int cmdidCut = 16;
  private const int cmdidPaste = 26;
```

```
protected override IList<MenuCommand> GetMenuCommands()
{
  // Add to the list from base.
  IList<MenuCommand> commands = base.GetMenuCommands();

  commands.Add(new DynamicStatusMenuCommand(
          new EventHandler(OnStatusCut),
          new EventHandler(OnMenuCut),
          new CommandID(
              new Guid(guidVSStd97),
              cmdidCut)));
  commands.Add(new DynamicStatusMenuCommand(
          new EventHandler(OnStatusPaste),
          new EventHandler(OnMenuPaste),
          new CommandID(
              new Guid(guidVSStd97),
              cmdidPaste)));
  commands.Add(new DynamicStatusMenuCommand(
          new EventHandler(OnStatusPaste),
          new EventHandler(OnMenuPaste),
          new CommandID(
              new Guid(guidVSStd97),
              cmdidPaste)));

  // other command handlers registered here.

  return commands;
}

// OnStatusXXX and OnMenuXXX methods go here in same class.
}
```

Finally, we need an `OnStatusXXX` handler for each of our commands. Each just returns a value to say whether the command can be used.

```
internal void OnStatusPaste(object sender, EventArgs e)
{
  MenuCommand command = sender as MenuCommand;
  command.Visible = command.Enabled = true ;
}
internal void OnStatusCopy(object sender, EventArgs e)
{
  MenuCommand command = sender as MenuCommand;
  command.Visible = true;
  command.Enabled = this.CurrentSelection.Count > 0;
}
```

Shape Containers

Diagrams in which one shape is contained within another are quite common—for example, state charts, use case diagrams, or component diagrams. By writing some custom code, you can create such diagrams. An essential requirement is that the model elements reflect the arrangement of shapes in some way, so that when the user moves a shape into or out of a container the corresponding relationship in the model changes too.

Depending on the effects required, you can use some of the existing nesting features built into the DSL Toolkit, or you can use a rule-based method of providing a similar effect. This section discusses the options. (And it's worth noting that this is one of the areas where the DSL Tools will evolve in future versions.)

Child Shapes

The graphical framework on which DSLs are built provides two relationships that make one shape a child of another: `NestedChildShapes` and `RelativeChildShapes`. Each of them makes the child shape move around with the parent.

Nested child shapes and connectors are restricted within the bounds of their parent—you cannot drag a shape outside its parent's boundary, and connectors stay within the bounds. The location of a `NestedChildShape` is measured relative to its parent.

The main shapes on the diagram are its nested children. To loop through all the shapes and connectors on a diagram:

```
foreach (ShapeElement shapeOrConnector in diagram.NestedChildShapes)...
```

(To get to the diagram from any shape, use `shape.Diagram`)

The shapes on a swimlane are also nested child shapes.

`ImageFields` and external text decorators are hosted on relative child shapes of their principals; `Port` shapes are relative children.

To avoid confusion, we'll talk about one shape "containing" another, and we use the word "nesting" only where we are using the `NestedChild-Shapes` relationship. There is more than one way of achieving containing behavior.

A DSL Using Nested Child Shapes

The essence of this model is shown in Figure 10-8. Each domain class is mapped to a shape, and each of the reference relationships is mapped to a connector. Notice that the **ExampleChild** class is embedded under **ExampleElement** and that there is a reference relationship between **Example-Elements**, and another between **ExampleChildren**.

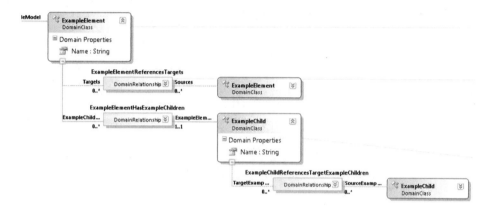

FIGURE 10-8: DSL using nested child shapes

Looking at the shape map for **ExampleElement**, its **Parent Element Path** property is

```
ExampleModelHasElements.ExampleModel/!ExampleModel
```

This tells us where the **ExampleElement** shape should be located. The path navigates back to the model; therefore it is the diagram—that is, the presentation view of the model—that should host the **ExampleElement's** own view.

Now let's look at the shape map for **ExampleChild**. In most DSLs, a child embedded an extra layer down would have a longer parent element path, navigating back through its immediate parent and ending up back at the model root so that its shape's parent is also the diagram.

But, in this case, the **Parent Element Path** only goes back to the **Example-Element**:

```
ExampleElementHasExampleChildren.ExampleElement/!ExampleElement
```

This tells us that the parent shape of the child's shape is expected to be the **ExampleModel**'s shape.

Now ordinarily, the current version of the DSL Tools disallows that scenario, because it is not yet fully supported—you get a validation error. However, by setting the "Has Custom Parent Element" flag in the shape map, we can defeat that restriction. In fact, setting the flag means we have to provide the custom code to say the same thing (and we might as well have left the parent element path blank):

```
internal sealed partial class FixUpDiagram {
private ModelElement GetParentForExampleChild(ExampleChild childElement)
{
  return childElement.ExampleElement;
}}
```

Now we can run the DSL and see the effects (Figure 10-9).

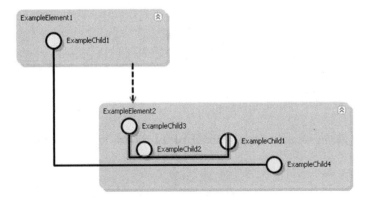

FIGURE 10-9: DSL with nested child shapes and non-nested connectors

We can add some nice behavior. Notice that we added an Expand/ Collapse decorator in the parent shape, just like in a compartment shape. Collapsing the shape hides the nested shapes and their connectors automatically (Figure 10-10).

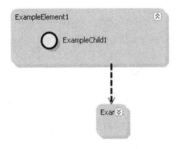

FIGURE 10-10: Using the Collapse button

To get this behavior, we just need to write this:

```
public partial class ExampleShape
{
  /// <summary>
  /// Decide what collapsing means for the bounds of this shape.
  /// </summary>
  protected override void Collapse()
  {
    base.Collapse(); // Remove child shapes
    this.ExpandedBounds = this.AbsoluteBounds;
    this.AbsoluteBounds =
    new RectangleD(this.Location, new SizeD(0.5, 0.5));
  }
  /// <summary>
  /// Decide what expanding means for the bounds of this shape.
  /// </summary>
  protected override void Expand()
  {
    base.Expand();
    this.AbsoluteBounds = this.ExpandedBounds;
} }
```

We can also turn on built-in behavior to resize the parent as the children move around:

```
  /// <summary>
  /// Ensure that nested child shapes don't go
  /// outside the bounds of parent by resizing parent.
  /// </summary>
  public override bool AllowsChildrenToResizeParent
  { get { return true; } }

  /// <summary>
  /// Ensure that parent shape is never resized too small
  /// to cause children to be outside of it.
  /// </summary>
  public override SizeD MinimumResizableSize
  {
    get
    {
      return this.CalculateMinimumSizeBasedOnChildren();
    }
  }
```

What happens is that as you move the children to the right or bottom, the parent shape expands, and as you move them to the left or top, they stop at the parent boundary. When you drag the parent's bounds inward, they stop before crossing a child.

Looking back at the connectors, we could hope to improve on their routing—they seem to more or less ignore the child shapes, passing right over them. Normally we'd expect the connectors to steer around obstacles. The reason here is that the connectors are located on the diagram, while the child shapes are located on their parent shapes. The connectors connect their ends to the child shapes, but the routing along the way ignores them.

(It is possible to get the connectors to find the lowest common parent of the elements they're connecting, but some hacking of the `Diagram.tt` template is required. In `VSSDK\VisualStudioIntegration\Tools\DSLTools\TextTemplates\Dsl\Diagram.tt`, comment out the loop near the end of `FixUpDiagram`. As recommended earlier, alter a local copy.)

In this scheme, a child is firmly fixed in its parent once it is there—you cannot easily move a child out of its parent.

Shape Containment Using Rules

Improved support for nested shapes is on the agenda for future versions. In the meantime, we can take another approach to shape containment that allows shapes to be moved between containers. While we expect this method to be rendered obsolete in future releases, it provides useful functionality in the interim, and has some tutorial value. (See the full version of the code on this book's website.)

This model implements a state chart (Figure 10-11). **States** and other **FlowElements** such as **StartPoints** and **EndPoints** are embedded in a **StateGraph**. They can be interconnected by **Flows**, and a **State** can contain other **FlowElements**.

The containment relationship will be represented on the diagram by the containment of one flow element shape inside another. As the user moves the shapes around, the links change, and the **Parent** property can be seen to change in the properties window. It is a reference relationship—this makes issues such as parent element paths easier to deal with, though we have to ensure there are no loops (see Figure 10-12).

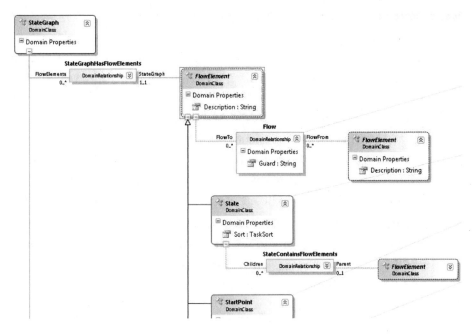

FIGURE 10-11: State Chart model

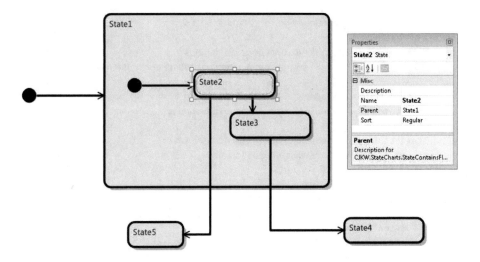

FIGURE 10-12: Running DSL with movable state shapes

Bounds Rule

Because we don't have the built-in feature that parents fully enclose their children, we have to write it ourselves. For this we can write a bounds rule (which we encountered earlier in this chapter). It deals with two cases.

- If the user has moved a shape (so that the height and width haven't changed but the location has changed), we ensure that it is either fully in or fully outside every other shape rather than straddling a border. The effect is that if you move a shape onto the boundary of another shape, it snaps to be either in or out.

- If the user is resizing a shape, then the bounds rule is called repeatedly with varying height and width. In this case, we stop the bounds from being dragged across any other shapes. This means that you cannot move a shape into or out of another shape without actually moving it.

A bounds rule is a class. To register a bounds rule, override `BoundsRules` in the shape's class, returning an instance of the rule.

```
public class StateShapeBoundsRule : BoundsRules
{
  public override RectangleD GetCompliantBounds
                (ShapeElement shape, RectangleD proposedBounds)
  {
    StateShape stateShape = shape as StateShape;
    if (stateShape == null) return proposedBounds;

    State state = stateShape.ModelElement as State;
    if (state == null) return proposedBounds;

    // Are we moving or resizing?
    if (!Equal(proposedBounds.Height,
                      shape.AbsoluteBoundingBox.Height)
      || !Equal(proposedBounds.Width,
                      shape.AbsoluteBoundingBox.Width))[1]
    { // resizing
        return RestrictResize(state, stateShape, proposedBounds);
```

---

1. Comparison between floating-point numbers is unreliable unless done with a function that allows for rounding errors, such as `Math.Abs(a-b) <= 0.001 * (Math.Abs(a) + Math.Abs(b))`.

```
        }
        else
        {
            return RestrictMovement(state, stateShape, proposedBounds);
        }
    }
}
```

We mustn't forget to register the rule:

```
public partial class StateShape
{
  public override BoundsRules BoundsRules
  { get { return new StateShapeBoundsRule(); } }
}
```

Change Rule

To ensure that the reference link to the parent is updated as the shapes are moved, we provide a change rule (one of the types of rule listed in Table 10-3), associated with the AbsoluteBounds property of NodeShape, the common base class of all shapes.

We looked at the outline of the rule earlier. It has two jobs: to rearrange the diagram so that the children move with a moved parent, and to rearrange the relationships so that parenthood in the model is reflected in containment in the shapes. Here is the entry point of the rule. Its sole public method will be called whenever any of the properties of any NodeShape changes.

```
[RuleOn(typeof(NodeShape), FireTime = TimeToFire.TopLevelCommit)]
public sealed class ContainerShapeChangesRule : ChangeRule
{
  public override void ElementPropertyChanged
                              (ElementPropertyChangedEventArgs e)
  {
    StateShape stateShape = e.ModelElement as StateShape;
    // Ignore other types of shape
    if (stateShape == null) return;

    // Don't fire when loading up from file
    if (stateShape.Store.TransactionManager.
                  CurrentTransaction.IsSerializing)) return;

    // Only interested in one domain property of this class.
    if (e.DomainProperty.Id == NodeShape.AbsoluteBoundsDomainPropertyId)
    {
      RectangleD oldBounds = (RectangleD)e.OldValue;
```

```
        RectangleD newBounds = stateShape.AbsoluteBoundingBox;

        HandleAbsoluteBoundsChange(stateShape, oldBounds, newBounds);
    }
}
```

The rule will be called whenever the bounds of any NodeShape change, but we're not interested unless this is a move rather than a resize:

```
private void HandleAbsoluteBoundsChange
     (NodeShape stateShape, Rectangle oldBounds, Rectangle newBounds)
{
  // have we moved or resized?
  double dw = newBounds.Width - oldBounds.Width;
  double dh = newBounds.Height - oldBounds.Height;
  double dx = newBounds.X - oldBounds.X;
  double dy = newBounds.Y - oldBounds.Y;

  // Moved or resized? If moving, height and width don't change.
  if (dw == 0.0 && dh == 0.0)
  { // moved

    // Keep children by moving them too
    MoveContainedStates(stateShape, dx, dy, dw, dh);

    // This shape may have moved in or out of parent
    UpdateParent(stateShape);
  }
 }
}
```

The shape may have moved in or out of a parent, so the domain relationship should be changed.

```
private void UpdateParent (NodeShape movedShape)
{
  // Navigate from shape to the state it's presenting.
  State state = movedShape.ModelElement as State;

  // Ignore if we've somehow got some other sort of shape.
  if (state == null) then return;

  // Loop over all the shapes in the diagram
  foreach (ShapeElement shapeElement in shape.Diagram.NestedChildShapes)
  {
    StateShape stateShape = shapeElement as StateShape;
    // Ignore other shapes and the moved shape.
    if (stateShape != null && stateShape != movedShape)
```

```
    {
        if (stateShape.AbsoluteBoundingBox.Contains
                            (movedShape.AbsoluteBoundingBox))
        {
            // this works because we keep smaller ones later in list
            closestFit = stateShape;
        }
    }
}
state.Parent = closestFit == null ? null
                                  : closestFit.ModelElement as State;

}
```

Notice the reference to `shape.Diagram.NestedChildShapes`. Every shape has a link to its containing diagram, and every diagram has a list of its shapes, `NestedChildShapes`. (This includes all the shapes we are dealing with—the containment scheme we use in this sample doesn't use the `NestedChildShapes` relationship, so all of the shapes form a flat list under the diagram.)

Move Children

The change rule should also move the children of each shape that has moved:

```
childShape.Location = PointD.Add(childShape.Location, offset);
```

But there is an excellent example here of difficulties caused by rules firing in no particular order. If the user moves only one shape, then the change rule moves its children; the same rule then fires on them, and they move their children, and so on. This works well—each parent must only move its children, and they will move theirs.

But suppose the user selects a whole group of shapes, including both children and parents, and then moves the whole group. Each child will get moved twice! Since there is no guarantee about whether the change rules for children or parent will be fired first, it is awkward to come up with a scheme that avoids the double move.

The solution is to use a separate inline-firing rule to note all of those shapes that are being moved. Inline rules execute as soon as the change has happened—the inline rule notes the shape in the top-level transaction's `Context`. When the more leisurely top-level commit rule comes along, it moves those children that have not been noted and leaves alone those children that have done their own moving.

The inline rule begins in the same way as the commit rule, but instead of actually moving the shape, just notes it in the transaction's Context. This is accessed, and created if necessary, by MovingShapes().

```
[RuleOn(typeof(NodeShape), FireTime = TimeToFire.Inline)]
public sealed class ContainerShapeInlineChangesRule :
            Microsoft.VisualStudio.Modeling.ChangeRule
{
  public override void ElementPropertyChanged
                            (ElementPropertyChangedEventArgs e)
  {
    NodeShape stateShape = e.ModelElement as NodeShape;
    if (stateShape == null) return;
    if (StateShapeBoundsRule.IsDeserializing(stateShape)) return;
    if (e.DomainProperty.Id == NodeShape.AbsoluteBoundsDomainPropertyId)
    {
      MovingShapes(stateShape.Store).Add(stateShape);
    }
  }

  public static List<NodeShape> MovingShapes(Store store)
  {
    if (!store.TransactionManager.InTransaction)
      return new List<NodeShape>();
    Dictionary<object, object> context =
      store.TransactionManager.CurrentTransaction.Context.ContextInfo;
    if (!context.ContainsKey("ContainerShapeChangesRule"))
    {
      context.Add("ContainerShapeChangesRule", new List<NodeShape>());
    }
    return context["ContainerShapeChangesRule"] as List<NodeShape>;
  }
}
```

The method in the commit-time rule that actually moves the shapes, called by HandleAbsoluteBoundsChange in the preceding code, should only do so if the shape is not already scheduled to be moved in this transaction:

```
private void MoveNestedStates
        (NodeShape shape, double dx, double dy, double dw, double dh)
{
  // Find the domain element that this shape represents.
  State state = shape.ModelElement as State;
```

```
        if (state == null) return;
        SizeD offset = new SizeD(dx, dy);

        List<NodeShape> moving =
          ContainerShapeInlineChangesRule.MovingShapes(shape.Store);

        // Children is the property of State that navigates the reference
        // relationship StateContainsFlowElements.
        foreach (FlowElement child in state.Children)
        {
          // Find the shape representing this FlowElement.
          foreach (PresentationElement pel in
            PresentationViewsSubject.GetPresentation(child))
          {
            NodeShape childShape = pel as NodeShape;
            // We want the one that's in the same diagram as our parent.
            if (childShape == null || childShape.Diagram != shape.Diagram)
              continue;

            // Only move it if it isn't already scheduled to move.
            if (!moving.Contains(childShape))
              childShape.Location = PointD.Add(childShape.Location, offset);
          }
        }
      }
```

Z Order

The change rule rearranges the front-to-back ordering ("Z Order") of the shapes so that smaller shapes are always on top of larger ones. This is desirable in a state chart, since whenever you move a smaller item over a larger one, you never want it to be obscured.

The Z Order is represented in the ordering of the diagram's NestedChild-Shapes list—later shapes are painted later, and thus are nearer the viewer. Connectors (instances of BinraryLinkShape) are all moved to the front.

Each shape also has a ZOrder property, a double that should be maintained in correct order.

SUMMARY

This chapter has covered a number of topics, using a variety of examples, which we hope give a flavor of the extent to which you can customize the DSL Tools. In particular, we've looked at the following:

- The basic mechanisms of extensibility
- Propagating change within and outside the store
- The interface to the VS Shell
- Creating menu commands
- Implementing cut and paste
- Representing relationships as containment of one shape in another

For more detail and code of all the techniques described in this (and the other) chapters, please download the solutions from the book's website.

■ 11 ■
Designing a DSL

Introduction

In Chapter 2, we discussed how a DSL is developed incrementally and bottom-up. You begin with specific application code and gradually parameterize it. First turn your existing code into a set of templates—so that if they were not modified, they would just generate the original code. Then gradually replace pieces of the templates by template expressions; the DSL develops alongside, as the means to express these statements' parameters.

We contrasted this with a top-down approach that begins by considering the domain as a collection of interrelated concepts—those represented in the DSL's domain model. That approach has a number of potential advantages. It gets much more quickly and directly to a substantial DSL; it tends to produce a more self-consistent and complete result; and it tends to ensure that variations are expressed in terms of requirements rather than implementation, so that incidental variations in implementation are factored out. However, we also observed a problem with top-down—that it often leads to impractical implementations if not combined with bottom up regularly. We concluded that, in practice, it is effective to alternate between top-down and bottom-up techniques, working incrementally to avoid the risk of a big upfront investment but occasionally standing back to check for consistency.

We stepped through a small slice of the development of the CJKW Issue Tracking DSLs, framework, and code generators, and we touched on many of these points but did not explore the process in any depth. That's the purpose of this chapter. Specifically, we discuss a range of techniques and options for:

- Identifying variability and discovering DSLs—A DSL is about the bits that vary, while your framework embodies the patterns of your architecture.
- Developing the domain model to capture points of variability.
- Defining the notation, using a familiar notation or notational conventions where applicable.
- Developing validation constraints—Identify dependencies between properties and spot mandatory or prohibited loops in your snapshots.
- Developing and evolving the framework—Understand the architecture of the code that your DSL targets, and encode that in a framework.
- Testing the DSL, the validation constraints and rules, generators and commands, and generated code.
- Evolving and migrating a DSL—Ensure old models can be used with new versions of the DSL.
- Recognizing a good DSL—Scope, minimality, familiar notations, moderate redundancy, good use of the syntactic space, using the users' terms.

Identifying Variability

CJKW has two mingled motivations for developing a generic framework, of which DSLs may be a part. (Your own emphasis may be on one or the other.) The first motivation is to maintain a *product line* of multiple similar products—all of their customers want Issue Tracking systems, but with different features. The second motivation is to facilitate variation through time of each product—each customer wants to be able to introduce new features at short notice. The first represents the ideal; go to customers with the product, the Issue Tracking system, and a list of features that customers can choose from to configure the product to suit their needs. CJKW would input the customer choices into the product factory, which creates the Issue Tracking system tailored to a specific customer's requirements. The second motivation, however, represents reality; the customer will always want to adapt the system to meet new requirements once it's been delivered, and these requirements are bound to include features that weren't predicted when setting up the original product line.

Fortunately, both problems can be mitigated by the same basic approach: separating out the parts that vary from the parts that remain constant, thereby making changes easier. And where the changeable parts form complex structures, DSLs may be created to express their instances.

Bottom-Up or Top-Down?

Identifying variability can be like performing a balancing act. If you follow agile programming principles to the letter, you should never create features based on future prediction (on the assumption that it is impossible to get right); you should instead wait until the actual need arises and then refactor accordingly. This tends toward a bottom-up way of working. On the other hand, you can accommodate all the variations you have seen so far, but then the next thing that comes along requires some change deep in what you had thought was the invariant part of the system. So some awareness of future needs may mean you can plan your refactoring in order to help with planning of resources and to ensure a smoother transition when major rearchitecture is required. An awareness of possible future needs tends toward a top-down way of working.

To date, CJKW's clients have required that different projects have different sorts of issue, with different fields and different sequences of states, but none has yet needed two sorts of issue within the same project. To make issue-types distinct from projects would require substantial work on the database schemas and surrounding code. The one client who would have it was able to accept that one real-world project would use two database projects, one for each sort of issue. Some team members have argued for doing the necessary refactoring upfront, but the cost is assessed as being fairly high, and to do all the refactoring now would pull resources away from directly revenue-earning work. Instead, a plan is drawn up to phase in the refactoring over time to meet the predicted needs of future business; it is expected that there'll be many more clients who have the same need, and by refactoring the product line to include this feature, they will be able to generate more business and be more competitive in the market. Although the plan is informed by the needs of the first client who wanted this capability, inevitably it has required a top-down analysis of the likely requirements in this area and some upfront design of the architecture of the refactored framework.

Feature Trees

One technique for thinking about and capturing variability top-down is feature trees. A feature tree[1] is a presentation of a set of requirements, some of which are optional. Because options are often interdependent, they can be presented as a tree. As a configuration tool, you have probably seen them in software installer wizards, under the "Custom Install" heading. (For example, the Windows Installer—you choose the features you require. OK, so you want IIS; do you want FTP, or Web Service? If you want Web Service, do you need a scripts directory? And so on.) As analytical tools, they are useful for setting out the options your clients have or could have.

Figure 11-1 is part of the feature tree CJKW creates for its Issue Tracking product line. Most items are optional—you make a set of selections to define a particular product from the line. A child item can be selected only if its parent is selected, together with additional dependencies shown by the dashed arrows. "X" marks mutual exclusion between choices.

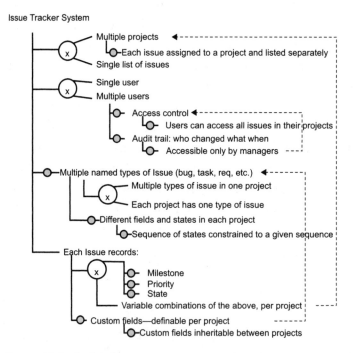

FIGURE 11-1: Feature tree

---

1. For more on feature trees, see K. Czarnecki, S. Helsen, U. Eisenecker, "Staged Configuration Using Feature Models," *Software Product Lines: Third International Conference*, Boston, MA, 2004.

For example, as a customer, I might decide that I don't need multiple projects, but I do need multiple users, although access control is not required. I'll have an audit trail, but must accept that because I haven't chosen access control I can't restrict the audit trail to managers.

The tree notionally includes every feature in the requirements document; some of them may turn out not to be optional after all. After some discussion, CJKW decides that Multiple Projects is a non-optional feature of every installation; this saves development effort, and in practice loses little flexibility—customers who want "single list of issues" need only create one project.

Development tasks can be mapped to the nodes in the tree that they enable. Development effort is required both for features and optional or XOR nodes. One task links each issue to a milestone, but more effort is required to make that optional per installation, and yet more is needed to make it optional per project.

A feature tree is about requirements, rather than design; each feature describes something that can be seen by the client of the system. In their first few customer-specific systems, CJKW's design choices evolved somewhat as the team gained experience. Many of the variations are about changes in design choices rather than changes in requirements—for example, using a list instead of an array at some point. These changes are not included in the feature tree.

Choices may be marked with how often or in what context they may vary—for example, Single/Multiple User—select on Installation; Custom Fields—select per issue type or project; Multiple Types of Issue per Project—currently fixed at false. Each project defines a single type of issue.

Feature trees are not only for features visible to end users. If you are designing something like a generic wizard builder, then your clients are the developers who call your subsystem, and your features are the behavior visible to them at your API.

Feature Trees and DSLs

Feature trees work well for binary or enumerated choices. A feature tree can work more or less directly as a DSL clothed in a suitable syntax. Many installers have feature trees that appear either in the form of expandable trees of checked options or as wizards.

But some variabilities are more complex structures that cannot simply be selected or deselected. Inspecting its feature tree, CJKW's developers identify that where customers opt for "Sequence of states constrained to a given sequence" and "custom fields definable per project," the users will need suitable notations for defining the detail of these choices. This is the origin of the two DSLs used in the project.

Developing the Domain Model

In Chapter 2, the Issue State DSL came about by observing that statecharts seemed a good fit with the problem, which was confirmed by the business analyst who was already drawing state diagrams informally when eliciting requirements from customers. Once that basic connection had been observed, the DSL was refined by sitting back and thinking about the domain model and notation as a whole, and by making changes incrementally to the definition (for example, adding properties to domain classes) as dictated by the needs of the code generators.

However, it's not always that easy. In this section, we describe a more systematic technique for creating the domain model aspect of a DSL. This technique tends to be useful to get you through cases where it's proving difficult to work out exactly what domain classes, relationships, and domain properties are required. The technique is adapted from a technique proposed in the Catalysis[2] approach to object-oriented analysis and design.

Sketch Domain Snapshots

The requirements scenarios describe the domain in words. To help clarify them, it is a very useful whiteboard technique to draw *snapshots*. A snapshot is an informal drawing showing a collection of elements and links at a particular moment in time. Only some elements and links will be instances of domain classes and relationships in the domain model of a DSL; the domain model can be inferred from them. Others represent instances in a running system generated from models expressed in the DSL; the instances are generated from the instances of the domain classes and relationships defining the

---

2.   Desmond F. D'Souza and Alan Cameron Wills, *Objects, Components, and Frameworks with UML: The Catalysis Approach*, Addison-Wesley, 1998.

DSL. Of course, when you start, you don't know which are which, and that's part of the analysis that needs to be done.

Project and Field Snapshots

Let's focus first on custom field definitions. In the feature tree and scenarios, we identified that a project administrator can determine what fields are available to users who create issues, and that these sets of fields are defined on a per-project basis. So we can draw some example fields associated with a typical project. Each field will have a name and a type. Associated with each project will be some issues; each issue has a description and—among other things—some values for the fields. Each field value associates a value of the correct type with a field and an issue. So the drawing looks like Figure 11-2.

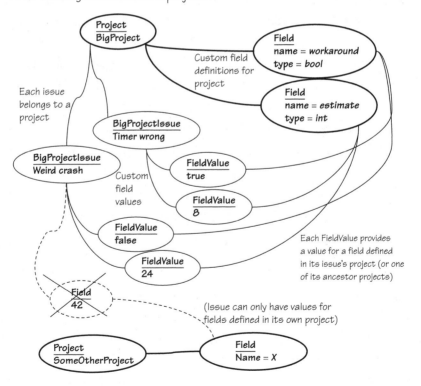

FIGURE 11-2: Snapshot—custom fields

Notice some of the principles we've followed:

- **Snapshots**. Draw a single instant in time. Illustrate a particular point in a requirement scenario. If there are widely differing configurations of relationships, use more than one snapshot to examine and discuss them.

- **Abstract**. The nodes and lines here say nothing about how they are implemented in a machine. Keep those questions separate.

- **Highlight variability**. The bold lines and entities drawn in bold are those that change less often. For example, once a project has been defined, the set of Issue Types allowed to it will change rarely, but issues will be added frequently. Distinguishing different frequencies of variability is the key to identifying which elements and links represent instances of domain classes and relationships.

- **Disallowed links**. Snapshots are particularly good at illustrating and providing insights about constraints—for example, that an issue's field values must be for fields belonging to the issue's own project. To illustrate these constraints clearly, show some disallowed links.

- **Sketches**. This is a whiteboard or paper exercise. Don't feel obliged to stick to a "correct" syntax. Feel free to draw smilies, stick figures, houses, and so on instead of ellipses.

- **Separate topic areas**. Don't crowd everything onto one diagram. Show different groups of relationships on different drawings.

- **Changes**. It can be useful to show on the diagram what changes are allowed—especially how relationships may change (see the Issue State snapshot in Figure 11-3).

Issue State Snapshots

Now let's move on to Issue State. The requirement is to allow an administrator to determine, for each project, the collection of states that an issue can take on, and what transitions are allowed between them. We draw a typical project and some states, as illustrated in Figure 11-3. Each project has an initial state that a new issue must take on, and each state has a set of permitted next states.

<u>Issue State</u>
After triage has approved a bug.

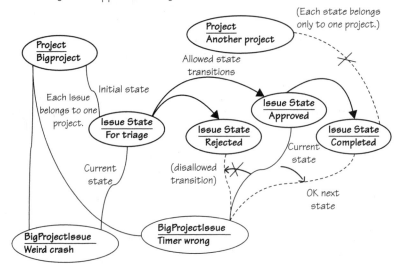

Each issue has a single current state, which must be one of those defined for its project.
Each project defines a number of states, and permitted transitions between them.
When a user changes an issue's current state, it must follow one of its project's transitions.

FIGURE 11-3: Issue Snapshot: Issue State

We should make some cautionary observations about snapshots. Because they are informal, they don't pretend to represent exactly or completely everything there is to say about the topic; they're just an aid to thinking. For example, is there always a single Initial State for each project, or can the project have more than one—from which a user must choose to create an issue? We can't tell from this snapshot—it might just be that there is only one in this particular illustration.

■ TIP Snapshots and filmstrips

Questions such as "How many initial states?" can be answered by producing a collection of snapshots representing the different possibilities (e.g., draw one where there is more than one initial state in a project) and by testing that against scenarios. One way to generate such a collection is to write out user stories and then develop a sequence of snapshots, a *filmstrip*, to illustrate the conceptual state of the domain at each step. An efficient way of doing this is to produce a single diagram and then use different colors to show the changes between each step—it

> works very well on the whiteboard and PowerPoint. Once you've done this a few times, you may find that you don't need to physically draw the snapshots—you can construct them in your head, and the user stories are sufficient. However, there are always difficult cases where the only way to sort it out for sure is to commit ink to surface.

Because at this stage the lines on the diagram represent conceptual relationships rather than actual implementation, we can always feel free either to leave off any redundant relationships to avoid clutter or to include redundant information if it makes things more clear. For example, we can see that the Completed state belongs to BigProject because you can follow a chain of transitions from the initial state; in an implementation, we would probably link each state directly to its owner project and record the transitions. Conversely, we have linked each issue both to a project and a state, but we could in theory have left out the project link, since each state belongs to only one project. We're exploring the scenarios that our DSLs will represent rather than an implementation.

Domain Model from Snapshots

The feature tree helped us identify the two areas where we might use DSLs. We have drawn some snapshots of the domain in typical situations in order to help us understand the real-world relationships that the DSLs will express.

In this step, we separate out parts of the snapshots that are relevant to a particular candidate DSL and create a model of the domain using the DSL Tools Domain Model Designer.

Project Definition Domain Model

The first DSL area covers the definition of fields that issues in a particular project can have. We pick out the less changeable parts of the snapshot— they are the projects and field definitions and their relationship, as shown in Figure 11-4.

At this stage, we have to make some distinctions that were unclear from the snapshots. What exactly are the multiplicities for fields in projects? What are the types that a field can have?

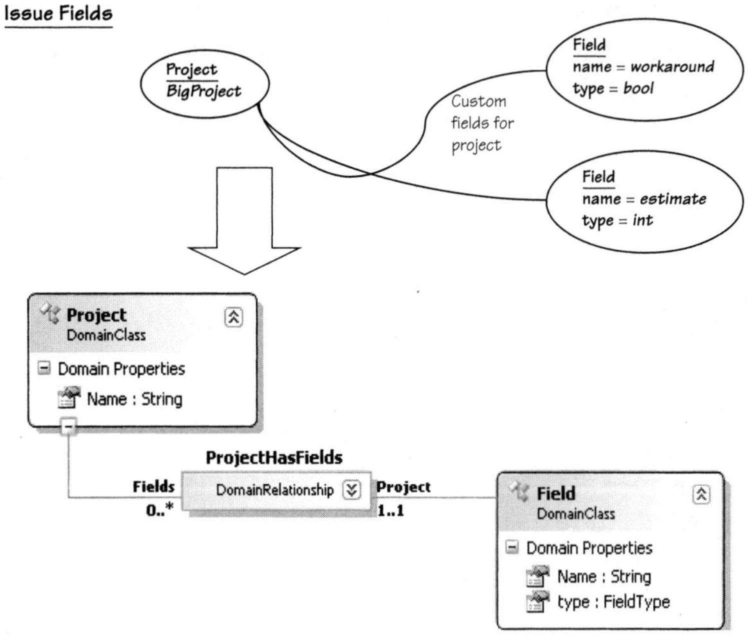

Issue Fields

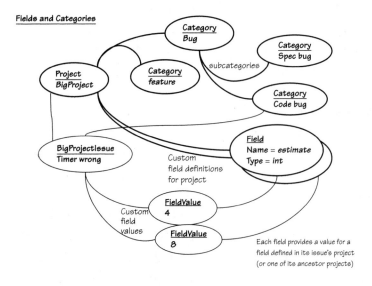

FIGURE 11-4: Inferring a domain model from a snapshot

We may also refine and extend the model from the initial sketches. The requirements call for each issue to be assignable to a *Category*; Categories are defined per project, and each can contain subcategories. We create a new snapshot to look like Figure 11-5.

Fields and Categories

FIGURE 11-5: Snapshot—categories and fields

This leads to another draft of the domain model in Figure 11-6. While drafting the model, we decide the domain class name "IssueCategory" will be more explanatory than "Category."

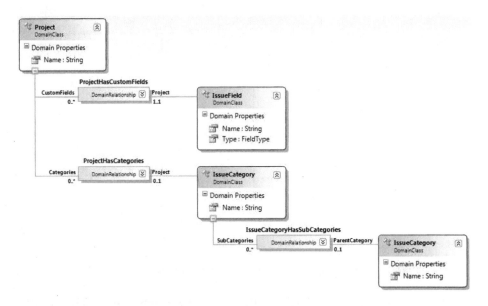

FIGURE 11-6: Domain model—categories and fields

Notice how, in the snapshots, we consider objects and relationships outside the scope of the domain model we end up with—here, the instance issues and field values. They are about the meaning of the DSL—in this case, how a model in the language defines structures and constraints to which the field values must conform. Considering context in the snapshots is most important for understanding the language.

Inherited Relationships

One last improvement can be made to this model. We have chosen the multiplicities on each role to fit the situations depicted in the example snapshots. But there is also another restriction. From the snapshot, you can see that an **IssueCategory** can belong to a **Project** or it can be a subcategory of another **IssueCategory**. Trying out variations on this snapshot would soon reveal that it cannot both belong to a project and be a subcategory, and would also raise the question of whether it could belong to two projects or be subcategories of different categories. Assuming that none of these situations is allowed, we conclude that an **IssueCategory** should only have one parent—whether it is another **IssueCategory** or a **Project**. To represent this information, we can create a class that abstracts the **IssueCategory**-parenting characteristics of **Project** and **IssueCategory**, as shown in Figure 11-7.

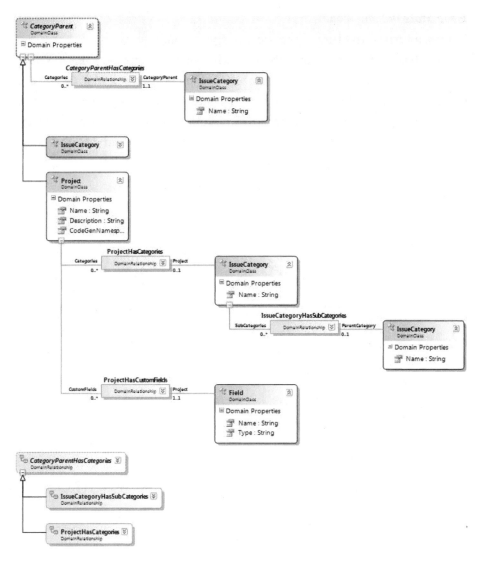

FIGURE 11-7: Domain model—CategoryParent

The relationship **CategoryParentHasCategories** from **CategoryParent** to **IssueCategory** has a multiplicity of 1 at the parent end. By forcing the other two relationships of **IssueCategory** (to parent **Project** and parent

IssueCategory) to be subrelationships of **CategoryParentHasCategories**, we force there to be only one element at a time playing the parent role in a relationship. Thus, each **IssueCategory** must either be embedded under a **Project** or under another **IssueCategory**, but not both.

Issue State Domain Model

Now we turn to the Issue State part of the domain, shown in Figure 11-8.

We've added an extra **IssueStateModel** root domain class in which the projects are embedded. Top level states are then embedded in projects, and other states embedded beneath them. The chain of states headed by the project seemed natural enough to the CJKW developers when they drew it on the whiteboard at first, but more experienced modelers may find it slightly odd. We'll see how this initial domain model is evolved as the notation is explored.

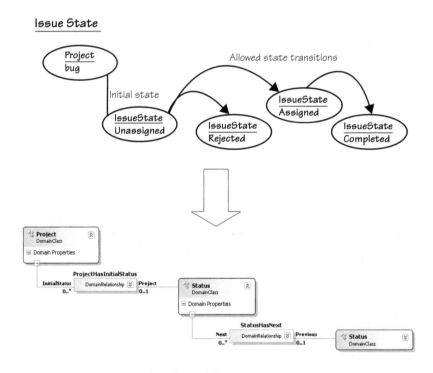

FIGURE 11-8: Issue State domain model

Developing the Notation

We have a domain model, which just defines the concepts that the language deals in; now we want to decide how it looks on the screen and what you can do with it in the designer. Given that notations in the DSL Tools are currently mostly restricted to nodes and lines, we might at first think that, looking at the snapshots we have drawn, we need only decide the shapes of the nodes. However, that isn't quite true—there are some decisions still to be made.

It's worth reiterating that no development process is linear. It is at this point that we converge with those who have known all along what their notation is going to look like, as we discussed in an earlier section. In fact, we generally move quite rapidly between trying out concrete notations, investigating the underlying domain model, and sketching snapshots of the surrounding context. Working with the domain model and snapshots helps ensure we are including everything we need the DSL to say; experimenting with concrete notation helps understand how we want to say it.

There are four ways to represent a relationship in concrete syntax:

1. **Connector**. Each link of the relationship maps to a connector on the diagram, with the related elements represented as shapes. This is how we have drawn all the relationships in the snapshots; it works for any relationship.

2. **Nesting**. A shape nesting inside a swimlane or other shape can represent a one-one or one-many relationship. For example, subcategories can be shown as shapes inside their parent categories.

3. **Compartments**. An item in a compartment list shows a chosen property of the other end of a one-many relationship. The disadvantages are that it only shows one line of information about the target and can't nest deeper than one level. The benefit is that it is very compact compared to having a complete shape per element.

4. **Explorer only**. The relationship is not shown on the diagram and just appears in the language explorer.

■ **TIP** Consider relationships first

The way you represent a relationship in concrete syntax can in turn influence how you represent related elements. So consider relationship first.

Project Definition Notation

Figure 11-9 shows some of the choices for the relationships between projects and categories and between projects and fields.

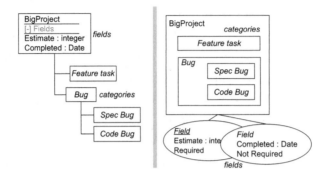

FIGURE 11-9: Project definition—syntax options

CJKW likes the nested categories (right picture in Figure 11-9) and the compartments for the fields (left picture in Figure 11-9). Fields as separate objects would be useful if they had other interesting relationships that could be drawn as connectors, but the compact compartment shape list seems most appropriate. Compartment listing wouldn't work for categories, because they can be nested indefinitely; connectors look OK, and would be especially useful if they had other interesting relationships.

Unfortunately, it is difficult[3] to nest shapes inside a compartment shape with version 1 of the DSL Tools, so if the fields are to be in a compartment list, then the categories will have to be outside the project. CJKW settles on a compromise in which the top categories are separate while subcategories are nested. Other project variables are represented in different compartments. See the example in Figure 11-10.

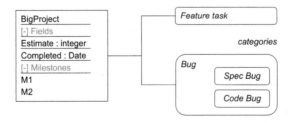

FIGURE 11-10: Project definition—concrete syntax example

---

3. It is possible, but significant custom code is required.

Reviewing the Domain Model

Now we complete entering the language into the DSL designer, and in doing so, we check that the domain model still can be mapped to the chosen concrete syntax and that the embedding links within any model form a tree. There should be no difficulties in this case.

Issue State Notation

Working from the domain model in Figure 11-8, we can consider a variety of alternatives for the IssueState concrete syntax. They include

1. The Next relationship and the InitialState relationship are represented by different kinds of connectors, as shown in Figure 11-11.

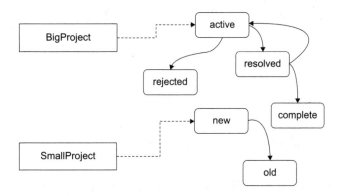

FIGURE 11-11: Projects and states in a flat diagram

This has the disadvantage that states from different projects could get intermingled. Since a state can't belong to more than one project, and transitions should not cross from one project to another, keeping them all in the same area seems potentially confusing.

2. Projects are represented by containers, with the states inside. Since a connector from the container to the initial state would look slightly odd, we mark the initial states distinctively instead, as shown in Figure 11-12. A disadvantage here is that multiple projects with complex state diagrams will take up substantial screen real estate.

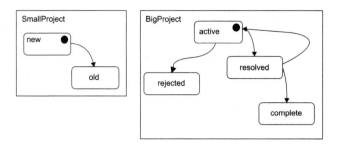

FIGURE 11-12: Projects contain states

3. Each project is represented by a separate model (in a separate file). Again, we mark the initial states distinctively (Figure 11-13).

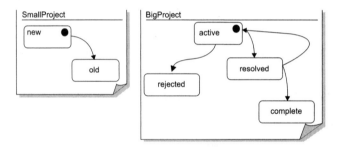

FIGURE 11-13: One project per model file

4. As scheme 3, but with one last refinement: Initial state is marked by a separate start mark rather than a decorator on the state, as shown in Figure 11-14.

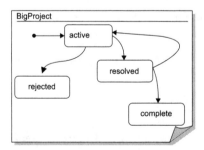

FIGURE 11-14: One project per model file

A benefit here is that it is slightly easier to read if we decide to allow more than one starting state—in that case, there would still be one start marker, with more than one pointer to states. It's also in tune with standard notion for statecharts.

CJKW chooses scheme 4.

Reviewing the Domain Model

To make this notation work the following must be there:

- The **Project** domain class is removed, because each model corresponds to a single project.
- The mapping from domain model to drawing will be easier to define if states all embed directly from the root element (rather than some being embedded in states, as in the draft model).
- A separate relationship between states is required to represent the transitions. This should be a reference relationship.
- To provide for the start mark, we need a separate type of element. It must have a unique qualifier/key pair among the other states.

We therefore arrive at the model in Figure 11-15.

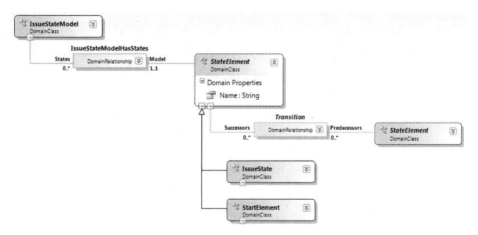

FIGURE 11-15: Refactored Issue State domain model

Again, there is one more improvement we can make concerning
relationships among the multiplicities. As it stands, the model permits start
elements to have multiple relationships to other states; we really want to
allow only one transition to leave a **StartElement**. We could enforce this
condition with validation constraints, but it is more effective to impose a
hard constraint by using relationship inheritance, as shown in Figure 11-16.

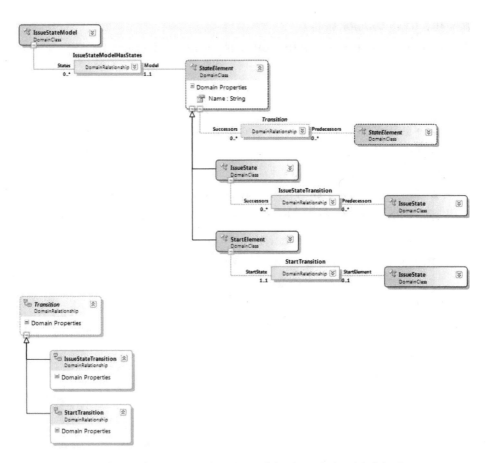

FIGURE 11-16: Refactored Issue State domain model using relationship inheritance

Familiar Notations

You are often quite soon aware of what your notation should look like. Why
did CJKW hit on statecharts for defining state transitions? Well, statecharts
are such a familiar notation with a long history that it would be difficult not
to. A starting template for statechart-like languages is provided with the
DSL Tools, and creating the DSL is the work of an afternoon—although as

we've seen, the framework that implements it is the time-consuming part. Of course, this used not to be the case—developing a graphical designer for a DSL used to be a big deal, before kits like the DSL Tools became available.

One of the objections sometimes raised against DSLs is that each new recruit has to learn an unfamiliar set of languages. This seems not to be a problem in practice. A clear notation adopting a familiar style is easy to pick up even if the details are different, and the constraints imposed by the toolbox and the validation conditions help to guide the newcomer. Even with textual languages, which can be much more complex than graphical ones, the user can be prompted by IntelliSense. In the end, learning a project's DSLs are no worse—and can be a lot easier—than learning an API, and unlike the API, the DSL can be accessible, if appropriate, to end users.

Adopt any notation that is already in use in the target domain, adding information if necessary. This has the considerable advantage of improving communication with your clients. To take a completely different example for a moment, supposing you write a navigation system for the London Tube; installed on a mobile phone, it will tell you the best route from any station to any other. Now suppose you make it generic—it can work for the Paris Metro, the New York subway—potentially, for any train system anywhere. But to work for a particular train system, it has to be parameterized, using a DSL to tell it about the stations and connections. Now what would the DSL that would help you convey that information to the navigation software look like? Of course, it looks like the subway map—the shapes and connectors it defines should allow you to create models that look just like the maps of the train systems you are trying to describe.

> ■ **TIP**
>
> Before constructing a concrete syntax from first principles, look to see what existing notations present themselves.

Defining Validation Constraints

Not all models that could be drawn in our language make sense. For example, it would not be useful if there were some states in an Issue State diagram that could not be reached from an Initial state.

Now that we have a domain model and notation for a DSL—at least a first draft—we should define validation constraints over the model. They will be checked when the user opens or saves the model, or explicitly asks for validation.

There are two objectives. The first is to minimize errors in tools that read the model. For example, since we generate a typed access API for Issue Fields, each field name must be a valid C# property name. A valid model is one that raises no errors when processed, so validation constraints should be determined with those tools in mind.

The second objective is to detect errors by finding inconsistencies. To this end, it can be useful to introduce redundancies into the language. For example, we could give Issue State an "End State" flag; the language user must set the flag for states that intentionally have no exit transition. This would help avoid unintentional loose ends.

Internal Consistency

Internal consistency means validation checks that can be performed on a model without reference to any external data. The following heuristics will help you discover constraints that should be written:

- Print a copy of the DSL's domain model (with all properties visible). Link in pencil all occurrences of the same class.
- Look for loops in the resulting diagram. The loop may involve any number of links—either relationships or inheritance. For each loop, draw an example set of instances, as they would be in the internal store. Ask yourself whether corresponding loops are disallowed or mandated in the instances. See Figure 11-17 for an example.
- Consider also branches off any loop, where the loop end of the branch has a multiplicity greater than 1. See Figure 11-18 for an example.

(Although this example serves to demonstrate the technique, our scheme to present each project's states in its own model—hence all states are directly embedded in a single root element of domain class IssueStateModel—means this particular constraint will not be broken without a software fault.)

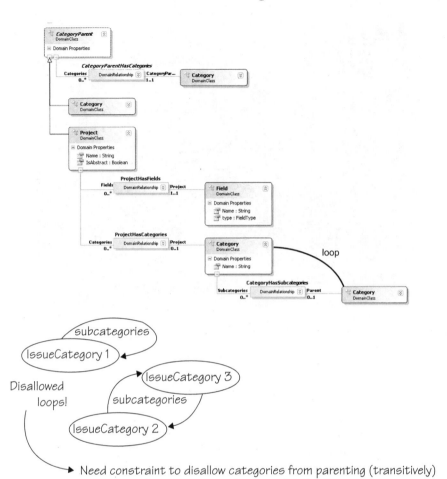

FIGURE 11-17: Loops in project definition model

- Consider whether each property should be unique in some scope, for example, **Field.Name** in the Field's Project.

- Consider whether there are format and range constraints for each property—may it contain spaces? May it be empty? Must it be a valid C# name?

- Consider whether each property should be constrained by the value of other properties. Equal? Not equal? Equal to some function? In some range or type?

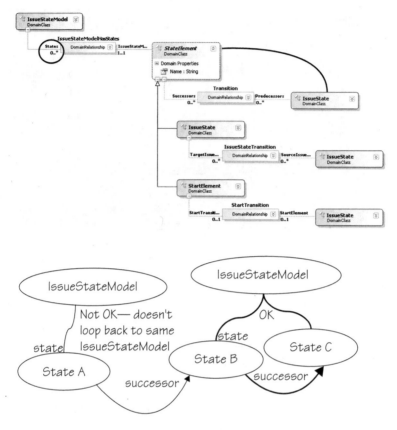

FIGURE 11-18: Loops in Issue State model

Consistency with External Data and Models

A model must also be consistent with external data. For example, each issue state may refer to a field defined for the project in the separate project fields model. Validation checks can be written to check directly against the other model or against the database they write to.

Most external checks are for validity of reference pathnames, items in databases, and so on. It is also possible to conduct the loop-checking exercise presented earlier by drawing instance diagrams that extend beyond the boundaries of your model and drawing references of any sort—names, URIs, database keys, and so on, as lines.

Developing and Evolving the Framework

Generation versus Interpretation

The biggest task in adopting a domain-specific development approach is in generalizing the software to produce a framework. Designing and implementing a DSL is now a relatively small amount of work, thanks to kits like the DSL Tools. In the typical scenario, as we've discussed, the project to create a product line has been preceded by a series of more specific products. Since the team's ideas about requirements and architecture have been evolving during that time, much of the implementation may be inconsistent between the specific instances, even where the requirements were similar. The task now is to bring them all together and separate out the necessarily variable parts from the invariant parts. Some of the variable parts may be driven from a DSL.

The project to develop the framework often coincides with a desire to rewrite the whole thing from scratch. If you have time, confidence in, and agreement on the new architecture, and confidence in continuing demand for your product, then great—have fun! But the "Big Rewrite" is always something of a risky project and usually has to go on in the back room while short-term needs are met using the old architecture. So it isn't always acceptable for the generalization project to be a major upfront investment.

There are two broad approaches to generalization that boil down to a difference in binding time: interpretation and generation. In frameworks that implement an interpretive approach, the metadata about the variable aspects of the requirements is stored live within the system. The CJKW Issue Tracker is essentially interpretive; the names and types of fields attached to the issues in each project are held in a table, and the core of the system is independent of them. In generated systems, the metadata is used to generate code from templates at build time. A mixed approach is often used.

Let's look at the relative advantages of the two approaches.

Performance

Interpretive systems are generally slower, both because they need to read the metadata as they go along and because they cannot be optimized to take advantage of particular configurations. In the Issue Tracker, all types of custom field value must be converted to and from a common form, and their types must be looked up in the field type table.

Upfront Investment

A generator template can be written by taking an existing instance and inserting parameters wherever there are points of variance; indeed, it's almost impossible to do it any other way. You can start with something that covers just a small range of variation from the initial instance and then gradually elaborate the template, adding branches where you need radically different structures or algorithms in the runtime system.

In contrast, to write an interpretive system, you must first invent a core data structure that will accommodate the whole range of cases.

For example, in a generated version of the Issue Tracker, the code and structures for custom fields would be stamped out from a loop in the template to work in the same way as the standard fields (such as priority and milestones). In the existing interpretive code, custom fields are kept in a separate table while the standard fields are dealt with relatively economically as columns in the main issue table.

Flexibility and Migration

Interpretive systems are able to change on the fly and can run multiple cases side by side within the application. In the issues database, it is relatively easy to accommodate several projects with different sets of custom fields. In a generated system, a separate module would be required to support each variation, and the system would have to be stopped and rebuilt.

Interpretive systems usually handle migrations more easily. For example, suppose we add more custom fields to a project in the issues database. In an interpretive system, the field values are kept in a generic table whose form will not change with the additional fields. It is therefore easy for the code to cope with the missing fields in old issues that predate the change—a generic mechanism for filling in default values will work for them all.

But in a generated system, we might well build the set of fields more intimately into all the data structures. The issues table in the database would have a column for each field; we would have to explicitly migrate old issues into the new database.

Range

In a generated system, data structures and algorithms can be varied radically to suit the metadata simply by changing the generators. In an interpreted system, each time you stretch it to accommodate a more general structure, you may lose performance and complicate the architecture.

For example, supposing we decide that, in addition to single-valued fields, we would like lists—so that the project administrator could decide that each issue can have, say, a list of owners. This is a change that goes outside the current range of the interpretive system. We need to rewrite the generic code and data structures. The table of field types, for example, will need a flag indicating whether it can be multivalued; and since (**field_id**, **issue_id**) no longer form a unique key to field values, we may need to change the values table.

Once the change has been made, the new structures and code underlie all the data in the generic architecture. The old database will need to be migrated to the new generic structure—even those projects that don't need the new feature. Any performance penalty applies equally to all the data.

In contrast, in a generated system, the new structures only apply where they are needed, and old databases that don't require the new features don't have to be migrated.

So the flexibility of interpretive systems applies only within the range that they are built for, and extending that range may require significant investment and could lead to the customization pit discussed in Chapter 1. So where the range of requirements is wide and liable to change, generation can be a better strategy.

Typing and Programmability

Compile-time type checking is one of the benefits of generated code. Even in a largely interpretive system, it can be useful to provide a generated wrapper. From the Project Definition language, we generate code that accesses untyped objects from the generic issues database and casts them appropriately. In the same way, much of the generated code in the DSL designer solution takes the form of wrappers and constructors; the underlying in-memory store provides a generic relational model in which type information is interpreted on the fly.

Typed code is much easier to write and read than the corresponding generic version. Compare "bug.Estimate" with something like "bug.Get-CustomFieldValue("Estimate"))"—the first version is not only more succinct, but the IDE helps you write it.

Evolving a Generic Framework

As we've seen, the quickest way to start generalizing a system can be to turn its existing code into templates and parameterize it piecewise. However, you need to very quickly start moving boilerplate into a common framework core in order to prevent the code generation code from becoming overly complex. For example, early versions of the DSL Tools had a lot of functional code generated from templates in the designer solutions. As we gained experience, more of the functionality was moved into a generic utility layer and then into the core framework.

Once you have a framework, we can envisage a number of different typical evolution paths for it. The path taken depends on initial circumstances, the stability of the requirements, and performance requirements.

Increasing Genericity

In this scenario, the code of a product line starts with one or two specific instances and then works through a number of template-generated versions in which there is an increasing set of variation points. Then boilerplate from the template is moved into the framework, and the generation templates are simplified. Finally, it moves toward an interpretive system tailored to the range of expected requirements, but it retains a layer of generated strong-typing wrappers. This happens cyclically and incrementally, so at any point in time there may be some parts of the framework that are interpretive and some that are refactored boilerplate.

Prototypes

In this route, there are more funds for upfront experimentation with the architecture. The project may begin with some small specific instances, but then it goes straight for an interpretive architecture, with a long period of design. Part of the rationale is that the result will be easy to experiment with on the fly. In practice, the range of cases covered is likely to match the actual requirements rather imperfectly (especially if the requirements are changing in the meantime), and so the initial version will be over-elaborate in some areas and difficult to stretch in others. For example, we might have started with an issues database that could handle multiple types of link between issues—which might never be needed—but doesn't deal with more than one type of issue per project, which probably will be needed.

Integrated Systems

If you are lucky, you have access to the source code of the whole system and can make choices about where on the generative-interpretive axis it lies. More often, though, systems are constructed from an ill-matched collection of existing parts for which there is no source code. In this case, all you have control of is a miscellany of configuration files and bits of plug-in code. Making a change at the requirements level involves multiple changes in these diverse pieces.

This is one of the great strengths of generative architecture—it provides a method of abstracting the actual requirements from these implementation details.

The degree to which the metadata is interpreted in the live system is determined by the components themselves, and it may differ between the components. For example, the Issue Tracking database is interpretive; from the Project Definition and State Transition designers, we generate SQL that transfers the metadata into the database. This metadata can be updated on the fly without harming the existing instance data or stopping the system. However, the type wrappers are compiled from generated code, so a client that uses them must be stopped when the metadata are updated.

Driving a Framework from the DSL

There are at least three ways of driving a framework from the DSL. These have already been considered in depth in other chapters, so we just provide a summary here:

* **Model as configuration file**. The model is serialized to a file; the generic framework reads the file on build, or in a setup operation. Variants of this involve adjusting the serializer to suit an existing framework, or processing the file with XML tools. Serialization was discussed in Chapter 6.

- **Model generates code**. In Visual Studio, the model is one file in a project; the project also contains multiple templates that read the model, generating code and other files. Templates are transformed before building, and most changes to the code are made by adjusting the model. When necessary, some custom code is added. Rarely, some change is needed to a template file. This is the architecture used by the DSL Tools for authoring DSLs and their designers and associated components. This was all discussed in Chapter 8, which also provided a sample of how to drive the Text Templating Engine from a command in order to provide more orchestrated generation.

- **Model drives external API**. A command associated with the DSL reads the model and drives a database or other system. The model may be entirely transferred into the external system by the operation, or it may update just relevant parts of the system. This would be used by the Issue Tracker to update the database from the model, for example. The implementation of custom commands was described in Chapter 10.

■ TIP Custom commands in Visual Studio

The approach to adding custom commands uses the raw Visual Studio extensibility mechanisms. Another possibility is to use the Visual Studio Guidance Automation Toolkit,[4] with which it is also possible to attach commands to DSLs—as well as other parts of the Visual Studio UI such as particular types of project and project item—and have them instantiated along with code files and templates in a project.

Testing

Automated tests are a very successful assurance against the introduction of errors as code is extended and refactored. Tests typically include

- Unit tests aimed at individual pieces of code written by the unit's developer, and including "mock" or stub interfaces to simulate the rest of the system.

---

4. http://msdn2.microsoft.com/en-us/teamsystem/aa718948.aspx

- Integration, or "end-to-end" tests, which take the system through scenarios at the user level and are designed to verify that the system requirements have been met.

- Combinatorial tests designed to try significant combinations of input values, particularly edge cases, to check correct behavior throughout the space and to check error handling.

- Performance tests that check capacity and response times.

There are several aspects of a DSL that need to be tested: validation constraints; generator templates; any generated code; menu commands; anything you have customized, such as serialization; and the DSL itself.

▪ TIP **Automating Tests**

Visual Studio Team System provides a good automated test framework that allows a developer to run unit tests on his or her project before checking in changes to the shared repository. There are also command-line utilities that build a VS project and run its tests, which can be used in an unmanned nightly or rolling build system (which continually tests the latest repository content). We divide up our development into tasks of a few days each and find these facilities invaluable for preventing regressions.

▪ TIP **Measuring Code Coverage**

Visual Studio's test kit includes a coverage tool, which monitors tests as they run, marking and counting the number of branches executed within the code under test. A typical expectation is that a suite of automated tests should achieve coverage of at least 70%–80%[5].

---

5. For generated code, this expectation applies to the proportion of the generating template that is covered, rather than the generated code. Since one template usually generates multiple variants of itself, the reported coverage of the generated code may be much smaller, and you will have to do some analysis to work out what coverage of the generating template that represents.

After a test has run within VS, you can right-click and select "Code Coverage Results," and get a view of the source code in which the executed branches are highlighted. This helps you adjust your tests to make sure most branches are exercised, which gives some assurance that the most common paths (the combinations of branches through the code) have been checked.

To get a coverage analysis, you first identify the compiled assembly to the coverage tool, under the "Test>Edit Test Run Configurations" menu in Visual Studio.

Validation Constraints

Your validation constraints should generate warnings for any invalid combinations of objects, properties, and links. In particular, any generators or other tools that process your models should be able to correctly process every model that passes validation.

A straightforward approach to validation tests is to hand-build one or more test models, with examples of each kind of error, as well as a representative selection of valid elements.

Validation tests can be automated from within a unit test by creating or loading test models and then calling validation through APIs.

■ TIP Create test models in code rather than reading them from a file

You could create test models by hand, and then have your automated tests read these in. But it is more flexible to write code that constructs a model instance in memory—when the DSL changes, it is quicker to change the code than to change the test models. Chapter 3 explained how to create models in memory. If you want to share the code between multiple tests, then put it in a helper class that all tests can access.

> **■ TIP** Use validation base classes for unit tests
>
> Chapter 7 explained how to use validation outside the IDE by using the `ValidationController`, `ValidationContext`, and `ValidationMessage` base classes directly. This approach can be used within unit tests to validate a model created in memory, with the error messages being passed to a log file that can then be compared to a baseline.

The test can dump the error list to a text file and compare it with a baseline (that is, a previous example of the same list that you have checked by hand). On the day some change alters the list of reported errors, the test will fail; the developer must either fix the fault or confirm that the new results are OK by copying them to the baseline file.

Your test models must also produce sensible results when your generation templates, custom commands, and any other tools are run against them. Models used to check these tools should therefore be checked to see that they pass validation; conversely, any test models that pass validation should be checked against the other tools.

> **■ TIP** Use snapshots to create test cases
>
> We earlier described how snapshots could be used to help design the domain model, and, indeed, validation constraints on that domain model. Snapshots provide a pictorial view of instances of the domain model, and the test cases for a validation constraint are, essentially, a set of domain model instances, some of which satisfy the constraint and some of which don't (counterexamples). So start with any snapshots that you created when working out the constraint in the first place, and encode those as test cases. Then create new snapshots to give increased coverage, paying particular attention to counterexamples (which will cause errors).

Generator Templates

You need to test your generating templates, which need to work with any model that passes the validation tests.

Once again, a straightforward method is to create one or more test models by hand. Then you run the template within Visual Studio using "Run Custom Tool" or "Transform All Templates," and check the generated result. For an automated test, you can either drive Visual Studio through its API or use the command-line interface to the text templating engine (which doesn't require VS). The test should compare the result with a baseline.

Before comparing against a baseline, you usually need to recognize and blank out some things that can vary from one run to another—Guids are a particular culprit, and Dates if they are initialized from "now."

When testing templates, we only want valid models. A possible starting point is to use the valid models created to test validation. Also, if you find that you are able to generate code that doesn't build from these models, it probably means that you've omitted a validation constraint. It is better to add a further validation constraint rather than write code in the template that looks for the invalid model and writes an error message to the output.

You can get a coverage analysis of a text template, but there are some complications. The text templating engine translates your template into a temporary C# file, and then compiles and executes it; the compiled code reads your model and writes the result file. Then the engine will normally delete both the temporary C# file and the compiled assembly. To get a coverage analysis, you need to be able to identify the assembly to the coverage tool, which entails precompiling the text template and keeping the translated source and compiled assembly afterwards so that you can see the analysis.

Generated Code

If your generator templates create code, or data files interpreted by code, you will want to test their behavior. A generated file will usually be part of a project containing several other generated or fixed files, just as the DSL Language project itself is. Generated code tests follow this sequence:

1. Create a copy of a project in which code generated from the templates is used.
2. Substitute the model file with a test model (which must be valid).

3. Execute the project's templates (either through the command-line version of the text templating host or by driving VS to run the "Transform All Templates" command).

4. Build the project (using MSBuild from a script or using the VS API).

5. Run the behavioral tests on the built assembly. (What the tests do depends on the nature of the project.)

6. Repeat from step 2, with another test model.

An alternative would be to generate both the target product code as well as unit tests for that code and then run the normal unit test and code coverage tools from Visual Studio.

Rules

Rules are used to maintain consistency across a model, propagating changes from one part to another. They were introduced in Chapter 3, used in Chapter 7, and discussed in more depth in Chapter 10. A rule can be tested in an instance of the DSL Tools Store, without running Visual Studio, by creating a model, making a change within a transaction, committing it (thereby causing rules to fire), and then checking that the resulting model incorporates the expected changes caused by the rules. This can be automated in a unit test using some of the techniques already described.

Language Definition

Does the DSL cover all the information your users need to capture? If you followed the method earlier in the chapter, you developed the language from specific requirements scenarios. But as you experiment and change the DSL, it is worth retrying those scenarios at intervals to ensure that you don't drift away from them. This is a manual test, because it depends on your judgment about the usability and scope of the language.

Evolving a DSL

After designing and using a DSL for a while, you will inevitably want to change it, and you will not want to lose the language instances that you have already created.

Changes in a DSL take one of the following forms:

- **Additions.** New properties in a class or relationship; new classes; new relationships. The deserializer will take care of these, filling in default values when reading objects from older files.

- **Deletions.** Properties, classes, or relationships removed. In this case, the deserializer will ignore the deleted elements.

- **Refactoring.** A structure is replaced by something that represents the same information in a different way. For example, we might replace the Issue State Transition by a class with a pair of relationships on either side. Here, the deserializer will see some additions and some deletions but will not be able to do the translation automatically.

- **Changes of property and relationship types** come under the refactoring heading.

Of these, the language author needs to worry about refactorings. The following tactics mitigate the pain of change to some extent:

- **Separate refactorings.** Identify and localize each refactoring, and plan separately how you will deal with each one. For example, one version change of the Issue State DSL might introduce a domain class to replace the **Transition** relationship, and might also introduce multiple issue types per project. As far as possible, we should keep those changes independent of each other.

- **Don't delete anything.** Instead of deleting the old structure, just add the new one—for example, have both the **Transition** relationship and the domain class replacing it coexist in the same model. Deprecate the old structure by removing its tools from the toolbox, and any merge directives or connection builders that might deal with its creation, so that new instances can't be created. Then use one of the tactics that follow this one.

- **Ensure the tools work with both structures.** During a migration period, ensure that the generating templates and other tools can work with both structures as much as possible. If the change is prompted by a changed requirement in what the tools generate, at least allow language users to edit and work with the old instances until they need to generate material from them.

- **Provide translation tools.** One way is to provide a command that scans a store and updates the model in place. It is possible to make this happen on opening a file of an older version.

  Another convenient method of translating instance models is to write a generating template that creates the serialized form of the new version of the DSL from models of the older version.

  XSLT can also be used to translate one model file into another, given that they are both XML files.

- **Validate** required fields. If you translate on opening an old file, make sure that your validation methods check any new fields so that the user is prompted to provide the required extra information.

- **Delete obsolete domain classes** when you're sure all the instances are updated.

- **Publish the update plan** to your language users so that they know when older structures will be obsolete.

Migration between language versions is an important and common problem. Having a forgiving file reader (deserializer) certainly relieves some of the pain, but you could do more. It is possible to conceive of tools that automate some of the above tactics. For example, one could maintain the history of changes to a domain model between versions and then use this information to generate a tool that does the conversion automatically.

What Makes a Good DSL?

A good DSL—one that helps the people who are using it—makes it easy to clearly represent information for a particular purpose. The following are some characteristics of a good DSL, many of them summarizing what we've discussed already:

- **Well-defined scope.** There is an easy-to-state single purpose for the DSL—for example, "to describe the permitted sequence of states of issues in a project."

- **Minimality.** There are no more concepts and relationships than are required for the ideas that need to be described with the DSL. If you can see a way to reduce the number without losing information, do so.

- **Familiarity.** If there is a notation already in use in the domain— railroad tracks? electrical circuits?—base your notation on that. If the type of information is normally associated with a particular style of diagram—statecharts—use the conventions familiar there. Adapt the notation where you need to.

- **Bring out the important bits.** The most important things should be the most obvious and easiest to change: names of states, transitions between them. Less important detail—for example, the target name-space of the generated code—can be left to the properties window. If you need to print out the full detail for some reviews, write a report template.

- **Moderate amount of redundancy.** Ensure that when the user has made an important distinction, it was intentional. For example, we flag an error if the user has not marked a state with no incoming transitions as "start." On the other hand, users don't like to have to say everything twice, so don't overdo it.

- **Use the syntactic space.** Most of the diagrams a user can draw should be meaningful. A language that is heavy with complex con-straints probably doesn't fit the conceptual space well and is difficult to remember how to use. The big advantage of a DSL is that the notation guides you through useful things to say.

- **Graphs are not syntax trees.** If you have an existing text notation, it is unlikely that its syntax tree will be the best graphical notation. See the example on regular expressions in the next section.

- **Allow for customization.** Your DSL will not cover all the cases that users will require. Provide for further customization through hand-written code, preferably without forcing the users to alter generating templates.

- **Use the users' language.** The language should be expressed in its users' terms, talking about their requirements—rather than its implementations. Talk about issues rather than tables. Where it's difficult to avoid bringing in some implementation concerns, try to package them up in a single domain class, or by exploiting categories in the properties window (see the end of Chapter 4). For example, in the DSL designer you'll find that properties that are mostly concerned with the form of the generated code are always gathered together under a "Code" category.

To illustrate the last few points further, we will consider the development of a different example.

Appropriate Notation: An Example with Regular Expressions

As software designers, we are always strongly aware of the tree-structured nature of just about everything we deal with. In designing a DSL notation, there is always an inclination to represent this tree directly in the syntax. However, this is not always the most usable option.

Chapter 1 mentioned regular expressions as an example of a textual DSL. Regular expressions have a very compact textual notation, and while very powerful for those who have learned the notation, occasional users can find them opaque. The goal in this example is to create a DSL in which regular expressions can be constructed with a graphical notation. The expected benefits include

- The toolbox guides construction of the expression.
- A pictorial model is easier to follow.
- Validation checks can be applied.
- Graphical presentation should be easier to learn and understand.

Reminder about Regular Expressions

Regular expressions can seem very arcane to the uninitiated, but the basic idea is simple. Suppose you are processing some text—let's say, an html file; and you want to find the next html element (between < and >); and you want to extract the tag and the parameter pairs of the element and get them into separate variables. So you call:

```
foreach (Match m in
    Regex.Match(yourHtmlString, theRegularExpression))
{ ... and each m is a match to part of the string ... }
```

The regular expression contains a sequence of characters that you expect to find in the string, and certain characters (parentheses, * + ? [ ] and one or two others) play special roles. * signifies a repetition of zero or many of what went immediately before, so that < * matches a < followed by any number of spaces, including none. + is similar, but insists on at least one occurrence. Square brackets match any single character in the range defined within, so that [A-Z]+ matches any sequence of at least one capital letter. Parentheses demarcate a match that you wish to capture into a variable, so that ([A-Za-z]+) should return to you a word made of one or more alphabetics. (?:...)* repeatedly performs the matches within the parentheses without capturing the whole thing to a variable. | specifies alternative matches. (?<name>...) matches a pattern that a later ${name} must match in the same way—so that the use of quote in the following example ensures that an opening quotation is matched with the same kind of closing mark.

This regular expression:

```
< *([A-Za-z]+) +(?:([A-Za-z]+) *= *(?<quote>"|')([^"']*)${quote} *)*/?>
```

matches, for example:

```
<  table bgcolor=  "#ffddff" border="1' >
```

as illustrated in Figure 11-19.

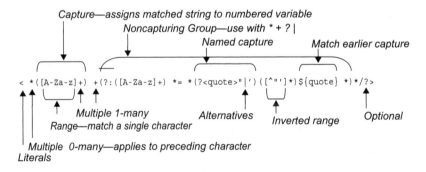

FIGURE 11-19: Interpretation of a regular expression

The objective of this DSL is to make a more accessible notation for regular expressions.

Candidate Notations

There are several notations that might be made to work, each of which takes a rather different approach. One of our major principles is to work from instances, so in the following we use an example that teases out the notational distinctions: `<a (?:b[cd]*e|[a-z]+)z`.

Candidate Notation 1: Regexp Tree

This notation (Figure 11-20) directly represents the abstract syntax tree of the regular expression. A sequence is represented by a vertical box, iterations are shown as a "*" in a circle, and alternatives are shown as a " | " in a circle.

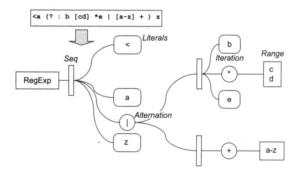

FIGURE 11-20: Regexp Tree notation

The difficulty is that it isn't very easy to follow how it matches up to a given input string. For one thing, you have to go back and forth between nodes and their descendants to follow the matching process.

Candidate Notation 2: Railroad Tracks

"Railroad tracks" (Figure 11-21) have been used for presenting parsing paths for many years (notably in the syntax definition of Pascal). Match by pushing a counter around as you follow the string; replicate the counter on going through a branch (small filled rectangle); delete a counter when it fails to match; the whole thing matches if you get a counter to the end.

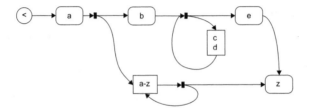

FIGURE 11-21: Railroad track notation

The big drawback to this notation is that there are a lot of possible graphs that don't correspond to regular expressions. While it is possible to write validations, contraventions are not always easy for the naïve user to spot, and it would be very irritating to constantly run into obscure error flags. In general, one of the expectations of a DSL is that it helps you to make statements that make sense within the domain.

The particular difficulty is that it allows you to make non-nested loops, and it can be quite difficult, depending on the layout of the graph, to see whether the constraint has been contravened or not, as illustrated in Figure 11-22 (which is invalid).

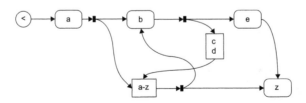

FIGURE 11-22: Invalid railroad track

Candidate Notation 3: Nested Boxes

This is a compromise solution in which arrows represent sequence, and nesting represents containment (Figure 11-23). The rule here is that paths can only converge or diverge at the branch points on either side of a box that contains the alternative paths. Each node otherwise just has at most one arrow entering and one leaving. There are also loop boxes with ports marked * or +.

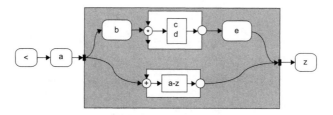

FIGURE 11-23: Nested box notation

This works just as well with the counter semantics while at the same time disallowing spaghetti branches. At the exit of a + or * loop box, you can move the counter around the box boundary back to the entry port. If the entry port is * or ?, you can avoid the content altogether by moving around the boundary straight to the exit. (The entry ports are decorated with arrows lined up with the box boundary to suggest this behavior.)

Candidate Notation 4: Nested Paths

This is another counter-following notation, but there are two kinds of link. Each node only has one entering link (Figure 11-24). To match a string to the expression, you follow the Next links, matching each character to the character in a box; if you match the last node to the string, the match has succeeded. If you come to a diamond or circle, you must first follow its Parts links, and match that (by getting to the last link)—if there are several Parts links, split the counters and a match to any one will do.

This notation is a bit more difficult to follow than the nested boxes, but (unlike candidate 2) all of the graphs you can draw make sensible regular expressions, and (unlike candidate 1) sequences of matches are represented by following Next links rather than working through a fan of sibling links so that you can understand the graph by pushing counters around it.

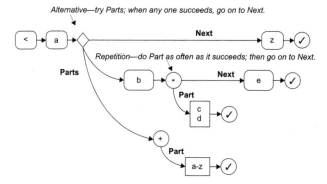

FIGURE 11-24: Nested path notation

Graphs Are Not Syntax Trees

Nested Boxes (or its pragmatic variant, Nested Paths) seem to be the best notation, but notice how far those notations are from the initial direct representation of the regular expression syntax tree. The first candidate would be the easiest to generate regular expressions from, but the better notations help a user to understand the concepts.

The same consideration will frequently apply when taking any existing text syntax—typically an XML file—and creating a diagrammatic representation of it. The syntax tree of the existing language is often not the best option.

SUMMARY

This chapter has presented a set of techniques and options around the process of designing DSLs for domain-specific development, picking up where we left off in Chapter 2 and benefiting from a much deeper knowledge of the mechanics of creating a DSL and associated code generators (Chapters 3–10).

On the topic of identifying variability, we summarized the top-down versus bottom-up approaches and introduced feature trees as a way for working top-down. We introduced the notion of snapshots to assist with the development a domain model, and described by example how a notation might evolve from initial ideas to the final definition, and the kinds of trade-offs that have to be made. Snapshots made a reappearance when considering how to identify and define validation constraints; we also identified some domain model patterns to watch out for as indicators that additional constraints may be required. We then moved on to the topic of frameworks, where we discussed more pros and cons of generation versus interpretation, and we provided some advice on evolving them. That was followed by some advice on how to go about testing a DSL and code generators, with cross-references to other parts of the book that have introduced coding techniques relevant to writing automated tests. There was then a brief section on what to watch out for when evolving a DSL, and tactics you can use to mitigate the pain were presented. The chapter concluded with some advice on how to recognize a good DSL, illustrating this with a comparison of possible graphical notations for regular expressions.

Conclusion

So you've downloaded the tools, read the book, and you're gung ho on implementing a domain-specific approach to development in your organization. What's the best way to go about this? Our advice would be to start small and bottom-up. Find a project where you reckon there's a lot of repetitive code being written, templatize it, and write a DSL to drive the templates.

As you start to scale, you'll probably need to orchestrate your code generation, for example, loop though a model and generate one file per model element. In Chapter 8, we described how, with some custom code, you could go about this—and the technique will take you some distance. However, you might also like to look up the *Guidance Automation Toolkit* (*GAT*)[6], which can be used for code generation orchestration as well as for automating other development tasks like unfolding project templates. GAT adopts a strategy of revealing automation steps to the developer in context and at the point that the developer needs them.

Once you've got two or three DSLs going, or even as you start to develop the second, you may find it necessary to get different DSLs to interact. For example, you may need to know how to have elements in a model of one DSL cross-reference elements in a model of another DSL (or even cross-reference elements in another model of the same DSL), to navigate those references in the UI, to know when the references are broken and be told how to fix them, and to visualize the references on the design surface.

---

6. See http://msdn2.microsoft.com/en-us/teamsystem/aa718948.aspx.

And then you will need to know how to exploit these cross-references in activities such as code generation and validation. It is possible to implement some of this yourself through custom code—a starting point would be, for example, storing cross-references as strings in properties on domain classes—and we are aware of customers who have done this. There is also a powertool available called the *Designer Integration Service* (*DIS*),[7] which can be downloaded for experimentation purposes, though it is not suitable for production tools.

At some point, you'll also need to integrate domain-specific development with your organization's general software development practices. We're not going to pretend this is an easy task, because it is likely to have significant impact on the development culture of the organization. Take, for example, the job of specifying the application to be built. You may find that the models you are producing, and from which significant code is being generated, don't need developer expertise to write down (at least not the initial drafts), and, further, that they could replace large tracts of informal specification. If that's the case, the specification task changes into one of defining the models that then get passed on and further refined by the development team, and then writing informal specs for those aspects that still need to be implemented as custom code. Are those who write specifications in your organization willing or able to change the way they work? There's also an impact on testing; if the code generators are tested, what aspects of the generated code that is embedded in the system being built needs testing? How does this impact the testing process familiar to the testers in your organization? The developers will also have less code to write, in particular, less rote code. This may suit some developers, but for others it may take them into uncomfortable zones—writing rote code is how they make a living. And what about the impact on the project planning process? What are the costs of specification, development, and testing when models and code generators are involved? Our best advice is to work very pragmatically and incrementally—do it a project at a time; take metrics (e.g., estimated versus actual cost) to inform the next project; get buy-in from a few individuals in different disciplines and then roll it out from

---

7. www.microsoft.com/downloads/details.aspx?FamilyID=bfba74af-4f28-44cc-8de5-
    0c3c55d21863&displaylang=en. There is also a link from the DSL Tools home page.

there; and build up a wiki of best practices, maintain it, and share it between projects.

So you've read the book and want to read more? What can we recommend? Just one book: *Software Factories: Assembling Applications with Patterns, Models, Frameworks and Tools*, by Jack Greenfield and Keith Short, with Steve Cook and Stuart Kent.[8] This book synthesizes a number of recent initiatives in software development (e.g., product lines, model driven development, domain-specific languages, patterns) into a theory for software development in the future and elaborates that theory in some depth. One can think about domain-specific development as a stylized form of the software factory approach, and the *Software Factories* book will certainly get you thinking about how it might evolve. Also, being a book of synthesis, it has a rich bibliography for those who wish to delve further.

Our job here is done. Our goal in writing this book was to explain what Microsoft's DSL Tools are for, and how to use them effectively. If you were already a user of the DSL Tools, then we hope this book has provided some useful new techniques to try out on your own projects, and clarified any aspects you didn't understand. If you're new to the DSL Tools, we hope the book has inspired you to download the tools and try the approach for yourself.

---

8. Wiley Publishing Inc., 2004

Index

Microsoft .NET Development Series

.NET Framework Standard Library Annotated Reference, Volume 1: Base Class Library and Extended Numerics Library — Brad Abrams — 0321154894

.NET Framework Standard Library Annotated Reference, Volume 2: Networking Library, Reflection Library and XML Library — Brad Abrams, Tamara Abrams — 0321194454

Essential Windows Presentation Foundation — Chris Anderson — 0321374479

.NET Web Services: Architecture and Implementation — Keith Ballinger — 0321113594

Visual Studio Tools for Office: Using C# with Excel, Word, Outlook, and InfoPath — Eric Carter, Eric Lippert — 0321334884

Visual Studio Tools for Office: Using Visual Basic 2005 with Excel, Word, Outlook, and InfoPath — Eric Carter, Eric Lippert — 0321411757

Graphics Programming with GDI+ — Mahesh Chand — 0321160770

Framework Design Guidelines: Conventions, Idioms, and Patterns for Reusable .NET Libraries — Krzysztof Cwalina, Brad Abrams — 0321246756

ASP.NET 2.0 Illustrated — Alex Homer, Dave Sussman — 0321418344

The .NET Developer's Guide to Directory Services Programming — Joe Kaplan, Ryan Dunn — 0321350170

Essential C# 2.0 — Mark Michaelis — 0321150775

The Common Language Infrastructure Annotated Standard — James S. Miller, Susann Ragsdale — 0321154932

Essential ASP.NET with Examples in C# — Fritz Onion — 0201760401

Essential ASP.NET with Examples in Visual Basic .NET — Fritz Onion — 0201760398

Building Applications and Components with Visual Basic .NET — Ted Pattison with Dr. Joe Hummel — 0201734958

.NET Internationalization: The Developer's Guide to Building Global Windows and Web Applications — Guy Smith-Ferrier — 0321341384

The Visual Basic .NET Programming Language — Paul Vick — 0321169514

A Developer's Guide to SQL Server 2005

Bob Beauchemin
Dan Sullivan

0321382188

Essential .NET Volume 1
The Common Language Runtime

Don Box
with Chris Sells

0201734117

The .NET Developer's Guide to Windows Security

Keith Brown

0321228359

Effective Use of Microsoft Enterprise Library
Building Blocks for Creating Enterprise Applications and Services

Len Fenster

0321334213

Software Engineering with Microsoft Visual Studio Team System

Sam Guckenheimer
with Juan J. Perez

0321278720

The C# Programming Language
Second Edition

Anders Hejlsberg
Scott Wiltamuth
Peter Golde

0321334434

Enterprise Services with the .NET Framework
Developing Distributed Business Solutions with .NET Enterprise Services

Christian Nagel

032124673X

Data Binding with Windows Forms 2.0
Programming Smart Client Data Applications with .NET

Brian Noyes

032126892X

Smart Client Deployment with ClickOnce
Deploying Windows Forms Applications with ClickOnce

Brian Noyes

0321197690

Essential ASP.NET 2.0

Fritz Onion
with Keith Brown

0321237706

Designing Forms for Microsoft Office InfoPath and Forms Services 2007

Scott Roberts
Hagen Green

0321410599

eXtreme .NET
Introducing eXtreme Programming Techniques to .NET Developers

Dr. Neil Roodyn

0321303636

Windows Forms 2.0 Programming

Chris Sells
Michael Weinhardt

0321267966

Essential Windows Workflow Foundation

Dharma Shukla
Bob Schmidt

0321399838

Programming in the .NET Environment

Damien Watkins
Mark Hammond
Brad Abrams

0201770180

Pragmatic ADO.NET
Data Access for the Internet World

Shawn Wildermuth

0201745682

.NET Compact Framework Programming with C#

Paul Yao
David Durant

0321174038

.NET Compact Framework Programming with Visual Basic .NET

Paul Yao
David Durant

0321174046

Register
Your Book

at www.awprofessional.com/register

You may be eligible to receive:

- Advance notice of forthcoming editions of the book
- Related book recommendations
- Chapter excerpts and supplements of forthcoming titles
- Information about special contests and promotions throughout the year
- Notices and reminders about author appearances, tradeshows, and online chats with special guests

Contact us

If you are interested in writing a book or reviewing manuscripts prior to publication, please write to us at:

Editorial Department
Addison-Wesley Professional
75 Arlington Street, Suite 300
Boston, MA 02116 USA
Email: AWPro@aw.com

Addison-Wesley

Visit us on the Web: http://www.awprofessional.com